T0305385

Valuation for M&A

Valuation for M&A

Building and Measuring Private Company Value

Third Edition

CHRIS M. MELLEN
FRANK C. EVANS

WILEY

Published by John Wiley & Sons, Inc., Hoboken, New Jersey.
Published simultaneously in Canada.

For general information on our other products and services or for technical support, please contact our Customer Care Department within the United States at (800) 762–2974, outside the United States at (317) 572–3993, or fax (317) 572–4002.

Wiley publishes in a variety of print and electronic formats and by print-on-demand. Some material included with standard print versions of this book may not be included in e-books or in print-on-demand. If this book refers to media such as a CD or DVD that is not included in the version you purchased, you may download this material at http://booksupport.wiley.com. For more information about Wiley products, visit www.wiley.com.

Library of Congress Cataloging-in-Publication Data:

Names: Names: Mellen, Chris M., author. | Evans, Frank C., author.
Title: Valuation for M&A : building and measuring private company value / Chris M. Mellen.
Other titles: Valuation for M & A | Valuation for M and A
Description: Third edition. | Hoboken : Wiley, 2018. | Series: Wiley finance | Revised edition of Valuation for M&A, c2010. | Includes index. | Identifiers: LCCN 2018008632 (print) | LCCN 2018011918 (ebook) | ISBN 9781119437345 (pdf) | ISBN 9781119437383 (epub) | ISBN 9781119437413 (oBook) | ISBN 9781119433835 (hardback)
Subjects: LCSH: Corporations—Valuation. | Consolidation and merger of corporations.
Classification: LCC HG4028.V3 (ebook) | LCC HG4028.V3 E93 2018 (print) | DDC 658.16/2—dc23
LC record available at https://lccn.loc.gov/2018008632

Cover Design: Wiley
Cover Images: © MaxxiGo/Shutterstock; © discpicture/Alamy Stock Photo

Printed in the United States of America.

10 9 8 7 6 5 4 3 2 1

Contents

Preface

"Value" is an expression of the worth of something, measured using two metrics: return and rate of return. To create and build value, businesses must pursue strategies that raise the return, reduce the risk, or combine the two. Conceptually, this seems obvious, but application is more difficult.

The mystery surrounding a company's value often causes executives to make bad investment and operational decisions. But these poor choices can be avoided. Accurate valuations are possible, and M&A deals can succeed for both buyers and sellers. The keys to success are in the pages that follow.

Through providing valuation advisory services to thousands of companies and corporate executives, we have developed the tools to accurately measure and successfully build value in companies. By employing these techniques, owners and managers can determine their company's value, what drives it, and how to enhance that value both in M&A and through daily operations.

In M&A transactions, sellers, buyers, and even their advisors struggle over the value of a business. Often they are frustrated by what they see as the other side's unrealistic expectations. These uncertainties abound:

- Do profits, often computed as EBIT or EBITDA, represent the company's true return to shareholders?
- Is the forecasted performance realistic?
- What is an appropriate rate of return or multiple, considering the investment's risk?
- Should the transaction be structured as an asset or stock deal?
- Has the seller properly prepared and packaged the company to get the best price?
- What personal issues are of critical importance to the seller?
- Has the buyer found the best target and accurately quantified potential synergies?
- Does the deal make sense at the quoted price?

Greater fundamental mystery exists in private companies – those not traded on a public stock market, including thinly traded public companies or divisions of large corporations. Most owners and managers operate these companies year after year without ever knowing the answers to these basic questions:

- What is the company worth?
- How much more would a strategic buyer pay to acquire it?
- What factors most affect the company's stock value?
- What is the owners' real return on investment and rate of return?
- Does that return justify the risk?
- Are owners better off selling, and if so, how and when?

Selling is just one of many options available to a business owner to exit the business. This third edition again takes a step back to discuss the now-maturing field of exit planning, explain the unique challenges of private company owner exit decisions and the exit-planning process, and discuss some exit alternatives in cases where selling may not currently be the right option for the business owner.

- What financial, nonfinancial, professional, and personal issues must an owner consider in evaluating whether to exit, and, if so, how?
- What exit options other than a sale are available to the business owner?
- What makes planning a private company investment different?
- Why should exit planning for a private company begin now?

There have been considerable changes in the economy since the prior editions were written. The economy has rapidly become more knowledge-based, where intangible assets are a more significant portion of a company's value, and more global. Financial reporting standards pertaining to M&A transactions have responded – and this third edition has also responded.

- What are the unique characteristics of foreign companies to consider in cross-border M&A?
- What are some of the key intangible assets owned by companies, and how are they valued?
- What are the important financial reporting considerations that must be addressed when completing a transaction?
- What are the unique challenges of measuring and managing value in high-tech start-ups to maximize shareholder value?
- What is a fairness opinion and why should a private company consider obtaining one in advance of an M&A transaction?

This book provides the tools to answer these and related questions. It is written for business owners, investors, and managers of private companies in the lower middle markets (i.e. companies generating between $3 million and $250 million in revenues) who lack the guidance of a stock price set by a free and active market. It does so in five new sections. The introductory chapter that comprises Part I introduces many of the concepts covered in this book on how both buyer and seller can win from an M&A transaction. Part II focuses on factors to consider when doing both a quantitative and qualitative assessment of a business in an effort to build company value in preparation for an M&A transaction. This part's four chapters introduce and explain how to measure private company return on investment, factors to consider in a market and competitive analysis, specific steps to take in preparing for an M&A transaction, and how to measure synergies to be gained following a successful transaction. Part III explains the valuation process for M&A purposes over eight chapters, which cover the three approaches to value and how to reconcile results when conducting a valuation analysis for a potential or actual M&A transaction. Part IV introduces and explains seven specialty issues as they relate to valuation for M&A, including: exit planning, deal structure, fairness opinions, financial reporting, intangible assets, start-ups, and cross-border M&A. Finally, Part V pulls together many of the concepts covered in this book with two case studies – one involving a distribution business and a second involving a public relations agency (professional services firm).

Our solutions to valuation and return on investment questions create accountability and discipline in the M&A process. Our techniques incorporate value enhancement into a private company's annual strategic planning to provide direction to shareholders in their investment decisions. In short, our book is a roadmap to building and measuring value in both operating a company and selling or buying one.

Many investors have heard about building value in a public company where the stock price provides the market's reaction to the company's performance. It is much more difficult to develop a successful strategy and measure performance and ROI accurately when no stock price exists. Difficult, but not impossible.

We invite our readers to employ these techniques to achieve accurate M&A valuations for private companies and to build value in daily operations. Trade the mystery for this roadmap to wealth.

Chris M. Mellen
Frank C. Evans
May 2018

Dedication and Acknowledgments

This book is dedicated to our dear friend and mentor, David Bishop, coauthor of the first edition. Through his formation of the American Business Appraisers national network, David brought us together and provided countless hours of education and guidance to elevate us in the business valuation profession. For that we are deeply grateful.

In addition to David, this book would not have been completed successfully without the help and support of many of our colleagues and of Sheck Cho at John Wiley & Sons. We would also like to thank Sid Shaver for his contribution of Chapter 20, "Cross-Border M&A"; Ken Sanginario for his contribution of Appendix 8A, "Using Specific Company Risk Strategically"; and Justin Johnson for his contribution of Appendix 13A, "Disciplined and Thorough Valuation Analysis Key to Avoiding Failed M&A Deals."

My thanks to exit planning advisor extraordinaire John Leonetti for his invaluable feedback and many suggestions on the exit planning chapter. I would also like to thank Roger Grabowski for his comments on the cost of capital chapter; Ray Rath, René Hlousek, and Darren Cordier for their edits and feedback on the initial financial reporting and intangible asset chapters in the second edition; Ed Hamilton for his update of the financial reporting chapter in this third edition; Charles Costa for his math checks on the exhibits and some general research; Patrice Radogna for her review of the new case study on the professional services firm; and Frank Mainville and Andrew Reddington for their critique and enhancements to the high-tech start-up chapter. And, most important, I owe my deepest gratitude to my family. To my wife, Kim, and my daughters, Sophia and Julia, thank you for your tolerance of my long hours while I was working on both the second and third editions of this book, and for the love, light, and support you bring to me every day!

Chris Mellen

My continuing thanks to my brother, Harry Evans, who helped so much with the first edition; to my friend and colleague, Frank Mindicino, for his unique knowledge and insights; and to my assistant, Shelly Myers, and my partner and daughter, Sarah DeKreek. Finally, to my wife, Lin, thanks for your love and support in so many ways.

Frank Evans

PART I

Introduction

CHAPTER 1

Winning through Mergers and Acquisitions

Buyers and sellers can create substantial value through merger and acquisition (M&A). Both can win from a transaction. That is the beauty of deal making. And that is much of the allure that has driven the tremendous volume of M&A activity worldwide over the past three decades.[1] Despite this volume, most businesses are not salable. M&A advisors disqualify roughly 65% to 75% of prospective sellers and, according to a U.S. Chamber of Commerce study, only 20% of the businesses that are for sale will successfully transfer hands to another owner. This would imply that only 5% to 7% of companies actually get sold![2]

This book focuses on private company business value, with particular focus on private (or closely held) companies in the lower end of the middle market (i.e. those generating between $3 million and $250 million in value).[3] What creates value? How do we measure it? How does a management team build it? How do they preserve it? How do they maximize it through a transaction? It is this focus that will improve the chances of selling a business. These concepts are equally important to buyers and sellers because both

---

[1] Chapter 5 presents a very necessary second view of the potential results of M&A.

[2] Looked at another way, the Tax Foundation reported in 2013, based on corporate tax return filings with the IRS, that there were approximately 9.1 million corporations in the United States (1.7 million C Corporations and 7.4 million S Corporations, plus another 23 million sole proprietorships). As noted at the beginning of Chapter 4, Mergerstat reported a total of 97,093 transaction announcements over the course of 10 years between 2007 and 2016, which represents approximately 1.1% of total S and C corporations.

[3] For purposes of this book, we define the middle market as companies with a total enterprise value of $250 million to $1 billion, lower middle market at $10 million to $250 million, lower-lower middle market at $3 million to $10 million, and small-cap or micro companies under $3 million.

can and should benefit from a deal. But different results frequently occur. Sellers may sell under adverse conditions or accept too low a price due to lack of preparation or knowledge. And every buyer runs the risk of purchasing the wrong business or paying too much. As seen during the Great Recession of 2007–2009, transactions during adverse economic times create their own sets of challenges. That is why understanding value – and what drives it – is critical in mergers and acquisitions.

Wise shareholders and managers do not, however, confine their focus on value to only M&A. They should be building value in their business while still running it. If you do not grow, you will ultimately decline. As Will Rogers famously said, "Even if you're on the right track, you'll get run over if you just sit there."

Value creation drives the strategic planning of shareholders and managers and, in the process, creates focus and direction for their company. Their M&A strategy supports and complements their broader goal of building shareholder value, and they buy and sell only when a given deal creates value for them.

This brings us back to the purpose of this book. It explains how to create, build, measure, manage, preserve, and maximize value in mergers and acquisitions in the context of the broader business goal of building value. Senior managers in most public companies focus on value every day because it is reflected in the movement of their stock price – the daily scorecard of their performance relative to other investment choices. Private companies, however, lack this market feedback and direction. Their shareholders and executives seldom understand what their company is worth or clearly see what drives its value. For this reason, many private companies – and business segments of public companies as well – lack direction and underperform.

Managing the value of a private company, or a division of a public corporation, is particularly difficult because that value is harder to compute and justify. Yet most business activity – and value creation or destruction – occurs at this operational level.

Being able to accurately measure and manage the value of smaller businesses or business segments is critical in the value-creation process. And this skill will pay off in M&A as well because most transactions involve smaller entities. Although we read and hear about the big deals that involve large corporations with known stock prices, the median M&A transaction size in the United States between 2012 and 2016 was approximately $43 million. Smaller deals involving closely held companies or segments of public companies are the scene for most M&A activity.

Therefore, every value-minded shareholder and executive must strive to maximize value at this smaller-entity level where daily stock prices do not exist. The concepts and techniques that follow explain how to measure and manage value on a daily basis and particularly in M&A. The discussion begins with an understanding of what value is.

Critical Values Shareholders Overlook

When buyers see a potential target, their analysis frequently begins by identifying and quantifying the synergies they could achieve through the acquisition. They prepare a model that forecasts the target's potential revenues if they owned it, the adjusted expense levels under their management, and the resulting income or cash flow that they anticipate. They then discount these future returns by their company's cost of capital to determine the target's value to them. Armed with this estimate of value, they begin negotiations aimed at a deal that is intended to create value.

If the target is not a public company with a known stock price, frequently no one even asks what the target is worth to its present owners. However, the value the business creates for the present owners is all that they really have to sell. Most, and sometimes all, of the potential synergies in the deal are created by the buyer, rather than the seller, so the buyer should not have to pay the seller for most of the value the buyer creates. But in the scenario just described, the buyer is more likely to do so because his or her company does not know what the target is worth as a stand-alone business. Consequently, the buyer also does not know what the synergies created by his or her company through the acquisition are worth, or what the company's initial offer should be.

Sellers are frequently as uninformed or misinformed as buyers. Many times the owners of the target do not know if they should sell, how to find potential buyers, which buyers can afford to pay the most to acquire them, what they could do to maximize their sale value, or how to go about the sale process. After all, many sellers are involved in only one such transaction in their career. They seldom know what their company is currently worth as a stand-alone business, what value drivers or risk drivers most influence its value, or how much more, if any, it would be worth to a strategic buyer. Typically none of their team of traditional advisors – their controller, outside accountant, banker, or attorney – is an expert in business valuation. They certainly have not seen as many businesses as an experienced business appraiser. Few of these professionals understand what drives business value or the subtle distinction between the value of a company as a stand-alone business versus what it could be worth in the hands of a strategic buyer.

The seller could seek advice from an intermediary, most commonly an investment banker or business broker. But these advisors typically are paid a commission – if and only if they achieve a sale. Perhaps current owners could achieve a higher return by improving the business to position it to achieve a greater value before selling. This advice is seldom popular with many intermediaries because it postpones or eliminates their commission.

With sound advice so difficult to find, sellers frequently postpone sale considerations. Delay is often the easier emotional choice for many entrepreneurs who identify personally with their company. But with delay, opportunities are frequently lost. External factors – including economic, industry, and competitive conditions that may dramatically affect value – can change quickly. Consolidation trends, technological innovations, or regulatory and tax reforms also can expand or contract M&A opportunities and value.

Procrastination also can hamper estate planning and tax strategies because delays reduce options. And the bad consequences are particularly acute when value is rapidly increasing.

Thus, buyers and sellers have very strong incentives to understand value, manage what drives it, measure it, and track it to their mutual benefit.

Stand-Alone Fair Market Value

With a proper focus on maximizing shareholder value, buyers and sellers begin by computing the target company's stand-alone fair market value, the worth of what the sellers currently own. This value reflects the company's size, access to capital, depth and breadth of products and services, quality of management, market share and customer base, levels of liquidity and financial leverage, and overall profitability and cash flow as a stand-alone business.

With these characteristics in mind, "fair market value" is defined by Revenue Ruling 59-60 of the Internal Revenue Service as "the *price* at which the property would change hands between a willing buyer and a willing seller when the former is not under compulsion to buy and the latter is not under any compulsion to sell, both parties having reasonable knowledge of the relevant facts."

Fair market value includes these assumptions:

- Buyers and sellers are hypothetical, typical of the market, and acting in their own self-interest.
- The hypothetical buyer is prudent but without synergistic benefit.
- The business will continue as a going concern and not be liquidated.
- The hypothetical sale will be for cash.
- The parties are able as well as willing.
- The hypothetical seller is not forced to sell (i.e. accept an offer that represents a "distress sale") and a buyer is not compelled to buy (i.e. necessary to earn a living).
- The reference is to "price" rather than "proceeds."
- The parties operate at arm's length, or independent of each other.
- Both parties have reasonable knowledge of the relevant facts.
- The seller must be willing to accept the price available under prevailing economic, industry, and market conditions as of the effective date.

The buyer under fair market value is considered to be a "financial" rather than a "strategic" buyer. The buyer contributes only capital and management of equivalent competence to that of the current management. This excludes the buyer who, because of other business activities, brings some value-added benefits to the company that will enhance the company being valued and/or the buyer's other business activities (e.g. being acquired by other companies in the same or a similar industry). Also excluded is the buyer who is already a shareholder, creditor, or related or controlled entity who might be willing to acquire the interest at an artificially high or low price due to considerations not typical of the motivation of the arm's-length financial buyer.

The seller in the fair market value process is also hypothetical and possesses knowledge of the relevant facts, including the influences on value exerted by the market, the company's risk and value drivers, and the degree of control and lack of marketability of that specific interest in the business.

While fair market value is impersonal in nature, investment value reflects the value to a particular buyer based on that buyer's circumstances and investment requirements. This standard of value includes the synergies or other advantages the strategic buyer anticipates will be created through the acquisition.

Fair market value should represent the minimum price that a financially motivated seller would accept because the seller, as the owner of the business, currently enjoys the benefits this value provides. The controlling shareholder in a privately held company frequently possesses substantial liquidity because he or she can harvest the cash flow the company generates or sell the company. The noncontrolling or minority shareholder generally possesses far less liquidity. As a result, the value of a noncontrolling interest is usually materially less than that interest's proportionate ownership in the value of the business on a control basis.

Prospective buyers who have computed stand-alone fair market value should also recognize that this is the base value from which their negotiating position should begin. The maximum value the buyer expects to create from the deal is the excess of investment value over fair market value.[4] So any premium the buyer pays above fair market value reduces the buyer's potential gain because the seller receives this portion of the value created.

---

[4] In practice, the term *intrinsic value* is sometimes used. *Graham and Dodd's Security Analysis* (Cottle, Murray, and Block, 5th edition, New York: McGraw-Hill, 1988, p. 41) defines intrinsic value as "the value which is justified by assets, earnings, dividends, definite prospects, and the factor of management." Intrinsic value is more broadly defined than fair market value, but is similar in that it reflects characteristics relating to the asset being valued, but not those related to a particular buyer that is part of investment value.

As discussed further in Chapter 14, sellers frequently are motivated by nonfinancial considerations, such as their desire to pass ownership of the company on to their children or long-term qualified employees, or, if they work in the company, to retire or do something else. When these non-financial considerations exist, it is particularly important for shareholders to understand the financial effect of decisions made for personal reasons. Opportunistic buyers can take advantage of sellers, particularly those who are in adverse personal circumstances. Once again, this fact stresses the need for a continual focus on value and implementation of a strategic-planning process that routinely considers sale of the company as a viable option to maximize shareholder value. This process accommodates shareholders' nonfinancial goals and provides the time and structure to achieve them and manage value as well.

Investment Value to Strategic Buyers

The investment value of a target is its value to a specific strategic buyer, recognizing that buyer's attributes and the synergies and other integrative benefits that can be achieved through the acquisition. Also known as strategic or synergistic value, the target's investment value is probably different to each potential buyer because of the different synergies that each can create through the acquisition. For example, one buyer may have a distribution system, product line, or sales territory in which the target would fit better than with any other potential buyer. Generally this is the company to which the target is worth the most. Well-informed buyers and sellers determine these strategic advantages in advance and negotiate with this knowledge.

The difference between fair market value and investment value is portrayed in Exhibit 1.1, which shows an investment value for two potential buyers. The increase in investment value over the company's fair market value is most commonly referred to as a control premium, but this term is somewhat misleading. Although the typical buyer does acquire control of the target through the acquisition, the premium paid is generally to achieve the synergies that the combination will create. Thus, this premium is more accurately referred to as an acquisition premium because the primary force driving it is synergies, rather than control, which is only the authority necessary to activate the synergy.[5]

---

[5] To address the diversity in practice among business appraisers in adjusting value to reflect benefits of control, the Appraisal Foundation developed a working group, which published *The Measurement and Application of Market Participant Acquisition Premiums* in 2017, intended mostly for valuations completed for financial reporting purposes, but containing perhaps the most comprehensive explanation of such premiums to date.

EXHIBIT 1.1 Fair Market Value versus Investment Value

Investment Value – 2	_____
Investment Value – 1	_____
Acquisition Premium	
Fair Market Value	_____

The obvious questions this discussion generates are:

- Why should a buyer pay more than fair market value?
- If the buyer must pay an acquisition premium to make the acquisition, how much above fair market value should the buyer pay (i.e. how large should the acquisition premium be, either as a dollar amount or as a percentage of fair market value)?

The median acquisition premiums for purchases of public companies in the United States have been about 33% over the last 10 years. These figures are not presented as a guideline or as a target. Premiums paid are based on competitive factors, consolidation trends, economies of scale, and buyer and seller motivations – facts that again emphasize the need to thoroughly understand value and industry trends before negotiations begin. For example, a company with a fair market value of $10 million has a much stronger bargaining position if its maximum investment value is $20 million than if it is only $12 million. To negotiate the best possible price, however, the seller should attempt to determine what its maximum investment value is, which potential buyer may have the capacity to pay the most in an acquisition, and what alternatives each buyer has, and then negotiate accordingly.

Generally speaking, buyers should begin their negotiations based on fair market value. Before they enter the negotiation process, where emotional factors and the desire to "do the deal" take over, buyers should establish their walk-away price. This is the maximum amount above fair market value that they are willing to pay to make the acquisition. Establishing the maximum price in advance encourages buyers to focus on value rather than on winning the deal. Naturally, the farther the price moves above fair market value toward that buyer's investment value, the less attractive the deal becomes. Value-oriented buyers recognize that acquisitions at a price close to their investment value require them to fully achieve almost all forecasted synergies – on time – to achieve the forecasted value. And the closer the acquisition price gets to their investment value, the less value the acquisition can create for the buyer's shareholders and the smaller the buyer's potential margin of error. When a seller demands too high a price, the buyer's better option is often to decline that deal and look for one with a better potential to create value.

This fact illustrates a fundamental but essential lesson in making any investment: Identify the distinction between a good company and a good investment. While a good company may possess many strengths, it will prove to be a bad investment if the price paid for it is too high. Conversely, a company with weaknesses may offer a good investment opportunity if the price is adequately low relative to the forecasted returns, particularly to the strategic buyer who possesses the strengths to compensate for the target's weaknesses.

Win–Win Benefits of Merger and Acquisition

In order for there to be a successful M&A transaction, three things need to be in line. First, the business itself must be ready. This means addressing many of the concepts discussed in the four chapters within Section II, Building Value. Next, the owner himself must be ready, as discussed with the mental readiness concept within Chapter 14. Finally, there needs to be a buyer ready to pay a multiple that the business owner will accept. That means that the business owner must have an understanding of what his business is worth, as covered in the eight chapters within Section III, Measuring Value.

To illustrate the win–win benefits of M&A to buyers and sellers, the next discussion summarizes the valuation of Cavendish Seafood Distributors, which is presented in detail in Chapter 21. Many of the technical steps in this illustration are explained only briefly. Each step is described in detail in the chapters that follow. Various technical issues will be introduced in italicized print with a reference to the chapter that explains how to handle these matters.

Cavendish was founded about 20 years ago by Lou Bertin, who had enjoyed a successful career as a restaurateur. Bertin, who had an MBA and always wanted to run his own business but was tired of the demands of running a restaurant, recognized a need for better distribution of seafood to restaurants in his home state. Armed with his entrepreneurial spirit, substantial expertise in running restaurants, $1.7 million of his and two 10% minority investors' equity cash, and a well-conceived business plan, he founded Cavendish.

As with most small companies, however, several major risks and constraints weighed heavily on Bertin. He is looking to retire or at least reduce his hours. And although Cavendish has been a successful venture, Bertin has seen his personal wealth increasingly tied to the fate of the company at a time in his life when he knows diversification is the much wiser investment strategy. *Should Bertin's 80% equity interest in Cavendish be valued, or some other investment? Would the valuation process or computation be different if he owned a 100% interest and there were no minority shareholders, or if all of the stock were owned by minority shareholders?* (See Chapters 12 and 14.)

Sales for Cavendish's latest year top $75 million, and earnings before interest and taxes (EBIT) adjusted to reflect ongoing operations will be about $7.5 million. *Is EBIT the best measure of return for Cavendish? Would it be more accurate to use revenue or net income before or after taxes or cash flow?* (See Chapter 6.) Cavendish is heavily leveraged. To move toward long-term stability, significant additional capital spending is required. Does the financial leverage affect value, and if so, how? (See Chapter 9.) Does the anticipated capital spending affect value, and if so, how do we account for it? (See Chapter 6.)

The company's product line is narrow by industry standards, although it has developed a loyal and rapidly growing base of restaurants and grocery stores. Cavendish's profit margins are negatively impacted by forces outside its control, such as increases in fuel prices and drops in demand from restaurants during economic downturns. *How can the valuation reflect these various risk drivers and value drivers? What if the buyer can eliminate some of these weaknesses?* (See Chapters 3 and 8.) Bertin's staff is comprised primarily of family members and people like him who had burned out of working in restaurants and were looking for a career switch to an industry with normal working hours. Bertin himself has lost the enthusiasm for the strategic planning the company would need to continue its historical growth performance. *Should an adjustment be made if some of these individuals do not materially contribute to the success of the company? Should an adjustment be made if anyone is paid above- or below-market compensation?* (See Chapter 6.)

Bertin has been routinely approached by investment bankers, private equity firms, and contacts within the food distribution industry about a sale of the company, and he is especially concerned about a possible recession in coming years given how long it has been since the economy was last in recession. In addition, one of Cavendish's major competitors, a company that is five times its size, is using its leverage to push Cavendish out of some of the urban markets in Cavendish's core territory. This more intense competition, coupled with concerns about economic conditions in the near future, has led Bertin to postpone planned price increases. *Can these competitive issues be identified by reviewing Cavendish's financial statements? What additional research, if any, is required? How are these competitive factors reflected in the valuation?* (See Chapters 3 and 8.)

Computation of Cavendish's Stand-Alone, Fair Market Value

As a lower middle market size company, Cavendish carries many risks, including limited capital, high financial leverage, a narrow product line, and very limited management. When combined with the company's loyal customer base, rapid sales growth, high product quality, and average profitability, these factors generate Cavendish's weighted average cost of capital rate of 19%, which reflects its risk profile and growth prospects.

Is a weighted average cost of capital the same as a discount rate? Is this the same as a capitalization rate? (See Chapters 7 and 9.) When the company's normalized net income to invested capital of $5.84 million for this year is divided by a 15% weighted average cost of capital (WACC) capitalization rate, the fair market value on a stand-alone basis of the enterprise is determined to be $40.5 million. Is this the value of equity? (See Chapter 6). *Why is only one year of earnings used to compute value? How does this reflect future year growth?* (See Chapter 7.)

Investment Value to Strategic Buyer

A larger public company that wants to quickly acquire a presence in Cavendish's market recognizes its strengths and weaknesses. Because the larger buyer frequently can eliminate many of Cavendish's limitations, it can increase Cavendish's sales growth and profits much more rapidly. Cavendish is also much less risky as a segment of the large company that possesses a broad array of market strengths. *How are these changes in risk reflected in the valuation? Who gets this value?* (See Chapter 3 and Appendix 13A.) *Is the transaction fair from a financial point of view? Should he invest in a fairness opinion so that he and the Company's two noncontrolling shareholders are comfortable with the transaction consideration?* (See Chapter 16.)

When owned by the strategic buyer, Cavendish's stand-alone EBIT could be increased over the next several years through more efficient operations and access to a broader market and an extensive distribution system. In the terminal period following the forecast, Cavendish's growth should be similar to that consistent with expectations for the food distribution industry. *How should the forecast and the years thereafter be used in computing value?* (See Chapter 7.)

After the deal is closed, the buyer will have to allocate the purchase price for financial reporting purposes. Part of this process will involve identifying and valuing Cavendish's intangible assets. *What financial reporting considerations will have to be made?* (See Chapter 17.) *What are the intangible assets owned by Cavendish, and how are they valued?* (See Chapters 17 and 18.)

While Cavendish has a WACC capitalization rate of 15%, Omni Distributors, the buyer, a large, well-known public company, has a WACC discount rate of about 12%. *How are capitalization rates and discount rates different, and when should each be used?* (See Chapters 7 through 9.) Because Cavendish operates in a new market for this buyer, has limited management and increasing competition, the buyer adjusted its discount rate for the added risk of Cavendish. *Should the buyer use its own discount rate to compute the investment value of Cavendish? If not, how should it be adjusted? How should this rate be affected by Cavendish's high financial leverage?* (See Chapter 9.) The discounting of Cavendish's expected future net cash flow to invested capital adjusted for synergies determined that Cavendish's invested capital is worth $69.7 million to one strategic buyer. What is net cash flow to invested capital, how is it computed, and how many years should be discretely forecasted? (See Chapter 6.) How does this discounting process reflect the potential adjustments to the return and the rate of return for the risk drivers and value drivers that have been considered? (See Chapters 7 and 8.) The $31.3 million excess of the $69.7 million investment value of invested capital over Cavendish's $38.4 million fair market value means this buyer could pay up to $31.3 million over stand-alone fair market value to acquire Cavendish. *What should be the minimum value considered by both the buyer and the seller to start the negotiations? How much above $38.4 million should this buyer be willing to pay to acquire Cavendish? Should this decision be influenced by competitors also bidding to acquire Cavendish? If the buyer ultimately pays $69.7 million to acquire Cavendish, is the buyer better off? How?* (See Chapters 1, 4, and 5.)

Cavendish's balance sheet shows assets of almost $44 million and equity of $15 million. How do these affect its value? (See Chapters 11 and 12.) Public companies in Cavendish's industry are selling at EBIT multiples ranging from 3 to 18, with a mean of 8. *Should these be considered, and how? Do the EBIT multiples generate equity value?* (See Chapter 10.) Another public food distributor recently sold for a 72% premium over its market value. *Should this transaction be considered in determining value?* (See Chapter 10.)

Since Cavendish is not a public company, should there be a discount for lack of marketability? Since Cavendish has noncontrolling shareholders, is a control premium or discount for lack of control applicable? (See Chapter 12.)

Can a buyer employ strategies to reduce risk in an acquisition? (See Chapters 4 and 18.) *How can buyers most effectively evaluate synergies?* (See Chapter 5.)

Can sellers employ a strategy to build value? Can they effectively plan in advance for a sale? (See Chapters 2 and 4.)

Buyers and sellers clearly have opportunities to gain through mergers and acquisitions. In order to create value, however, they must be able to measure and manage it. This process begins with the ability to identify and quantify those factors that create value. Most often, this must be done in a privately held company or a division of a public corporation where stock prices do not exist.

As you will see in this book, there are many factors that go into the valuation of a business. Valuation is both an art and a science. It is both a quantitative and a qualitative assessment of a business. But to boil it all down into one sentence: Business valuation is about the risk of achieving a company's expected future cash flows. Or even more simply, it is about risk and return. The chapters to come explain how to build operating value in a private company and how to create, build, measure, manage, preserve, and maximize value in mergers and acquisitions.

PART II

Building Value

CHAPTER 2

Building Value and Measuring Return on Investment in a Private Company

So much has been written about value and creating value that these concepts have acquired many meanings. Buyers and sellers must recognize how strategies affect value to achieve maximum benefit from purchase or sale decisions. It is even more important for owners and executives to understand how value is created or destroyed as they manage their daily operations where no immediate sale is anticipated. To manage value creation effectively in closely held companies, segments of public companies, and thinly traded public companies, that value must first be measured. Doing so requires precision in the definition and measurement of investment, return, rate of return, and value to accurately compute value and return on investment. Yet each of these metrics is almost always measured and reported incorrectly for nonpublic entities. As a result, their true economic performance and any resulting value creation or destruction is unknown, and investors seldom even know that they are misinformed.

Public Company Value Creation Model

The path to understanding value creation in private companies begins with an understanding of the public company model. It estimates future net cash flow returns and provides a value through a stock price that reflects investor perception of the company's relative level of risk.

Value creation and return on investment (ROI) are reasonably clear for investments in common stock of public corporations. Investors anticipate future cash returns (net cash flows) that they receive in dividend payments and appreciation when the stock is sold. Stock appreciation is a function of the anticipated cash return in the next period and the subsequent expected growth in that return. Thus the value of common stock in a public company ultimately can be reduced to dividend cash receipts and the anticipated growth in those cash receipts, which is reflected in stock appreciation.

This theory of common stock valuation based on anticipated cash receipts is widely accepted, yet many investment decisions are made based on irrelevant investment or price data. With current stock price information available for public securities, some investors focus on the amount they originally invested in the security while other investors focus on its current value. The latter is the right choice. In accounting language, their original investment is a sunk cost – it is irrelevant to their current decision because it is not a future return, and it cannot be changed by any choices that investors can make. The current value of the security *is* relevant because it represents the investors' current choice versus alternative investments. Investors should focus on this value because the decision to hold the stock is a decision not to invest that current value in some other way.

With the return correctly identified as net cash flow and the focus on current rather than historic value, risk is quantified. Varying levels of risk are reflected in the relationship between the stock price and its expected return. Higher-risk investments must produce higher rates of return, as investors select from the universe of potential risk-versus-return choices to achieve their investment goals. With daily stock market prices and periodic company performance measures conveniently available, investors focus on publicly traded stocks and study the current stock price and future cash flows.

This is where past earnings measures enter the analysis. The commonly quoted price-to-earnings (P/E) multiple compares the current stock price to a prior period's net income, but increasingly investors recognize that future circumstances may differ from the past. This is most evident in how the media currently reports on earnings disclosures. A public company's announced earnings are routinely compared against the market's expectations, which emphasizes the dependence of value on the future, while historical data is used primarily to assess the reliability of forecasts.

Historical data about rates of return of publicly traded stock can provide substantial insight about investor risk-versus-return expectations and the resulting rates of return that investors can expect. These annual rates of return earned by investors are based on these relevant amounts:

- Investments expressed as beginning of period cash outlays.
- Return expressed as the net cash inflow for that period.

Using this data, which is prepared in annual studies by Duff and Phelps[1] and described in Chapter 8, investors can compare their expectations against the average historical performance of past investments in public securities.

Thus the public company model computes the relevant current value based on relevant anticipated future net cash flow returns, with the relationship between them expressed as a multiple or percentage to quantify the company's risk. This procedure allows alternative investments to be analyzed and compared. Stock price movements reflect investor reaction to changes in either the company's expected net cash flow or risk, or both.

Computing Private Company Value Creation and ROI

We have now reviewed how the market measures change in the value of publicly traded companies. It focuses on future cash flow returns, current economic and industry conditions, as well as the company's internal capabilities to determine the company's risk profile, and through this process the company's value is determined. Individual investors, institutional investors, analysts, and the leadership of public companies constantly engage in this process with the consensus of their conclusions being reflected in the daily changes in every public company's stock price.

The secret to accurate valuation and ROI investment analysis for private companies, including divisions of public companies and thinly traded public companies, is to adapt the public security investment model to the unique characteristics of the nonpublic entity. However, this must be exercised with caution. Specifically, there are vast differences between public and private companies. As a result, public and private capital markets are not substitutes. They differ in terms of risk/return, liquidity, access to capital, liability, management, and behavior, among others. Nonetheless, although private capital market theory is developing, the mainstream private capital markets, including private company owners and their advisors, still draw parallels and look to the public company model to understand and determine their private company value. That said, we have introduced the key metrics involved – investment, return, rate of return, and value.

Investment

Which of the next points constitutes the correct measure of your investment in your private company?

---

[1] Duff & Phelps, LLC, *2017 Valuation Handbook: U.S. Guide to Cost of* Capital (Hoboken, NJ: Wiley, 2017).

1. The initial investment you and other shareholders made in the company plus any subsequent investments.
2. Your investments in the company plus any profits reinvested (this would be the book value of equity on your balance sheet).
3. The current market value of all the tangible assets that you use in the operations of your business.

The first two answers presented are clearly incorrect, although they are frequently used in return on capital employed (ROCE) measurements. Those numbers represent costs incurred in the past that may or may not have any relationship to value today. If these investments are low relative to value today, they generate a higher ROI; if they are high relative to value today, they generate a lower ROI. In either case, past investments are irrelevant (they are a sunk cost) because *the key measure for current decisions is the value of your investment today.*

The third choice listed, the current value of the tangible assets used in your operations, is an appropriate measure of investment if your company generates inadequate profits and no intangible value. *In an underperforming company with no intangible or goodwill value, your investment consists primarily of the current value of the company's tangible assets.* From our experience working in the middle market, nearly half of the private companies we see fail to generate their potential profits and intangible value.

An underperforming business is generally worth little or no more to its current owners than its tangible asset value, even though it may have valuable customers or technology and a good reputation. Because it fails to convert these qualities into adequate profits, they create no intangible value for the current owners unless they are sold to a buyer at a premium price that reflects intangible value that buyer hopes to create.

Most of the value in successful companies lies in their intangible assets. In fact, in a survey of 147 purchase price allocation analyses completed by the authors for financial reporting purposes of companies that had sold, an average of 23% of the purchase consideration was allocated to fixed assets and working capital, meaning that 77% of the value in these companies was in their intangible assets, including goodwill.[2] Houlihan Lokey found similar results in a 2016 survey of 455 transactions where an average of 29% of the purchase consideration was allocated to tangible assets, 35% to identifiable intangible assets, and 36% to goodwill.[3]

If your business generates sufficient profits to create operating or goodwill value (i.e. if you generate profits beyond your required rate of return), your company possesses intangible value and your investment must be

---

[2] Specifically, 39% of the purchase consideration was allocated to identifiable intangible assets and 38% to goodwill.
[3] Houlihan Lokey, *2016 Purchase Price Allocation Study*, published September 2017.

measured differently. For companies that generate profits in excess of their cost of capital, the owner's investment in the business is the present value of the company's anticipated future returns, a fourth point above to the question of what constitutes the correct measure of your investment in your private company. The higher those anticipated returns are, the higher the owner's investment will be.

For example, consider Microsoft. Its value today has nothing to do with what people put into the company some years ago, or the profits it reinvested, or whatever its tangible assets are worth. The value of Microsoft stock trading in the market today is solely a function of the anticipated future returns – dividends and stock appreciation – that shareholders expect to receive. This traditional model used to value public companies is the same one that is used in valuing profitable private companies.

Traditionally, owners associate their investment in their business with a cash outlay they made to acquire or expand the business. However, once they own it, they must recognize that every day they choose not to sell the company, they are by default electing to reinvest in it at whatever the company's current market value is. And when the company's operations have created operating value beyond whatever outlays were initially made by investors to acquire or expand the company, those prior amounts become irrelevant to their current investment decision. Only the current market value matters.

To summarize, as you consider your investment in your private company, either that investment is limited to the current market value of the tangible assets in the business, if it incurs losses or if its profits are inadequate; or the investment is the present value of its future returns if the company's operations generate intangible value. For profitable companies, this investment measure is harder to compute, but it is an invaluable tool for owners making investment decisions.

Return

Think of an investment you have made in a public company and what return you get from that investment. Obviously, it is limited to dividends and appreciation in the stock value. As an investor, you do not get the company's income, or its earnings before interest and taxes (EBIT) or earnings before interest, taxes, depreciation, and amortization (EBITDA). If the company borrows money effectively, the returns to investors include any benefits created by this lower-cost debt financing.

Private company returns must be measured the same way. The return that an investor in a private company should focus on is the spendable cash that the company generates after allowing for payment of all expenses and taxes and all reinvestment requirements for working capital and capital expenditures. This amount, which is sometimes called free cash flow, is the net cash flow on the capital invested in the business. It is computed as:

Net Income after Taxes
Add: Interest expense, net of income tax
Add: Noncash charges – depreciation and amortization
Less: Capital expenditures
Less: Increased Investment in Working Capital
         Net Cash Flow to Invested Capital

Curiously, net cash flow to invested capital appears on no financial statements, and private company owners almost never see it. But it represents the critical cash that can be taken from the business by debt and equity capital providers after all of the company's needs have been met. It is the capital providers' true return.

Note that in providing this explanation, we are using the return to debt and equity capital providers. This is necessary because the equity in a business benefits from the availability of debt capital and appropriate use of debt can improve return on equity. *Therefore, the proper computation of "return" for strategic planning and value creation purposes should be the net cash flow return to debt and equity capital rather than just equity capital.* There is a detailed discussion of calculation of net cash flow in Chapter 6.

Rate of Return

The third critical metric for value measurement and calculation of ROI, rate of return, must be understood because every investment carries a different level of risk. Proper investment choices must consider the risk or likelihood that the investment's future return will be achieved. This *required* rate of return is also known as a cost of capital, a required rate of return, or a discount rate, and is used to quantify the likelihood that future returns will be achieved. Fundamental investment theory states that investors will accept higher risk in investments only if they have an opportunity to earn a higher return. Therefore, the higher the perceived risk in an investment, the higher the rate of return must be on that investment. Mathematically, higher rates of return cause greater discounting of anticipated future returns, which reduces their value. Thus the greater the risk, the greater the discount rate and the lower the value. Conversely, lower risk would carry a lower discount rate and a higher value.

Note the distinction between your company's *required* rate of return, which reflects its relative level of risk, and your company's *actual* rate of return, which reflects its historical performance and is used to compute the company's *actual* ROI. Your actual return may be above or below what you should be earning based on your investment's risk. The required rate of return is the benchmark you must achieve to create value. Because companies employ both debt capital and equity capital – and hybrids such as preferred stock or convertible debt – the cost of each of these capital sources must be computed. Some companies can take on more lower-cost debt because they have greater collateral or more reliable returns that enable creditors to lend more money. The relative amounts of debt and equity vary by company and by industry and affect the company's cost of capital. The quality of management, level of competition, and other competitive factors also affect the likelihood that a company will achieve a forecasted revenue, income, and cash flow, and all of these factors also affect its cost of capital. A private company's weighted average cost of debt and equity capital – its weighted average cost of capital (WACC) – typically varies from about 12% to 24%, depending on the company's risk profile and capital structure. This risk profile is quantified through an analysis of the economy, industry, and company to assess its overall competitive position and likelihood of success. This process yields the company's *required* rate of return, or WACC, which is used to discount its future returns to compute its present value.

Just as the current measure of the first two ROI metrics – investment and net cash flow to invested capital – requires careful calculation, so does the estimate of the company's rate of return. But without this precise measure of risk, the return on future investments cannot be accurately quantified. There is a detailed discussion on calculation of cost of capital or rates of return in Chapters 7 through 9.

Value

Value can be a dangerous term. If it is not properly defined, it can easily be misinterpreted, and this lack of precision can yield bad investment decisions.

Based on the prior discussion, it should be clear that investment in – *and the value of* – a private company can be computed as the greater of the current value of its tangible operating assets (if it generates inadequate returns), or the present value of its future returns discounted at a *required* rate of return that reflects their relative level of risk. For an adequately profitable company, the present value of its future returns will exceed the tangible value of its operating assets with the excess representing the company's operating or intangible (sometimes called goodwill) value. This is the value of the business in the hands of its present owners or to a financial buyer who would only bring cash to a deal to acquire the company. It is the company's *fair market value*, and it represents the owner's current investment in the business. The owner elects to make this investment in the company every day that he or she decides not to sell the business.

Investors should understand that same company may have a higher *strategic (or investment) value* – perhaps significantly higher – to a strategic investor who, in buying the company, could create higher returns, a lower capital investment, or lower risk through the acquisition and ownership. Wise investors never lose sight of the fact that an alternative to continued ownership of their private company is its sale to a strategic buyer who could create synergies and value enhancement. Through a sale, the seller often can share in these synergistic benefits.

In addition to the distinction between fair market value and strategic value, investors should also focus on the distinction between the value of their company as a whole – 100% of it – and the value of a fractional interest in it.

An investment in most public companies can be liquidated in a few days because those shares are traded on an active market. For most private company investments, this is not the case, unless the private company owner owns 100% of the business and it is in an industry where purchases and sales of companies frequently occur.

Those who own a minority or lack of control interest in a private company must recognize that their lack of control of the company's operations, combined with the lack of a ready market for the company's stock, renders their investment relatively less attractive. *Lack of control and the accompanying lack of marketability can diminish value by 25% to 50% or even more of the proportionate share of the value of the company as a whole.* This is described further in Chapter 12. Thus, a further step that private company owners must take in assessing their individual ROI is to consider any diminution in value that occurs from lack of control and lack of marketability. Investors who ignore these factors in planning an exit strategy for their private company investments are frequently disappointed as they learn of the weaknesses in the bargaining position of a minority shareholder in a private company.

Illustration of Correct Calculation of Value Creation and ROI for Invested Capital

To illustrate the theoretical model that has been described, the next example, presented in Exhibits 2.1 through 2.5, provides basic information about Companies A and B and computes investment, return, actual rate of return, and value for each for a year, and then computes the increase in value that occurs during that year and the resulting return on investment that is achieved. In reviewing this example, please note that this illustration does not provide a detailed justification for the required rate of return (WACC) that is used. This explanation is provided in detail in Chapters 7 through 9.

Illustration of Correct Computation of Private Company ROI

The next data pertains to two private companies, A and B. Shareholders of each company invested $1 million to buy their stock. Both had a market value of tangible invested capital (net operating assets) of $10 million on their balance sheets at the beginning of the current year, as shown in

Exhibit 2.1 (i.e. their balance sheets were identical). Companies A and B had similar risk profiles, so both had the same WACC capitalization rate of 12.5%, as computed in Exhibit 2.3. They also each paid interest at a rate of 5% and combined federal and state income tax at a rate of 27%. Company A's *forecasted* net cash flow to invested capital at the beginning of the current year was $937,000 while Company B's was $1.392 million, as shown in Exhibit 2.2, and both of these returns were expected to grow 4% annually over the long term. Exhibit 2.4 calculates investment and value at the beginning of the year, and Exhibit 2.5 makes the calculations at the end of the year and then calculates ROI for the year.

EXHIBIT 2.1 Balance Sheet: Beginning of Current Year

			Companies A & B		
	Book Value ($000)	*Market Value ($000)*		*Book Value ($000)*	*Market Value ($000)*
Cash	1,000	1,000	**Accounts Payable**	2,000	2,000
Accounts Receivable	2,000	2,000	**Notes Payable**	6,000	6,000
Inventory	3,000	3,000	**Total Liabilities**	8,000	8,000
Fixed Assets (net)	4,000	6,000	**Total Equity**	2,000	4,000
Total Assets	10,000	12,000	**Total Liabilities & Equity**	10,000	12,000
Less: Accounts Payable	–2,000	–2,000	**Less: Accounts Payable**	–2,000	–2,000
Net Operating Assets	**$8,000**	**$10,000**	**Invested Capital**	**$8,000**	**$10,000**

EXHIBIT 2.2 Forecasted Net Cash Flow to Invested Capital for Current Year

	Company A ($000)	Company B ($000)
EBITDA	2,700	3,300
Depreciation	–800	–900
Interest	–300	–300
Pretax Income	1,600	2,100
Income Tax	–432	–567
Net Income	1,168	1,533
Add: Net Interest Expense	219	219
Add: Depreciation	800	900
Less: Capital Expenditures	–900	–1,000
Less: Working Capital	–350	–260
Net Cash Flow to Invested Capital	**937**	**1,392**

(continued)

(continued)

EXHIBIT 2.3 Weighted Average Cost of Capital (Required Rate of Return) Beginning of Current Year

Capital Source	After Tax Cost	Weight	Weighted Average Cost
Debt	3.7%	30%	1.1%
Equity	22%	70%	15.4%
WACC Discount Rate			16.5%
Less: Long-term Growth Rate			−4.0%
WACC Capitalization Rate			12.5%

EXHIBIT 2.4 Calculation of Investment (and Value) as of the Beginning of the Current Year

	Companies A and B
Fair Market Value of Net Tangible Assets from Balance Sheet	$\underline{\$10,000,000}$
	Company A
Present Value of Forecasted Net Cash Flows for the Current Year	$\dfrac{\$937,000}{12.5\%} = \$7,500,000$
	Company B
Present Value of Forecasted Net Cash Flows for the Current Year	$\dfrac{\$1,392,000}{12.5\%} = \$11,100,000$

Conclusion: While inadequate net cash flow returns prevent Company A's operating value from exceeding the $10 million current value of its net tangible assets, the value of Company B is $11.1 million based on its cost of capital, anticipated profits, cash flow, and growth. These are the key measures of "investment" that shareholders should consider. The shareholders' original investment of $1 million and the current book value of equity and invested capital are irrelevant in computing investment and ROI.

EXHIBIT 2.5 Calculation of Actual Return on Invested Capital for Current Year for Companies A and B

Based on each company's actual performance in the current year, and their competitive position at year-end, Company A is expected to generate net cash flow to invested capital of $1,100,000 next year and Company B is expected to generate $1,500,000, with both cash flows expected to grow at 4% annually over the long-term. Assuming neither company paid out dividends or distributions, Company A and Company B had net tangible assets at fair market values of $10,750,000 and $13,000,000 respectively at year end. While Company A's risk profile (required rate of return) remains at 16.5% at year-end, Company B has strengthened its management and its balance sheet, which reduced its risk (required rate of return) from 16.5% to 15.5%. Using this information, the value of each company at the end of the current year is computed as follows:

Company A	Company B
$\dfrac{\$1,100,000}{(16.5\% - 4\%)} = \$8,800,000$	$\dfrac{\$1,500,000}{(15.5\% - 4\%)} = \$13,000,000$

The total return to debt and equity capital providers for the current year is then computed as follows:

	Company A	Company B
Value of the Investment at the End of the Year	$10,750,000	$13,000,000
Value of the Investment at the Beginning of the Year	$10,000,000	$12,000,000
Invested Capital Appreciation	$750,000	$1,000,000
Add: Actual Net Cash Flow for Current Year (Company B only)	$0	$1,100,000
Total Return for Current Year	$750,000	$2,100,000

Each company's actual return on invested capital for the current year is computed as follows:

Company A	Company B
$\dfrac{\$750,000}{\$10,000,000} = 7.5\%$	$\dfrac{\$2,100,000}{\$12,000,000} = 17.5\%$

Total Return for Current Year
Value of Investment at Beginning of Year

In this illustration, the computation of actual ROI for Company A is based on the value of its net tangible assets, which includes the net cash flow earned during the year. Because Company B created value from its operations, its actual return to capital providers includes both the excess cash flow of $1,100,000 generated during the year (comparable to public company net after tax interest expense plus dividend payments) and the appreciation at year-end of $1,000,000 based on the market's pricing of its anticipated future cash flows. Can the calculation of ROI be considered reliable when one of its two major components is based on an estimate of future performance? The estimated performance must be based on sound, objective judgment for the ROI conclusion to be credible. The ROI of public companies, however, also includes capital appreciation based on anticipated performance, so the process presented is the standard method used for public companies. Because building value is a financial objective in every company, capital appreciation must be considered to accurately compute ROI.

Calculation of Actual ROI for Equity

In the preceding illustration, we computed actual ROI for invested capital, which includes both debt and equity capital. Private company owners should also focus on return on equity; this computation is similar to the example just presented. To compute actual ROI for equity, investment and value would include the calculated market values of equity at the beginning and end of the year, net cash flow would be to equity holders so it would be before consideration of interest expense and after debt principal proceeds or payments, and the required rate of return would be the equity discount rate. The topic of invested capital versus equity is explained in further detail in Chapter 6.

The company's actual rate of return on equity will be higher than its actual rate of return on invested capital as long the company generates a return on borrowed capital that is higher than that capital's net after tax cost. Key factors that affect a company's actual rate of return on equity versus invested capital include its level of profitability, its tax rate, its cost of debt and cost of equity, the relative levels of debt and equity in its capital structure, and the anticipated change, if any, in that capital structure. Private company owners and their chief financial officers should annually evaluate these variables as they assess the company's performance, its growth potential, and long-term need for capital to determine a capital structure that maximizes the company's long-term ROI. In doing so, however, owners should also look at their personal income needs, wealth, investment portfolio, and risk tolerance, including their need for diversification and liquidity. Owners of controlling interests in private companies, in particular, should strive for the capital structure for their private company that enables them to best achieve their personal financial goals. When their private company investment fails to serve their personal financial needs, they should consider selling out and investing in alternative ways that better meet their needs while still balancing personal nonfinancial considerations.

How Debt Financing Affects ROI

What are the pros and cons of financing with varying levels of debt, and how do investors determine the optimum level? Describing debt financing as "financial leverage" is really quite accurate because the debt funds enable the owners to lever or increase the return they earn on their equity. The rub, however, is that the leverage effect can also lower the investors' return. Exhibit 2.6 illustrates how debt can affect rates of return on equity.

Investors should draw several conclusions from a review of the results shown in Exhibit 2.6:

- Because the interest cost of debt is fixed, it must be paid regardless of earnings levels. When earnings are low, the interest expense limits or even can eliminate the return to equity.

EXHIBIT 2.6 Balance Sheet ($000s)

Investors are considering three capital structures - A, B, and C - to provide $10 million of capital for their company. Assuming a high interest rate environment where the interest cost is 10%, an income tax rate of 27%, and a stock price of $1,000 per share, note how the earnings per share (EPS) varies with the capital structures at the three different levels of earnings before interest and taxes (EBIT).

Net Operating Assets

Total		10,000

Liabilities and Equity

Capital Structure	A	B	C
Interest-Bearing Debt	0	3,000	6,000
Equity	10,000	7,000	4,000
Total	10,000	10,000	10,000

Calculation of Earnings per Share with Different Capital Structures at Different Levels of Earnings ($000s) Except Earnings per Share

Capital Structure	A	B	C	A	B	C	A	B	C
EBIT	800	800	800	1,600	1,600	1,600	2,400	2,400	2,400
Interest Expense (10%)	0	300	600	0	300	360	0	300	600
EBT	800	500	200	1,600	1,300	1,000	2,400	2,100	1,800
Income Tax Expense (27%)	216	135	54	432	351	270	648	567	486
Net Income	584	365	146	1,168	949	730	1,752	1,533	1,314
Number of Shares	100	70	40	100	70	40	100	70	40
EPS	$5.84	$5.21	$3.65	$11.68	$13.56	$18.25	$17.52	$21.90	$32.85

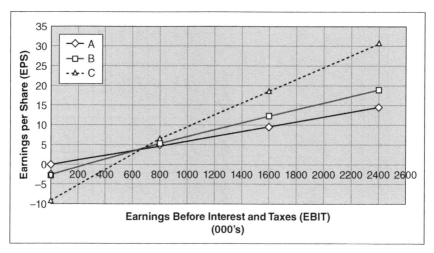

EXHIBIT 2.7 Increased Volatility in Earnings per Share Created by Variation in Amount of Financial Leverage

- Because the interest cost of debt is fixed, when earnings are strong, the equity holders collect all of the increased earnings; the creditors get none of the increase.
- The lower-risk, lower-return nature of debt forces creditors (bankers, primarily for private companies) to focus on collateral and cash flow. They must protect their limited return on the downside, because they get no share of the added return on the upside.

As shown in Exhibit 2.6, the degree of financial leverage also creates volatility in equity returns. When earnings varied from $800,000 to $2.4 million under the lower leverage of capital structure A, the resulting earnings per share ranged from $5.84 per share at an EBIT of $800,000 to $17.52 per share at an EBIT of $2.4 million. With the higher debt in capital structure C, however, earnings per share varied much more, from $3.65 to $32.85 over the same range of EBIT.

This volatility, which is portrayed graphically in Exhibit 2.7, clearly illustrates both the risks and rewards of financial leverage. And it emphasizes to the private company owner the critical need to clearly understand the company's competitive position. The stronger your long-term position appears to be, the more stable your resulting earnings and cash flows should be, which enables you to take greater advantage of debt financing. A less certain or weaker ability to compete requires safer financing with less debt.

Higher-growth companies frequently need capital for expansion, and their owners can benefit from the many choices of funding that the market offers. In addition to traditional debt, there are sources of subordinated debt and hybrid debt/equity funds that offer risk/reward combinations to fit almost any need. Whether an investor class wants a minimum level of fixed returns, protection on the downside, potential on the upside, or incentives to management to share in stock value enhancement, financing mechanisms exist. Each offers different levels of risk and return to match an individual investor's circumstances, considering the company's financing capabilities.

These financing options are also very beneficial when private companies have owners with major differences in their age, wealth, liquidity, desire for corporate control, and appetite for risk. Such owners are not limited to a one-size-fits-all capital structure. A blended structure can meet multiple needs, and this structure can be changed to fit changing investor circumstances and needs.

This is often critically important for investors nearing retirement who should reduce their private company investment to decrease their risk and increase both their portfolio diversification and their liquidity.

The message here should be clear: *Private company owners should review their capital structure annually as well as before any major capital expenditure, refinancing, or ownership change is contemplated. With a clear understanding of the risk/reward consequences of creative financing, owners can both increase their ROI and better achieve their other financial goals in the process.*

Operating Options to Enhance ROI

Once the mechanics of private company ROI are understood, the next step is to devise a strategy to improve the company's ROI. The key factors to enhance ROI should now be clear:

- *Option 1. Investment (current value).* Reduce the investment in net operating assets employed without causing returns to decrease or risk to increase. Illustration: Through more frequent inventory turns, reduce the required investment in inventory from a market value of $3 million to $2.5 million, and pay out the $.5 million to shareholders. The company's net cash flow and value remain the same, it requires less capital investment to generate that cash flow, and shareholders receive an added return.
- *Option 2. Return (net cash flow).* Increase forecasted net cash flow returns without increasing the investment in the company or its risk. Illustration: Through improved advertising, increase net cash flow by $100,000, which, when capitalized at 10%, yields $1 million in increased company value.

- *Option 3. Rate of return (risk).* Decrease the company's risk without increasing shareholder investment or impairing net cash flow returns. Illustration: By introducing a new product line that appeals to more customers, the company reduces its heavy reliance on its major customer. This reduced customer concentration cuts the company's WACC capitalization rate from 10% to 9.5%. When the forecasted return of $1.2 million is capitalized at 9.5%, company value is increased by $0.63 million.

Conclusion: ROI can be enhanced through any combination of reduced investment, improved returns, or lower risk. Wise shareholders constantly pursue strategies to achieve these value enhancements. These shareholders also should recognize that a primary – if not the most important – contribution of a company's board and senior management is to devise and execute successful strategies to enhance ROI. These strategies should be presented and reviewed annually as the centerpiece of the company's strategic planning process.

Common Owner Questions and Concerns about Managing and Maximizing ROI

- *Do investors in public companies also focus on net cash flow to invested capital in computing ROI?* Professional public company investors and managers focus primarily on net cash flow to equity, which is the return they actually receive. It consists of dividends and appreciation in stock value. Because public company investors can easily sell their common stock investment and generally cannot influence the company's capital structure and its level of debt, they focus on cash flow after borrowing rather than on net cash flow to invested capital, which is before borrowing.
- *How does a company's actual performance versus expectations affect value?* As this discussion has explained, anticipated future profits, if they are adequate, and the likelihood of achieving them determine a company's value. When a company's actual performance is above or below anticipated performance, investors use this new information to determine their new expectations and ultimately the value of the company's stock. So investors continually monitor a company's historical performance but generally make their investment decisions based on anticipated future performance. This same continual process of assessing actual versus anticipated performance occurs with public companies, where actual profits are always compared against the level that was expected.
- *Does a key change in a company's competitive position, such as a breakthrough in technology, the emergence of a new strong competitor, or the*

loss of a key person, affect value? When does such a change occur? The value of publicly traded stock moves up and down every day based on changing competitive factors, and the same thing actually occurs with private companies. It simply is noticed much less, or not at all, because the value of private companies is generally not monitored on a regular basis. Changes in stock value for public and private companies occur as soon as investors are aware of new competitive information.

- *When should shareholders focus on a company's value to a strategic buyer versus its fair market value?* Shareholders are wise to always monitor the interest strategic buyers may have in their company and the price buyers would pay based on synergies they believe they could achieve through an acquisition. Shareholders should pay particular attention to the level of interest expressed by strategic buyers when they believe their company's strategic position, and therefore its competitive advantages, is about to decline. At that time, strategic buyers may be able to overcome this weakness and pay an attractive price to do so.

- *Since a lower cost of capital, which reflects lower risk, generates a higher value, can investors create value by increasing debt to lower their company's cost of capital or WACC?* While this makes theoretical sense, it fails a reality check. Value is a function of what the market will pay for an asset; a property's current capital structure is generally of little interest to buyers because buyers bring their own capital. Thus buyers could independently bring the benefits of financial leverage that debt creates, so buyers should not be expected to pay any premium to the seller for the debt financing the seller possesses. While debt financing cannot artificially raise a company's value, it can increase investor's ROI, as this chapter has explained.

- *Does growth automatically create value?* Many shareholders and corporate executives are surprised to learn that value is not automatically created when a company increases its revenues or assets. Increased size does not necessarily lead to greater cash returns or reduced risk. Even profitable growth generally requires cash investments for working capital and fixed assets, both of which reduce the company's expected net cash flow. Therefore, growth increases value only when it reduces risk or creates positive net cash flows, after consideration of capital reinvestment requirements.

- *How much can a company's risk profile change, and can this change be accurately measured?* Procedures to calculate rates of return are presented in Chapters 8 and 9. While they do involve judgment and reflect perceptions of anticipated future risk, the process of quantifying rates of return can be reliable and accurate, particularly for established businesses. In the middle market – companies with sales ranging from

$10 million to several hundred million dollars – there is less stability than in the largest public companies. Therefore, the market price of these companies is much more volatile. For example, as explained further in Chapter 8, the volatility in the price of the smallest 10% of companies traded on the New York Stock Exchange is approximately 50% greater than in the largest 10% of those companies. So the risk profile of middle-market companies can change significantly. Information and techniques are available to measure and quantify the effect of these changes on stock value.

- *A private company investment earns an actual rate of return of 10%, although, based on its risk profile, it should be generating a required rate of return of 18%.* Why would this company's owner consider selling this investment if his financial advisor informs him that he can expect to earn only about 6% long term on his sale proceeds from investing them in a conservative portfolio to fund his requirement? Assuming the financial advisor's estimated long-term return of 6% to fund a retirement is correct, the owner should still consider selling for these reasons.

1. His current investment in the private company is underperforming, so it is not building value.
2. Even more important, his private company is a much higher risk investment, and because of this risk, there is a strong possibility that the value of this investment could decline rapidly.
3. The owner also should recognize that it is likely that his wealth is concentrated in this single high-risk investment and he lacks the diversification that someone moving toward retirement should have.
4. He lacks liquidity in this private company investment. If he owns less than a controlling interest in it, this lack of control in the company and the accompanying lack of marketability decrease the value of his investment and his flexibility in managing that investment, as explained in Chapter 12.

- *Some successful private company owners avoid borrowing because they "do not want to have to pay interest to the bank." Is there a danger in this attitude?* The primary danger is not in the owner's reluctance to borrow, although this discussion has explained how prudent use of debt can increase return on equity. Far more important is for private company owners to recognize that all capital bears a cost and, therefore, should generate a return. Equity capital is not "free" because the investor does not have to pay herself an annual return on it. On the contrary, because equity is a much higher risk capital than debt – probably at least three times as high – it should earn its required rate of return, or the owner should seek a more attractive investment elsewhere.

Analyzing Value Creation Strategies

A company's value-creating historical performance and future potential can be monitored through use of the return on investment tool called the DuPont analysis. Developed by scientists at DuPont about a century ago to track that company's performance in its diversified investments, this analysis looks at profit margin and asset turnover as the building blocks to return on assets.

The DuPont formula involves the accounting measures of return and investment that this discussion has criticized as being potentially misleading. It employs accounting measures of income and investment at book value that can distort performance and value assessment. However, with proper adjustments and careful interpretation, the DuPont analysis can help to identify and quantify value drivers and ultimately develop strategies to improve return on investment and create value.

The DuPont analysis identifies the building blocks of profit margin and asset turnover that lead to return on net operating assets in the equation shown in Exhibit 2.8.

The profit margin, also known as return on sales, measures the margin of profit on a dollar of sales by comparing a measure of income to revenue. Nonoperating or nonrecurring items of income or expense should be excluded for the purpose of this analysis. Interest expense, net of its income tax benefit, should be added back to income to prevent financing costs from influencing the analysis of operating performance. The result is the company's normalized net income after taxes but before financing costs, known as net income to invested capital (I/C). Strategies to improve profit margin include increasing revenues or decreasing expenses. The search to achieve these goals should focus management on analysis of profit margin value drivers, as shown in Exhibit 2.9.

In assessing each of these functional areas to improve profitability, management should refer to the company's strategic plan and the strengths, weaknesses, opportunities, and threats (SWOT) analysis, which is described further in Chapter 3. Those SWOTs should help both to identify and to assess the likelihood of improving profitability through changes in any of these functional areas.

Most managers and shareholders can clearly see the relationship between revenue enhancement or expense controls and profitability, and

EXHIBIT 2.8　DuPont Analysis

Profit Margin	Net Operating Asset Turnover	Return on Net Operating Assets
$\dfrac{\text{Net Income to I/C}}{\text{Sales}} \times$	$\dfrac{\text{Sales}}{\text{Net Operating Assets}} =$	$\dfrac{\text{Net Income to I/C}}{\text{Net Operating Assets}}$

how this can lead to value creation. Far fewer see the importance of efficiency in asset utilization, known as *asset turnover.* This building block focuses on the capital employed relative to the sales volume generated. Improvements here can be achieved through strategies that increase revenues proportionately more than any accompanying increase in assets or decrease assets proportionately more than any accompanying decrease in revenue. This conceptual goal can then be executed through improvements to the management of major assets, as measured by the accounts receivable collection period, inventory turnover, and fixed asset turnover. The primary resources and functions that comprise total assets are shown in Exhibit 2.10.

In assessing each of these activities to improve efficiency in asset utilization, management should return again to the SWOT analysis to determine the likelihood of improving performance in that activity, considering the company's internal capabilities and its external environment.

In traditional DuPont analysis, the profit margin measured as a percentage is multiplied by the asset turnover, expressed as a number of times, to yield the return on assets. This rate of return, expressed as a percentage, will receive less emphasis here than in the traditional analysis because

EXHIBIT 2.9 Profit Margin Value Drivers

Value Drivers	Income Statement Accounts
Markets	Sales
Customers	
Advertising and Marketing Policy	
Volume	
Pricing	
Production Capacity	Cost of Goods Sold
Production Efficiency	
Product Design	
Raw Material Choices and Costs	
Labor Costs	
Overhead Costs and Utilization	
Warehousing and Distribution Costs and Efficiency	Operating Expenses
Marketing, Advertising, and Selling Costs	
General Administration Policies and Costs	
Attributes	Income Taxes
Strategies	
Rates	

of its reliance on accounting measures of return and investment. In this focus on value, current and proposed strategies to improve profit margin and asset turnover should be analyzed to determine their effect on investment, net cash flow, and risk. The net cash flow is determined by sales volume, operating margins, tax rates, and investment requirements for working capital and fixed assets. Risk is reflected in the SWOT analysis and the company's competitive position, given its strategic advantages and disadvantages. Risk is ultimately quantified through the WACC, which reflects the company's risk-adjusted cost of debt and equity and the relative amount of each financing source employed. The components of this value creation

EXHIBIT 2.10 Asset Turnover Value Drivers

Value Drivers	Balance Sheet Accounts
Customer Base	Accounts Receivable and
Industry Practices	Collection Period
Credit Policy	
Collection Procedures	
Discounts and Allowances	
Credit Loss Exposure	
Supplier Capabilities	Inventory and Turnover
Purchasing versus Handling versus Carrying Costs	
Customer Loyalty and Stock-out Risks	
Production Requirements	
Distribution Capabilities	
Obsolescence Threats	
Supplier Base and Purchasing Power	Accounts Payable,
Industry Practices	Accrued Expenses
Payment Policy	and Payment Period
Cash Flow Capacity	
Discounts and Allowances	
Credit Availability	
Current and Anticipated Capacity	Fixed Assets and Turnover
Production and Scheduling Efficiency	
Warehousing and Distribution Efficiency	
Capital Constraints	
Vendor/Supplier Capacity and Reliability	
Make or Buy Options	

EXHIBIT 2.11 Components of Value Creation

analysis are summarized in Exhibit 2.11. The competitive analysis that supports the WACC is presented in Chapter 3, and the techniques to quantify the WACC are explained in Chapter 9.

The left-to-right flow in Exhibit 2.11 can be summarized in this way:

- Revenues less expenses yield the margin of profit on each dollar of sales.
- Revenues versus assets reflect the sales volume achieved compared to the resources employed to reveal efficiency in asset utilization.
- Margin and turnover are combined to generate the net cash flow to invested capital (NCF$_{IC}$), which is the cash return to debt and equity capital providers.
- The SWOT analysis considers the company's external environment and internal capabilities.
- The cost of debt and equity funds to the company is determined by its external environment and internal capabilities.
- The company's net cash flow return to debt and equity providers is discounted or capitalized by the WACC, which is its combined cost of debt and equity, to yield the operating value of the entity.

Once this information for a business has been gathered and organized, the key to value creation is to identify those strategies that most effectively improve net cash flow or reduce risk. In this process, managers frequently are tempted to stray toward strategies that create sales or asset growth without considering the effect on net cash flow. These growth strategies also frequently increase the company's risk profile as they move it away from its core business or into new and less familiar markets. So each strategy must be quantified in terms of its cash flow and risk consequences while management candidly assesses the company's ability to execute the strategy given competitive conditions.

How Do These Value-Building Concepts Compare to Strategies Generally Referred to as Economic Value Added?

They are quite similar. While some applications of economic value added employ proprietary adjustments and methodologies, the conceptual goals are always to pursue strategies that:

- Increase net cash flow through some combination of increased revenues, decreased expenses, and more efficient asset utilization.
- Reduce the company's risk, relative to its expected returns, and thereby decrease its cost of capital.

Value creation in a private company should now be intuitively obvious. It employs the public company model but requires increased management attention and measurement precision in the absence of a published stock market price. The key is to pursue strategies that create cash flow and present the highest likelihood of success. Achieving these goals requires an understanding of, and relentless attention to, the risk and return fundamentals that have been described. To begin this process, we next look in further detail at how to analyze a company's strategic position to assess and quantify risk.

CHAPTER 3

Market and Competitive Analysis

We have established that a company's value is determined by its expected net cash flow and relative level of risk. To both measure value and manage valuation creation, we must accurately assess the competitive environment in which the company operates. Doing this includes analyzing both the external and the internal conditions that influence performance. Many companies routinely perform these steps in their annual strategic planning process. What most nonpublic entities fail to do, however, is tie the results of their strategic plan to the ultimate goal of creating shareholder value. Whether valuing a company for merger and acquisition, performance improvement, or any other reason, competitive analysis is an essential step.

Many people see valuation as primarily a financial calculation. They analyze historical financial performance, position, and cash flow, compute financial ratios, and compare them to industry averages. Based on this information, they prepare spreadsheets that forecast future performance. Armed with this data, they compute the company's value and often feel confident in their assessment.

This process overlooks a major weakness of financial statements: They portray the *results* of a company's past financial performance but not the *causes*. A company's success is generally dependent on its ability to produce products or services efficiently, in appropriate quantity and quality, on time at a reasonable cost, and to market, sell, and distribute them effectively at a sufficiently attractive price. This success depends on numerous external and internal factors that must be assessed as part of the valuation process. Therefore, a solid *qualitative* assessment of the company is at least as important as a *quantitative* assessment. In other words, a proper valuation involves both a *quantitative* and a *qualitative* assessment of a business. This chapter explains how to perform market and competitive analysis to assess a company's strategic position and ability to compete in its market against its peers.

Test Yourself on Risk and Value Drivers

Companies in many industries are valued based on multiples of earnings, cash flow, or revenue. A key point to remember is that the appropriate multiple for the target company depends on its strengths and weaknesses. Strong appraisal skills require an instinct for those factors that tend to influence these multiples up or down. Test yourself *from the buyer's and the seller's perspective* in assessing whether the next 20 factors would *generally* increase or decrease a company's value and resulting multiple. The answers are shown in the paragraph that follows the list.

1. Possess strong brand name or customer loyalty
2. Sales concentrated with a few key customers
3. Operate in a well-maintained physical plant
4. Operate in a small industry with a limited customer base
5. Generate a high sustainable net cash flow to shareholders
6. Have compiled or reviewed rather than audited financial statements
7. Possess competitive advantages, such as technology, location, or an exclusive product line
8. Operate with deficient working capital and generally limited financial capacity
9. Generally favorable future economic and industry conditions
10. Operate with limited management on whom the company is heavily dependent
11. Sell a diverse mix of products to customers located in broad geographic markets
12. Sell commodity-type products that possess little differentiation from competitors
13. Operate in large, high-growth industry
14. Substantial excess capacity exists in the industry
15. High barriers in industry impede entry by new competitors
16. Continual threat posed by substitute products and technological obsolescence
17. Possess strong position in niche industry
18. Sell products through brokers, creating limited knowledge of or contact with product end users
19. Are either the most efficient low-cost producer or high-quality producer, or both
20. Possess history of litigation with customers, suppliers, and employees

> When companies in an industry are selling, for example, at four to eight times some level of earnings, that range allows for major variation in value. The odd-numbered risk and value drivers listed would generally move a company toward the higher end of the multiple range while the even-numbered items generally have a negative effect, resulting in lower multiples. The significance of these drivers varies by company, and the appraisal must subjectively weigh each. Finally, in assessing a driver, remember that while it may exist in an assessment of the company on a stand-alone basis, it may be eliminated through an acquisition, creating a synergistic benefit.

Linking Strategic Planning to Building Value

Companies engage in annual strategic planning to provide purpose and direction for the business. In the first stages of planning, the company typically establishes a mission, which, in addition to defining the company's purpose, helps its management and employees to identify those key constituencies, often referred to as stakeholders, to whom the company is primarily accountable for its long-term success. A typical mission statement would read:

> Our mission is to produce the highest-quality products and services for our customers, while generating the highest possible return on investment for our *stockholders*, while providing a safe, productive working environment for our employees, while operating as a constructive corporate citizen in our *community*.

The mission statement is intentionally general and, as demonstrated, can fit almost any for-profit entity. Management and employees can reconsider it annually to focus on exactly why the company exists and whom it must serve to be successful in the long term.

From this company-wide statement of purpose, the company's annual strategic plan develops. It begins with broad, long-term goals established by the board of directors and senior management. From this general direction, the planning process progresses throughout the organizational structure, with each business segment preparing intermediate and short-term objectives and plans, which must be consistent with the long-term corporate objectives established by the board. They are submitted, evaluated, resubmitted, and ultimately approved in a process that should provide the company with both direction and consensus at all management levels.

Accompanying the plans at each segment level are budgets, which are financial expressions of how the goals, objectives, and targets will be achieved.

Throughout all levels of the planning process, an essential step is preparation of a competitive analysis. This analysis is typically done by evaluating the company's internal factors and external environment to identify any strengths, weaknesses, opportunities, and threats (SWOT) that exist. The internal analysis considers the company's capabilities, including production capacity and efficiency, marketing, sales and distribution effectiveness, technological capability, and the depth, quality, and availability of management and employees – these are the strengths and weaknesses. The external analysis examines those factors outside the company that will influence its performance and competitive position, including economic and industry conditions – these are the opportunities and threats. The SWOT analysis attempts to define the competitive environment in which the company operates to identify the optimum strategy for success considering these conditions. That is, the SWOT analysis enables management to formulate a strategy that will minimize the effect of a company's weaknesses on its business while maximizing its strengths based on conditions in the industry and the capabilities of the company relative to its competition. Ideally, a company will match its strengths against market opportunities that result from its competitors' weaknesses or voids.

When preparing competitive analysis for a valuation, the same SWOT analysis should be performed. It identifies and assesses how the company operates, how it interacts with and relies on its suppliers and customers, and how it performs relative to its competitors. From this we determine how risky the company is relative to its competitors, considering the industry and economic conditions in which it operates. As the competitive analysis progresses, we identify the causes behind the results reflected on the company's financial statements. That is, we identify why the company performed the way it did given its competitive environment. And because investment is always forward looking, the competitive analysis ultimately is used to assess the company's *anticipated* performance. While history provides a track record, value is primarily a function of the future.

The factors that are identified in the competitive analysis are frequently referred to as value drivers and risk drivers. *Risk drivers* cause uncertainty for the company. *Value drivers* reflect the company's strengths that enable it to both minimize risk and maximize net cash flow returns. Cumulatively, identifying the risk and value drivers establishes the company's strategic advantages and disadvantages. They are ultimately quantified in the discount rate that reflects the company's overall level of risk and in the forecast of expected net cash flows, considering the company's competitive position.

Top 10 Value Drivers

It is critically important for a business owner to identify and understand the value drivers – factors that increase cash flows and reduce risk – associated with business. While many value drivers are identified throughout this chapter and book, we consider the following 10 to be most essential to increasing cash flows and reducing risk, thereby enhancing overall company value.

Capital Access. The smaller the company, the more limited its access to debt and equity capital. The company will need to assess the kind of capital needed to achieve its goals. Questions to ask:

- How is the company currently leveraged?
- How do bank covenant restrictions impact the business and its future plans?
- Do shareholders have to provide equity or personally guarantee loans?
- Is bringing in an outside investor and issuing preferred stock a viable option?

Customer Base. A solid and diversified customer base is essential for the ongoing viability of a business. When companies grow and prosper by providing exceptional service to their largest customers, dependency may increase to the point where too great a percentage of revenues are concentrated with too few customers; companies must manage the allocation of customer concentration to reduce the risk of losing a large source of revenues.

- What percentage of the company's revenues do its top five customers comprise?
- What amount of revenue is recurring?
- What is the economic useful life of its customer base?

Economies of Scale. As production output increases, businesses typically achieve lower costs per unit. Whether through quantity discounts or spreading capacity costs over higher volumes, larger companies possess distinct advantages in certain operations and markets.

- Is the company effectively exploiting its internal economies of scale (i.e. cost savings that accrue regardless of the economic environment or industry in which it operates)?

(continued)

(continued)

- What are the company's growth opportunities such that it can realize more economies of scale?
- Can the company enter into a consortium, joint venture, or out-source to increase buying power and reduce expenses?

Financial Performance. Financial analysis assists in measuring trends, identifying the assets and liabilities of a company, and comparing the financial performance and condition of the company to other, similarly positioned firms. Internally prepared and compiled financial statements may hamper management's assessment of performance, causing potential buyers to possibly question the quality of this data.

- How does the company compare in terms of liquidity, activity, profitability, and solvency measures?
- What financial controls are in place?
- Are the financials audited or reviewed by an outside CPA?

Human Capital. A company's employees are at the heart of an organization. Key value drivers include the knowledge, skills, experience, training, and creative abilities that employees bring to a business, and the health of its company culture.

- What are the quality control procedures?
- How effective are the production/service capabilities?
- How is the company managed?
- What is the depth and breadth of management?
- Are there any key person dependencies in terms of technical knowledge, production skills, or customer contacts?
- Is there a management succession plan?
- What rights do individual shareholders have?

Market Environment. Each business is impacted by economic trends and developments in the industry in which it operates. Management must understand how the industry is impacted by economic factors and how the industry is structured to minimize the impact of macro trends on the business.

- What is the company's market share?
- Where is it positioned in the market?
- Does management have an understanding of its niche and unique offering?

- Does the company have diverse offerings that can modulate the impact of economic swings?

Marketing Strategy and Branding. Marketing is the link between customers' needs and their response to a company's products/services. Strong branding will not only improve company sales by increased market recognition, it will also provide a clear direction that will improve operational efficiency when tied to the company's mission.

- How does the company market itself?
- What are its marketing and sales capabilities and shortcomings?
- How effective and known is its brand?
- What is its social media presence?
- How effective is its website?
- Is the brand tied to the company's mission statement and its strategic direction?

Product/Service Offering. Specialty companies frequently derive their strength from focusing in niche markets, but concentration may create risks from lack of diversification and overdependence on limited markets. Some specialty companies may find their largest customers adopt a policy to deal only with suppliers who offer a broad range of products, forcing them to either expand their product offerings or sell out to a larger company. Increasing diversification reduces risk, which improves value.

- What is the company's mix of offerings?
- How subject is any concentrated offering to economic and industry swings?
- What products/services can be offered that differ from existing ones but that use similar human capital, production capability, customer base, etc. to diversify?
- What opportunities exist for vertical or horizontal integration?

Strategic Vision. Most companies put together a one-year budget, but few attempt to put together a business plan or long-term forecast. Valuation is all about future expectations and company management needs a strategic vision to create value. Management must take a look at all the information they have gathered from reviewing their company to divulge a strategic vision that can be passed along to the future owner, which provides additional support and assurance of continuity of, and even increase, sales.

(continued)

(continued)

- What is management's long-term outlook?
- When did the company last put together a formal business plan?
- Is the company's strategy in tune with its customers' demographics, tenure, needs, and demands?

Technology. Companies with fewer monetary resources often lack adequate research and development resources, finding it difficult to keep pace with technological changes in their markets. Such companies often face an inescapable need to incur large amounts of capital expenditures in the near future or allocate resources to a limited number of product development projects. This inevitably results in product or service obsolescence, adverse impact on future growth, and loss in market share. In the meantime, larger companies are in a better position to demonstrate technological expertise by developing products that address emerging customer needs such that customers may choose their state-of-the-art products, despite the availability of lower cost, lower performance technology.

- How much resources does the company allocate to R&D?
- Is their use of technology up to date?
- Are there impending technological changes that could negatively impact the company's product/service offering?

Assessing Specific Company Risk

The development of the discount rate is explained in Chapter 8. The primary element in this rate that incorporates the competitive analysis is known as unsystematic risk (or alpha), which measures the company's specific risk relative to that of its peers. Unsystematic risk generally involves assessment at three levels:

1. Economic
2. Industry
3. Company

Competitive analysis begins at the macroenvironmental level. It proceeds to focus more specifically, first on the subject company's industry and then preferably on the subject company's subsection of that industry.

The analysis then concludes with a review of the company itself. It is generally forward looking as it considers the future conditions in which the company must operate.

Macroenvironmental Risk

The examination begins by exploring the outlook for conditions in which all companies will operate. These conditions include political, regulatory, socioeconomic, demographic, and technological factors, but the primary focus is on the economic climate. Specific economic factors include the general rate of economic growth – gross national product or gross domestic product – and extend to the rate of inflation, interest rates, unemployment rates, and similar factors. The markets served by the company and its customer base frequently determine the breadth of this analysis. For example, a company that serves a national or international customer base must consider that economic climate, whereas when a company's customer base is primarily local, the state and local climate becomes the focus.

The extent of analysis of regulatory, political, cultural, and technological factors is dependent on the influence that these issues exert on the company's performance. Companies operating in industries such as health care, where regulatory influences traditionally have been substantial, require extensive examination on how these factors will affect overall performance. Similarly, these issues must be considered if major regulatory or political changes are anticipated. Technological changes also should be examined in proportion to their anticipated effect on a company's performance. Those companies that rely heavily on technology for growth and success or those that are particularly vulnerable to technological improvements require more concentrated analysis of these factors.

Most of the macroenvironmental factors are beyond the company's immediate control, but they all must be analyzed to assess their effect on its performance.

Industry Analysis

Analysis at the industry level examines the overall attractiveness of operating in a selected industry and the company's relative position versus its competitors in that industry. Whenever possible, broader industry definitions are more specifically defined. For example, the healthcare industry could be reduced to nursing homes and then, within that category, personal care versus assisted-living facilities. Similar industry subdivisions could reduce food services to restaurants, to fast food versus full menu, and then to with versus without alcoholic beverages. Keep in mind that the size of an industry affects the analyst's ability to make these subdivisions. Larger industries typically have trade or professional organizations devoted to industry research for their members' benefit.

Initially at the industry level and eventually extending to the company level, strategies must be formulated and implemented to direct the company toward success. The objective is to exploit the company's strategic advantages while minimizing the consequences of its disadvantages.

Various methodologies or frameworks for conducting strategic analysis have been developed. One of the best known is described in *Competitive Strategy* by Michael E. Porter,[1] which provides a framework to analyze rivalry and structure within an industry. This includes analysis of barriers to entry and the threat of new entrants, the bargaining position and influence of customers and suppliers, and threats posed by substitute products or services. Porter describes generic strategies, including class leadership, differentiation, and focus, that represent the alternative strategic positions that companies may assume in an industry.

The purpose of the industry analysis is to identify and analyze how industry factors will affect a company's ability to compete. Since this analysis is forward looking, it examines the company's likely performance given its strategic advantages and disadvantages. The strategic analysis should recognize the concept of positioning based on varieties, needs, access, and trade-offs between these activities.

Porter built on this model in many subsequent works, including his classic article, "What Is Strategy?" In that article, Porter discussed "Reconnecting with Strategy," which explains the challenge for established companies to redefine their strategy in this way:

> Most companies owe their initial success to a unique strategic position involving clear trade-offs. Activities once were aligned with that position. The passage of time and the pressures of growth, however, led to compromises that were, at first, almost imperceptible. Through a succession of incremental changes that each seemed sensible at the time, many established companies have compromised their way to homogeneity with their rivals. The issue here is not with the companies whose historical position is no longer viable; their challenge is to start over, just as a new entrant would. At issue is a far more common phenomenon: the established company achieving mediocre returns and lacking a clear strategy. Through incremental additions of product varieties, incremental efforts to serve new customer groups, and emulation of rivals' activities, the existing company loses its clear competitive

[1] Michael E. Porter, *Competitive Strategy* (New York: The Free Press, 1980).

position. Typically, the company has matched many of its competitors' offerings and practices and attempts to sell to most customer groups.

A number of approaches can help a company reconnect with strategy. The first is a careful look at what it already does. Within most well-established companies is a core of uniqueness. It is identified by answering questions such as the following:

- Which of our product or service varieties are the most distinctive?
- Which of our product or service varieties are the most profitable?
- Which of our customers are the most satisfied?
- Which customers, channels, or purchase occasions are the most profitable?
- Which of the activities in our value chain are the most different and effective?

Around this core of uniqueness are encrustations added incrementally over time. Like barnacles, they must be removed to reveal the underlying strategic positioning. A small percentage of varieties or customers may well account for most of a company's sales and especially its profits. The challenge, then, is to refocus on the unique core and realign the company's activities with it. Customers and product varieties at the periphery can be sold or allowed through inattention or price increases to fade away.

A company's history can also be instructive. What was the vision of the founder? What were the products and customers that made the company? Looking backward, one can reexamine the original strategy to see if it is still valid. Can the historical positioning be implemented in a modern way, one consistent with today's technologies and practices? This sort of thinking may lead to a commitment to renew the strategy and may challenge the organization to recover its distinctiveness. Such a challenge can be galvanizing and can instill the confidence to make the needed trade-offs.[2]

Industry analysis is an essential step in both the company's annual strategic planning process and in a business valuation. Management must clearly understand the relative attractiveness of an industry, the market and structural characteristics most likely to change that level of attractiveness, and the resources necessary to compete successfully in that environment. Industry analysis and strategic planning constitute a unique body of knowledge with

---

[2] Reprinted by permission of *Harvard Business Review* from "What Is Strategy?" by Michael E. Porter (November–December 1996). Copyright © 1996 by the Harvard Business School Publishing Corporation.

which the business appraiser must be familiar in order to properly assess a company's likely performance. Those lacking this background should acquire the benefits that this insight can provide before addressing significant valuation or merger and acquisition decisions.

Company Analysis

The analysis of strengths and weaknesses within the company should take into consideration the external economic and industry factors that have been described. That is, the internal assessment should reflect the company's external environment, including SWOT.

A proper internal analysis will look at the company's historical performance, paying particular attention to the competitive factors – the causes – that created the results portrayed on the company's financial statements. With this history in perspective, the analysis then looks at anticipated future economic and industry conditions, how those conditions differ from the past, and the company's ability to compete in this expected environment. The DuPont analysis described in Chapter 2, with its focus on profit margin and efficiency in asset utilization, should be applied to forecasted future performance. Each of the company's major functional areas, including purchasing, design and production, sales, marketing and distribution, and general administration, should be evaluated from margin and asset-efficiency viewpoints. This analysis should be done for each business segment to assess return on investment. Ultimately, the return should be quantified as net cash flow to invested capital and the rate of return as a weighted average cost of capital (WACC), with these factors determining value creation.

In assessing revenues, breakdowns must be made by product or service line, reflecting anticipated volume and prices, given external conditions and the company's internal competitive advantages and disadvantages. The other factors affecting the company's net cash flow include cost of sales, operating expenses, income taxes, and the funding of fixed assets and working capital. These factors also must be assessed in light of the company's internal capabilities and external environment. Internal capabilities, including purchasing, design and engineering, production, and accounting and data processing, should be assessed in light of the company's competition. A qualitative assessment of the company's history, personnel, production capacity, and technology versus that of its competition and factors identified in the industry analysis feed into the metrics measured by the DuPont analysis. From this, the company's ability to generate the forecasted return is evaluated and its risk profile measured against its likely competition is also assessed.

This returns us to the SWOT analysis, which was performed earlier in assessing external factors. A similar examination is now made of internal capabilities and limitations to identify the company's competitive advantages and disadvantages. The results of these internal strengths and weaknesses, when considered against the external opportunities and threats, are quantified in the forecast that supports the company's strategic plan. The risk profile that reflects the internal and external uncertainties in the plan is then quantified in the company's rate of return or WACC.

Competitive Factors Frequently Encountered in Nonpublic Entities

As will be discussed, traditional financial analysis includes the measure of a company's liquidity, activity, profitability, and solvency. The DuPont analysis, which was described in Chapter 2, analyzes profitability primarily as a function of profit margin and asset turnover. Financial leverage measures the extent to which the company is financed with debt. It is often combined with coverage ratios, which compare various measures of the company's income or cash flow against fixed debt payments that it must service. And liquidity ratios measure the company's ability to pay current debt with current assets. These factors affect companies of all sizes, whether they are publicly traded or privately held.

The next factors, which are discussed in more detail in Chapter 8, tend to be particularly important to nonpublic entities. Buyers and sellers must carefully distinguish the effect of each on stand-alone fair market value versus investment value to a strategic buyer. Many of these create substantial strategic disadvantages to the company on a stand-alone basis, but they can be eliminated or greatly mitigated if the company is acquired and becomes a segment of a larger business.

- Lack of access to capital.
- Ownership structure and stock transfer restrictions
- Company's market share and market structure of the industry
- Depth and breadth of management
- Heavy reliance on individuals with key knowledge, skills, or contacts
- Lack of strategic vision
- Marketing and advertising capacity
- Breadth of products and services
- Purchasing power and related economies of scale
- Condition of facility and upcoming capital expenditure needs
- Customer concentration
- Vendor and supplier relations and reliance
- Distribution capability
- Ability to keep pace with technological changes
- Ability to protect intellectual property

- Increasing threat of foreign competition
- Litigation, environmental, and adverse regulatory issues
- Depth, accuracy, and timeliness of accounting information and internal control

Financial Analysis

The analysis of a company's financial statements is performed to assist in measuring trends, identifying the assets and liabilities of the company, and comparing the financial performance and condition of the company to other, similarly positioned firms. Financial analysis commonly includes a comparison of the company's financial and operating ratios with those of a sufficiently similar industry peer group to aid the valuation process by enhancing the evaluation of the company's operations with respect to operational performance common to the industry. When used, the industry norms are obtained from sources such as trade associations, tax return databases, associations of credit-granting officers, specific similar companies whose operating statements are filed with government agencies, or other similar sources. The most common measures of a company's financial performance are liquidity, activity, profitability, and solvency.

Liquidity Measures

Liquidity ratios measure the quality and adequacy of current assets to meet current obligations as they become due. Two commonly used liquidity measures include the current and quick ratios.

The *current ratio* is an indication of a company's ability to service or meet its current obligations. Generally, the higher the ratio, the more assurance exists that the retirement of current liabilities may be made. The composition and quality of current assets is a critical factor in the analysis of a particular company's liquidity. The current ratio is:

$$\text{Current Ratio} = \frac{\text{Current Assets}}{\text{Current Liabilities}}$$

The *quick ratio*, defined as current assets minus inventory divided by current liabilities, is a more conservative liquidity measure that expresses the degree to which a company's current liabilities are covered by its most liquid current assets. As such, inventory is excluded from the numerator. This results in a ratio equal to cash and equivalents, plus accounts receivable, prepaid expenses, and other current assets, over current liabilities. The quick ratio is calculated as:

$$\text{Quick Ratio} = \frac{\text{Current Assets} - \text{Inventory}}{\text{Current Liabilities}}$$

Days in accounts payable measures the average number of days it takes a company to pay its funds. This measure indicates short-term creditworthiness of a company and how much it depends on trade credit for short-term financing. It is calculated as:

$$\text{Days in Accounts Payable} = \frac{365 \times \text{Average Accounts Payable}}{\text{Cost of Goods Sold}}$$

Activity Measures

Activity ratios express the relationship between the company's level of operations (typically in terms of revenues) and the assets needed to maintain the operations. Several measures are used to analyze how well a business is utilizing its assets and how efficiently it is managing the activity of the business. Generally, a higher ratio indicates more efficient operations since relatively fewer assets are required to maintain a given level of operations. The results enable individuals to assess management performance in these areas.

With regard to receivables, two activity measures include the receivables turnover measure and the days in receivables indicator. The *receivables turnover* measures the number of times accounts receivable turn over during the year. The higher the turnover of receivables, the shorter the time between the recognition of revenue and cash collection. Receivables turnover is calculated as:

$$\text{Receivables Turnover} = \frac{\text{Revenues}}{\text{Average Receivables}^3}$$

Days in receivables is another indicator of a company's success in collection of earned income. This figure expresses the average time in days that receivables are outstanding, measuring the company's success in the collection of accounts receivable. Generally, the greater the number of days outstanding, the greater the probability of delinquencies in accounts receivable. Similarly, it could indicate that the composition of contract performed during the year was such that the average duration was longer and the period of time from revenue recognition under the percentage of completion method to the date invoiced increased. It is calculated as:

$$\text{Days in Accounts Receivable} = \frac{365}{\text{Receivables Turnover}}$$

---

[3] Note that the average referred to in these ratios typically represents the average of the amount reflected on the balance sheet as of the date of the analysis and that reflected one year earlier.

The *inventory turnover* measures the company's inventory management efficiency by calculating the number of times the average inventory is converted into receivables or cash during the year. Inventory turnover is calculated as:

$$\text{Inventory Turnover} = \frac{\text{Cost of Goods Sold Average}}{\text{Inventory}}$$

Days in inventory measures the average number of days goods are in inventory. This ratio measures short-term sales potential. If it is above the industry norm, it means that the company may be carrying excessive inventory. If it is below the norm, it indicates that the company may not have enough resources to meet changes in demand and is losing business as a result. Given that manufacturing companies have three stages of inventory (i.e. raw materials, work in process, and finished goods), this calculation is more complex as compared to a retail company with only finished goods inventory. It is calculated as:

$$\text{Days in Inventory} = \frac{365}{\text{Inventory Turnover}}$$

Working capital turnover is a measure of a company's sales to its underlying working capital. This ratio measures how efficiently working capital is employed. A low ratio may indicate inefficient use of working capital; a very high ratio position signifies overtrading (representing a vulnerable position for creditors). Working capital turnover is calculated as:

$$\text{Working Capital Turnover} = \frac{\text{Revenues}}{\text{Average Working Capital}}$$

Days in working capital measures the average number of days required to convert working capital into revenues. The fewer the days required, the more efficient working capital is being used by a business. It is calculated as:

$$\text{Days in Working Capital} = \frac{365}{\text{Working Capital Turnover}}$$

The activity ratios presented thus far are short term and operating in nature. There are also a couple of activity ratios that are long term and investment in nature.

Fixed asset turnover is a measure of a company's revenues to its fixed assets. This ratio measures how efficiently a company's long-term capital investments are being employed. Specifically, this ratio reflects the level of revenues generated or maintained by investments in productive capacity.

Care must be taken when considering this ratio due to timing of a company's purchase of assets as compared to its peers. Fixed asset turnover is calculated as:

$$\text{Fixed Asset Turnover} = \frac{\text{Revenues}}{\text{Average Fixed Assets}}$$

Total asset turnover is a measure of a company's revenues to its underlying asset base. This ratio measures how efficiently a company's asset base is being employed. Specifically, this multiple indicates the number of times assets turn over in generating a level of revenues. It is a key component in measuring return on assets. Total asset turnover is calculated as:

$$\text{Total Asset Turnover} = \frac{\text{Revenues}}{\text{Average Total Assets}}$$

Profitability Measures

An operating goal of any business is to produce profits. Companies are acquired with the expectation that they will earn profits. Value is based on the cash flow-generating capacity of a company. Operating and profitability ratios allow an assessment of management's primary function. There are two general ways to assess profitability: (1) return on revenues and (2) return on investment.

Return on revenues, typically calculated by dividing net income by revenue, more broadly allows for the measurement of profitability at varying levels. The gross margin measures gross profit, profit after deduction of a company's cost of goods sold, as a percentage of revenues. The operating margin measures operating income, gross profits less operating expenses, as a percentage of revenues. The predebt operating margin measures earnings before interest and taxes (EBIT) as a percentage of revenues. The pretax margin measures pretax income as a percentage of revenues. The profit margin measures net income as a percentage of revenues. These margins are typically presented in a common-size income statement, which looks at all levels of expense and profitability as a percentage of revenues.

Return on investment (ROI) can be quantified both as a return on assets (ROA) and a return on equity (ROE). As discussed in Chapter 2, these measures are potentially misleading in terms of assessing performance and value creation, due to their measurement of income and investment at book value.

Solvency Measures

In evaluating a company's long-term risk and return prospects, it is essential to analyze its capital structure. Solvency can be assessed using coverage ratios, leverage ratios, and distress ratios. While financial leverage allows companies to accrue excess returns for their shareholders when the rate of return on the investments financed by debt is greater than the cost of debt, it creates additional risk in the form of fixed costs that negatively affect profitability if demand declines. Coverage ratios measure a company's ability to service debt, whereas leverage ratios measure the amount of debt in a company's capital structure, and distress ratios assess the risk of bankruptcy. These measures are important in measuring a company's ability to service its debt obligations as well as in measuring the degree of leverage that exists in a company.

Coverage ratios measure a company's ability to service debt. The most common ratio is EBIT divided by interest expense, often referred to as *times interest earned*. This ratio measures a company's ability to meet its interest obligations. The higher the ratio, the greater the company's ability to service its debt. A higher ratio may also signal a company's ability to take on more debt.

$$\text{Times Interest Earned} = \frac{\text{EBIT}}{\text{Interest Expense}}$$

Leverage refers to the amount of debt in a company's capital structure. The greater the amount of debt in the capital structure, the higher the degree of leverage that exists in a company. Higher degrees of leverage indicate businesses that are more susceptible to changes in the economy and risk to creditors if current levels of equity deteriorate.

The *debt ratio* is calculated by dividing the company's total debt (including current liabilities) by its total assets. This ratio calculates the percentage of total funds provided by creditors. This measure helps determine debt capacity, the amount of debt necessary to finance the total assets of the company. The lower the ratio, the greater the cushion against creditors' losses in the event of liquidation.

$$\text{Total Debt} = \frac{\text{Debt Ratio}}{\text{Total Assets}}$$

Total debt to equity is calculated by dividing total debt (current and long term) by stockholders' equity. This ratio expresses the relationship between capital contributed by creditors to that contributed by owners. It expresses the degree of protection provided by the owners to the creditors. The lower the ratio, the greater the percentage of assets financed or paid with capital contributed or retained by the owners of the company instead of external financing through the use of debt.

$$\text{Debt to Equity} = \frac{\text{Total Debt}}{\text{Total Equity}}$$

Alternatively, it can be calculated to total capital:

$$\text{Debt to Total Capital} = \frac{\text{Total Debt}}{\text{Total Capital (debt + equity)}}$$

These ratios measure a company's liquidity, profitability, and leverage independently. A tool exists that combines key aspects of these analytical measures to assess the risk of a company in terms of financial distress. The *Z-score*, developed by Edward Altman, is a well-known financial distress prediction model. In assessing a company's level of financial distress, five ratios are used together and each ratio is weighted. These weighted averages are used:

1.2 × (working capital to total assets) +
1.4 × (retained earnings to total assets) +
3.3 × (EBIT to total assets) +
0.6 × (market value of equity to book value of debt) +
1.0 × (revenues to total assets)

A score greater than 2.99 is preferred; a score less than 1.81 indicates significant risk of bankruptcy.

Summary

The purpose of financial analysis is to draw meaningful conclusions from a comparison of the company's performance to its past performance and to composite industry data. However, it is possible, and no indication of trouble, to have variation from company to company, even within the same industry. This is often because not every company has the same line of products or services, or the same capital structure. Nor is every company in the industry at the same point in its evolution and development. In most cases some difference between the subject's figures and the composite industry figures is to be expected.

In closing, financial statements reflect past results and not potential future performance. Financial analysis begins to bridge that gap by bringing to focus problems and opportunities for future improvement necessary to enhance value and be better prepared for the merger and acquisition process.

Conclusion

Although business valuation involves many financial calculations, it is not primarily a financial activity, particularly when valuation is done for merger and acquisition purposes. The value estimate must consider the company's competitive environment. This analysis should closely parallel the SWOT analysis performed in annual strategic planning. From this investigation, the company's strategic advantages and disadvantages are identified and assessed to determine its optimum strategy for success. This must be done in computing both the company's fair market value on a stand-alone basis and its investment value to strategic buyers because the company's competitive position frequently changes dramatically in an acquisition. The process of quantifying these competitive factors into a rate of return is described in Chapters 8 and 9 and into a multiple is described in Chapter 10.

CHAPTER 4

Merger and Acquisition Market and Planning Process

For buyers and sellers to be most effective in merger and acquisition (M&A), they should have an understanding of the volume, terms, and trends taking place in M&A to avoid being misled by transactions reported in the media. Most transactions involving privately held companies require only limited reports on the change in ownership, sale price, or strategic objectives. People usually hear only about the largest transactions involving major public companies. Yet such transactions make up just a small percentage of the total activity and may not present a representative picture of the M&A market. The following statistics, reported in the 2017 edition of *Mergerstat® Review*, provide valuable background and perspective. As the introduction to that source states: "The *Mergerstat® Review* includes formal transfers of ownership of at least 5% of a company's equity and where at least one of the parties is a U.S. entity."[1]

As Exhibit 4.1 indicates, M&A activity in the United States slightly lagged the economic cycle, increasing steadily and dramatically throughout the 1990s in both volume and value, decreasing during the recession that began in 2001, picking up again in 2003, only to decline again in 2008 as the financial markets collapsed. Deal flow started to pick up again in 2010 and took off in 2014, reaching all-time highs in terms of both number of net transaction announcements (12,012) and total deal value offered ($1,975,380 million) in 2015, followed by a slight decline in 2016. This data reflects a total of 97,093 transaction announcements over the last ten years, between 2007 and 2016.

Exhibit 4.2 illustrates the importance of privately owned sellers, which had increased as a percentage of the total transactions from 40% in 1990 to a peak of 59% in 2015 and 2016. Privately owned sellers comprised of

---

[1] *Mergerstat® Review 2017* (Portland, OR: Business Valuation Resources, 2017), 15.

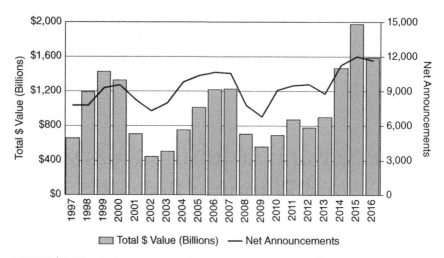

EXHIBIT 4.1 Trends in Mergers and Acquisitions: 1997–2016

Source: Reprinted with permission from FactSet Mergerstat, LLC (www.mergerstat .com), p. 19.

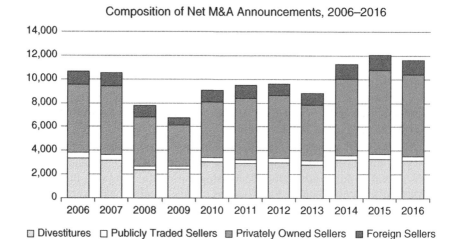

EXHIBIT 4.2 Composition of Net Merger and Acquisition Announcements: 2006–2016

Source: Reprinted with permission from FactSet Mergerstat, LLC (www.mergerstat .com), p. 27.

51% to 59% of total transactions between 2006 and 2016. Clearly the heaviest activity is in the acquisition of privately held companies. Although the average transaction price during the period from 1997 to 2016 ranged from approximately $155 to $581 million, the median transaction size during this time ranged from about $21 to $60 million, according to Mergerstat. The magnitude of the middle market also becomes clearer with Exhibit 4.3, which shows that around two-thirds of the transactions in recent years have had a purchase price of less than $100 million. Of the privately owned sellers, the average purchase price during the period 2012 to 2016 ranged from $93 to $188 million, with the median purchase price ranging from $19 to $34 million.

For privately owned sellers, this source cited two primary motives to sell. The first and most frequent reason was lack of a successor to take over the business. The second reason was increasing demand for the company's products or services, causing the need to sell to obtain adequate resources for expansion.

Mergerstat also presents pricing information in the form of median price to earnings (P/E) multiples offered for acquisitions of public and private companies. These multiples clearly increase with the size of the transaction

EXHIBIT 4.3 Net Merger and Acquisition Announcements Purchase Price Distribution: 2007–2016

Source: Reprinted with permission from FactSet Mergerstat, LLC (www.mergerstat .com), p. 29.

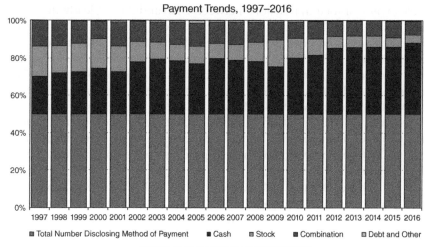

*Other includes stock options and stock warrants.

EXHIBIT 4.4   Payment Trends: 1997–2016

Source: Reprinted with permission from FactSet Mergerstat, LLC (www.mergerstat
.com), p. 33.

and generally tend to be lower when the terms of sale call for a cash payment
rather than for payment in the form of stock or some combination of cash,
stock, and debt.

Exhibit 4.4 reveals the more popular payment terms employed in
recent years. This increased use of cash is accompanied by a corresponding
decrease in stock and some combination of payment, suggesting the
market's increasing awareness of the riskiness of those payment forms.

The M&A data presented clearly emphasizes the importance of privately
owned companies and middle-market-size companies in the U.S. economy,
although transactions involving these companies receive less publicity
than those concerning public firms. With these companies comprising
such a large portion of total deal activity, it is essential that buyers
and sellers understand how to both measure and build value in these
businesses.

Common Seller and Buyer Motivations

It is advantageous to know why the other side in a transaction is considering
the deal. This knowledge should aid both in assessing the strength of one's
negotiating position and in structuring the proposal to meet the other side's
financial, strategic, and personal objectives.

Common Seller Motives

- Personal desire to leave due to age, poor health, family pressure, burnout
- Owners' need for estate planning
- Lack of a successor, including conflicts among family members and owners or loss of key people
- Need for additional capital to finance growth
- Weak or declining performance or growing financial difficulties
- Presence of strategic disadvantages that cannot be overcome as a stand-alone business
- Trends in globalization
- Market or industry conditions that create strong sale prices

Common Buyer Motives

- Expand product lines or geographic markets
- Obtain better growth opportunities
- Enhance profitability and cash flow through revenue enhancement or cost reduction
- Enhance competitive strengths or reduce weaknesses
- Acquire needed technology or capacity faster than through internal expansion
- Prevent competitors from entering the market
- Take out a competitor
- Obtain control over a source of scarce resources or supply for production or quality control purposes
- Better employ surplus capital or management
- Diversify to minimize risk

Why Mergers and Acquisitions Fail

Because most of the M&A activity in the United States involves privately held companies, data on the buyers' success in these transactions is limited. Much more information exists when the companies involved are public. The results of these transactions are described extensively in *The Synergy Trap: How Companies Lose the Acquisition Game*, by Mark L. Sirower, which, in addition to an in-depth analysis, includes a summary of acquisition performance in the United States over many years.[2] There are numerous reasons why deals

---

[2] The general conclusion is that well over half of the acquisitions of public companies destroy value for buyers while sellers frequently are rewarded with the premiums they received. Mark L. Sirower, *The Synergy Trap: How Companies Lose the Acquisition Game* (New York: The Free Press, 1997).

fail, which, of course, vary by the transaction and circumstances involved. The most common causes tend to be:

- *The price paid is too high.* This frequently results from the failure to distinguish the *target* from the *investment.* Even the best company can be a poor investment if the price paid exceeds the present value of its anticipated future returns.
- *Make-it-happen pressure from the executive level.* This often results from executives' desire to move too quickly or to make their mark on the company without adequate analysis of the effects of the transaction on value.
- *Exaggerated synergies.* Anticipated revenue enhancements, cost reductions, operating efficiencies, or financing benefits are overestimated.
- *Failure to integrate operations quickly.* Because the price for the synergies is paid up front, they must be achieved on time to yield benefits and create value. To succeed, an M&A transaction must have a solid integration plan that must be effectively communicated to all those impacted by it so that it can be executed quickly; otherwise value will leak away.
- *Failure to accurately assess customer reaction.* The newly combined company may force certain customers to seek a different source of supply to avoid buying from what has become a competitor or to avoid excessive reliance on one source of supply.
- *Failure to consider first-year negative synergies.* Mergers or acquisitions often cause disruptions, including name changes, internal corporate clashes, additional regulatory requirements, strained shareholder relations, negative public perception of the effect on consumers or of closing facilities, and the cost of severance packages and closing facilities, all of which should be quantified as part of the analysis.
- *Failure to estimate and recognize stand-alone fair market value.* For private companies that lack an established value, buyers may look only at investment value, including synergies, and ignore the target's lower value on a stand-alone basis.
- *Inconsistent strategy.* Inaccurate assessment of strategic benefits may occur.
- *Inadequate due diligence.* In the precombination phase, ineffective strategic planning or assessment of value drivers and risk drivers or pressure to win negotiations prevails over sound decision making.
- *Incompatibility of corporate cultures.* Lack of communication, differing expectations, and conflicting management styles all contribute to lack of execution.
- *Distraction from existing business.* Failure to anticipate or effectively react to competitors' response to the acquisition, including inattention

to ongoing operations and loss of key personnel of acquirer or target, affects profitability.

- *Inadequate risk analysis.* Discussed in Chapter 6, this involves the failure to rigorously assess the likelihood of success of a transaction or to consider management discretion in future periods.

Much of the literature on M&A cites "chief executive hubris," the desire to grow for the sake of growth, inexperience, and overly complacent corporate directors or shareholders as factors contributing to this poor track record. While much less information is available on the success of M&A activity involving closely held companies, many of these same conditions are present in middle-market transactions. In addition, there is an overwhelming misunderstanding of what value is, how it is created, and how it must be carefully measured and analyzed in M&A.

Sales Strategy and Process

As discussed, the success of buyers and sellers in negotiating a deal is dependent on understanding the transaction from the other side's perspective. Doing this includes recognizing their financial, strategic, and personal motivations and the process they are experiencing in the negotiation. From a business owner's perspective, this is discussed extensively in Chapter 5. A sale is just one of many options a business owner has to exit her business. The next discussion describes steps that a seller should go through before an M&A transaction takes place.

Step 1: Identify Potential Consequences of Inaction

Most sellers have never sold a company. This inexperience, combined with the frequent emotional reluctance to sell, inhibits adequate preparation. Seller inexperience with the sale process typically causes underestimation of the consequences of lack of preparation. Too often sellers equate selling a company with the effort required to sell their inventory or home. The company, of course, is far more complex – financially, operationally, and emotionally – so much more preparation is needed to successfully complete the sale.

The principal consequence of inaction is lost opportunity. These losses occur most commonly on four fronts, and each can have huge long-term consequences to the seller.

1. Failure to address key nonfinancial issues
2. Failure to identify what drives value
3. Failure to recognize the importance of timing
4. Failure to prepare the company for a sale

FAILURE TO ADDRESS KEY NONFINANCIAL ISSUES   Key nonfinancial issues most commonly concern people issues and usually include one or more of these key groups: family members, other owners, and employees. Closely held companies frequently have one or more family members who work in the company, often in key management positions. Their financial and professional future may be greatly influenced by a sale decision, so these matters must be discussed. The key decision criteria here are often personal as well as financial, and painful choices are frequently required.

Partners and employees also may be affected favorably or unfavorably by the decision, and allowances for these personal and financial consequences may be necessary.

The natural inclination with these people issues is to ignore them, usually by postponing any decision at all. Ignoring issues seldom eliminates them, frequently exacerbates them, and often narrows options when the issues are finally confronted at a later date.

FAILURE TO IDENTIFY WHAT DRIVES VALUE   Business executives often are so immersed in the day-to-day challenges of running the company that they lose sight of the bigger value maximization goals that were described in Chapters 1 and 2. Without routine attention to what drives long-term value, particularly stand-alone versus strategic value, major sale opportunities may be missed. Unless the annual strategic planning process is tied to value creation, it frequently fails to drive value and return on investment.

FAILURE TO RECOGNIZE THE IMPORTANCE OF TIMING   Companies and industries go through a natural progression of growth, development, and other changes that create strategic strengths and weaknesses. Ongoing worldwide trends in consolidation, reduced regulation, and globalization are only a few of the external factors that may create one-time opportunities that must be recognized to maximize return. Inattention to these factors may not only result in an excellent opportunity missed; it could render the company uncompetitive or unsalable for more than tangible asset value.

FAILURE TO PREPARE THE COMPANY FOR A SALE   Because companies are operating entities that face changing competitive conditions, they are seldom ready on short notice to obtain the optimum sale price. Advanced planning, often over a period of years, may be necessary to capitalize on the company's strengths and minimize its weaknesses. Inattention to the sale process usually prevents adequate planning.

The conclusion here should be clear: Inaction virtually guarantees lost opportunities and a lower sale price. Proactive planning, with a relentless focus on value, is a must.

Step 2: Identify Key Nonfinancial Issues

As briefly addressed in the last section, key nonfinancial issues are usually personal issues involving other owners or employees, some of whom may be family members or close friends. Often, resolving these issues to the seller's satisfaction may carry negative financial consequences. When these issues are present, recognize that some decisions are made for reasons that cannot be justified financially. It may be helpful to separate these issues into categories, such as financial, strategic, and personal, then set goals based on their separate criteria in seeking an overall succession plan. Procrastination frequently results when shareholders attempt to apply a financial measure to a personal decision.

A common example of the difficulty that can arise occurs with confusion between ownership succession and management succession. While the former is easily accomplished without long-term consequences by transfer of shares through a gift or sale, the latter is far more complicated. Management succession requires careful assessment of the qualifications of the successor, and this transfer can have a huge influence on the future performance of the company.

Resolution of nonfinancial issues typically involves different measurement criteria and may necessitate professional consultation.

Step 3: Assemble an Advisory Team

The logical, and often correct, first step for the business owner contemplating a sale is to contact the company's accountant, attorney, and banker. Before doing so, however, the business owner should consider the perspective and qualifications of these advisors. While they may be loyal and proven advisors on routine company matters, they may lack the expertise or experience to handle the sale of the business properly. Tax and legal advice is critical, so advisors, whether internal or external, should routinely handle M&A transactions. Also recognize that these trusted advisors may bring to the sale decision a natural reluctance to see it happen because of their resulting loss of a client. Although this does not mean they would not provide appropriate advice, sellers need to be served by an enthusiastic, aggressive team that is determined to achieve their goals.

Other external advisors should include a valuation consultant and an intermediary. The valuation and transaction advisory services are frequently provided by the same party – usually an investment banker; consider what skills they bring to the transaction. The intermediary may be great at the sale process but have little technical valuation knowledge. This could result in the seller not receiving the best advice about value maximization strategy, preparing the company for sale, or even on how to achieve the highest possible price. Conversely, the valuation consultant may possess little M&A experience or industry contacts, which are essential in the sale of certain kinds of businesses.

With regard to independence, when the valuation consultant and the intermediary are not the same person or from the same firm, the valuation consultant's job is solely to provide valuation-based strategic planning and a value estimate or range of values. The valuation consultant in this case is providing a specific fee for service and does not have the potential upside of earning a commission from a potential sale. As such, the buyer or seller working with the valuation consultant can be more confident that the results from the valuation analysis are unbiased and independent. In general, the more profitable a company is, the more helpful valuation and transaction advisors can be in achieving the maximum sale price as a function of the company's profits. Much of the value in this case would be intangible; here skilled advisors are essential. Less profitable or underperforming companies often sell at asset value, where little more than brokerage services are needed.

The independent valuation advisor often offers substantial benefits over having this service provided internally. A company's chief financial officer or controller may believe that, as a financial expert, he or she is competent to prepare a valuation. These skills require years of experience. Because a valuation consultant typically charges a fee for service rather than a percentage of the transaction consideration, if valuation consulting services related to M&A and/or exit planning is part of his practice, that consultant may very well have been involved in more M&A transactions than an intermediary. Corporate executives, because of their involvement in the company's operations, may lose perspective in assessing key competitive factors. Less experienced appraisers also frequently have difficulty distinguishing between stand-alone fair market value and investment value in the valuation and analysis process.

Industry conditions also can influence the need for and choice of a transaction advisor. For some businesses, the biggest challenge is finding one or more qualified buyers. In other cases, it is assessing with which buyer the fit would be best or which can afford to pay the highest price. And in every case, deal structure and negotiation skills are essential.

As discussed further in Chapter 15, the seller must focus relentlessly on the after-tax cash proceeds received in the sale. Advisors may offer many options on how the sale is structured, with the maximum return potentially received in a wide variety of forms.

Therefore, tax advice is essential. Subsequent investment advice from the seller's wealth advisor on how to handle the sale proceeds should also be obtained.

Step 4: Identify Likely Alternatives

Once the key nonfinancial issues have been identified and addressed and the professional advisory team is assembled, the next step for the seller is to identify the possible transfer alternatives. These typically include:

- Sale to an outside party
- Sale to an inside group
- Transfer through gifting
- Transfer through an estate plan

Each of these alternatives offers pros and cons to achieve the owner's financial and nonfinancial objectives. Naturally, they carry different risk and return consequences that should be fully explored with the advisory team. Again, it should be recognized that some of the owners' most important objectives may be nonfinancial, and these must be fully explored and discussed. Especially where family members are involved, there must be a candid assessment made of the company's ability to compete under a new management team. Where hand-picked successors are family members who are unlikely to succeed, these difficult issues should be addressed in advance to prevent likely future failure. Also recognize that decisions made for personal reasons may carry significant financial consequences. Although the owners have the right to make these decisions, they also must recognize their effect on the sale price, the company, and its various stakeholders.

Step 5: Preparation and Financial Assessment of Alternatives

With the likely alternatives identified, the advisory team should make a more detailed assessment of the financial consequences of each alternative, including:

- *Evaluate legal issues in preparation for the sale.* This legal audit should include a review of the corporate by-laws, stock certificates, transfer restrictions, title to assets, ownership and protection of intellectual property, contracts in place, leases and debt covenants, and ongoing litigation.

- *Compute stand-alone fair market value and estimate investment values to assess the likely benefits to be achieved from a sale to various types of strategic buyers.* This synergy premium should be considered in assessing the financial consequences of other transfer options.
- *Address the need to prepare the company for a sale.* The valuation of the business will have identified the drivers that most heavily influence the company's value, and from this the timing of the sale can be considered. Economic and industry conditions may not be ideal at the present time, or the company may greatly benefit by pursuing short-term strategies that better position it to achieve a maximum sale value. Preparation may take from up to a few months to a year but should allow the owners to present the company in the most advantageous possible way. Thus, to achieve the best possible price and terms, the seller should compute the stand-alone fair market value and estimate each potential buyer's (e.g. private equity buyer, private equity buyer seeking a platform company, corporate strategic buyer seeking a vertical acquisition, corporate strategic buyer seeking a horizontal acquisition) investment value prior to committing to the sale process.
- *Reevaluate the tax issues and options that accompany each alternative.* Once again, while recognizing the seller's objective to achieve selective nonfinancial goals, he or she should focus on the after-tax proceeds that result from the sale, however it is structured.
- *Make a firm decision and stick to it.* Once the personal issues have been identified and addressed and the advisory team has identified the likely alternatives, including the personal and financial consequences of each and the steps necessary to achieve the desired value, a well-informed decision can be made. At this point, the owner should be comfortable with the decision, recognizing that most choices carry some unwanted consequences and that the best choice seldom achieves every goal.
- *Do not second guess.* Because entrepreneurs and others involved in middle-market companies frequently identify personally with the company and its success, the decision to sell frequently involves strong emotions. A sale is not by definition a failure, even if the company has been underperforming. It is a decision to achieve a variety of personal and financial goals that, if reached in a rational and systematic manner, simply represents sound management. It may also be progressive – the company's best next step in its life cycle.
- *Prepare the company for sale.* Many of the details in the preparation and sale process are managed by the transaction advisor. Several points can be mentioned here that should be recognized in advance:
  - Strengthen the reliability of the financial statements, especially if the company is solidly profitable with a sound balance sheet. Do not give

a buyer any reasons to doubt the company's reported performance. Have five years of audited financial statements prepared by a reputable accounting firm, with detailed supporting documents available for the due diligence process.

- Clean house. Remove any bad debts, obsolete inventory, unused plant and equipment, and nonoperating assets that may create questions or doubts or impede the sale process. Distribute excess cash to shareholders. Resolve contingent liabilities and related legal and regulatory issues that are outstanding. Dress up the company physically, from repair and maintenance to painting and landscaping.
- Maintain confidentiality while negotiating contracts or less formal agreements to keep key employees.
- Rely on the intermediary. Often the negotiating process is long and difficult and requires hard bargaining. The seller does not want to expend valuable negotiating leverage early in this process. An intermediary should handle these initial steps, conserving the seller's negotiating capacity to the end of the process when it is needed most.

Step 6: Preparation of Offering Memorandum

An essential step in the sale process is preparation of the company's *selling brochure or offering memorandum*. This document presents the seller's strategic plan, including its long-term operating goals and objectives. While the selling brochure should be grounded in reality and defendable under intense scrutiny by buyers, it is also intended to present the most favorable, realistic picture of the company as an acquisition target.

A properly prepared offering memorandum presents more than details about the target and its industry. It provides insight into the seller's strategic position and potential, given industry circumstances. It also should indicate management's ability to design a coherent and effective strategy to maximize the company's performance and value.

A significant goal of the offering memorandum is a clear expression of the strategic advantages of the company as an acquisition candidate as well as what processes, skills, and proprietary systems can be transferred to the buyer. The unstated message in this description should be the justification for why potential buyers cannot afford to pass up this acquisition.

An offering memorandum consists of these parts:

- Executive summary
- Description of the company

- Market analysis
- Expected future performance
- Deal structure and terms

EXECUTIVE SUMMARY Experienced M&A participants would agree that the most critical part of an offering memorandum is the executive summary. Intended to catch the potential buyers' attention, it must provide a compelling case for why the company is an attractive acquisition. In just a few pages, this summary should present the company's history and current market position, major products and services, technological achievements and capabilities, and recent financial performance. The company's strategic advantages should be emphasized, particularly how they can be exploited by an acquirer. Although descriptive, the well-written executive summary is a sales document that effectively promotes the company as an acquisition target.

DESCRIPTION OF THE COMPANY This section of the selling brochure usually begins with a description of the company's history and extends to a forecast of its projected operations. It usually includes a detailed description of:

- Major product or service lines
- Manufacturing operations, capabilities, and capacities
- Technological capabilities
- Distribution system
- Sales and marketing program
- Management capabilities
- Financial position and historical performance
- Current capitalization and ownership structure

MARKET ANALYSIS The offering memorandum also should include a market analysis, which is a discussion of the industry or industry segment in which the company operates, including an overview of key industry trends, emerging technologies, and new product or service introductions. This assessment of the market typically describes the company's current position relative to its competition and strategic advantages that will allow it to maintain or improve this position. Key competitors are often described with a constant focus on the company's future and its strategy to grow and improve its performance.

EXPECTED FUTURE PERFORMANCE After this history of the company and strategic analysis, the brochure presents a forecast of future operations, including income statement, balance sheet, and statement of cash flows plus the assumptions that support this projection.

DEAL STRUCTURE AND TERMS The offering memorandum should present essential information about deal structure, specifics on any items excluded from the sale, and any restrictions on payment terms. For example, disclosure of any specific tangible or intangible assets that the seller intends to retain can be identified as well as restrictions on any debt that can be assumed by the buyer or the seller's willingness to finance any or all of the transaction.

The offering memorandum frequently is preceded by an initial teaser letter that may be narrowly or broadly sent to potential buyers. It provides a brief description of the company, which it may or may not specifically identify. The teaser provides only an overview of the company's finances. Its purpose is to stimulate interest, emphasizing where the company is, how it got there, and, most important, where company management believes the company can go. It invites potential buyers to request additional information – the offering memorandum.

Exhibit 4.5 portrays a seller's deal timetable that involves a 12-week sale process. This should be viewed as a goal – 12 weeks would be very fast. The timetable reflects the many steps in the sale process, emphasizing the importance of planning, preparation, and the benefits of good professional advisors.

For many middle-market shareholders, the sale of their company is the largest financial decision they will ever make. Businesses are complex entities involving people, products, customers, and technologies operating in continually changing industries, economies, and regulatory environments. Their strategic position and value is constantly changing. This value is difficult to measure in the first place, and owners should not only know what their company is presently worth on a stand-alone basis but what it could be worth to strategic buyers when synergistic benefits are considered.

Sale opportunities may be continually available at an attractive price. It is much more likely, however, that a buyer or an ideal population of likely buyers may have to be identified and enticed to consider an acquisition of the company. Anticipating the wants and needs of these prospective buyers, the target may have to be positioned to maximize its attractiveness. This process may require considerable time as well as careful timing to exploit ideal sale conditions in the industry or the economy.

EXHIBIT 4.5 Deal Timetable

Develop and Implement Marketing Strategy	Solicit Initial Bids	Bid Evaluation and Detailed Due Diligence	Conduct Negotiations and Solicit Final Bids	Closing
■ Collect data ■ Conduct due diligence ■ Prepare marketing materials ■ Prepare normalization adjustments and valuation ■ Select, prioritize candidates ■ Develop approach strategy ■ Determine list of potential buyers and gather detailed contact information ■ Obtain confidentiality agreement from all parties ■ Complete working group list ■ Create nonconfidential company teaser, confidential offering memorandum, and other marketing materials (including company investor presentations)	■ Continue calling process ■ Facilitate information flow between buyers and company to expedite buyers' evaluation ■ Select buyers to meet with management ■ Organize data room ■ Management meets with interested buyers ■ Buyers conduct preliminary financial, legal, and accounting due diligence ■ Prepare for detailed due diligence ■ Solicit and receive buyers' nonbinding preliminary indications of interest	■ Establish price ■ Establish form of consideration ■ Establish timing ■ Establish terms and conditions ■ Determine ability of buyer to complete transaction ■ Estimate prospects of combined entity ■ Select final bidders and conduct on-site due diligence ■ Distribute draft of definitive agreement and final bid request letter to interested parties ■ Leverage competitive process to generate increased transaction value ■ Determine one or two bidders with whom to enter into negotiations	■ Establish exclusivity ■ Prioritize key objectives ■ Negotiate and execute definitive agreement ■ Announce transaction ■ File regulatory documents (if necessary) ■ Obtain buyer shareholder approval (if necessary)	

EXHIBIT 4.5 (*Continued*)

- Commence target blitz with nonconfidential company teaser
- Obtain signed confidentiality agreements from interested parties and distribute confidential offering memo
- Commence calling process

4 Weeks ⟷ 3 Weeks ⟷ 2 Weeks ⟷ 3 Weeks ⟷ Thereafter

12 Weeks

The message here should be clear: Selling at an attractive price requires a lot of luck or, in most cases, careful advance planning. Failure to plan carefully greatly increases the likelihood that the owners will fail to achieve some or all of their financial and personal goals.

Acquisition Strategy and Process

The acquisition strategy should fit the company's overall strategic goal: increase net cash flows and reduce risk. In strategic planning over the long term, to achieve this goal, shareholders and management frequently face the choice of internal development (i.e. organic growth) versus merger or acquisition. To drive the company toward its strongest competitive position, resources constantly must be shifted from underperforming activities or those with less potential to those that provide greater benefits. In shifting resources, management can move them among existing operations, into developmental activities, or into acquisitions.

The primary reason for acquiring or merging with another business is to produce improved cash flow or reduced risk faster or at a lower cost than achieving the same goal internally. Thus the goal of any acquisition is to create a strategic advantage by paying a price for the target that is lower than the total resources required for internal development of a similar strategic position.

Forms of Business Combinations

Business combinations can take any of a number of forms. In an *acquisition*, the stock or assets of a company are purchased by the buyer. A *merger*, which is primarily a legal distinction, occurs through the combination of two companies, where the first is absorbed by the second or a new entity is formed from the original two. A less drastic form of combination is a *joint venture*, which typically involves two companies forming and mutually owning a third business, most often to achieve a specific limited purpose. The lowest form of commitment in a strategic combination would be an *alliance*, which is a formal cooperative effort between two independent companies to pursue a specific objective, or the *licensing* of a technology, product, or intellectual property to another organization. Thus, in terms of control, investment, and commitment, acquisition provides the strongest position, followed by a merger. When less commitment is desired, joint ventures, alliances, or even licensing arrangements can be adopted.

The planning process should identify the strategy behind combinations as well as the anticipated benefits from them. In assessing these benefits, the different types of potential acquisitions usually fall into one of these categories:

- *Horizontal acquisitions.* By acquiring another firm in the same industry, the buyer typically aims to achieve economies of scale in marketing, production, or distribution as well as increased market share and an improved product and market position.
- *Vertical acquisition.* Moving upstream or downstream, the buyer looks to acquire a supplier, distributor, or customer. The objective typically is to obtain control over a source of scarce resources or supply for production or quality control purposes, improved access to a specific customer base, or higher-value products or services in the production chain.
- *Contiguous acquisitions.* Buyers may see opportunities in adjacent industries where they can capitalize on related technologies, production processes, or strategic resources that may serve different markets or customer bases.

The strategic planning process described in Chapter 3 identifies the company's competitive position and sets objectives to exploit its relative strengths while minimizing the effects of its weaknesses. The company's M&A strategy should complement this process, targeting only those industries and companies that can improve the acquirer's strengths or alleviate its weaknesses. With the acquisition plan focused on this goal, management can reduce the cost and time involved in analyzing and screening investment opportunities that arise. Opportunities that fail to meet these criteria can be rejected more quickly as inconsistent with the overall strategic plan. Thus acquisition should be viewed as only one of several alternative strategies to achieve a basic business objective. When less investment or commitment is preferred, alliances, joint ventures, or licensing agreements may be a more appropriate form of combination.

Typically, a major advantage of an acquisition over internal development is that it accomplishes the objective much quicker. In addition, the acquisition helps to reduce risk when the acquirer is moving beyond its core business. An established business brings with it one or more of these benefits:

- Track record
- Management
- Competencies
- Products
- Reputation
- Brands
- Customer base

Internal development may lack all of these benefits. The target also may carry weaknesses, which should diminish its stand-alone value. These attributes should be considered against the buyer's competencies to assess their effect on future performance.

Acquisitions also may provide bounce-back, synergistic benefits that the acquirer can leverage by spreading that benefit over its larger base of business. These benefits are described further in Chapter 5.

Acquisition Planning

The acquisition plan should tie very closely to the company's overall strategic plan. Whenever the acquisition plan starts to drift from the strategic plan, whenever its connection to the strategic plan tends to blur or become less well defined, stop! That is a clear warning to return to the company's basic strategy and goals and investigate whether this acquisition fits. Relentless discipline in this process is rewarded with less time and cost spent studying targets that are not a logical fit.

STEP 1: TIE ACQUISITION PLAN TO OVERALL STRATEGIC PLAN Maintaining focus also means requiring every proposal to pass the firm's primary value creating goal: It should increase net cash flow or reduce risk, or both, and the details of the forecast and valuation should support this conclusion.

From the company's strategic plan and the strengths, weaknesses, opportunities, and threats (SWOT) analysis that supports it, the company's competitive position – its strategic advantages and disadvantages – are identified. In a company's day-to-day operations, it attempts internally to improve on its strengths, eliminate or minimize its weaknesses, and take advantage of market opportunities. Business combinations, whether acquisitions, mergers, alliances, joint ventures, or licensing agreements, are generally undertaken to achieve the same goals, but typically faster or at a reduced cost. Thus the acquisition plan originates in the strategic plan when objectives can be achieved more effectively through some form of combination rather than internal development. Acquisitions also may be made for defensive purposes, such as to keep a competitor out of a market, to eliminate a weak competitor that could be acquired and strengthened or that depresses prices, or to protect a technology.

STEP 2: FORM EFFECTIVE ACQUISITION TEAM The makeup of the acquisition team can influence its likely level of success. Teams tend to be more effective when comprised of managers from several functional areas, including marketing and sales, operations, distribution, and finance. Each of these disciplines provides a different focus on a target as these managers bring different concerns to the evaluation process. Teams comprised solely of financial executives often overlook operational issues while those consisting only of generalists frequently exhibit a lack of attention to detail. For this reason, a blend of background and knowledge combined with open discussion of each member's concerns usually results in a more thorough and accurate analysis.

Larger companies have M&A or corporate development departments; those that lack this capacity internally may have to add external legal, tax, and valuation advisors. These outside advisors often bring the added benefit of objectivity and creativity as well as a portfolio of experiences and business contacts that internal team members may lack.

STEP 3: SPECIFY ACQUISITION CRITERIA The acquisition team's strategy should flow from the company's overall strategic plan, but specific objectives for each acquisition should be required to both justify and focus the process. Typically, these objectives should lead to acquisition criteria and should leverage the acquirer's current strategic advantages, including surplus cash, management, technology, market strengths, or production capacity. Most strategic goals also include a minimum required rate of return on capital invested. The return should be measured as net cash flow with equal attention given to the timing of the cash inflows and their anticipated rate of growth. Adherence to specified goals and the company's track record of success also improves when managers' compensation is tied to the achievement of these specific measurements.

Typical acquisition criteria include parameters on the size, location, and market position of the target or its products as well as performance goals. For example, the required market position may be to be first or second in sales in a given market, or the high-quality or low-price leader in the industry. In establishing these criteria, the target's current and forecasted growth must be assessed against these parameters.

The criteria also should be assessed from the perspective of risk tolerance. That is, management should consider the potential least favorable and most favorable outcomes and the company's ability to respond to downside conditions.

STEP 4: CONSIDER TARGET WEAKNESSES VERSUS ACQUIRER'S STRENGTHS As acquisition criteria are evaluated, managers should be encouraged not to quickly reject targets that display weaknesses. Companies frequently come on the market because of strategic disadvantages ranging from lack of capital to inadequate distribution. These limitations often have reduced the company's growth and returns, and, in the process, they decrease its value. This may make it a more attractive acquisition target, particularly when the buyer possesses the capabilities to eliminate the problem. Thus the acquisition criteria must consider not only the strategic strengths and weaknesses of the target as a stand-alone but how it will perform when incorporated into the acquirer's operations. The acquisition parameters also should define whether the company will evaluate troubled companies and under what circumstances.

STEP 5: DEFINE SEARCH PROCESS The acquisition strategy also should define the discovery or search process. Less aggressive companies may consider only those potential acquisitions brought to them by intermediaries or owners looking to sell. This approach probably will miss many opportunities, particularly those unknown candidates that are not being considered by any other buyer. The search strategy sources and resources should be defined, including establishment of the minimum information required to evaluate a candidate.

STEP 6: SELECT SEARCH CRITERIA AND FIND TARGET COMPANIES Following the decision to pursue mergers or acquisitions, set the criteria for the target of your hunt. In other words, select the search criteria.

The primary criteria that should be on any list are:

- *Industry.* Generally this is the same industry or a similar industry to that in which the acquirer is currently active. A relevant question is whether only vertical acquisitions are of interest or if horizontal prospects are also to be considered.
- *Products or services.* Often acquirers desire products or services that have a significant presence in the market. Thus they seek to acquire a target that has a better brand name or an expanded line of products or services, particularly higher value components or lines.
- *Revenues.* Revenues are usually evaluated based on size, and usually the target will be smaller than the acquirer.
- *Earnings.* Acquirers should decide if they require a desired minimum amount of earnings, or whether losses (see the next bullet point) are also acceptable, if correctable. A target with losses will likely be dilutive to the acquirer's earnings in the short run; however, this is often less significant than indicated by the M&A market's fixation on whether earnings are immediately dilutive. Negative earnings can be corrected if they are a result of weak management or an inability to fund growth

or to modernize plant. Often a target with correctable losses can be acquired at an attractive price.

■ *Whether turnarounds are considered.* Turnaround situations can include anything from a target that has recently experienced losses to one in bankruptcy. Some acquirers are willing to look at turnarounds while others rule them out by policy. In a seller's market, when there are many buyers looking at every attractive company available to be acquired, the willingness to consider turnarounds can assist the acquirer. Usually there are fewer possible buyers for turnarounds, and the sellers tend to be more realistic about price. The more conservative prices paid for turnarounds also may provide the acquirer more time to achieve synergies.

■ *Geographic area.* Most buyers want to acquire targets in a given geographic area. With the globalization of markets and the continuing reduction in trade barriers, acquirers are increasingly interested in targets throughout the world. The decision on where expansion should next take place should be based on the acquirer's overall strategic plan.

■ *Whether target's management should be retained.* Most often this choice is influenced by the acquirer's depth of competent management. When a company has excess management worthy of a promotion, it may seek to acquire a region or product line for them. Growth strategies, however, should always be tied to value creation.

When the M&A market is hot, the price required to acquire a successful company is higher. Often these higher prices can be justified only through an earn-out used to bridge the higher price the seller feels is appropriate based on the future outlook versus the lower price the buyer feels is appropriate based on the target's current status and performance. Earn-outs are discussed further in Chapter 15.

■ *Private companies or public companies.* Generally, this choice is most dependent on whether the acquisition is consistent with the acquirer's strategic plan.

■ *Ideal fit.* A target is usually an ideal fit when its product or service naturally fits the acquirer's marketing, sales, and distribution system and its geographic requirement. Such a fit allows fast and efficient integration. Buyers must be cautioned, however, that even the best fit remains a poor investment if the price paid is too high compared to the risk-adjusted returns.

Having selected the criteria to judge targets, the next step is to find prospective targets. The more common ways to locate targets include:

■ *Industry contacts.* Although hit and miss, targets sometimes are found through personal relationships within the desired industry. This process works better when the desired targets are in the same industry as the acquirer because this increases the number of companies and trade associations with which the acquirer has contacts.

- *Business intermediaries.* Business broker and investment banking firms[3] represent companies available for acquisition as well as acquirers. Providing such firms with the acquirer's criteria informs them that the acquirer is looking and supplies guidance as to what is desired. The acquirer should recognize that the use of intermediaries may generate many inappropriate prospects. It can be expected to result in two types of pressure:

    1. The intermediary's fee, or the major portion of the fee, is earned only when a deal occurs; hence, the intermediary's primary objective is to "make a deal happen."
    2. Often the intermediary will create a sense of urgency (i.e. a pressure for the acquirer to act in haste to avoid missing the deal).

        Acquirers should resist these pressures, as well as the encouragement to bid a higher price than the analysis of the strategic benefits and synergies of the deal warrants. For nearly all acquirers there is, at any time, an ample number of possible acquisitions. Buyers should not be rushed into offering too much, acting too fast, or feeling the need to do any specific deal.

- *Searching for the right target.* With a well-defined criteria sheet, an acquirer can search for and approach companies to determine their level of interest. This process is more difficult than waiting for intermediaries to identify targets, but it often identifies targets that are not represented by any intermediary. Through this search, exceptional targets may be identified and competitive bidding against other buyers is avoided.

Some business valuation professionals and intermediary firms offer a service to locate and make the initial contact with companies not on the market but that fit your criteria. The advantages of outsourcing include:

- The task becomes a contracted performance with a timeline in contrast to something the acquirer will do whenever the time can be found.

---

[3] The distinction between the two is that investment banking firms are usually larger with a team of M&A experts usually servicing companies with revenues in excess of $10 million. Their fees are typically higher than those for brokers and they typically require an initial retainer, monthly fees, and a success fee. Business brokers are usually individuals or very small teams with lower overhead who typically do not have the extent of resources that investment banks have, and thus tend to charge lower fees and service smaller companies.

- When a valuation firm provides this service, it can use its familiarity with the company and contact with its executives to begin the process of estimating the target's stand-alone market value.
- The contact by the outsourced professional can sidestep the attempts of prospective targets to qualify the acquirer before the acquirer has determined his or her level of interest.

Understandably, targets want to know whether a potential acquirer is a cash buyer or wants management to stay. Early contacts by acquirers lead to the targets asking this type of question at a time when the buyer's focus should be on learning more about that specific target. Appraisers can easily deflect or delay these questions by explaining that at the time they lack the authority to address them.

STEP 7: ESTABLISH GUIDELINES ON INITIAL CONTACT PROCEDURE   A search strategy also should provide guidelines on how contact with a prospect should be initiated, including control of:

- Who in the acquiring company has access to this information
- What information about the acquirer may be released
- Strategic goals of the acquirer that can be discussed
- Personnel permitted to participate
- Authority to sign nondisclosure agreements
- Minimum information to request from the target

Many of these information-related concerns can be simplified through use of an intermediary, which enhances confidentiality for both parties and frequently speeds the process. In gathering initial information, one option that may be attractive to both the buyer and seller is for the buyer to authorize preparation of a valuation of the target. In return for cooperation with the valuation, the buyer promises to provide the seller with a copy of the appraisal of the company's fair market value on a stand-alone basis. This information helps to educate the current owners on what their company is worth and, more important, why that value is appropriate. Armed with this information, the acquirer also can compute investment value inclusive of anticipated synergies, which enables the acquirer's management to make an informed decision on whether to proceed with negotiations.

STEP 8: ESTABLISH PROCEDURES TO REVIEW THE ACQUISITION TEAM'S RECOMMENDATION   Another step to implement in the acquisition process includes checks on the negotiating manager's ability to close the deal. Too often acquisition team members, due to their proximity to the transaction, become emotionally involved and lose their objectivity. The company can protect itself from this process by establishing a committee to review acquisition team proposals or by designating a senior manager who must grant approval. This review process is a safeguard to prevent members of the M&A team from personally associating with the transaction and overpaying as a result.

With this acquisition-planning strategy in place, the primary challenge is discipline. Rigorously examine each proposal to ensure its fit within the broader corporate strategy, then analyze that target's forecasted risks and net cash flow benefits relative to the price the company must pay to obtain them. Establish in advance of the negotiations the walk-away price where the project is rejected because the risk-adjusted returns do not justify the price. Armed with this decision-making process, success in acquisitions is much more likely.

STEP 9: DETERMINE TONE OF LETTER OF INTENT The letter of intent (LOI) represents the parties' preliminary agreement to agree. In tone and content, it can be either hard or soft; the latter option is recommended. This soft approach represents a good-faith intent to consider all issues when the letter is executed but to recognize that additional issues may (probably will) emerge that must be subsequently resolved. A soft letter often can be completed in a few drafts over a few weeks. Hard letters of intent usually must be much more detailed, require extensive negotiation at a relatively early stage in the purchase/sale process, and can take many revisions and weeks to reach agreement. They often resemble the definitive agreement that defines the final terms of sale.

Due Diligence Preparation

As part of the advance planning, both buyers and sellers should prepare for the inevitable due diligence that must precede any acquisition. Buyers should inform sellers with their LOI of the information that they will need. Sellers should begin this preparation in the initial stages of the sale planning process so that all necessary information is conveniently and promptly available for prospective buyers. Preparing for due diligence also will assist sellers to recognize buyers' concerns and issues that sellers must address to make the company as attractive as possible to prospective acquirers. Exhibit 4.6 provides a summary of a typical due diligence request list.

Merger and acquisition activity has been very heavy for middle-market-size companies. Although they receive much less publicity because the buyers and sellers are often privately held, as mentioned, these transactions constitute most of the deal activity in the United States.

EXHIBIT 4.6 Due Diligence Request List

A. Company Overview
____ Discussion on company strengths, weaknesses, opportunities, threats
____ Dialogue on the company's sustainable competitive advantages, including: synergies, preemptive position in supply or distribution channels, product distinctiveness/technology advantages, economies of scale, pricing advantages
____ Most recent business plan and strategic planning documents
____ Copies of published corporate literature and press articles
____ Employment benefit plans, contracts, and compensation agreements that exist and/or are contemplated
____ Employee head count (current, historical, and projected)
____ Resumes of key employees and division organization chart including all functional groups
____ Listing of the company's major facilities, including a brief description of location, size, age, utility, and whether they are owned or leased
____ Discussion on any regulations to which the company's operations are sensitive

B. Ownership
____ Cap table – i.e. list of stockholders, option and warrant holders, holders of phantom stock; including date of purchase/grant, price, number of shares
____ Financing history, including shares, price, amount raised, dates
____ Summary of recent stock option grants, if any, including shares, exercise price, dates
____ Any valuations (409A, 718, 83(b)) done in compliance with share-based compensation
____ Details of transactions in the company's stock during the last 5 years

C. Historical and Projected Financial Information
____ Five years of historical financial statements, by quarter
____ Breakdown of sales by top 10 customers for the last 5 years
____ Breakdown of sales by product/service line, including price and volume detail
____ Breakdown of operating expenses by product/service line
____ Summary of significant accounting policies
____ Marketing plan for at least one year
____ Detailed budget plan for at least one year
____ Financial projections for five years
____ Breakdown of significant historical and projected capital expenditures
____ All management letters from auditors (if any), plus management responses (if any)
____ Receivables aging analysis for last two years
____ Listing of bad debts for last 5 years
____ Fixed asset register or depreciation schedule
____ Details of any contingent liabilities (such as guarantees or warranties) or off-balance-sheet financing (such as letters of credit)

(continued)

EXHIBIT 4.6 (*Continued*)

D. Products and Services
_____ Description of products/services
_____ Description of business model, pricing policies, volume projections
_____ Current market share data
_____ List of top suppliers

E. Sales and Marketing
_____ Discussion of sales and distribution by product/service line
_____ Sales force productivity statistics and sales plan for each department or product line for the most recent year
_____ Advertising and promotion plan and budget
_____ Current marketing materials and sample advertisements
_____ Website statistics

F. Technology
_____ Description of technology processes
_____ Overview of process and historical and projected expenditures
_____ List of proprietary technology
_____ Description of licensed technology from outside parties

G. Intellectual Property
_____ List and/or description of patents, licenses, copyrights, trade names
_____ Copies of technology licensing agreements
_____ Royalty payments paid or received
_____ Background on research and development investments
_____ Information on any internally developed software

H. Legal
_____ Articles of incorporation
_____ Corporate by laws
_____ Shareholder agreements
_____ Employment and/or non compete agreements
_____ Termination agreements with ex-employees
_____ List of partnerships and affiliations, including any agreements
_____ Contracts with unions
_____ Details of any litigation, including pending or threatened lawsuits

I. Other
_____ Copies of bank loan arrangements and lease contracts
_____ List of companies previously contacted and any documentation, including draft definitive agreements
_____ Details of any environmental issues that could have a material impact on the company
_____ Copies of any business appraisals completed for the company within the last 5 years

In many respects, M&A activity for middle-market companies is not well-organized, a notable exception being private equity. Many sellers, and to a lesser extent buyers, may be involved in just one transaction in their careers. Their legal, tax, valuation, and intermediary advisors also may possess limited expertise or experience. Although some industries are consolidating with heavy M&A activity, in other industries, prospective buyers and sellers frequently have difficulty identifying ideal prospects with which to do a deal.

These circumstances combine to emphasize the importance to buyers and sellers of understanding value and what drives it, knowing the market, and recognizing the advantages of advance planning and preparation to achieve successful deals.

CHAPTER 5

Measuring Synergies

Buyers can destroy substantial value through merger and acquisition (M&A). That is the ugly, risky potential outcome that every buyer must have the discipline to confront continually. Since so much of the allure of M&A centers around synergy, this chapter addresses what it is and how to measure it.

The Acquisition Strategy and Process section in Chapter 4 emphasized that a company's acquisition plan should tie closely to the overall strategic plan of the business. At its core, that plan should drive the company to strategies that increase its net cash flow to capital providers and minimize its risk. The typical acquisition is actually a capital budgeting decision where the buyer acquires brands, processes, and technologies as well as tangible assets. Resources are allocated based on the anticipated future returns they are projected to generate, adjusted for the risk profile of the investment.

Acquisitions should be made to increase shareholder value. They may expand the company's products or markets, provide a new technology, increase its efficiency, or raise its growth potential. None of those results, however, should be the ultimate goal. The acquisition should increase shareholder value by reducing the company's risk or increasing its net cash flow to invested capital. This reminder of the company's essential purpose is made because potential acquisitions often create distractions that may cause managers to lose their focus on shareholder value.

To further emphasize this point, consider the return-of-investment implications when one public company pays a premium to buy another public company. When Buyco pays $90 per share to acquire 100% of Sellco, which had been trading for a market price prior to the acquisition of $60 per share, Buyco is paying $30 per share more – a 50% premium – than what its shareholders would have to pay to acquire the same stock on the open market. Implicit in the acquisition decision is the message to shareholders that Buyco can create value above this premium through the acquisition. Thus, their decision presumes that it is in the shareholders' best interest to pay this premium in advance based on management's ability to deliver the expected synergies. For shareholders to end up better off in this scenario, management must create substantial returns to justify the premium paid. Success is not impossible, but such lofty goals, in light of investment alternatives, mandate sound acquisition valuation and analysis.

In addition to their focus on shareholder value, executives and board members also must recognize that M&A is usually the company's largest form of discretionary spending. Such a decision often has a greater effect on shareholder value than any other, and few other events in the life of a business can change value so quickly and dramatically. Acquisitions generally commit a company to the selected strategy for a long period of time. As implementation occurs, it becomes increasingly difficult to abandon that commitment, particularly if the market's initial reaction is negative. Finally, because the company typically has paid a premium over fair market value for the acquisition, it often is aiming to achieve difficult synergies, which creates a heightened level of uncertainty about the success of the investment.

Synergy Measurement Process

These risks in M&A are not presented to discourage making acquisitions; rather, the point is to impress on buyers the need to fully understand how to evaluate potential acquisitions with value creation as the goal.

Synergy Defined

Achieving synergy begins with a clear understanding of what it is. Defining synergy as "a combination of businesses that makes two plus two equal five" or "the wonderful integration benefits from combined strategies and economies of scale" is imprecise and misleading.

In his book, *The Synergy Trap: How Companies Lose the Acquisition Game*, author Mark L. Sirower provides this definition and discussion of synergy:

> Synergy is the increase in performance of the combined firm over what the two firms are already expected or required to accomplish as independent firms.
>
> Where acquirers can achieve the performance that is already expected from the target, the net present value (NPV) of an acquisition strategy then is clearly represented by the following formula:

$$NPV = \text{Synergy} - \text{Premium}$$

In management terms, synergy means competing better than anyone ever expected. It means gains in competitive advantage over and above what firms already need to survive in their competitive markets.[1]

Thus, the acquiring and target firms already have built into their stock values investors' expectations of the increase in value that each company can achieve while operating as a stand-alone business. *Synergy* is the improvement in excess of these anticipated improvements, which makes success in the acquisition process a much more elusive goal. And the odds of successful achievement of this goal are generally reduced by the size of the acquisition premium paid. If most of the value-creating potential from the acquisition is paid to the sellers in the form of a premium, little potential value creation exists for the acquiring firm.

This fact raises the related issue of identifying which party, the buyer or the seller, creates the synergies. Typically, the buyer enables the competitive advantages of the combined enterprise, including revenue enhancements, cost reductions, or technology improvements, over the performance of the individual entities. So the synergy value is usually created by the buyer.

Exceptions do exist. When a target possesses a technology or proprietary process that the buyer can adapt and employ over its larger volume base, this bounce-back synergy is created primarily by the seller. Although the buyer brings the enhanced customer base over which the benefit can be extended, the target creates a benefit and value far beyond what it is worth as a stand-alone entity.

Sources of Synergy

Synergistic benefits generally result from five potential sources:

1. Revenue enhancements
2. Cost reductions
3. Process improvements
4. Financial economies
5. Risk reduction

REVENUE ENHANCEMENTS Revenue enhancements may result from higher unit sales, which usually are achieved by the combined entity serving a broader market or offering an expanded product line, or both. Selected price increases also may be achieved, particularly when the combined entity

---

[1] Mark L. Sirower, *The Synergy Trap: How Companies Lose the Acquisition Game* (New York: The Free Press, 1997), p. 20.

creates strategic advantages, such as being the sole supplier for a technology or product.

Forecasted revenue enhancements should be viewed with caution. They are often dependent on many external variables, particularly customer and competitor response. Both may be difficult to predict, and, to a large extent, they are beyond the control of the combined entity. For example, customers may have a policy that prevents excessive reliance on any one source of supply. Competitor reaction also should be anticipated, including new product offerings and price discounts.

Revenue enhancements can be achieved when the combined company offers a broader line of products or services, often by leveraging the distribution system of the new entity. The expanded or improved product line also may qualify the combined company to compete for business that was not available to either the acquirer or the target operating as stand-alone businesses.

COST REDUCTIONS Estimates of the second synergy source, cost reductions, tend to be more predictable and reliable than revenue improvements. Through consolidation of functions, positions and related fixed assets and overhead are eliminated. The magnitude of this benefit tends to be larger when the target is similar to the acquirer in operations and markets served.

To succeed with cost reductions, particular attention must be paid in advance to job titles and account classifications. Because these tend to vary among companies, identifying which specific functions can be eliminated becomes more difficult. Salaries and wages, in particular, require vigilance because while positions may be cut, the individuals who held them sometimes survive in the new entity in a different department or job title.

TECHNOLOGY AND PROCESS IMPROVEMENTS Process improvements occur when the combined entity adopts the most efficient or effective practices employed by the target or acquirer. These enhancements frequently result from technological or process improvements that can be leveraged over the broader base of the combined entity. The improvements can create enhanced revenues or cost reductions as well as more efficient operations or more effective marketing and distribution.

FINANCIAL ECONOMIES The fourth synergy source, financial economies, is often misunderstood. The value of a target cannot be enhanced by attributing to it a lower cost of capital through use of more debt financing. Since any acquirer could achieve this benefit, such financial manipulations seldom have genuine value-creating potential. However, the combination may lower the combined entity's financing costs and may allow for efficiencies in lease terms, cash management, and management of working capital.

The combined entity also may create certain tax benefits, such as use of net operating loss carryovers or the ability to incorporate in a jurisdiction that provides favorable tax rates. Acquirers are cautioned, however, to recognize that most financial economies cannot materially improve a company's strategic position and seldom should be the driving force behind a transaction.

RISK REDUCTION The target's cost of capital can be reduced through acquisition by a larger company that eliminates many of the risks that exist in the target as a stand-alone business. The target can eliminate several risks typically seen in smaller companies – such as key person dependency, customer concentration, failure to keep pace with technological changes, and position relative to its competitors – by becoming a segment of a company that possesses a broad array of market strengths.

Key Variables in Assessing Synergies

In assessing the potential savings from each of these synergy sources, members of an M&A team should focus relentlessly on three variables that can dramatically influence the accuracy of the estimated synergy and value calculation.

1. *Size of synergy benefit.* The synergy value should be quantified in a forecast of net cash flows that includes estimates of revenues, expenses, financing and tax costs, and investments in working capital and fixed assets. Each component of the forecast, particularly all estimated improvements, must be challenged rigorously. Acquisition team members must resist the natural inclination to buy into the deal emotionally, which so often leads to overly optimistic revenue and expense estimates. Each element in the forecast must be estimated accurately.
2. *Likelihood of achievement.* The business combination will project various benefits, some of which have a very high likelihood of success while others may be long shots. For example, the likelihood that the administrative costs associated with the target's board of directors can be eliminated is about 100%. Conversely, achieving certain sales goals against stiff competition is probably far less definite. These differences must be noted and allowed for in the forecast. Computing the probability of various outcomes, such as optimistic, expected, and pessimistic,

or through a Monte Carlo simulation, helps to quantify the range of possible outcomes. In particular, management should be sensitive to downside projections and their consequences.

3. *Timing of benefits.* The buyer's M&A team must recognize that while the acquisition usually occurs as a single transaction, its benefits accrue over a forecast period that may cover many years. The value of the acquisition and its success are critically tied to achieving the improved cash flows according to the forecasted time schedule. Any delays push cash flows farther into the future and reduce their present value. Temptations to accelerate the timing of revenue enhancements or cost savings must be avoided, with the timing of each assumption challenged just as the amounts are. The history of M&A is littered with stories of how unrealistic acceleration of improvements to enhance the attractiveness of an acquisition led to overestimation of synergy value. The M&A team that succumbs to this pressure is first and foremost fooling itself.

The clear point here is to stress the importance of objectivity and rigorous due diligence in the examination of forecasted synergies. Investors anticipate improvements in the performance of both the acquirer and the target in the values they establish for each company as stand-alone entities. The synergies related to the acquisition must reflect improvements beyond those already anticipated. The value of these synergies must exceed the premium over the acquirer's fair market value in order to create value. Thus, every forecasted synergy must be challenged aggressively in terms of the estimated amount, the likelihood of achievement, and when that benefit will occur. Companies that overlook this process are inviting unpleasant surprises and disappointment in the future.

Synergy and Advance Planning

The acquisition planning process described in Chapter 4 emphasized the need to tie the acquisition plan to the company's overall strategic plan. Within this context, each acquisition should be evaluated in light of the likelihood of achieving the forecasted synergies. Mark L. Sirower describes the Cornerstones of Synergy as the following four elements of an acquisition strategy that must be in place to achieve success with synergies:[2]

1. *Strategic vision.* Represents the goal of the combination, which should be a continuous guide to the operating plan of the acquisition.

---

[2] Ibid., p. 29.

2. *Operating strategy.* Represents the specific operational steps required to achieve strategic advantages in the combined entity over competitors.
3. *Systems integration.* Focuses on the implementation of the acquisition while maintaining preexisting performance targets. For success, these should be planned in considerable detail in advance of the acquisition to achieve the timing of synergy improvements.
4. *Power and culture.* With corporate culture changing with the acquisition, the decision-making structure in the combined entity, including procedures for cooperation and conflict resolution, must be determined and implemented. Success in the integration requires effectiveness throughout the newly combined organization, which forces the need for clarity of purpose.

Synergy has acquired almost a mythical reputation in M&A for the rewards that it reputedly provides. Watch out for these rewards. In some cases, they may indeed be a myth.

Business combinations can provide improvements, but these must be in excess of the improvements that investors already anticipate for the acquirer and target as stand-alone companies. These anticipated stand-alone improvements are the first hurdle that any combination must surpass. When the acquirer pays a premium to the target's shareholders, the present value of any benefits provided by the combination must be reduced by this premium. Thus, the higher the premium paid, the lower are the potential benefits to the acquirer. Acquirers also must recognize that in handing over initial synergy benefits to the seller in the form of the premium payment, they have left themselves the challenge of achieving the remaining synergies, which are often the most difficult.

Synergies must not be mythical. They must be harshly contested, accurately forecasted, and appropriately discounted net cash flows that reflect their probability of success under carefully constructed and reviewed time schedules.

PART III

Measuring Value

CHAPTER 6

Valuation Approaches and Fundamentals

Accurate valuation requires appropriate application of the available approaches to determine value, a clear understanding of the exact investment in a business that is being sold or acquired, and a clear measure of the returns that the company generates. Therefore, to enhance precision in the valuation process, this chapter introduces the three valuation approaches, the invested capital model to quantify the investment in the business to be valued, the net cash flow to most accurately measure the company's return to capital providers, the adjustments to the company's financial statements to most accurately portray economic performance, and the mathematical techniques to manage investment risk.

Business Valuation Approaches

Businesses vary in the nature of their operations, the markets they serve, and the assets they own. For this reason, the body of business valuation knowledge has established three primary approaches by which businesses may be appraised, as illustrated in Exhibit 6.1.

According to the *International Glossary of Business Valuation Terms*, the income approach is "a general way of determining a value indication of a business, business ownership interest, security, or intangible asset using one or more methods that convert anticipated benefits into a present single amount. The market approach is "a general way of determining a value indication of a business, business ownership interest, security, or intangible asset by using one or more methods that compare the subject to similar ('guideline') businesses, business ownership interests, securities, or intangible assets that have been sold." Finally, the asset (or cost) approach is "a general way of determining a value indication of a business, business

EXHIBIT 6.1 Business Valuation Approaches and Methods

ownership interest, or security by using one or more methods based on the value of the assets of that business net of liabilities."

Within each of these three approaches, there are several methods. For example, within the income approach, there are the single-period capitalization method and the multiple-period discounting method more commonly known as the discounted cash flow (DCF) method, among others.[1] Within the market approach, there are the guideline public company method and the transaction multiple method, among others. Within the asset approach, there are the adjusted book value method and the liquidation value method, among others. Within each of these methods, there are several valuation procedures. The discounted cash flow and discounted future earnings are technically procedures within the multiple-period discounting method of the income approach. The capitalization of cash flow and capitalization of earnings are technically procedures within the single-period capitalization method of the income approach. Any of the common multiples seen (such as price to earnings, total invested capital to earnings before interest and taxes [EBIT], etc.) are procedures within either the guideline public company method or the transaction multiple method of the market approach.

The income approach is described in Chapter 7, with Chapters 8 and 9 devoted to the development of appropriate rates of return within that approach. Chapters 10 and 11 introduce the market approach and asset approach. Business valuation theory requires that the appraiser attempt to

---

[1] This is not meant to be an exhaustive list of the many methods and procedures within the three valuation approaches. However, it is important to note that additional valuation methods and procedures exist. As an example, for very small businesses, where the owner runs the business on a fulltime basis and the business generates under $2 million a year in revenues, a seller's discretionary cash flow method within the income approach and a direct market data method within the market approach may be more applicable than the methods explained in this book.

use each of the three approaches in every appraisal assignment, although doing so is not always practical. For example, a company may lack a positive return to discount or capitalize, which may prevent use of the income approach. Use of the market approach may not be possible because of the lack of similar companies for comparison. The asset approach, in the absence of the use of the excess earnings method (which is generally not employed for M&A appraisals), cannot accurately portray general intangible or goodwill value that is not shown at market value on a company's balance sheet. Thus each of the approaches brings constraints that may limit its use or effectiveness in a specific appraisal assignment. It is even more important, however, to recognize that each approach brings a unique focus on value and what drives it. The income approach most often looks at future returns discounted to reflect their relative level of risk; the market approach establishes value based on the price paid for alternative investments; the asset approach establishes value based on a hypothetical sale of the company's underlying assets. The strengths and weaknesses of each method, the nature of the appraisal assignment, and the circumstances present in the company being appraised and the industry in which it operates determine which of the approaches can be used and the relative reliability of the results from application of that approach. How to evaluate these results is discussed in Chapter 13, and Exhibit 13.1 provides a summary of the circumstances in which each approach is generally most applicable.

In providing this overview of the approaches to business valuation for M&A, this discussion assumes, unless stated to the contrary, that the business being appraised is a viable, going concern. Those companies intending to liquidate or that are in long-term decline may require different assumptions and valuation procedures.

Using the Invested Capital Model to Define the Investment Being Appraised

For M&A, the investment in the company is generally defined as the invested capital of the business, which is the sum of its interest-bearing debt and equity. This quantity is computed in Exhibit 6.2.

Subtracting the payables from the current assets yields the company's net working capital. Nonoperating assets are also removed, with a corresponding decrease in owner's equity. This leaves the net operating assets that are used in the business and the interest-bearing debt and equity – the invested capital – that is used to finance them.

Keep in mind that all of the company's general intangible characteristics, including employees, customers, and technology, will be included in the

EXHIBIT 6.2 Computation of Invested Capital

Balance Sheet	
Assets	*Liabilities*
	Payables
(Nonoperating assets excluded)	Interest-bearing Debt
	Equity
Total Operating Assets*	Total Liabilities and Equity*
Less: Payables	*Less*: Payables
Net Operating Assets	Invested Capital

*All operating assets and liabilities should be adjusted to market value.

calculation of the value of invested capital. Invested capital is also referred to as the enterprise value of the company on an operating basis because the whole business – including the net operating tangible and intangible assets – is being appraised. A major reason why invested capital, rather than just equity, is valued for M&A is to prevent potential distortions that could be caused by variations in the company's capital structure. In addition, a company may not be run at its optimal capital structure. Invested capital is frequently referred to as a debt-free model because it portrays the business before the relative levels of debt and equity are determined. The objective is to compute the value of the company before considering how operations are financed with debt or equity. Each buyer may choose to finance the company in a different way. This choice, however, should not affect the value of the business. Its operations should have the same value regardless of how they are financed. Also note that any debt related to the acquisition is excluded from invested capital because the value should not be distorted by transaction-related financing choices.

Since the invested capital model portrays the company on a predebt basis, the company's returns – income or cash flow – must be calculated before debt, and its cost of capital or operating multiples must consider both debt and equity financing sources. These points are described in Chapters 9, 10, and 11 after further discussion on returns and rates of return.

Why Net Cash Flow Measures Value Most Accurately

As we discussed in the first two chapters, value creation in a business ultimately can be defined as the risk-adjusted net cash flow that is made available to the providers of capital. Whether the company's stock price increases as a result of a new technology, an improved product line, more efficient operations, or a similar reason, all of these will produce increased cash to capital providers. Thus value inevitably can be traced to cash flow, which is why in the context of valuation a commonly used phrase is "Cash is king." Investors and managers are used to seeing a company's performance expressed as some level of earnings – before or after interest or taxes. The first difficulty with earnings, of course, is that they do not represent the amount that can be spent. As such, earnings frequently fail to show the true amount that is available to capital providers. For example, a company may have an impressive EBIT, but if most or all of this is consumed in interest, taxes, or reinvestments into the company for the working capital or capital expenditures needed to fund anticipated operations, there may be no cash return available for capital providers.

For closely held companies, earnings often are presented as net income before or after taxes. Because this is a return to equity – after interest expense has been recognized – it reflects the present owner's preferences for relative levels of debt versus equity financing. Buyers want an accurate picture of the true operating performance of the company prior to the influence of financing, so returns to invested capital rather than equity should be presented.

Computation of Net Cash Flow to Invested Capital

Because financial statements usually are prepared in compliance with generally accepted accounting principles (GAAP) for reporting to external parties, net cash flow to invested capital (NCFIC) does not appear anywhere in the statements, including the statement of cash flows. It can, however, easily be computed, as Exhibit 6.3 illustrates.

In reviewing this computation, the benefits of net cash flow become more apparent. It represents the amount that can be removed from the business without impairing its future operations because all of the company's internal needs have been taken into consideration. This is why net cash flow is frequently referred to as *free cash flow*.

NCF_{IC} is the only return that accurately portrays the company's true wealth-creating capacity. It reveals the company's return before principal and interest on debt to prevent distortions that could be caused by different borrowing levels. It is a measure of cash flow rather than earnings because investors can spend only cash, not earnings. NCF_{IC} is the net return after taxes and also after providing for the company's internal need for capital expenditures and working capital. Thus it represents the true cash flow available to providers of debt and equity capital, after payment of taxes and the company's internal reinvestment requirements.

EXHIBIT 6.3 Net Cash Flow to Invested Capital

Math Symbol	Component
	Net income after taxes
+	Interest expense, net of income tax (interest expense × [1 − t])
=	Net income to invested capital
+	Noncash charges against revenues (e.g. depreciation and amortization)[a]
−	Capital expenditures (fixed assets and other operating noncurrent assets)[a]
+ or −	Changes in working capital[a,b]
+	Dividends paid on preferred shares or other senior securities, if any[c]
=	Net cash flow to invested capital

[a]In a forecast, these amounts should be at levels necessary to support anticipated future operations, not simply averages or actual amounts from the past or next year's expected amounts.

[b]Remember that the invested capital model is "as if debt free," so any interest-bearing debt in the current liabilities should be removed. Generally speaking, doing so will reduce the dollar amount of the growth in working capital.

[c]In most appraisals this item is zero because usually there are no preferred or other senior dividend-receiving classes of securities.

As is explained further in Chapter 7, the company's net cash flow can be forecasted in discretely identified future years or for a long-term period.

In computing the net cash flow for the long term or terminal period (i.e. into perpetuity), specific relationships between components in the net cash flow computation almost always should be maintained. Capital expenditures should exceed the depreciation write-off of prior-period capital expenditures to reflect inflation and growth. Similarly, the change in working capital should cause a decrease in net cash flow, because the cash outflow required to fund increases in accounts receivable and inventory should exceed the cash inflow provided by increases in accounts payable and accrued payables.

Frequent Need to Negotiate from Earnings Measures

The M&A market, particularly for middle-market and smaller businesses, is seldom well organized. As mentioned earlier, many participants are involved in only one or perhaps a couple of transactions during their entire career, and most advisors – accountants, attorneys, and bankers – do not frequently encounter such transactions. The lack of an organized market and inexperienced participants often leaves sellers hunting for potential buyers and buyers searching through contacts and industry associations or mailing lists for potential companies in which to invest.

In this environment, expectations are often unrealistic, and misinformation abounds as participants look for shortcuts or simple formulas to compute value quickly and conveniently. Values based on multiples of EBIT or earnings before interest, taxes, depreciation, and amortization (EBITDA) usually fill the resulting void. Sellers, in particular, like these measures because they produce relatively high return numbers that look and sound impressive. The problem, of course, is that these are not real returns because income taxes and the company's internal reinvestment needs have not yet been paid. That is, neither EBITDA nor EBIT represents cash that could be available to capital providers.

So how does either party – a seller who wants to know what a company is really worth, regardless of negotiating strategy, or a buyer negotiating with a seller who is quoting such numbers – handle the likely confusion that will be present? The key is to consistently make all value computations using net cash flow to invested capital. With this process the party will be employing the true return available to capital providers along with the most accurate and reliable rates of return. When sellers or their intermediaries quote unsubstantiated EBIT or EBITDA multiples, buyers must demand an explanation of how the multiples were determined. The informed participant, whether buyer, seller, or intermediary, generally will recognize the lack of justification for unrealistic multiples and, more important, be able to explain why they do not accurately reflect value.

Among the most common ways that EBIT or EBITDA multiples distort value include:

- *Inaccurate return.* The computation of EBIT or EBITDA is unrealistic in comparison to historical or future performance, considering likely industry and economic conditions.
- *Confusion of strategic value with fair market value.* Investment bankers or brokers may quote an EBIT multiple that was derived from one or a few transactions where the buyer paid a particularly high price. Unusual synergies unique to that transaction may have justified that multiple, but it seldom represents the market, particularly where such synergies are not available to other buyers.
- *Inappropriate guideline companies.* The selection of multiples from public companies that are much larger or industry leaders that are not sufficiently similar to the target company result in an inappropriate comparison.

- *Inappropriate date*. The selection of multiples from a transaction that is not close to the valuation date may reflect different economic or industry conditions. Similar distortions can occur by mixing returns and multiples – for example, deriving a multiple for net income and applying it to EBIT.
- *Choice of average multiple*. Indiscriminate use of the mean or median multiple derived from a group of companies will distort the indication of value when the target company may vary substantially from the average of that group.

The solution: When savvy investors find they must negotiate from earnings multiples, they determine value using NCFIC and then express that value as a multiple of EBIT or whatever other measure of return the other party prefers to use.

The second compelling reason to choose net cash flow rather than a measure of earnings results from the choices available in developing a rate of return (discussed further in Chapter 8). This rate or its inverse, a multiple, is applied to the return in a discounting, capitalization, or multiplication process to compute value. The reliability of the value determined is clearly dependent on the accuracy and dependability of the two primary variables in the equation, the return and the rate of return or multiple. The public markets provide the basis for highly reliable, long-, intermediate-, and short-term rates of return on net cash flow based on many years of historical experience. In the U.S. market, readily available data dates back to 1926 and reflects actual cash returns that creditors and investors have received and the resulting rates of return that have been earned on their investments. These rates reflect buyers' *prospective* choices – that is, the current prices paid for the anticipated future net cash flow returns on investment. This data provides appraisers with an excellent perspective on investors' risk-versus-return expectations and an accurate indication of their required rates of return on investments with varying levels of risk.

It is important to emphasize that no similar historical rate of return data is available on the other return measures that are frequently reported, including EBITDA, EBIT, net income before taxes, and net income after taxes.[2] None of these measures reflects net cash returns that actually could be available to shareholders. And all are merely measures of historical performance with no investment amount attached to them. As such, there is no way to tie these historical results to prices that investors paid for the anticipated future return on those investments. Chapter 8 illustrates potential errors and distortions from the use of historical rates.

---

[2] However, as will be discussed in Chapter 8, this is changing thanks to surveys and resulting research on required rates of return in the private capital markets in the Pepperdine Private Capital Markets Project.

Financial Statement Adjustments

Adjustments to a target's financial statements, commonly referred to as normalization adjustments, convert the reported accounting information to amounts that show the true economic performance, financial position, and cash flow of the company. Differences between amounts shown on the financial statements and market values most commonly result from one or more of these causes:

- Elections to minimize taxes, including excess compensation, perquisites, rent, or other above-market payments made to owners or other related parties
- Adjustments required to change the basis of accounting, including conversion from cash to accrual or from one inventory or depreciation method to another
- Adjustments for nonoperating and/or nonrecurring items, including asset surpluses or shortages, personal assets carried on the company's balance sheet, or personal expenses paid by the business, and items of income or expense that are not part of ongoing operations
- Differences between the market value of assets and the amounts at which they are carried on the company's books

The significance of many of these normalization adjustments is greater in the valuation of smaller companies. Midsize or larger businesses may have characteristics that require adjustment, but the effect may be immaterial. For example, $100,000 of above-market compensation could result in a significant change in value to a company with $1 million of annual sales, but it may be immaterial to a business with sales of $100 million. Smaller companies also more frequently have financial statements that have been compiled or reviewed, rather than audited, or use the cash basis of accounting rather than the accrual basis. Thus, smaller companies frequently require more adjustments, and the relative impact of the adjustments tends to be greater.

Adjustments can be made to both the income statement and the balance sheet, or one can be adjusted without a corresponding change to the other. For example, a nonrecurring gain or loss can be removed from the income statement without any required adjustment to the balance sheet.

Most often in M&A the buyer is acquiring a controlling interest in the target. This gives the buyer the authority to control and, if desired, manipulate the company's income. Minority owners, however, generally lack the authority of control. For this reason, the first category of adjustments listed is referred to as the *control adjustments* and generally should be made only when a controlling interest in a company is being appraised. Typical control adjustments include:

- Above- or below-market compensation, in any form, paid to controlling shareholders
- Above- or below-rent paid on real estate or equipment owned by the controlling shareholder and leased to the company
- Related or favored parties on the payroll who are paid above- or below-market compensation
- Assets such as automobiles, airplanes, condominiums, memberships, and so on that are owned and/or paid for by the business for the benefit of controlling shareholders but that would not need to be provided to an arm's-length employee hired to provide the same services
- Insurance premiums for policies on which the corporation is not the beneficiary
- Cash surrender value of life insurance
- Above- or below-market loans to and from the corporation to controlling shareholders

In those less common M&A valuation circumstances where the target is a minority equity interest, the decision not to make control adjustments to income may result in a very low or zero value for that minority interest. This low value often reflects the disadvantages of the minority owner versus that of the control owner. (The value of the minority interest can be increased by provisions in a shareholder agreement that restrict the majority owner's access to the company's cash flow.) Alternatively, the return to the controlling shareholder can be used after control adjustments, and then a discount for lack of control can be applied to the resulting value. Doing this is not recommended, and frequently it distorts value because the discount for lack of control may not reflect the magnitude of that particular company's minority versus control income difference. These adjustment points are discussed further in Chapters 11 and 12.

Adjustments to the Balance Sheet

Adjustments to the balance sheet primarily reflect the need to convert assets from book value to market value. In the context of the going-concern enterprise, market value is usually the value of the asset "in place in use" as opposed to either the historical cost and depreciation-based book value or value in contemplation of a liquidation. Asset surpluses or shortages also must be considered; industry norms often are used to determine the desired balance. Nonoperating assets, such as airplanes or condominiums for the owner's personal benefit or real estate not used in the company's operations, should be removed from the balance sheet, with the net effect of these changes charged to an equity account, most typically retained earnings. When real property used by the business is owned by related parties, the rent paid should be compared to market rates to determine if adjustments to income are required. Whether these assets will be included in a sale also should be considered.

Specific adjustments to balance sheet accounts are listed and explained in detail in Chapter 11.

Adjustments to the Income Statement

Adjustments are made to the income statement to convert the company's reported financial performance to its true economic performance. Buyers typically purchase a business to obtain the company's future returns. These returns usually are portrayed in a forecast when the acquisition is under consideration so buyers can assess the company's historic performance and, more important, its future. The forecast frequently requires these income statement adjustments:

- *Nonrecurring revenue or income items.* One-time revenue or income sources, such as a gain on a sale of assets, insurance proceeds, a large sale to a customer under circumstances that are not expected to recur, or a gain from a property condemnation should be subtracted from the company's income because they do not reflect the ongoing profitability of the business.
- *Nonrecurring expense or loss items.* Expenses not expected to recur, such as losses on sale of assets, moving expenses, restructuring costs, or other one-time charges that do not reflect the company's ongoing performance should be added back to income.
- *Nonoperating items of income or expense.* Interest or dividend income beyond amounts earned on transaction-level cash balances, rental income on assets not used in the business, and nonoperating expenses that are not part of the company's core business should be added or subtracted from income. Examples of nonoperating expenses include: charitable donations; education-related payments for nonworking family members; nonworking family members on the company payroll; nonbusiness entertainment or travel; nonbusiness membership dues; automobiles leased for nonworking family members; personal use of credit cards and expense accounts; nonbusiness gifts; landscaping or maintenance expenses related to the owner's home; utilities for the owner's home; purchase of personal furniture, jewelry, or other assets; and estate planning and other personal legal fees.

■ *Owner perquisites.* Payments made by the company to shareholders or other parties favored by them in the form of salaries, bonuses, and fringe benefits of any kind that are above or below market rates should be adjusted to market levels. When such individuals are paid a market-rate compensation but fail to provide adequate service that is required by the company's operations, no adjustment should be made if the buyer anticipates replacing that person with a competent substitute.

Adjustments to the target's historical income statements are made to allow more accurate interpretation of historical performance and also to help to identify any inappropriate items that may be included in a forecast. These adjustments should be considered in both the income and the market approaches in choosing the return stream used to compute the company's value.

Managing Investment Risk in Merger and Acquisition

Much of Chapters 8 and 9 is devoted to deriving discount rates that accurately reflect the risk associated with a specific investment. Based on the underlying theory of the capital asset pricing model, these techniques allow business appraisers to determine an appropriate rate of return for an investment, given general economic, industry, and specific company conditions. Although these techniques are clearly the most accurate in assessing the cost of capital for a business and gauging general company and market risk, additional risk analysis tools are available. M&A investment decisions, with appropriate computation of rates of return, constitute a variation of capital budgeting analysis on which more advanced statistical techniques can be employed to further inform management of the possible outcomes from an investment decision.

Traditional Statistical Tools

Business valuation techniques assess company and market risk. For example, the data cited later in this book develops discount rates based on the probability-weighted statistical expected value for each increment of return. In addition, various traditional statistical parameters are used in evaluating investment risk, including:

■ *Expected value.* Expected value is a weighted average of the forecasted returns with the weights being the probabilities of occurrence.
■ *Variance and standard deviation.* Variance is a standard statistical measure of the variation of the distribution around its mean. The standard deviation is the square root of the variance. It is the conventional

measure of the dispersion, or the "tightness," of a probability distribution. The tighter the distribution, the lower this measure will be, and the wider the distribution, the higher it will be. In the normal bell-shaped distribution, approximately 68% of the total area of the distribution falls within 1 standard deviation on either side of the mean. From this we conclude that there is only a 32% chance that the actual outcome will be more than 1 standard deviation from the mean. Similarly, the probability that the outcome will fall within 2 standard deviations of the mean is approximately 95%, and the probability that it will fall within 3 standard deviations is over 99%.

- *Coefficient of variation.* The coefficient of variation is a statistical measure of the relative dispersion of a distribution. It is computed as the ratio of the standard deviation of a distribution to the expected value of the distribution and measures the risk per unit of expected value.

An effective method for evaluating uncertainty is the *decision tree,* so called because the resulting chart resembles a tree with its trunk on the left and its branches extending toward the right. Each fork in the decision tree represents an event or a decision from which two or more outcomes are possible. By assigning a probability of occurrence to each branch, an expected value can then be calculated for each terminal branch of the tree.

Monte Carlo Simulation

Traditional statistical techniques frequently accompany M&A decisions, but Monte Carlo simulation (MCS) may also be beneficial. MCS is a statistical technique involving ranges of assumptions and outcomes. Each simulation applies random variables produced by statistical distributions of possible values for each of the variables and can be run using software such as Crystal Ball or @Risk.

In a merger and acquisition analysis, value is often a best estimate, single valuation, similar to budgeting for routine business decisions. Typically a spreadsheet analysis can demonstrate how the value would change if various inputs would change. However, it may also be useful to consider these questions to supplement the valuation results:

- The valuation result is the best estimate available, but how likely is it that the target company is worth more than the investment value? In other words, if we base our decision on that value, how confident are we in our concluded value based on the relied-on distribution for the assumptions and resulting distribution of expected values?
- How much plus/minus variation from the traditional value is realistically possible?

- Which variables or decisions in this analysis create most of the risk? And which create most of the opportunity? Of those that are controllable, how much can we reduce the risk and increase the opportunity by taking preemptive action?
- In a friendly acquisition, how can we use the data derived from our risk analysis to negotiate a better deal?

The MCS process involves three steps:

1. Identify the problem's critical elements – those variables that can cause significant swings in the valuation.
2. Quantify the uncertainty associated with each variable through a probabilistic approach.
3. Develop a model to describe the relations among the elements.

The results of the model are then used to assess the potential for achieving various results, such as estimated synergies or operational targets, as well as to identify areas of risk and opportunity. While MCS may provide answers to important questions, the reliability of its results is heavily dependent on the ability to accurately quantify the uncertainty of key variables; so the key assumptions must be carefully assessed.

Real Option Analysis

Traditional capital budgeting techniques require that uncertainties related to an investment be identified and quantified in advance. Because of the long-term and speculative nature of M&A investments, however, the company may encounter continually changing conditions, including variations in the project's risk profile or the emergence of new information. When an investment involves substantial uncertainty, whether in markets, technology, or competition, and there is a likelihood of continually evolving new information and changing competitive conditions, management may need decision tools that allow it to react as conditions change. The use of real options allows management to account for uncertainty as it gradually emerges over the life of an investment by valuing business strategies as chains of options or a series of decisions. *Real option analysis* (ROA) ties computation of the value of an investment to the expected way it will be managed in the future, with this future decision process guided by continual knowledge of the investment's value as it varies over time.

Investors and managers may encounter scenarios where traditional valuation methodologies generate inadequate or negative returns and values. Most commonly, these returns accompany substantial future uncertainty, which leads owners and managers to conclude that they should not fully commit to an investment. Although that investment may offer potential for attractive returns, rapidly changing market conditions, technical developments, and similar uncertainties render the returns too unlikely (too much of a long shot) to merit a full investment at the present time.

Traditional valuation methods, such as the discounted cash flow method, rely on forecasted investments and returns over a discrete number of periods, discounted at a fixed cost of capital. In the real world, management can react to new information or changing market conditions as they occur. Recognizing new strategic advantages and disadvantages, management would alter its strategy. Traditional valuation models that reflect circumstances and facts known at the outset of a potential investment cannot reflect this management flexibility to change course over time. The traditional model would generate an inadequate or negative value that concludes the forecasted benefits are inadequate given the investment risk.

Real options view the investment as a series of choices rather than a single decision. Financial option theory, primarily the Black–Scholes Option Pricing Model,[3] was developed to determine the equilibrium value of a stock option. These options *give the holder the right, but not the obligation*, to make a purchase at an agreed-on price before an agreed-on future date. Thus with the option, the investor has purchased the opportunity to share in the upside potential of an investment's performance while limiting the downside risk. Investors will choose to exercise the option only after considering future information that was unavailable at the time of the initial investment. If unfavorable conditions exist at the future date, the option is not exercised and the option cost is forfeited.

Quite logically, ROA was initially adopted in industries where very large investments were required, payoffs occurred over many years, and the likelihood of failure in any specific project was high. These conditions exist in oil and gas exploration as well as mining, where most initial searches do not result in a positive return. Similar conditions exist in sectors of the pharmaceutical industry, where the likelihood of success at the outset of a research and development effort is quite low.

This real option risk management methodology may serve as a strategic investment tool to assist in analyzing M&A targets or investments in start-up companies or research and development. In addition, ROA may offer benefits in the next situations, each of which should first be evaluated using the traditional techniques:

- Substantial uncertainty exists.
- There is a high likelihood that better information or competitive conditions will emerge from which management could increase value by changing strategy.

---

[3] Fischer Black and Myron Scholes, "Pricing of Options and Corporate Liabilities," *Journal of Political Economy* 81 (May–June 1973): 637–654.

- Investment benefits are expected to be derived from potential big payoffs in the future rather than current returns.

Since these criteria exist in many if not most M&A investments, ROA is most often used to evaluate start-ups or acquisitions that may substantially change the manner in which the acquirer or target conduct its operations. For example, initial investments in research and development are often made on a platform basis, not to achieve an immediate return, but to create the opportunity to make follow-on investments or develop new product options as further information emerges.

Investment in a real option typically involves the acquisition of a package of rights to a license, patent, or similar benefit. This investment usually constitutes a smaller initial outlay but allows management to be proactive to favorably influence the value of their option. That is, investors who have made a relatively small initial outlay can then take steps to influence the return on an investment, its risk profile, its holding period, or its value during that period, all of which affect the value of their real option. This methodology recognizes and quantifies this management flexibility by identifying the key factors that affect value and risk over time. The real option provides its holder with the opportunity to react to uncertainties as they unfold by either exercising the option or declining to do so. In the process, management can proactively decide to:

- Invest further
- Expand operations or markets
- Increase uncertainty through, for example, an investment in a new market
- Change the return on an investment through variations in revenues or expenses
- Extend the option period
- Sell and withdraw from the investment entirely
- Do nothing

With the financial option, the key variables in the Black–Scholes Option Pricing Model that affect value are:

- Time to expiration
- Risk-free interest rate
- Exercise price
- Stock price
- Uncertainty of stock price movements
- Dividends

These same criteria can be applied to real options in M&A or similar investment decisions with slight variations in the economic variables. For example, the exercise price is comparable to the present value of the committed operating costs of the project; the stock price is the equivalent of the present value of the expected returns from the project. Similarly, dividends are analogous to the payout or decline in the value of the investment during the holding period.

So, management could attempt to improve its strategic position and create value by influencing one or more of the real option variables. For example, it could try to extend the level or duration of regulatory barriers or invest in additional technology during the expiration period. It could also affect the exercise price or stock price by changing the company's cost structure to affect its revenues, expenses, and ultimately cash flow. In many new and emerging markets, management can actually encourage competitor investment and innovation to speed the development of new markets, products, or customers, or invest further to create additional hurdles for competitors. Thus with real option investments, greater uncertainty can actually increase the value of an option. With the option providing the ability but not the obligation to exercise, increased uncertainty may bring with it additional opportunities that are not yet well enough defined for an investment decision. The option provides the flexibility to management to wait for further information after which it can either exercise the option at what appears to be the optimum time or decline to exercise at all. Thus, real option analysis captures and quantifies the investor's ability to pay an upfront fee to acquire the flexibility or right to make an additional future investment at a price defined today, but only after analyzing future information that may make the investment more or less attractive.

While traditional valuation theory can be highly effective in assessing company and market risk, some M&A decisions may be clarified through use of additional analytical tools. MCS and ROA, however, require training and experience for proper application and interpretation.

Conclusion

Accurate business valuation requires precision in measuring both the investment and the return on investment. In M&A, invested capital is most often the quantity being valued, and net cash flow provides the most accurate indication of the company's performance. To make sure that the company's financial statements accurately portray the company, normalization adjustments may have to be made to the income statement or the balance sheet to eliminate the effects of nonoperating and nonrecurring items or nonmarket based compensation to shareholders.

Risk management techniques are also available for use in valuation for M&A. Most commonly these involve traditional statistical parameters that include expected value, variance, standard deviation, coefficient of variation, and decision trees. Where substantial risk exists and specific variables can be accurately quantified, MCS and ROA, when properly applied, may provide managers with additional information for decision making.

CHAPTER 7

Income Approach: Using Expected Future Returns to Establish Value

The theory of the income approach is compelling: The value of an investment is computed as the present value of future benefits discounted at a rate of return that reflects the riskiness of the investment. That makes great sense and applies to almost any operating business that generates a positive return.

Successful application of the income approach is more difficult, of course, because each of the key determinants of value – the return and rate of return – must be estimated. In the process of making these estimates, the analyst should carefully analyze the key variables, including prices, volume, and expenses that affect the return, and the risks that each carries. Investments made without the rigor and detail of this process are frequently those that overlook major costs or risks, or carry assumptions that are unrealistic and would not have withstood careful investigation.

Why Values for Merger and Acquisition Should Be Driven by the Income Approach

The income approach is arguably far more effective in computing value for merger and acquisition (M&A) than either the market or asset approaches. The acquirer is investing now to get future net cash flows that are uncertain – that is, carry risks – and the income approach conveniently quantifies these key determinants of value.

Conversely, the market approach usually employs price to earnings (P/E), earnings before interest, taxes, depreciation, and amortization (EBITDA) or similar multiples of a return of the latest historical period rather than an estimate of the future. Market multiples also tend to be less precise than the accuracy that can be achieved through the income approach with forecasted returns and a discount rate. For example, a P/E or EBITDA multiple that is applied to a single year's earnings cannot accurately reflect anticipated variations in those earnings over future years. When properly employed, multiples reflect general investor preferences and are often quoted by industry sources or sellers. Analysts should understand them and compare their results to the primary conclusion, which should be calculated through the income approach.

As previously discussed in more detail in Chapter 4, acquisition analysis should be an integral component of the company's overall strategic plan, which is supported by a budget and forecasted financial statements. Just as the budget forces managers to quantify and defend the financial consequences of their plan, the forecasts and underlying assumptions employed in the income approach to determine value require the same analysis and defense. Whether acquisition benefits arise from revenue enhancement, cost reductions, process improvements, or lower capital costs, the income approach will quantify the assumption and allow it to be debated and evaluated. The income approach also clearly quantifies the timing of these anticipated benefits and reflects how value declines as benefits are pushed farther into the future.

This approach also allows buyers and sellers to compute a company's stand-alone fair market value and its investment value to one or more strategic buyers. With this distinction clearly portrayed, buyers and sellers can easily see synergistic benefits and make informed decisions.

As discussed at the end of the previous chapter, M&A valuations may include application of probability or real option analysis. Each of these analyses can be conveniently incorporated into the forecast structure used in the income approach. The forecast also can easily be modified or updated as circumstances change, and forecasts provide an excellent budget that encourages postinvestment analysis and control.

When studying the income approach, this question inevitably arises: Does the value determined by the income approach include the value of the tangible assets owned in the business, and if so, how?

The values determined by the income approach and the market approach do include the value of all tangible and intangible assets employed in the operation of the business. The business uses these assets to generate its return and could not produce that return if these operating assets were not available. Therefore, the value determined by the income and market approaches includes the value of the tangible and intangible operating assets owned by the business.

If the business owns excess operating assets or nonoperating assets, these assets can be valued separately, and this value can be added to operating value to determine the value of the whole enterprise. This process is discussed in Chapter 11.

Two Methods within the Income Approach

Although this discussion of the income approach has assumed use of a multiple-year forecast, a forecast of only one year also can be used. This difference in the number of years – one versus multiple – creates the distinction between the two primary methods within the income approach.

Single-Period Capitalization Method

The first and simpler method involves the capitalization of the return for a company for one year, which is why it is called the *single-period capitalization method* (SPCM). Since this method involves computing value based on the return of only one year, it can produce a reliable value only if the return chosen is representative of the company's anticipated long-term future performance. Therefore, analysts should not automatically use the return for the latest historical year or an average of recent years if these are not an accurate indication of the future. The rate of growth in the single-period return is computed through the capitalization. This mathematical process requires a second critical assumption: that the return will grow approximately at the selected annual rate to infinity.

The formula for the SPCM is:

$$PV = \frac{r_0(1 + g)}{d - g}$$

where:

PV = Present value
r = Historical or current year return used as a base return, without the next year's growth
g = Proxy for long-term sustainable growth
d = Discount rate
$d - g$ = Capitalization rate

The key variables in this formula, r, g, and d, are discussed in detail in Chapter 8. At this point, recognize that the discount rate reflects the riskiness of the investment while the long-term growth rate reflects how the return is expected to grow annually to infinity. Thus, the capitalization rate, computed as $d - g$, is derived from the discount rate as a function of these two factors. Capitalization rates also can be expressed as a multiplier or multiple by dividing one by the capitalization rate. Capitalization rates can be derived from stock market prices in the market approach (which is explained and illustrated later). This source for these rates is not recommended, however,

EXHIBIT 7.1 Illustration of Capitalization Computations

To Calculate Value:		
$\dfrac{\$\,\text{Return}}{\text{Capitalization Rate}}$	=	$ Value
$\dfrac{\$1,500,000}{15\%}$	=	$10,000,000

To Convert a Capitalization Rate to a Multiple:		
$\dfrac{1}{\text{Capitalization Rate}}$	=	Multiple
$\dfrac{1}{15\%}$	=	6.67 times

Effect of Different Capitalization Rates on Value:		*Multiple*
$\dfrac{\$1,500,000}{30\%}$	=	$5,000,000	3.33
$\dfrac{\$1,500,000}{20\%}$	=	$7,500,000	5.00
$\dfrac{\$1,500,000}{10\%}$	=	$15,000,000	10.00
$\dfrac{\$1,500,000}{8\%}$	=	$18,750,000	12.50
$\dfrac{\$1,500,000}{5\%}$	=	$30,000,000	20.00

because of the volatility of market multiples and the stronger reliability of capitalization rates derived from discount rates. Exhibit 7.1 illustrates these relationships and shows how variations in the capitalization rate affect value and the related size of the multiple.

As with many simple formulas, users must understand the underlying assumptions or they may substantially distort value. The formula can employ a historical, current, or forecasted return, and frequently the forecasted return is computed as shown in the exhibit by multiplying the latest period's return by 1 + g, the anticipated long-term growth rate.

The SPCM is simple and convenient, so it is used often as a way to determine an initial indication of value. It also must be recognized that the cap rate can be the reciprocal of the well-known price earnings multiple when historical earnings is the return stream chosen.

The key to proper application of the SPCM is to never lose sight of the critical assumptions that underlie this method. The less realistic these assumptions are for a particular company, the less reliable will be the results of the SPCM. The return employed in the computation – the numerator – must be a realistic measure of the company's long-term, sustainable performance. Also, the growth rate, g, must be a realistic expectation of that company's ability to achieve annual growth in that return into perpetuity.[1] Where material variations in annual growth are likely, the SPCM becomes less accurate and can substantially distort value.

Which Return on Investment Would You Prefer, 20% or 40%?

The choice may depend on the definitions of return and investment. Return is the benefit to the investor and is usually some measure of income or cash flow. Investment generally is common stock equity, invested capital, specific assets, or another security, such as preferred stock or a stock option. To avoid error, the return must be matched correctly with the rate of return as shown in the table below.

Watch out for distortions. For example, using the single-period capitalization calculation and the 20% equity cap rate, $10,000,000/20% yields a $50,000,000 equity value while $12,000,000/20% yields a $60,000,000 equity value and $20,000,000/20% yields a $100,000,000 equity value. The $50,000,000 equity value is the only correct choice. The other values result from matching a capitalization rate of return that applies to net cash flow with different returns. Remember, it is imperative to match the return with the correct rate of return.

Using Rates of Return to Compute Equity Value

Return on Equity	Amount	Equity Value
Net income before taxes	$20,000,000	$20,000,000/40% $50,000,000
Net income after taxes	$12,000,000	$12,000,000/24% $50,000,000
Net cash flow to equity	$10,000,000	$10,000,000/20% $50,000,000

---

[1] By the term *perpetuity*, we mean indefinite or very long-term, not infinite. With present valuing, once calculations go beyond 20–30 years given the discount rates applicable to most private companies, there is not a material difference in the resulting value calculation. For example, at a discount rate of 15%, the present value of $100 over 20, 30, and 100 years is $626, $657, and $667 respectively. At a discount rate of 25%, the present value of $100 over 20, 30, and 100 years is $395, $399.50, and $400, respectively.

Discounted Cash Flow Method

An alternative to the simplicity of the SPCM is to apply a multiple-period discounting model. The concept of discounting is based on the premise that the value of a company can be determined by forecasting the future financial performance of the business and identifying the surplus cash flow or earnings that the business generates. The assessment of such future returns requires that the risks associated with a company's operations be analyzed and that such risk be reflected in calculating the present value of those future returns. The procedure by which cash flows are used as a measure of the returns generated by the business is commonly known as a discounted cash flow (DCF) analysis. The procedure by which earnings (i.e. net income) are used as a measure of the returns generated by the business is known as a discounted future earnings (DFE) analysis. For purposes of this book, we will use the term *DCF method*, as it is commonly referred to in practice.

Through use of a multiple-year forecast, the DCF overcomes both of the potentially limiting SPCM assumptions. The forecasted future returns, which typically range from 3 to 10 years, can portray future returns that may not be representative of the company's anticipated long-term performance. It also can accurately reflect variations in the return over the life of the forecast, from, for example, changes in revenues, expenses, or capital expenditures. Specifically, it is most applicable for companies forecasting unsustainable growth over the next several years, erratic changes in cash flows, or temporary declines given an economic or industry recession. Thus, when material return variations are anticipated, the DCF should be employed and the SPCM rejected. At the same time, it should be recognized that the methods will generate identical results if the returns forecasted in the DCF reflect the long-term growth rate used in the SPCM computation.

Because M&A decisions normally involve large amounts of money and carry long-term consequences for buyers and sellers, the DCF generally should be used unless the subject company has very stable earnings and constant growth is the likely outcome.

As commonly developed, the DCF has two stages, but there are instances where three stages may be more applicable. The first is a forecast of a specific number of years, and the second stage is a method for estimating the terminal value (i.e. the value for all years after the forecast period). The DCF is portrayed mathematically as

$$PV = \frac{r_1}{(1+d)^1} + \frac{r_2}{(1+d)^2} + \frac{r_3}{(1+d)^3} + \cdots + \frac{r_n}{(1+d)^n} + \frac{\dfrac{r_n(1+g)}{d-g}}{(1+d)^n}$$

where:

PV = Present value

   r = Return (generic term for whichever type of earnings or cash flow is selected)

   d = Discount rate

   g = Long-term sustainable growth rate

   n = Last period in the forecast, which should be a sustainable, long-term return

d − g = Capitalization rate

Note the implicit *end-of-year convention* assumes the return is received at the end of each year. For start-up companies or ventures into emerging industries, it may be difficult to forecast with a high level of confidence beyond just a few years. Conversely, for established companies in mature industries, relatively accurate forecasts can be made for periods as long as 7 to 10 years. While there is no prescribed number of years to forecast, it should extend long enough to reflect anticipated variations in the company's return, and it should end with a stable or sustainable return.

In preparing forecasts, the advisor or analyst may first go to company management. If management forecasts are to be relied upon, they must only be accepted if in the advisor's judgment they reflect existing and expected economic, industry, and company performance as well as overall relevant market data and prevailing market attitudes (i.e. that they are reasonable). Scenarios may also be completed reflecting management's optimistic and pessimistic outlook in addition to its most likely. In addition to the preparation of a forecast of what is expected to happen, additional projections may be prepared showing the results of scenarios involving acquisition by different types of synergistic buyers, the infusion of additional capital by a private equity investor, etc.[2]

---

[2] Under the American Institute of Certified Public Accountants (AICPA) Professional Standards, *AT Section 301 Financial Forecasts and Projections*, a *forecast* is what is expected to happen while a *projection* is what might happen under certain hypothetical assumptions.

Questions to Consider in Understanding the Assumptions behind Forecasts[3]

- Is expected growth in revenue due to an increase in price or volume or both?
- How does expected growth in revenue of the company compare to industry growth?
- Is revenue growth achievable given the current conditions of company operations?
- How are new products or services considered in forecasted revenue? If so, are corresponding expenses reasonable?
- Are new products under development? What is the basis for research and development expenses? Are forecasted capital expenditures consistent with the revenue growth assumptions?
- Are operating expenses consistent with historical levels? Did management differentiate between fixed and variable costs?
- If there are variable costs, what do costs vary against?
- Are forecasted results consistent with historical results? If not, why?
- Do the forecasts consider any synergies from revenue enhancement and/or cost savings?
- Is it reasonable for management to forecast a much higher or lower growth rate compared to guideline companies or other industry metrics?
- Is it reasonable for management to forecast a much higher or lower profit margin compared to guideline companies or other industry metrics?

Once a stabilized return is achieved, the DCF capitalizes all returns beyond the discrete forecast period as the *terminal value*, based on the assumption that the subject private company has a perpetual life under a going-concern premise. As portrayed in the last equation, the terminal value is computed by increasing the stabilized return in the final year of the forecast by the anticipated long-term sustainable growth rate as of the end of the forecast, capitalizing that return, and then computing the present value of the capitalized return as of the end of the forecast period. This is commonly referred to as the Gordon Growth Model. Alternatively, in M&A, the terminal value is also commonly determined by way of an exit multiple (e.g. a multiple of Year 5 EBITDA), discounted to present value.

---

[3] American Society of Appraisers Business Valuation Committee Special Topics Paper #3, "The Use of Management's Prospective Financial Information by a Valuation Analyst," *Business Valuation Review*™ (Spring, 2017): 5.

Several questions frequently emerge about the DCF formula:

- How long should the forecast be?

    Although five years is typically applied, it could be three years or 10 years or any other number of years. The forecast should be long enough to portray all anticipated variations in the company's return and until a stabilized return is achieved. The stabilized or sustainable return is necessary because it is used in the terminal value computation, which should reflect long-term relationships between the various elements in the company's return.
- Why do we discount the capitalized value in the terminal computation?

    The terminal value represents the value of all of the future returns beyond the discrete forecast period. This capitalized value then must be discounted, using the end-of-year present value factor for the final period in the forecast.
- What proportion of the total value should the terminal value be?

    There is no correct answer to this question because the terminal value will vary depending on the particular circumstances, such as the long-term growth rate, of each investment. The relative size of the terminal value increases as the forecast period decreases and becomes increasingly less important as the forecast lengthens. Depending on the discount rate, after a forecast of about 10 years, the terminal value is much less significant.

The DCF formula assumes that the returns generated by the investment are received by the company at the end of each period. Since most investments generate returns that are received throughout the year, the DCF formula often is revised by the *midyear discounting convention* and is portrayed in the next equation:

$$PV = \frac{r_1}{(1=d)^5} + \frac{r_2}{(1+d)^{1.5}} + \frac{r_3}{(1+d)^{2.5}} + \ldots + \frac{r_n}{(1+d)^{n-.5}} + \frac{\frac{r_n(1+g)}{d-g}}{(1+d)^n}$$

where:

PV = Present value

r = Return (generic term for whichever type of earnings or cash flow is selected)

d = Discount rate

g = Long-term sustainable growth rate

n = Last period in the forecast, which should be a sustainable, long-term return

$d - g$ = Capitalization rate

The midyear convention assumes the return is received evenly through-out each discretely forecasted year. A minority of practitioners prefer to use the midyear convention in the computation of the terminal value, in which case the discount factor would change in the last equation from n years to $n.5$ years. Otherwise, the discount factor in the terminal year should equal that of the last forecast year.

Three-Stage DCF Model

The DCF just discussed is a traditional two-stage model, which includes the financial projections for the discrete forecast period and a terminal value to reflect the company's ongoing operations beyond the last forecasted year. For many early-stage companies, an interim stage is sometimes applicable. For example, an early-stage company might be expected to go through five years of considerable growth and five more years of still relatively high, but declining, relative annual growth. As stated in the previous section, fore-casts should extend long enough to reflect anticipated variations (including unsustainable levels of growth) in the company's cash flows. And, as dis-cussed in the next section, it would be difficult after the initial five years of projections to accurately estimate the appropriate long-term sustainable growth rate. As a result, another level is added to reflect this stage of higher, but not sustainable, growth.

For early-stage companies, small changes in the assumptions regard-ing sustainable long-term growth in economic benefits may result in large changes in indicated values. To minimize this phenomenon, a three-stage model involving the aforementioned interim stage is applicable. As seen in Exhibit 7.2, cash flow growth in Year 5 is forecasted at 56%. An interim stage for Years 6 through 10 reflects gradually declining rates of growth in cash flow of 40%, 30%, 20%, 15%, and 10% in each successive year. This is based on an assessment of the company's expected position at that time and considers long-term industry forecasts.

Therefore, the value of this company under a three-stage DCF model is equal to the present value of the cash flows for Years 1 through 5, plus the present value of the cash flows for the interim period of Years 6 through 10, plus the present value of the terminal value reflecting the company's ongo-ing operations, or $3.4 million. If a two-stage DCF had been used instead, capitalizing cash flows after Year 5 at the long-term sustainable growth rate of 4%, the resulting value would have been $2.2 million.

In certain cases, a fourth stage may be applicable. In addition, different discount rates may be applied to the different stages given their distinctive levels of risk.

EXHIBIT 7.2 Three-Stage DCF Model

I. Present Value of Cash Flows in First 5 Years:

	20x1	20x2	20x3	20x4	20x5
Revenues	$4,300,000	$7,600,000	$11,250,000	$15,100,000	$19,250,000
Less: Cost of Sales	938,500	1,540,375	2,290,375	3,165,375	4,165,375
Equals: Gross Income	$3,361,500	$6,059,625	$8,959,625	$11,934,625	$15,084,625
Less: Operating Expenses	3,233,406	5,718,401	8,237,000	10,840,456	13,455,595
Equals: Operating Income	$128,094	$341,224	$722,625	$1,094,169	$1,629,030
Less: Income Taxes at 27%	34,585	92,131	195,109	295,426	439,838
Equals: Net Income	$93,509	$249,094	$527,516	$798,744	$1,189,192
Plus: Depreciation	21,775	34,651	41,343	46,067	58,948
Less: Capital Expenditures	45,000	43,200	48,400	62,200	82,700
Less: Increase in Working Capital	60,000	66,000	73,000	115,500	124,500
Net Cash Flow	$10,284	$174,545	$447,459	$667,110	$1,040,939
Annual Cash Flow Growth Rate		*NM*	*156%*	*49%*	*56%*
Times: Present Value Factor (30% discount rate, mid-year convention)	0.8771	0.6747	0.5190	0.3992	0.3071
Equals: Present Value of Cash Flows	$9,019	$117,759	$232,218	$266,315	$319,654
Present Value of Cash Flows in First 5 Years (A)					**$944,965**

(continued)

EXHIBIT 7.2 (Continued)

II. Present Value of Interim Cash Flows in Subsequent 5 Years:	20x6	20x7	20x8	20x9	20y1
Net Cash Flow	$1,457,315	$1,894,509	$2,273,411	$2,614,423	$2,875,865
Annual Cash Flow Growth Rate	*40%*	*30%*	*20%*	*15%*	*10%*
Times: Present Value Factor (30% discount rate, mid-year convention)	0.2362	0.1817	0.1398	0.1075	0.0827
Equals: Present Value of Cash Flows	$344,243	$344,243	$317,763	$281,098	$237,852
Present Value of Interim Cash Flows in Subsequent 5 Years (B)					**$1,525,198**

III. Present Value of Terminal Year (Value beyond 20y1):	Terminal Yr.
Net Cash Flow for Terminal Year	$2,990,900
Capitalization Rate (30% Discount Rate − 4% Long-term Growth Rate)	26%
	$11,503,462
Times: Discount Factor (equal to Year 10)	0.0827
Present Value of Terminal Year (C)	**$951,408**

| **Indicated Fair Market Value of Equity (A+B+C, rounded)** | **$3,400,000** |

Establishing Defendable Long-Term Growth Rates and Terminal Values

In both the SPCM and the DCF, the computation of value is influenced by the size of g, the long-term growth rate of the company's return. Both computations assume that the return will grow at this rate forever, so an unrealistic growth rate can substantially distort value.

The factors most commonly considered in determining the growth rate include:

- General economic conditions
- Growth expectation for the company's industry, including consideration of growth expectations for industries in which the company's products are sold
- Synergistic benefits that could be achieved in an acquisition
- The company's historical growth rate
- Where the company is in its business life cycle
- Management's expectations as to future growth considering the company's competitive condition, including changes in technology, product lines, markets, pricing, and sales and marketing techniques

In evaluating these factors, it is essential to keep in mind that the SPCM and the terminal value in the DCF involve perpetual models – they assume the returns extend indefinitely. A good way to begin selection of the long-term growth rate is by considering macroeconomic factors. In the United States, for example, population growth is less than 2%, and growth in gross national product is usually less than 3%. Thus, the weighted average growth rate of all industries is about 3% in the long term. With this macroeconomic benchmark in mind, move to the specific industry and determine its historical and forecasted long-term growth. From that, if appropriate, move to that segment of the industry in which the target company operates and perform a similar analysis. National data can be used for companies that sell nationwide, but smaller firms that operate regionally or locally should be analyzed based on the performance in these specific areas. Remember that the growth rate chosen is applied to the company's return – earnings or cash flow – so product mix, prices, and margins should be used to assess the reasonableness of the growth rate chosen.

Companies that possess a track record of double-digit growth reflect competitive advantages that have allowed them to capture market share and grow rapidly. When these competitive factors suggest that continued very high growth should be anticipated for the foreseeable future, this result should be reflected in a forecast for that high-growth period. This high-growth performance logically should decline as market forces take over; that is, competitors enter the market, introduce new technologies, and bring cost savings and pricing pressure that eliminate the company's strategic benefit. Rates of growth also tend to decline as companies increase in size.

In *Competitive Strategy*, Michael Porter outlined four stages of an industry's life cycle: (1) introduction, (2) growth, (3) maturity, and (4) decline.[4] This observation is also applicable both to specific businesses and to products. Both revenues and earnings typically begin slowly at the introduction phase, then expand rapidly during the growth phase. After leveling out at maturity, they then begin a gradual decline. Therefore, applying unrealistically high or unsustainable growth assumptions may result in an earnings or cash flow stream that is overly optimistic and that indicates too high a value when capitalized.

Values often are inflated by long-term growth rates that suggest a company will maintain its competitive advantages forever. For example, in an industry that is growing at an annual rate of 3%, an SPCM or DCF computation that includes a long-term growth rate of 10% assumes that the target company will perpetually grow at over three times the industry rate, capturing additional market share forever. Sellers or their agents frequently attempt to inflate value through unrealistically high long-term growth assumptions, so these numbers always should be reviewed.

It is important to remember that the growth rate assumed in calculating the terminal value and subtracted from the discount rate to derive a company's capitalization rate must be sustainable. It is a compound growth rate sustainable into perpetuity. If a relatively high short-term growth rate is used as the conversion factor, the company will be incorrectly overvalued. In situations where a capitalization rate cannot be properly determined as of the date the company is being valued, a traditional two-stage DCF should be applied. In situations where a capitalization rate cannot be properly determined as of the end of a forecast period of, say, five years, a three-stage DCF should be considered. A company may be able to far outpace its competitors in the early stages or in any one given year, but not into perpetuity.

In determining the growth rate, several specific macro factors must be considered:

- The growth rate is nominal (i.e. it includes the rate of inflation).
- In the vast majority of cases, the growth rate ranges between approximately 2% (i.e. the long-term expected rate of inflation) and in very rare instances, 6%.
- In most cases, the growth rate ranges between 3% (to reflect some growth above inflation) and 5% (which approximates the real growth in gross domestic product plus inflation, given that competitive forces and

---

[4] Michael Porter, *Competitive Strategy* (New York: The Free Press, 1980).

EXHIBIT 7.3 Effects of Varying Long-Term Growth Rates on Value in the SPCM

	Key Facts	
Annual Return:	$6 million	
Discount Rate:	15%	
Long-term Growth Rates:	3%, 6%, 9%	

3% Growth	6% Growth	9% Growth
$\dfrac{\$6\,\text{million}}{15\% - 3\%} = \$50\,\text{million}$	$\dfrac{\$6\,\text{million}}{15\% - 6\%} = \$66.7\,\text{million}$	$\dfrac{\$6\,\text{million}}{15\% - 9\%} = \$100\,\text{million}$

other economic factors make it very difficult for a company to sustain much more than this into perpetuity).

- A growth rate less than 2.5% implies that the company is not expected to keep pace with inflation over the long term.
- A growth rate above 6% assumes that the company is expected to transcend competitive market forces, an achievement that has been made by very few companies.

In summary, long-term growth rates should not always be 3%. The forecast should, however, be scrutinized carefully with rigorous attention to the details that most affect growth, including markets, products, volume, and prices. Where unsustainable growth is anticipated, it should be reflected in the forecast of DCF.

The explosive effect on value from what may appear to be modest changes in the long-term growth rate is illustrated in Exhibit 7.3.

DCF Challenges and Applications

The DCF is often criticized or even not applied because, it is argued, it is very difficult to forecast what a company will be able to generate in cash flows beyond a year or two. While this point is valid – nobody has a crystal ball – valuation is a prophecy of the future. As such, *everything* in valuation is a forecast. Whether an SPCM or DCF or market multiple is used to estimate value, all are a form of a forecast. A higher EBITDA multiple, for example, is a forecast of expected higher growth and/or profitability. In essence, putting together forecasts, if possible with the input of company management, and applying those forecasts to develop a DCF analysis and resulting indication of value or range of values is a crucial part of M&A due diligence for both buyer and seller. With regard to middle market and lower middle market companies – the focus of this book – there are, in the opinion of the authors, very few exceptions to this. In fact, preparing multiple sets of forecasts and projections under various scenarios is good practice in valuation for M&A. A transaction occurs when the expectations of both buyer and seller meet within a range of values.

The income approach is the most widely used technique to value businesses for M&A because it is appropriate for almost any enterprise that generates a positive return. This approach is grounded in widely accepted economic theory that value can be computed by discounting future economic benefits at a rate of return that reflects their relative risk. The challenge in this process is to develop reliable returns and rates of return to use in computing the value. Both of the methods within the income approach, SPCM and DCF, offer advantages. While the SPCM is quick and convenient, the DCF allows for more detail and accuracy. The value generated by either method is dependent on the choices made for the returns and rates of return used in the formula, and each requires selection of a realistic long-term growth rate. Selection of the returns and the particular benefits of use of net cash flow to invested capital were described in Chapter 6; Chapter 8 explains how to develop defendable rates of return.

CHAPTER 8

Cost of Capital Essentials

A *discount rate*, also known as a cost of capital or a required rate of return, reflects risk, which, simply stated, is uncertainty. It is the expected rate of return that the market requires to attract funding to an investment. Based on the principle of substitution, it is a market-driven opportunity cost that depends on the riskiness of the underlying investment. Discount rates are determined by the market of alternative investment choices available to the investor with the rates varying over time as economic and risk characteristics change.

Cost of capital is further described in the *Ibbotson SBBI 2013 Valuation Yearbook* published by Morningstar, Inc.

> The cost of capital (sometimes called the expected or required rate of return or the discount rate) can be viewed from three different perspectives. On the asset side of a firm's balance sheet, it is the rate that should be used to discount to a present value the future expected cash flows. On the liability side, it is the economic cost to the firm of attracting and retaining capital in a competitive environment, in which investors (capital providers) carefully analyze and compare all return-generating opportunities. On the investor's side, it is the return one expects and requires from an investment in a firm's debt or equity. While each of these perspectives might view the cost of capital differently, they are all dealing with the same number.
>
> The cost of capital is always an expectational or forward-looking concept. While the past performance of an investment and other historical information can be good guides and are often used to estimate the required rate of return on capital, the expectations of future events are the only factors that actually determine the cost of capital. An investor contributes capital to a firm with the expectation that the business's future performance will provide a fair return on the investment. If past performance were the criterion most important to investors, no one

would invest in start-up ventures. It should also be noted that the cost of capital is a function of the investment, not the investor.

The cost of capital is an opportunity cost. Some people consider the phrase "opportunity cost of capital" to be more correct. The opportunity cost of an investment is the expected return that would be earned on the next best investment. In a competitive world with many investment choices, a given investment and the next best alternative have practically identical expected returns.[1]

Because businesses are usually financed with both debt and equity, the cost of each must be determined. Debt is less expensive than equity because it tends to be less risky, and the interest cost of debt is usually tax deductible. Returns on equity are not guaranteed, so they are more risky than debt and more difficult to quantify. Exhibit 8.1 portrays key distinctions between the characteristics of debt and equity, particularly in closely held corporations.

These differences in the rights and accompanying risks of capital providers cause commensurate differences in the cost of each source of capital. The resulting capital costs, or rates of return, are used to determine the value of the business. A lower-risk investment requires a lower rate of return, and the lower rate generates a higher value in the discounted cash flow (DCF) method or single-period capitalization method (SPCM) computation. Conversely, for a higher-risk investment, shareholders require a higher rate of return, which leads to a lower value, as illustrated with the SPCM in Exhibit 8.2.

Cost of Debt Capital

A company's cost of debt is usually its after-tax interest rate, assuming the company is profitable so that the interest expense can be deducted. When determining cost of debt, one must ensure that the company's cash flows are sufficient to service the debt and the company can continue to maintain its debt covenants. When the company's long-term debt is carried at approximately the current market rate of interest, then the book value and the market value of that debt are the same. When, however, the company carries debt securities that have interest rates that are materially above or below market rates as of the valuation date, the market value of the debt may vary from its book value, and adjustments should be made for the difference. Since this seldom occurs, particularly in closely held companies,

---

[1] Morningstar®, Ibbotson® *Stocks, Bonds, Bills and Inflation* (SBBI®) *2013 Valuation Yearbook* (Chicago: Morningstar, 2013), pp. 21–22.

EXHIBIT 8.1 Comparison of the Characteristics of Debt versus Equity

Characteristics	Corporate Bonds or Loans—Lesser Risk to the Investor	Common Stock—Greater Risk to the Investor
Safety of Principal	Guaranteed principal protection when held to maturity, although bond market values vary with interest rate levels.	No principal protection.
Income	Guaranteed fixed annual interest return.	Dividend payments dependent on financial condition, management preferences, and board approval.
Liquidation Preference	Priority in liquidation frequently exists over general creditors and over all equity holders.	Last priority in liquidation behind all creditors and other equity holders.
Collateral Provided	Often, depending on nature of loan and provisions.	Rarely.
Management Control	No management control, but creditor approval may be required for certain corporate actions.	Degree of control depends on size of interest, voting rights, and prevailing legal restrictions and agreements.
Appreciation	No potential for return beyond fixed interest payment.	Potential for return limited only by company performance, but may vary depending on degree of control, ownership structure, and legal restrictions and agreements.

Source: Frank C. Evans, "Making Sense of Rates of Returns and Multiples," *Business Valuation Review* (June 1999): 51–57. Reprinted with permission from *Business Valuation Review*, Copyright © 1999.

this discussion assumes that the market value and book value of the debt are the same unless it is specified to be different.

Historic average interest rates that reflect relative levels of investment risks that do not pertain to any specific date or economic conditions are illustrated in Exhibit 8.3.

EXHIBIT 8.2 Effects of Varying Rates of Return on Value

Higher risk and required rate of return yields lower value	Medium risk and required rate of return yields middle value	Lower risk and required rate of return yields higher value
$\dfrac{\$6\,\text{million}}{24\%} = \$25\,\text{million}$	$\dfrac{\$6\,\text{million}}{18\%} = \$33.3\,\text{million}$	$\dfrac{\$6\,\text{million}}{12\%} = \$50\,\text{million}$

Conclusion: The level of risk must be accompanied by a commensurate rate of return, which affects value. The higher the risk and associated rate of return, the lower the value will be.

EXHIBIT 8.3 Cost of Debt

U.S. Government Treasuries (Risk-free Rate)	Other Government Debt Instruments	Higher-Grade Corporate Bonds	Lower-Grade Corporate Bonds	Secured Loans to Privately Held Companies	Secured Loans to Privately Held Companies	Unsecured Loans to Privately Held Companies
2%	--->					12%

Cost of Preferred Stock

The cost of preferred stock is typically the market yield, which is the dividend rate of return on the security. Preferred stock can carry features that can make it callable, convertible, cumulative, or participating, all of which can affect the rate of return on the security.

Cost of Common Stock

The cost of common stock, which is generally referred to in this discussion as *equity*, is more difficult to determine because it carries no fixed return and its market value can vary dramatically. For this reason, the cost of common stock usually is expressed as the total of several elements, and every equity discount rate includes these three fundamental components:

1. *Risk-free rate.* The rate on an investment free of default risk. The common proxy for this component for long-term investments is the rate of return on long-term U.S. Treasury Bonds.
2. *Equity risk premium.* The addition to the risk-free rate of return for the increased risk inherent in equity over debt.
3. *Specific-company premium.* The adjustment to the rate for the specific risk profile of the subject company.

EXHIBIT 8.4 Cost of Common Stock

Large-Cap (S&P 500) Public Company	Mid-Cap and Lower-Cap Public Company	Micro-Cap Public Company	Larger/Stronger Private Company	Venture Capitalists and Smaller/Weaker Private Company		
10%	15%	20%	25%	30%	35%	40%

Typical costs of common stock when measured by net cash flows to equity investors, which do not pertain to any specific date, industry, or economic condition, are illustrated in Exhibit 8.4.

Fundamentals and Limitations of the Capital Asset Pricing Model

The cost of equity for public companies usually is quantified through the capital asset pricing model (CAPM), a branch of capital market theory that describes and quantifies investor behavior. An extensive discussion of CAPM is available in finance textbooks.

The CAPM can be used to determine the cost of equity in a privately held company. The most common application is for those businesses that are viable candidates to become public companies. The CAPM often is inappropriate for valuing private companies because the assumptions that underlie it are either inconsistent with or not sufficiently similar to investor circumstances surrounding such an investment.[2] To emphasize this point before reviewing the elements of the CAPM, consider the assumptions that underlie it:

- All investors are single-period expected utility of terminal wealth minimizers who choose among alternative portfolios on the basis of each portfolio's expected return and standard deviation.
- All investors can borrow or lend an unlimited amount at a given risk-free rate of interest, and there are no restrictions on short sales of any asset.
- All investors have identical estimates of the expected values, variances, and covariances of returns among all assets (i.e. investors have homogeneous expectations).
- All assets are perfectly divisible and perfectly liquid (i.e. marketable at the going price).

---

[2] For more comprehensive critiques of CAPM, see Shannon P. Pratt and Roger J. Grabowski, *Cost of Capital: Applications and Examples,* 5th ed. (Hoboken, NJ: Wiley, 2014), Chapter 13.

- There are no transaction costs.
- There are no taxes.
- All investors are price takers (i.e. all investors assume that their own buying and selling activity will not affect stock prices).
- The quantities of all assets are given and fixed.[3]

It should be obvious that many of the assumptions underlying the CAPM do not fit the typical investment in a closely held company. Such investments are seldom fully diversified, are often highly illiquid, and frequently carry significant transaction costs, and many times investor behavior is motivated by tax considerations. For example, while CAPM assumes a fully diversified portfolio, it is applied in valuation to assess the value of an investment in a single company. This distinction necessitates inclusion of the specific-company risk premium in the modified CAPM (MCAPM) that is discussed later in this chapter. These differences make the CAPM less effective in appraising closely held business interests, particularly of smaller companies. However, in order to quantify the cost of equity capital effectively, the mechanics of CAPM must be understood. They are summarized next and begin with recognition of the three factors essential in the development of a discount rate:

1. Risk-free rate
2. Equity risk premium
3. Specific-company risk premium

The CAPM formula quantifies these as:

$$R_e = R_f + \beta(ERP)$$

where:

R_e = Rate of return expected – the proxy for the market's required rate

R_f = Risk-free rate of return – a fixed return free of default risk

B = Beta – a measurement of the volatility of a given security in comparison to the volatility of the market as a whole, which is known as systematic risk

ERP = Equity risk premium – long-term average rate of return on common stock in excess of the long-term average risk-free rate of return

---

[3] Jay Shanken and Clifford W. Smith, "Implications of Capital Markets Research for Corporate Finance," *Financial Management* 25 (Spring 1996): 98–104.

Simply stated, the required rate of return on equity – the cost of common equity capital – is equal to the sum of the risk-free rate plus the equity risk premium, as modified by beta. While the equity risk premium quantifies the higher return that investors require for the added risk of equity over the risk-free rate, beta theoretically measures systematic specific-company risk. Beta quantifies *systematic risk* as the volatility in the market price of the subject stock versus the overall riskiness or volatility of the stock market. The beta for public companies is routinely reported by several data sources, although there are slight variations on how each source computes it. So for the stock of public companies, which have a market price that can be tracked continually compared to the movement of the market as a whole, the required rate of return, or R_e, demanded by investors can be computed accurately by CAPM. To compute the cost of equity of a larger privately held company or a thinly traded public company that carries a market price that may not accurately express investor expectations, CAPM also can be used. In this procedure, analyze the betas – the expressions of volatility – of a portfolio of public companies that are similar to the target company; from that analysis, an appropriate beta for the target can be derived.

An application of CAPM to derive a cost of equity capital is illustrated in Exhibit 8.5, which does not apply to any specific company, date, or economic conditions.

The computation can be interpreted in this way. The risk-free rate or cost of safe money as of the appraisal date is 3%. On average, over the long term, investors in large-cap stocks require an equity risk premium (ERP) of 6% over the long-term average risk-free rate. Although the market as a whole reflects systematic risk of 1.0, a study of the volatility, as measured by beta, of specific public companies reveals that those companies are more volatile than the overall market. Based on the similarity of the subject company to the sample of public companies from which the beta was derived, the overall market rate of return of 6% is increased by 20%, to 7.2%. When added to the risk-free rate, this yields a required rate of return on the common stock in the subject company of 10.2%.

Public companies are usually much larger and more diversified than closely held companies. As a result, establishing an appropriate beta that

EXHIBIT 8.5 CAPM Derivation of a Cost of Equity

	Basic Data	
R_f	as of the valuation date	= 3.0%
ß	based on analysis of guideline public companies in that industry	= 1.2
ERP	historical average	= 6.0%
	CAPM Computation	
R_e	= R_f + ß(ERP)	
10.2%	= 3.0% + 1.2(6.0%)	

expresses the risk profile of the closely held target based on the volatility of a group of public companies in that industry is very difficult, if not impossible. Usually CAPM requires too many factors about the subject company to be quantified through beta.

Modified Capital Asset Pricing Model

To overcome these limitations, the modified CAPM was developed, which includes two additional premiums that add precision to the process of estimating a required rate of return.

The MCAPM is expressed as:

$$R_e = R_f + \beta(ERP) + SCP + SCRP$$

where:

R_e = Rate of return expected – the proxy for the market's required rate

R_f = Risk-free rate of return – a fixed return free of default risk

β = Beta – a measurement of the volatility of a given security in comparison to the volatility of the market as a whole, which is known as systematic risk

ERP = Equity risk premium

SCP = Small-company premium – increase in the required rate of return to compensate for the risk associated with smaller size

SCRP = Specific-company risk premium – increase or decrease in the required rate of return caused by specific strengths or weaknesses within the subject company, which is known as unsystematic risk

The SCRP, also referred to as *alpha*, is intended to reflect *unsystematic risk*, which is the risk that emanates solely from the target company rather than from the market. In the MCAPM, it can be difficult to distinguish those risk factors that are captured in the beta (which reflects systematic risk in the market) from those that should be included in the alpha (reflecting risk that is specific only to the subject company).

The MCAPM is most effective in developing a cost of equity capital when a group of public companies that are reasonably similar to the target can be identified. When a population of, say, three to six similar public companies is available, analyze their operating and financial characteristics and compare them to the target. Assess the systematic risk reflected in their betas, considering conditions within that industry or segments of it, and then analyze specific company factors or alphas. When this information

EXHIBIT 8.6 MCAPM Derivation of a Cost of Equity

	Basic Data		
R_f	as of the valuation date	=	3.0%
ß	based on analysis of guideline public companies in that industry	=	1.2
ERP	historical average	=	6.0%
SCP	historical average	=	5.6%
SCRP	determined through SWOT analysis and other risk assessments	=	5.0%

MCAPM Computation

$$R_e = R_f + ß(ERP) + SCP + SCRP$$
$$20.8\% = 3.0\% + 1.2(6.0\%) + 5.6\% + 5.0\%$$

is available, the cost of equity can be computed from the MCAPM with reasonably reliable results.

An application of MCAPM to derive a cost of equity capital is illustrated in Exhibit 8.6, which does not apply to any specific company, date, or economic conditions. The source of the SCP and SCRP are explained later in this chapter under "Summary of Rate of Return Data."

The result of this MCAPM computation is an equity cost of 20.8%, which is 10.6% higher than the result of the CAPM application in Exhibit 8.5, which totaled 10.2%. The 10.6% difference results from application of the SCP and the SCRP factors in the MCAPM computation. The illustration in Exhibit 8.6 assumes that a smaller, more risky business is being valued that requires a 10.6% additional rate of return over the larger company profiled in Exhibit 8.5, which was less risky and had a required rate of return of 10.2%.

Build-Up Model

An alternative to using CAPM or MCAPM to determine a cost of equity commonly used by business appraisers is the build-up model, which recognizes the same three fundamental elements of any cost of equity:

1. Risk-free rate
2. Equity risk premium
3. Specific-company risk premium

The build-up model conceptually follows the MCAPM formula but eliminates the beta factor by assuming a beta of 1, which is the overall market's average volatility. Therefore, all differences in the risk profile of the subject company compared to the market as a whole must be reflected in the size premium and the specific-company premium. Implicitly this assumes that a company's specific risk factors that would cause its beta (if it had a beta) to be greater or lesser than 1 will be captured in the SCRP. Mathematically, this formula would appear as:

$$R_e = R_f + ERP + SCP + SCRP$$

Although each factor in the formula has been defined, they will be described in more detail. The most common reference source for this market data is *Valuation Handbook – U.S. Guide to Cost of Capital*, written annually by Duff & Phelps, LLC and published by John Wiley & Sons, Inc. (the *Valuation Handbook*).[4]

Risk-Free Rate

This rate, theoretically free of the risk of default, is the foundation of the derivation of a company's cost of capital. The risk-free rate is most commonly expressed in the U.S. market as the rate of return on U.S. Treasury bonds of 20-year duration.[5] When Ibbotson Associates initially started compiling data on market rates of return, they selected this 20-year duration for its studies, which start in 1926, for several reasons:

- Ibbotson wanted a long-term time horizon.
- Ibbotson wanted to include the Great Depression, as it was part of what could happen in the long term.
- The year 1926 was the oldest year for which there were reasonably reliable records of the details needed for the study.
- The 20-year U.S. Treasury bond was the longest-term bond, consistent with the assumption that a business is a going concern with a very long-term expected life.

---

[4] Duff & Phelps began authoring the *Valuation Handbook* in 2014 (data through year-end 2013). Morningstar had published the *Morningstar/Ibbotson SBBI®* *Valuation Yearbook* through 2013 (data through year-end 2012) containing much of this data. Prior to 2007, this was published by Ibbotson Associates. Printed publication of the Duff & Phelps *Valuation Handbook* was discontinued in 2018 and converted to an online delivery service known as Duff & Phelps Cost of Capital Navigator. See www.duffandphelps.com for more details.

[5] The St. Louis branch of the Federal Reserve Bank provides a proxy for the 20-year constant maturity Treasury bond on its website – https://fred.stlouisfed.org/categories/115.

Duff & Phelps, LLC, which now compiles data on market rates of return, also develops risk premiums for shorter time horizons (e.g. 1963). Overall, for the fair market value or investment value on a going-concern basis of a business, these long-term rates are almost always used to reflect the long-term nature of these investments. The risk-free rate typically used is that which is effective as of the valuation/transaction date. However, there is a strong argument for using a normalized rate that reflects the sustainable average return of 20-year Treasuries, especially during major economic swing periods (e.g. in late 2007 when U.S. Treasury bond rates fell due to a flight to quality as the financial crisis began).

Equity Risk Premium

The ERP recognizes the additional risk over the risk-free rate associated with investing in a portfolio of large publicly traded common stocks, commonly known as the large-cap stocks. Although historic data is used to derive this premium, it is forward-looking and the historic data is considered an acceptable proxy for a future ERP. This data is compiled annually and published in the *Valuation Handbook* introduced earlier in this chapter.[6]

Small-Company Risk Premium

The SCP reflects the additional increment of risk associated with investing in the common stock of smaller public companies, where size is determined based on market value of equity. Over the long term, smaller-cap stocks have been much more volatile but have provided higher returns than larger companies, which is why small-cap stocks and funds are popular with some investors.

Specific-Company Risk Premium

The SCRP component reflects the risks specific to the company and its industry. It in part quantifies both the qualitative assessment of the business (i.e. its strengths, weaknesses, opportunities, and threats) and the amount of additional premium a prudent investor would require in order to compensate for any additional investment risks incurred as compared to investing in a "typical smaller public company." Although it is determined judgmentally, it can be both accurate and defendable. It should reflect the analysis of the

---

[6] For more comprehensive explanations of the equity risk premium and deriving ERP estimates, see Shannon P. Pratt and Roger J. Grabowski, *Cost of Capital: Applications and Examples, 5th edition* (Hoboken, NJ: Wiley, 2014), Chapters 7 and 8.

competitive conditions in which the company operates, including external industry factors and internal company factors not captured in the return to which the rate will be applied. The ability to relate the competitive analysis of the company to the selection of this premium is critical to establishing a credible and defendable rate of return for use in valuing a business. Appendix 8A introduces a cloud-based platform – the Value Opportunity Profile – that helps identify areas where root causes of specific-company risk exist.

Risk and value drivers and their importance vary by company. For example, poor inventory turnover could cripple the profitability of a retail or wholesale business, but it may be immaterial to a service company. Recognizing that judgment is always required, next we list common specific-company risk factors introduced in Chapter 3 and briefly discuss each.

- *Lack of access to capital.* The smaller the company, the more limited its access to debt and equity capital. Especially when comparing closely held companies to their public counterparts, remember that they frequently face limits in the amount of debt or equity capital that they can raise. This fact also must be considered in assessing their growth prospects or ability to diversify. Also note that when an owner personally guarantees a business loan, the company's effective interest rate probably exceeds its stated rate.
- *Ownership structure and stock transfer restrictions.* The stock of privately held companies, without a public stock market for trades, often is unmarketable, particularly for minority ownership interests. Shares of stock in closely held companies frequently carry restrictions that tightly limit the conditions under which they can be transferred. Rights of first refusal at a specified price are common, and minority shareholders in particular often face restrictions that severely limit the marketability of their investment.
- *Company's market share and the market structure of the industry.* Smaller companies frequently operate in niche industries or segments of industries where market share can be a significant strategic advantage. Market leaders may possess special strength, such as a proprietary technology that provides brand awareness or pricing power. The structure of the industry also must be examined. For example, a company with a 20% market share may be able to dominate an industry when no other company possesses more than 5% of the market. However, a 20% market share where two competitors each control 40% leaves the company in a much weaker position.
- *Depth and breadth of management.* Smaller and even middle-market companies frequently possess gaps in their management team, leaving them weak in one or more functional areas. These factors must

be assessed in considering the company's strength at core functional levels, including quality control, production capability, marketing and sales capacity, and so on.

- *Heavy reliance on individuals with key knowledge, skills, or contacts.* It is not unusual in smaller companies for one person or a few individuals to possess essential technical knowledge, production skills, or customer contacts. This characteristic commonly increases the risk profile of a small or middle-market company in comparison with larger businesses because the company's success is tied to the presence of these key individuals.

- *Lack of strategic vision.* While many companies put together a one-year budget, few think beyond a year. Very few companies put together a business plan. A lack of long-term vision increases the risk of a company's ability to grow its revenues, profitability, and cash flow. It can promote confusion among employees about the direction of the company, short-term thinking, and many other problems that undermine company value.

- *Marketing and advertising capacity.* Smaller companies that compete against much larger rivals or national chains often lack the financial capacity or marketing expertise to properly inform their potential customer base about the advantages that they offer. Independent retailers, for example, may have as good or even better prices than the national chains against which they compete. The chains, however, possess the capacity to promote the image of their low pricing, which is a competitive advantage that the independents usually lack. Thus, due to their inability to inform their potential customers, the independents may lose market share even when they possess superior products, customer service, or prices.

- *Breadth of products and services.* Specialty companies frequently derive their strength from focusing in niche markets, but this product concentration creates risks from lack of diversification and overdependence on limited markets. Some specialty companies may find their largest customers adopt a policy to deal only with suppliers that offer a broad range of products, forcing them to either expand their product offerings or sell out to a bigger company.

- *Purchasing power and related economies of scale.* Due to their size, smaller companies often cannot achieve the cost or production efficiencies of their larger competitors. Whether through quantity discounts or spreading capacity costs over higher volumes, larger companies possess distinct advantages in certain operations and markets.

- *Condition of facility and upcoming capital expenditure needs.* A proper valuation includes an assessment of the location and desirability of facilities, the degree of obsolescence, adaptability to other uses, deferred maintenance, the underlying land value and quality of title, among other factors to determine upcoming capital expenditure needs. Given more limited resources, these factors tend to have a larger impact on smaller companies.

- *Customer concentration.* This problem plagues many small and middle-market companies, which frequently grow and prosper by providing exceptional service to their largest customers. In the process, however, they sometimes become overly reliant on these customers, who constitute too great a percentage of their total sales.

- *Vendor and supplier relations and reliance.* In order to specialize and create certain competitive advantages, smaller companies frequently subcontract major operations or production components to suppliers on whom they may become overly dependent. Lack of control over the timing, quality, or pricing of needed resources is a common result.

- *Distribution capability.* Larger companies with broad product lines typically possess regional or national distribution systems to protect their market share and product image. Independents frequently must rely on brokers or face much higher distribution costs as a percentage of sales. For example, independent food manufacturers that supply grocery chains lack the ability of broad-line national companies to influence in-store shelf spacing decisions and as a result receive the least attractive locations. This lack of direct access to customers may limit the independent's ability to provide them with the necessary attention and services to retain their loyalty. Lack of direct customer contact also prevents feedback on evolving customer wants and needs and limits branding potential.

- *Ability to keep pace with technological changes.* Companies with fewer monetary resources often lack adequate research and development resources, thus finding it difficult to keep pace with technological changes in their markets. Such companies that lack technology often face an inescapable need to incur large amounts of capital expenditures in the near future or allocate resources to only a limited number of product development projects. This inevitably results in product or service obsolescence, adverse impact on future growth, and loss in market share. In the meantime, larger companies are in a better position to demonstrate technological expertise by developing products that address emerging customer needs such that customers may choose their state-of-the-art products, despite the availability of lower-cost, lower-performance technology.

- *Ability to protect intellectual property.* Many companies have proprietary technology processes that comprise a significant aspect of their intellectual property. These companies primarily rely on trade secret laws, confidentiality procedures, and licensing arrangements. However, smaller companies often face difficulty in providing assurance that the steps taken to protect the intellectual property will be adequate to prevent misappropriation of their technology.

■ *Increasing threat of foreign competition.* A smaller company facing increased foreign competition is often resource-constrained to adapt to changes brought about by foreign competitors in terms of pricing, costs, product changes, and volume.

■ *Litigation, environmental, and adverse regulatory issues.* While all companies face these issues, a smaller company with fewer resources impacted by these factors will be more at risk to achieve expected future cash flows if faced with a lawsuit, liability associated with environmental contamination, or adverse change in regulations.

■ *Depth, accuracy, and timeliness of accounting information and internal controls.* Public companies face heavy accounting reporting requirements to regulatory agencies, the process of which generally improves the information available to their management. Such data is frequently lacking in smaller businesses, a fact that may hamper management's assessment of performance, and potential buyers may also question the quality of this data.

Caution should be exercised when considering these SCRP factors. Some may have been considered in the selection of the growth rate or in the returns through a higher cost of sales or operating expenses. The objective of this care is to avoid double counting by incorporating the same factor in both the rate and the return. A similar concern for avoiding double counting should be observed when qualifying any applicable discounts and premiums.

In addition to this list of factors that are often particularly important to small and middle-market companies, every business should be evaluated in terms of profitability and growth. These issues are reflected primarily in the forecast of the company's return in either the SPCM or the DCF. More important, the factors that cause these results need to be carefully examined in determining the SCRP.

Build-Up Model Using Duff & Phelps Size Study Data

As mentioned earlier and as will be explained in more detail, the rate of return data compiled in the *Valuation Handbook* uses market value of equity as one measure of size in conducting historical rate of returns research following the methodology used by Ibbotson. This data is now reported in the *Valuation Handbook* as the *CRSP Decile Size Premia Study*.[7]

---

[7] The size premia data reported is measured from 1926 to the end of the most recent year.

An alternative equity discount rate, presented in the *Duff & Phelps Risk Premium Report Size Study* (D&P Report),[8] determines a forward-looking cost of equity based on historical rates of return,[9] employing size-based portfolios of publicly traded companies, determined utilizing eight measurements of size. These include three measures of equity size (market value of common equity, book value of common equity, and average net income before extraordinary items for previous five fiscal years) and five measures of company size (market value of invested capital, total assets, five-year average EBITDA, sales, and number of employees).

Duff & Phelps segments the population of public stocks into 25 size-ranked categories or portfolios based on each of the eight size measures. These stocks comprise New York Stock Exchange (NYSE), American Stock Exchange (AMEX), and National Association of Securities Dealers Automated Quotations (NASDAQ) listed companies. Excluded are financial services sector companies, non-operating holding companies, American Depository Receipts (ADRs), companies that have been publicly traded for fewer than five years, companies with sales under $1 million in any of the previous five years, and companies with a five-year average EBITDA of zero or less.

The purpose of using size measures other than market value equity alone is to avoid potential selection biases of the market value of equity. For example, a firm that is highly leveraged may have a low market value of equity but can be quite large when using all other measures of size. In addition, firms may have a low market value of equity because they are risky and investors require a high discount rate. These firms are not necessarily risky because they are small, but rather small because they are risky.

The D&P Report provides average historical equity risk premiums since 1963. The equity risk premium is determined by calculating the average rate of return of each portfolio over the sample period and then subtracting the average income return on long-term Treasury bonds over the same period to arrive at an average historical equity risk premium. As the average historical equity risk premium is calculated for 25 portfolios segmented based on the eight size measures, it incorporates the size premium. Therefore, it is appropriate to add the equity risk premium to the average long-term Treasury bond as of the effective valuation date, with no further adjustment for size. The data shows a clear inverse relationship between size and historical rates of return.

---

[8] The reader is encouraged to review Chapter 19 of Shannon P. Pratt and Roger J. Grabowski, *Cost of Capital: Applications and Examples*, 5th edition (Hoboken, NJ: Wiley, 2014). The data is updated annually on the *Valuation Handbook*. CRSP stands for the Center on Research in Security Prices of the Booth School of Business, University of Chicago; CRSP provides the raw return data. The size premia data reported is measured from 1963 to the end of the most recent year.

[9] The measure of returns is based on dividend income plus capital appreciation and represents returns after corporate taxes (but before owner-level taxes).

EXHIBIT 8.7   Application of D&P Report to Estimate Cost of Equity

	Portfolio Rank #20		Portfolio Rank #25	
	Average	Smoothed Average ERP	Average	Smoothed Average ERP
Market Value of Equity	$1,313,000,000	10.37%	$121,000,000	14.02%
Book Value of Equity	$577,000,000	9.96%	$76,000,000	12.07%
Five-Year Average Net Income	$52,000,000	10.32%	$5,000,000	12.97%
Market Value of Invested Capital	$1,696,000,000	10.19%	$163,000,000	13.47%
Total Assets	$1,363,000,000	10.22%	$161,000,000	12.76%
Five-Year Average EBITDA	$164,000,000	10.10%	$17,000,000	12.55%
Gross Sales	$1,181,000,000	10.29%	$129,000,000	12.64%
Number of Employees	2,908	10.33%	305	12.65%
Average Premium		10.22%		12.89%
Risk-free rate, current		3.00%		3.00%
Cost of Equity		13.22%		15.89%

Source: Duff & Phelps, LLC, *2017 Valuation Handbook: U.S. Guide to Cost of Capital* (Hoboken, NJ: Wiley, 2017), Appendix 4: Risk Premium Report Study Exhibits, Exhibits A.1 through A.8.

   In applying the data from the D&P Report, the smoothed, average historical equity risk premium, which is based on a fitted regression line on the average historical risk premiums for the 25 portfolios, is used, as suggested by Duff & Phelps for the smaller size categories. For illustration, Exhibit 8.7 presents the data for two hypothetical companies – one that fits in Portfolio Rank 20 for each of the eight size measures and the other that fits in Portfolio Rank 25, the smallest ranking.

Summary of Rate of Return Data

An understanding of the general process used in the *Valuation Handbook* helps to explain several points made in this chapter and in Chapters 6 and 7, including why these rates, without further adjustment, are applicable only to next year's net cash flow to equity. The research assumes that a portfolio of large company stocks, such as the large-cap stocks of the NYSE or Standard & Poor's (S&P) 500, was purchased on January 1 of each year beginning in 1926 and sold on December 31 of each year. Each year's investment would have a rate of return based on the aggregate increase in the portfolio's share values plus dividends that were paid in that year. This process is repeated for each year from 1926 through the most recently completed year. These annual returns are the return of the market, or Rm. For each of the same years, the income return for the 20-year Treasury bond, called the Rf, is determined. Subtracting the Rf from the Rm for each year produces the equity risk premium for each year. The ERPs for all years are totaled and divided by the number of years to indicate the long-term arithmetic average ERP. This is the rate of return shown for the ERP in each *Valuation Handbook.*

A similar process is used for the small-company premium using NYSE companies or companies from the major U.S. exchanges, divided into 10 groups based on total market capitalization in the CRSP Decile Size Premia Study. Each group, called a decile, contains 10% of the total companies traded in that year on the NYSE. The small-company premium (SCP) is calculated by taking the actual return of each decile and subtracting the return predicted by CAPM. The betas increase as the deciles get smaller. This increase reflects the greater volatility of the return of smaller companies, so the returns estimated by CAPM also increase. Even as betas increase, however, they do not explain fully the returns achieved by these deciles, especially the smallest ones. To clarify the factors influencing the SCP, the return due to beta is removed to isolate the SCP due solely to size and exclusive of any specific riskiness of the company.

When using data from the *Valuation Handbook*, it is essential that every reader consult the text itself to thoroughly understand the material presented. In reviewing consider:

- On September 30, 2016, the largest decile of public companies comprise approximately 66% of the total market value of all NYSE companies, which emphasizes the dominance of the largest public firms.[10]
- The microcap stocks, deciles 9 and 10 of the CRSP Decile Size Premia Study, comprise only 0.92% and 0.40%, respectively, of the total market capitalization of public companies.[11] The ninth-decile stocks possess a total equity value of up to $567,843,000 and the tenth-decile stocks of up to $262,891,000,[12] illustrating how much larger the microcap stocks are as compared to the vast majority of privately held companies.
- The beta for decile 1, the largest public companies, is 0.92 for the 1926 to 2016 period, which indicates that these largest companies are more stable than the market as a whole. Conversely, decile 10 has a beta of 1.39, which shows these companies to be about 39% more volatile than the market as a whole.[13]

---

[10] Duff & Phelps, LLC, *2017 Valuation Handbook: U.S. Guide to Cost of* Capital (Hoboken, NJ: Wiley, Inc., 2017), pp. 7–9, based on data presented in Exhibit 7.1.
[11] Ibid.
[12] Ibid., pp. 7–10, based on data presented in Exhibit 7.2.
[13] Ibid., pp. 7–11, based on data presented in Exhibit 7.3.

- This volatility, which is generally interpreted to indicate risk, is reflected in the arithmetic mean return of companies from each decile. As the companies become smaller and their volatility increases, their returns over the long term also increase, reflecting investor demands for higher returns to compensate for the higher risk that they accept.
- The long-term arithmetic mean return on the largest public companies was 11.05% at the end of 2016. This return gradually increases with each successive decile, with the largest proportionate increase in the smaller half of the tenth decile, where the average long-term return is 20.27%, while the average return for microcap stocks was 18.04%.[14] This reflects the confidence company size gives to investors and the higher returns they demand from companies that lack size.

Private Cost of Capital

The methods used to develop cost of capital described thus far in this chapter are based on market data from the public markets, given the widespread acceptance and practice of using public market data to value privately held businesses. However, acknowledging the vast differences between public and private capital markets, a growing school of thought recognizes the equally vast flaws of this practice. Simply stated, public and private capital markets are not substitutes. Public and private capital markets differ in terms of risk and return characteristics, liquidity, management involvement, timing of equity pricing, market participant behavior, access to capital, diversification of holdings, market efficiencies, expected holding period, and cost of capital. In *Private Capital Markets*, Rob Slee explains the unique characteristics and needs of private companies, moving away from the corporate finance theory of the public markets when analyzing and valuing private companies.[15] Given the proliferation of capital alternatives and private business-transfer techniques over the last 30 years in the private capital markets, coupled with recognition of the vast differences between the two markets, private capital market theory is providing an alternative and more correct manner to derive private cost of capital (PCOC).

PCOC is the expected rate of return, stated on a pretax basis, that the market (i.e. the universe of investors who are reasonable candidates to provide funds to a particular private investment) requires in order to attract funds to a particular investment. Therefore, discount rates emanate from the return expectations of the providers of capital to private companies. To develop needed empirical evidence to derive a PCOC applicable to valuing private companies, Slee collaborated with John Paglia, PhD and Pepperdine

---

[14] Ibid.
[15] Robert T. Slee, *Private Capital Markets: Valuation, Capitalization, and Transfer of Private Business Interests,* 2nd edition (Hoboken, NJ: Wiley, 2011).

University in 2009 to develop a web-based survey of various providers of capital regarding how much capital is typically accessible, what the required returns are for extending capital, and outlooks on demand for various capital types, interest rates, and the economy in general. This survey has expanded and in 2017 added a survey of 11 types of investors, advisors, and capital providers including investment bankers, private equity investors, bank and asset-based lenders, mezzanine investors, limited partners, venture capitalists, angel investors, business appraisers, brokers, factoring facilities, and business owners.

Exhibit 8.8[16] presents the Pepperdine Private Capital Market Required Rates of Return, demonstrating the central 50% (i.e. the spread between the first quartile [25th percentile] and the third quartile [50th percentile]) of the surveyed expected returns to the capital providers in the private capital markets as measured by annualized gross financing costs. The PCOC is applied to the subject company's EBITDA when using rates from both debt and equity capital. It is applied to the subject company's pretax earnings before depreciation and amortization when using rates from just equity capital.

The PCOC model is as follows:[17]

$$PCOC = \sum_{i=1}^{N} \left[(CAP_i + SCAP_i) \times \frac{MV_i}{\sum_{j=1}^{N} MV_j} \right]$$

where:

N = Number of sources of capital
CAP_i = Median expected return for capital type i
$SCAP_i$ = Specific CAP risk adjustment for capital type i
MV_i = Market value of all outstanding securities i

There are four steps in applying the PCOC model:[18]

1. Review the credit boxes described in the most current Pepperdine survey to determine the appropriate capital types by which to compare. Select the appropriate median expected return (CAP) from the survey results for each qualifying capital type.

---

[16] Craig R. Everett, *2017 Private Capital Markets Report*, Pepperdine Private Capital Markets Project, p. 3.
[17] Slee, *Private Capital Markets*, p. 151.
[18] Ibid., pp. 152–155.

EXHIBIT 8.8 Pepperdine Private Capital Market Required Rates of Return – 2017

		1st Quartile	Median	3rd Quartile
Bank	$1M cash flow loan	6.0%	6.5%	8.0%
Bank	$5M cash flow loan	5.1%	5.5%	6.5%
Bank	$10M cash flow loan	4.4%	5.3%	5.9%
Bank	$25M cash flow loan	3.8%	5.0%	5.0%
Bank	$50M cash flow loan	3.5%	4.0%	4.3%
Asset-based Lending	$1M loan	9.4%	14.0%	15.8%
Asset-based Lending	$5M loan	10.0%	10.0%	12.3%
Asset-based Lending	$10M loan	8.6%	10.0%	12.0%
Asset-based Lending	$25M loan	6.5%	8.0%	8.0%
Asset-based Lending	$50M loan	5.5%	5.5%	6.3%
Mezzanine	$1M loan	18.0%	24.0%	24.5%
Mezzanine	$5M loan	15.0%	17.0%	17.5%
Mezzanine	$10M loan	13.0%	15.5%	20.0%
Mezzanine	$25M loan	11.5%	14.5%	16.5%
Mezzanine	$50M loan	10.8%	13.5%	16.0%
Mezzanine	$100M loan	9.5%	10.0%	13.0%
Private Equity Group	$1M EBITDA	21.8%	27.5%	33.8%
Private Equity Group	$5M EBITDA	21.0%	25.5%	31.5%
Private Equity Group	$10M EBITDA	21.0%	23.0%	30.0%
Private Equity Group	$25M EBITDA	20.8%	21.0%	28.8%
Private Equity Group	$50M EBITDA	16.5%	21.0%	21.0%
Private Equity Group	$100M EBITDA	14.0%	20.5%	21.0%
Venture Capital	Seed	25.0%	35.0%	60.0%
Venture Capital	Startup	25.0%	35.0%	55.0%
Venture Capital	Early Stage	15.0%	25.0%	50.0%
Venture Capital	Expansion	15.0%	25.0%	50.0%
Venture Capital	Later Stage	15.0%	25.0%	50.0%
Angel	Seed	45.0%	60.0%	67.5%
Angel	Startup	35.0%	40.0%	52.5%
Angel	Early Stage	30.0%	35.0%	47.5%
Angel	Expansion	30.0%	35.0%	45.0%
Angel	Later Stage	25.0%	35.0%	35.0%

Note: Data reflects annualized gross financing costs for each major capital type and its segments. The data reveal that loans have the lowest average rates while capital obtained from angels has the highest average rates. As the size of loan or investment increases, the cost of borrowing or financing from any of the following sources decreases.

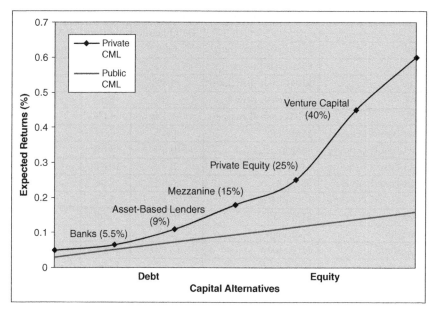

EXHIBIT 8.9 Private versus Public Capital Market Lines

2. Determine the market value of each capital type.
3. Apply a specific capital type risk adjustment to the selected median capital type based on a comparison of subject results to the appropriate survey credit box, using first and third quartile returns as a guide to this adjustment
4. Calculate the percentage of capital structure component by its CAP, and then add the individual percentage to derive the PCOC.

Exhibit 8.9 illustrates the Pepperdine Private Capital Market Line, demonstrating expected returns to the capital providers in the private capital markets as compared to the public capital market line.

International Cost of Capital

It has long been known that investment risk will vary from country to country based on political, regulatory, and economic conditions. Chapter 20 provides an overview of the international cost of capital adjustment methods, together with sources of more specific information.

How to Develop an Equity Cost for a Target Company

The foregoing discussion describes four models for determining a required rate of return on common stock in a private company: CAPM, MCAPM, the build-up model, and PCOC. The CAPM is seldom appropriate because of its underlying assumptions. If in studying the market one has identified several publicly traded companies that are sufficiently similar to the target, MCAPM may be an acceptable methodology. When this data is available, a beta for the target company is derived from the betas of the guideline companies. In the CAPM or MCAPM formula, the ERP is multiplied by β to reflect the risk characteristics of the guideline public companies, including the risk profile of the industry in which they operate. After studying the relative strengths and weaknesses of these companies and comparing them to the target, further adjustments should be made for size and specific-company risk factors, which are expressed as the SCP and SCRP premiums in the MCAPM formula.

In the application of this formula, even experienced appraisers struggle to distinguish between the amount of risk that is captured in the beta compared to that which is expressed in the SCP and the SCRP. As a result, the size of the SCRP adjustment is usually smaller when used in MCAPM than when used in the build-up model where there is no security-specific beta factor. To avoid this confusion or the potential of double counting factors, many simply employ the build-up model instead of MCAPM.

When the build-up model is used, the beta is assumed to be 1 so it is eliminated from the computation. If the target company appears to have an equity value of less than $100 million, one of the tenth-decile size premiums is probably the more appropriate choice for the SCP. For companies with equity values below $200 million, the combined ninth- and tenth-decile or microcap premium would most likely be more appropriate for the SCP. For even larger companies, selection of a low-cap premium or use of the MCAPM methodology is another possibility. Alternatively, use of the eight size measurements presented in the D&P Report affords a more thorough analysis and determination of an appropriate premium, with application of Portfolio Rank 25 for the smallest of companies.

Once the size premium is determined, the analyst has established a base rate of return of either about 14% if the tenth decile (aggregate market capitalization of around $100 million) is used or about 17% to 20% with the lower half of the tenth-decile premiums, which should be understood to mean: If an investor acquires a broad portfolio of tenth-decile-size companies, holds that investment for the long term, and makes the average return earned over approximately the past 90-plus years[19] in the United States, that investment will earn a net cash flow return (after corporate taxes but before the investor's personal taxes) of either 14% or 17% to 20% while enjoying the high liquidity of a public security.

The investment in the target company must be considered against that benchmark. Most closely held companies are smaller than microcap-size public companies, and most possess less management depth, narrower product lines, smaller markets and customer bases, and less access to capital. With this in mind, review the external and internal analysis of the target, identify the specific risk drivers and value drivers of the target, and compare them against the appropriate public company decile benchmark. From this, each risk driver or value driver of the target company can be quantified to determine the SCRP.

Less experienced appraisers are naturally confused about the magnitude of the SCRP adjustment. That is, should a specific value driver or risk driver cause the SCRP to change by 1%, 2%, or more? To provide a sense of perspective, look at the conclusions that the market – millions of investors spending billions of dollars over a period of 90-plus years – has made. What the market has essentially said is that the cost of relatively safe money, R_f, which includes an assumption of inflation, was between 2% and 3% in 2017. Investors have further stated through their actions that they will accept the greater risk of ownership of large-cap–size common stocks but only if they receive the ERP, approximately an additional 5% to 6% in the long term (conclusions are different in the intermediate and short term), or about twice the risk-free rate. Throughout history, investors have further stated that they will assume the additional risk of buying much smaller tenth-decile–size public stocks but that they demand an additional 5% to 10% in return for taking that additional step up the risk ladder. Thus investors in the market have moved from risk-free investments, to big public company stocks, to small public company stocks in approximately 5% to 8% increments. With the size of these relative risk increments as a guide, the selection of the specific-company premium is the appraiser's assessment of the size of the final step that the investor takes, versus other market alternatives, when buying the target company.

In the end, it is important to reiterate that the cost of capital being derived should be that of the target company, not the buyer. It must match the risk of the target company attaining the expected future cash flows on a stand-alone basis. In addition, and if it is not obvious in our discussion earlier in this chapter on cost of debt and the data presented in Exhibit 8.3, the cost of capital applicable to valuing the target company is not that which is used to finance the transaction; it is typically much higher.

---

[19] The 90-plus-year timeframe is in reference to 1926, the year in which Ibbotson started tracking rate of return data, as discussed earlier in this chapter.

Reconciling Discount Rates and P/E Multiples

One final point should be made in considering the cost of capital. The target is most often a private company, and the investor is most often acquiring a controlling interest in it. Yet the rates of return just quoted are for publicly traded securities where investors typically own minority interests. Any differences in control versus lack of control should be calculated in the relevant returns to which the rate will be applied or, when appropriate, in any discounts and premiums that may be applied later in the appraisal process. They should not be reflected in the derivation of these equity rates of return.

Buyers and sellers often are surprised to see equity capital costs of 25% or even higher. This can lead to doubt or disbelief in these rates.

During the 2000s, prior to the market collapse at the end of 2008, the average price-to-earnings (P/E) multiples for S&P 500–size U.S. companies was about 25 times, which implies a required rate of return of 4%. Why would anyone invest in common stock, even of an S&P 500–size company, to earn a return of only 4%? Are the much higher equity discount rates for closely held companies that result from the MCAPM or build-up models of about 25% realistic?

The journey from 4% to 25% is very logical if taken in steps that recognize the distinctions between the alternative investments. Begin by recognizing the advantages that S&P 500 companies have in terms of size, market share, access to capital, depth of management, breadth of product lines, brand names, and distribution systems, which often extend worldwide. When compared with the typical closely held company, even one of middle-market size, these differences tend to be very large.

Next, consider growth expectations. Investors do not buy stock at 25 times annual earnings expecting to earn 4%. Instead, they expect the stock to increase in value with the high implied growth rate continuing for something less than an infinite number of periods. As discussed in Chapter 7, the short-term versus long-term differences in the anticipated growth rate are a scenario that the SPCM cannot effectively portray. The reciprocal of the capitalization rate used in the SPCM, which is a P/E multiple, suffers from the same limitations. The competitive advantages that some large corporations possess provide long-term growth potential, but the duration of this advantage probably lies somewhere in the range of 4 to 10 years rather than infinity. However, with the stock market's traditional reporting mechanism being a multiple of a single year's earnings, high P/E multiples may result. The clear factor driving the multiple is the implied earnings growth and its resulting stock value appreciation.

Technical errors also create confusion. The 4% rate computed as the reciprocal of the P/E multiple of 25 is actually a capitalization rate, not a discount rate, for historical earnings, not for future net cash flow. Because P/E multiples, like capitalization rates, are applied to a single year's return, they reflect anticipated growth.

Exhibit 8.10 reconciles the 4% rate that results from a P/E multiple of 25 with an equity discount rate of approximately 25%. The key unknown needed to explain much of the difference is the implied long-term growth increment of 10% for large-company stocks.

EXHIBIT 8.10 Conversion of a Public Company P/E Multiple to a Discount Rate for Net Cash Flow to Equity for a Closely Held Company

Typical S&P 500 public company P/E multiple	25 times
Conversion of P/E multiple to cap rate for historical earnings (1/25 times)	4%
Conversion to cap rate for future earnings by multiplying by one plus implied growth rate for next year of 5%	× 1.05
Cap rate for future earnings	4.2%
Conversion from net earnings to net cash flow to equity cap rate based on long-term relationship between them calculated to be 20%	1.20
Cap rate for future net cash flow to equity	3.5%
Conversion to discount rate for next year's net cash flow to equity by adding implied growth rate of large public company	+10.0%
Discount rate for future net cash flow to equity before premiums for size and specific company risk factors (approximates arithmetic mean return for large-cap stocks)	13.5%
Tenth-decile premium from 2000 Ibbotson's *Stocks, Bonds, Bills and Inflation*®	4.5%
Premium for specific risk factors typical of a closely held company	7.0%[a]
Discount rate for future net cash flow to equity	**25.0%**

Source: Frank C. Evans, "Tips for the Valuator," *Journal of Accountancy* (March 2000): 35–41. Reprinted with permission from the *Journal of Accountancy*, Copyright © 2000 by American Institute of CPAs. Opinions of the authors are their own and do not necessarily reflect policies of the AICPA.

[a]An increment is included in the 7% to recognize the risk associated with the difference in investment liquidity between private closely held companies and the freely and actively traded S&P companies. This difference is commonly recognized through the application of a lack of marketability discount applied to the indicated value. It is provided for in this exhibit as that difference is part of the reconciliation of the public P/E to the ultimate private rate of return, amended through an application of a lack of marketability discount.

Conclusion

Determining an appropriate cost for the specific elements of capital in a business is one of the most complex areas in the valuation process. The cost of equity in a privately held company is least understood because such stock lacks both an ongoing market price and a fixed rate of return. The required rate of return or discount rate for common stock in a privately held company can be determined precisely through application of the appropriate methodology and selection of appropriate market-based rates of return. Professional judgment is required to quantify specific-company risks. This process is greatly aided by experience. In establishing the equity discount rate, the strategic strengths and weaknesses of the target that were identified and assessed in the competitive analysis of the company and the industry are quantified as the rate of return that is used to discount or capitalize the estimated future returns of the company to determine its value. Thus, the discipline of rigorously evaluating and determining the equity cost can result in an accurate valuation that reflects the risk and value drivers identified for that target.

Appendix 8A   Using Specific Company Risk Strategically

By Ken Sanginario[20]

In many private company valuation engagements, a deeper and broader analysis of the factors that drive the specific-company risk premium (SCRP) could provide significant added value to the subject company management for both valuation-based strategic planning and valuation for M&A, as well as establish an even more defensible determination of the SCRP and overall conclusion of value. By assessing a broader population of risk factors, the business appraiser can demonstrate a level of rigor beyond that which is typically exercised by business appraisers. Then, by individually connecting each assessed factor to the calculation of the SCRP, the business appraiser can provide great insights to company management regarding the impact on value of improving any of the assessed factors.

If we think about risk and quality as two sides of the same coin, the concept of using the valuation process to help companies understand, and drive, all the factors that improve quality and reduce risk becomes much easier to envision. The market for valuations could become widely expanded to include strategic valuation engagements for companies that may not even be thinking about getting a valuation. Business appraisers can position themselves to become broad-based business advisors, simply by doing what they already do, but at a more granular level. If the deeper analysis is conducted in a standardized manner, it can also provide an added layer of quality control and scalability in a valuation practice of multiple professionals.

In the private capital markets, where few companies reach peak performance, and where efforts to sell companies fail far more often than they succeed, the need and opportunity for companies to better understand and address the factors that comprise specific-company risk are compelling. Many private companies could nearly double in value purely by reducing the SCRP through a disciplined, methodical approach to identifying and addressing the qualitative factors that drive it. Think of it as a due diligence analysis, far in advance of the real thing, and a program to move toward eliminating all the weaknesses that constrain growth or cause M&A transactions to fall apart. The result for companies could be much improved performance, and higher success rates of sale transactions than the markets currently experience.

Instances where a deeper analysis would provide added value include any engagement where the subject company:

---

[20] Ken Sanginario is the founder of Corporate Value Metrics, creator of the Value Opportunity Profile® (VOP), and developer of the Certified Value Growth Advisor® (CVGA) training and certification program.

- Is motivated to reach peak performance;
- Is considering an exit, or an acquisition, within three to five years;
- Has recently been acquired, or has recently made an acquisition;
- Wishes to better align its senior management team around growth strategies;
- Is underperforming and facing any of the myriad related challenges, such as:
  - Lack of access to capital or other financial issues;
  - Pressures of industry disruption or commoditization;
  - Struggling to attract new and/or retain existing customers;
  - Inability to recruit or retain quality talent at any level;
  - Weak brand identity and outdated marketing strategies; or
  - Many others.

Many of the common specific-company risk factors are described here in Chapter 8. However, each factor also consists of underlying drivers that can be identified and addressed, in order to mitigate the overall factor. It might seem like an overly granular proposition but, in recent years, a cloud-based platform – the value opportunity profile (VOP) – was developed by Corporate Value Metrics to make the process easy and efficient.

The premise of the VOP is that every company is comprised of eight primary operating categories that must be fully functioning, and in balance with each other, in order to reach peak performance and maximum value. The eight categories are:

Planning	Leadership	Sales	Marketing
People	Operations	Finance	Legal

At the highest level, each of the eight primary categories is equally important, since the weakest of the eight categories will be a constraint to overall performance, growth potential, and value creation.

The primary categories in turn consist of subcategories that can be individually assessed to identify relative strengths and weaknesses. The subcategories represent potential areas where root causes of specific-company risk exist. By assessing each subcategory to determine how close the company is to functioning at a theoretical best-in-class level in that category, and scoring the results, business appraisers will be able to better explain why their client's values are what they are. More importantly, business appraisers and their clients will have a roadmap of what needs to improve in order to reduce risk, improve quality, establish better company balance, and maximize value. It gives companies the clarity to establish continuous improvement programs that are focused on the areas that will have the most impact on overall value and growth potential.

The VOP helps the business appraiser to assess each subcategory through a series of standardized questions that the business appraiser poses to the company's senior management in a group setting. The questions are asked in a manner that allows them to be typically answered on a scale of 0–10, with a score of 10 meaning that the company is at a best-in-class level in that category. The questions for each category may be different for different industries, but the overall categories are the same for all companies, as they represent the fundamentals of all businesses.

In total, the VOP provides nearly 400 questions that are answered in a one-day management retreat. Each question is directly linked to the calculation of specific-company risk, providing a level of rigor that is unmatched in the valuation profession. The enhanced defensibility of the SCRP, and overall conclusion of value, is only one of several benefits to the approach that the VOP provides. Additional benefits include enhanced consistency and scalability of the valuation process in a multiprofessional office and, most importantly, the ability to conduct what-if analysis on the company's valuation.

By selecting any weak area of the company, the business appraiser can instantly determine the impact on the company's value by improving that weak area. The calculations work by reducing the specific-company risk within an overall range. In turn, the reduced risk impacts the discount and capitalization rates by reducing the risk-adjusted cost of equity, the risk-adjusted cost of debt, and shifting the capital structure to allow more debt in the mix, assuming the cash flows can support it. The overall result is that companies can understand how to drive quality and value in a disciplined, methodical manner, over an extended period of years, rather than waiting until they need to improve quickly in order to achieve certain immediate goals.

The following tables present the framework of the value opportunity-profile process. Exhibit 8A.1 outlines the eight primary categories of the VOP with the related subcategories for each. The eight primary categories are weighted equally in their respective impact on the SCRP, and the subcategories within any given primary category are weighted equally to each other.

One may debate that certain subcategories, such as customer concentration, should have a super-weight, given their importance. However, the premise of the VOP is that there are various factors in other subcategories that would likely impact customer concentration, if they were well-developed. An example might be that a well-developed, overall strategic plan, with integrated sales and marketing strategies, would help to reduce or eliminate customer concentration. The VOP views the enterprise

EXHIBIT 8A.1 Value Opportunity Profile

Master Framework – Eight Primary Categories with Related Subcategories

Planning	Leadership	Sales	Marketing
Strategic Planning	Board of Advisors	Sales Team	Marketing Team
Target Market	Management Team	Sales Strategy	Marketing Strategy
Competition	Communication	Sales Operations	Market Positioning
Barriers to Entry	Company Culture	Projections	Branding
Product/Market Development	Succession Planning	Customer Base	Financial Investment

People	Operations	Finance	Legal
Organizational Structure	Operations Team	Finance Team	Legal Structure
Organizational Strategy	Operating Strategy	Finance Strategy	Intellectual Property
Continuous Learning	Supply Chain	Reporting/Analysis	Contract Management
Incentive Programs	Quality Assurance	Financial Health	Filings/Licenses
Policies/Procedures	Operating Efficiencies	Balance Sheet	Litigation
Organizational Scalability	Policies/Procedures	Internal Controls	
	Operating Scalability	I.T. Systems	
		Risk Management	

as an integrated organization, rather than as a disconnected group of silos and, hence, the linear weighting of all factors.

Exhibit 8A.2 outlines a sampling of the underlying factors that the VOP addresses within each subcategory, for a manufacturing company example (different versions exist for different industries). Each of the factors would be addressed by a facilitator's questions, followed by the subject company's management team discussing and debating how well-developed the company is in that category on a 0–10 scale. Once all questions are answered, the VOP calculates all scores and rolls the results through the embedded financial module that is separately populated in the VOP, to determine the overall discounted or capitalized cash flow calculation of value. The interview process with the management team provides great value, by itself, to the subject company, as it is often the first time the management team has been exposed to the different perceptions that each has regarding the company's direction and objectives.

EXHIBIT 8A.2 Value Opportunity Profile

Detailed Framework – Sample Subcategories (not all-inclusive) with Sample Factors to Be Assessed

Planning

Strategic Planning	Target Market	Competition
Fully developed?	How well established?	Direct competition
Written?	How old?	Indirect competition
Management input?	Geographic range	Position in market
Current?	Growing/shrinking?	Margin pressures
Independent review?	Specific economic factors	
Actively using?		

Leadership

Board of Advisors	Management Team	Communication
Exists?	Recognized team?	Written mission/vision?
Regular meetings?	Regular meetings?	Short-/long-term goals?
Management collaboration	All departments represented?	Tactical plans developed
Subcommittees	Educational levels	Plans fully integrated
Diversity of skills	Experience in industry	Performance measures
Veto authority?	Experienced in stage	Clear communication

Sales

Sales Team	Sales Strategy	Sales Operations
Composition	Written strategy?	Planning process?
Experience levels	Aligned w/mission, vision?	Tracking/reporting results?
Turnover	Integrated tactical plans?	Collaboration w/other departments
Adequacy for future	Clear objectives	Sales conversion metrics
	Distribution strategy	Incentive plans
		Market development program

EXHIBIT 8A.2 (*Continued*)

Marketing

Marketing Team	Marketing Strategy	Market Positioning
Composition	Written strategy?	Competitive analysis?
Experience levels	Aligned w/mission, vision?	Advantages understood?
Support of sales process	Integrated tactical plans?	Pricing strategy
	Clearly defined market	Defined customer experience
		Process for qualifying leads
		Tracking customer loyalty

People

Organizational Structure	Organizational Strategy	Continuous Learning
Qualified H.R. Exec resource	Written strategy	Formal training programs
Full organization chart	Aligned with overall plan	Education reimbursement
Job descriptions	Integrated tactical plans	Regular reviews
Designed around tactical plans	Standards for interviewing	Best practices process
Balanced for throughput	Standards for reviews	

Operations

Operating Region	Operations Team	Operating Strategy
Risks in Regions Where	Qualified C-Level Resource	Written Plan and Strategy
▪ Company operates ▪ Customers operate ▪ Supplies are sourced	▪ Qualifications of team ▪ Lean principles ▪ Company in transition?	▪ Aligned with overall plan ▪ Integrated tactical plans ▪ Tracking of key drivers

EXHIBIT 8A.2 (*Continued*)

Finance

Finance Team	Finance Strategy	Planning/Analysis/Reporting
Qualified financial executive	Full, written strategy	Annual audit or review
Education and credentials	Tracking key metrics	GAAP financial statements
Experience in industry	Targeted capital structure	Monthly reporting process
Experience at stage	Targeted cost of capital	Forecasting and projections
	Plan for financing growth	Comprehensive analysis
		▪ Product-line profitability
		▪ Customer profitability

Legal

Legal Structure	Intellectual Property	Contract Management
Appropriate entities established	Assets identified/protected	Standard terms/conditions
Reviewed by attorney	New intellectual property development	Review/approval process
Reviewed by tax advisor	Protections expiring	Nondisclosure agreements
		Noncompete agreements
		Employment agreements

CHAPTER 9

Weighted Average Cost of Capital

Chapter 6 introduced the concept of invested capital, which is the total of the company's interest-bearing debt and equity. Also known as business enterprise value (BEV) or enterprise value, this is the quantity most commonly used in a transaction to define the investment in the company that is being appraised. As emphasized previously, because operations are usually financed with debt and equity, its discount rate should include the cost of both debt and equity, which is referred to as the weighted average cost of capital (WACC). Therefore, when using either the single-period capitalization method (SPCM) or the discounted cash flow (DCF) method to compute the value of invested capital, a return to debt and equity is discounted or capitalized by the cost of debt and equity, the WACC.

The WACC reflects the combined cost of debt and equity with the weights of these capital sources based on their market value rather than book value. Typical WACC rates are shown in Exhibit 9.1; note that they do not pertain to any specific date, industry, or economic conditions, but rather provide an indication of the magnitude of the range.

The company's WACC declines as it employs more of the lower-cost debt with proportionately less of the higher-cost equity. Once the WACC applicable to the approximate optimum capital structure is achieved, additional debt causes the WACC to rise, reflecting the added risk higher financial leverage creates.

One of the more common finance questions relates to whether and how variations in the relative level of debt affect the value of a company. The presence of little or no lower-cost debt could create an artificially expensive all-equity WACC, even after allowing for the absence of financial leverage. That many privately held companies avoid debt may reflect the failure by some investors to recognize that equity capital bears a cost (i.e. requires a return) and that the added risk associated with equity

EXHIBIT 9.1 Weighted Average Cost of Capital

Large Cap (S&P 500)	Mid-Cap to Micro-Cap	Larger/Stronger Private Company	Smaller/Weaker Private Company		
7%	12%	15%	20%	25%	30%

capital demands a higher rate of return than debt. However, one should also recognize the increased flexibility and the decreased risk that an all-equity capital structure creates, which may make the company more attractive to some buyers.

In considering the effect of financial leverage, continuously focus on those characteristics that create value for the business. Capital is only one of many factors of production, and it is often relatively easy to replicate. For this reason, value is seldom significantly increased or decreased by variations in the capital structure of a business. That is, investors generally cannot manipulate value in a material fashion through adjustment to the capital structure of the company. Remember, buyers can refinance operating debt at their own lower-cost debt financing, so they will not pay a premium price to acquire a leveraged company.

To prevent these potential distortions in value, the invested capital model should be employed rather than the equity model to determine value on a predebt basis (i.e. before financing considerations). Further, it is usually informative to compare the debt-to-equity ratio of the subject company to industry standards – but only if these standards are based on market values, not book values – to get a better understanding of market practices. In the process, however, remember that because privately held companies usually lack the access to capital that is available for a public firm, they may have less debt capacity.

Iterative Weighted Average Cost of Capital Process

Determining the appropriate debt-to-equity weightings to use in the WACC computation is generally simple for publicly traded corporations because the market values of the debt and equity is readily available information. The market values of the debt of a public company are usually equal to the book value, unless a note or bond carries an interest rate that differs substantially from current market rates. Equity value can be determined by multiplying the company's stock price times the number of shares outstanding. The resulting market values of the debt and equity determine their weights in the WACC computation.

EXHIBIT 9.2 Iterative Process for a Typical Corporation (Fundamental Data)

Total Assets	$2,200,000	
Other Liabilities (trade and accrued payables)	$200,000	
Interest-Bearing Debt	$800,000	
Total Liabilities	$1,000,000	
Equity	$1,200,000	
Debt-Equity Mix (at book values)		
Interest-Bearing Debt	$800,000	40%
Equity	$1,200,000	60%
Invested Capital	$2,000,000	100%
Net Cash Flow Available to Invested Capital		$500,000
Forecasted Long-Term Growth Rate		3%

The debt and equity discount rates previously discussed are inserted into a block format to compute the WACC in a computation that students usually see in their first university finance course. In valuing closely held businesses, however, the computation can be more complex and errors are commonly made. So we begin with a simple illustration of the WACC and build on it to emphasize how to avoid the pitfalls that can occur.

Exhibit 9.2 contains the fundamental data that will be used in computations for the next nine exhibits, and Exhibit 9.3 shows the initial computation that yields a WACC of 13.75%.

EXHIBIT 9.3 Weighted Average Cost of Capital

Applicable Rates

Equity Discount Rate	20%
Nominal Borrowing Rate	6%
Tax Bracket	27%

Capital Structure at Book Values

Debt	40%
Equity	60%

Computation of WACC

Component	Net Rate	Ratio	Contribution to WACC
Debt @ Borrowing Rate $(1 - t)$	4.4%	40%	1.75%
Equity	20.0%	60%	12.0%
WACC Applicable to Invested Capital Based on Book Values			13.75%

EXHIBIT 9.4 Single-Period Capitalization Method: Net Cash Flow Available to Invested Capital Converted to a Value for Equity (Amounts Rounded), Second Iteration

Net cash flow available to invested capital	$500,000	
WACC capitalization rate (13.75% – 3.0%)	10.75%	
Fair market value of invested capital		$4,700,000
Less: Interest-bearing debt		$800,000
Indicated fair market value of equity		$3,900,000

Because a privately owned company lacks a going market price for its stock, the market value of equity, and the resulting debt-equity weightings, cannot be determined. If the incorrect debt and equity weights are used in the WACC computation, distortions to value can occur, as Exhibit 9.4 illustrates, based on the data from Exhibits 9.2 and 9.3.

The computation in Exhibit 9.4 yields an invested capital value of $4.7 million, from which is subtracted the interest-bearing debt of $0.8 million to yield what appears to be a correct equity fair market value of $3.9 million. Further study of the data, however, reveals that the conclusion contradicts the 40% to 60% debt-to-equity weightings on which the computation is based. That is, the 40% debt and 60% equity weightings from Exhibit 9.3 produced the $3.9 million equity value, which equals 83% of the resulting $4.7 million value of invested capital as seen in Exhibit 9.5. At this point in the computation we do not know what the appropriate debt-to-equity weightings should be, but we should recognize that they cannot simultaneously be 40% to 60% and 17% to 83%.

EXHIBIT 9.5 Debt–Equity Mix, Second Iteration

Invested capital	$4,700,000		100.0%
Debt	$800,000		17.0%
Equity	$3,900,000		83.0%

Computation of WACC

Second Iteration

Component	*Net Rate*	*Ratio*	*Contribution to WACC*
Debt @ Borrowing Rate (1 – t)	4.4%	17.0%	0.7%
Equity	20.0%	83.3%	16.6%
WACC Applicable to Invested Capital			17.3%

EXHIBIT 9.6 Single-Period Capitalization Method: Net Cash Flow Available to Invested Capital Converted to a Value for Equity (Amounts Rounded), Third Iteration

Net cash flow available to invested capital	$500,000	
WACC capitalization rate (17.3% − 3.0%)	14.3%	
Fair market value of invested capital		$3,500,000
Less: Interest-bearing debt		$800,000
Indicated fair market value of equity		$2,700,000

The solution is to perform a second iteration using the new debt-to-equity mix of 17% to 83%.[1] As illustrated in Exhibit 9.5, this yields a WACC of 17.3%, which is much higher than the 13.75% WACC originally computed.

The debt and equity weights that result from the new WACC cap rate of 14.3% in Exhibit 9.6 are shown in Exhibit 9.7. Once again a contradiction results, but the magnitude of the distortion has been reduced.

Exhibit 9.7 leads to the need for a third iteration in Exhibit 9.8 with the resulting debt-to-equity weights in Exhibit 9.9.

EXHIBIT 9.7 Debt–Equity Mix, Third Iteration

Invested capital	$3,500,000	100.0%
Debt	$800,000	22.9%
Equity	$2,700,000	77.1%

Computation of WACC

Third Iteration

Component	Net Rate	Ratio	Contribution to WACC
Debt @ Borrowing Rate (1 − t)	4.4%	22.9%	1.0%
Equity	20.0%	77.1%	15.4%
WACC Applicable to Invested Capital			16.4%

---

[1] The authors gratefully acknowledge the pioneering development of this procedure by Jay B. Abrams, "An Iterative Valuation Approach," *Business Valuation Review* 14, no. 1 (March 1995): 26–35, and *Quantitative Business Valuation: A Mathematical Approach for Today's Professionals* (New York: McGraw-Hill, 2001), Chapter 6.

EXHIBIT 9.8 Single-Period Capitalization Method: Net Cash Flow Available to Invested Capital Converted to a Value for Equity (Amounts Rounded), Fourth Iteration

Net cash flow available to invested capital WACC capitalization rate (16.4% − 3.0%)	$500,000 13.4%	
Fair market value of invested capital		$3,700,000
Less: Interest-bearing debt		$800,000
Indicated fair market value of equity		$2,900,000

EXHIBIT 9.9 Debt–Equity Mix, Fourth Iteration

Invested capital	$3,700,000	100.0%
Debt	$800,000	21.6%
Equity	$2,900,000	78.4%

This fourth iteration produced debt and equity values and corresponding weightings of 21.6% debt and 78.4% equity that were approximately consistent with the 22.9% debt and 77.1% equity weightings on which the underlying WACC computation was based. For simplicity, amounts in this illustration were rounded, and additional iterations could continue to reduce the remaining variation. The essential conclusion is that the debt and equity weights used in the WACC must produce consistent debt and equity values, or the debt-to-equity weights are not based on market values.[2]

Although this example used the SPCM to demonstrate that the iterative process will achieve the desired results, multiple iterations are used most often in application of the DCF method. With its multiple-year forecast, it involves more computations, but conceptually the process is the same.

Shortcut Weighted Average Cost of Capital Formula

There is a shortcut to this iterative process when using the SPCM. The fair market value of equity is the dependent variable in the next formula in which the remaining factors typically are known.

$$E_{FMV} = \frac{NCF_{IC}}{C_E - g} - D^*(C_D - g)$$

[2] David M. Bishop and Frank C. Evans, "Avoiding a Common Error in Calculating the Weighted Average Cost of Capital," *CPA Expert* (Fall 1997): 4–6. Reprinted with permission from *CPA Expert*. Copyright 1997 by American Institute of Certified Public Accountants, Inc.

where:

E_{FMV} = Fair market value of equity
NCF_{IC} = Net cash flow to invested capital
D = Total interest-bearing debt
C_D = After-tax interest rate
C_E = Cost of equity
g = Long-term growth rate

Although the return in this formula is net cash flow to invested capital, it could be a different return, such as net income to invested capital. To prevent distortions to the value of equity, any change in this return must be accompanied by a commensurate change in the cost of that return (i.e. discount rate). Use of a different return is illustrated in the case study in Chapter 21.

This formula is presented with the data from the preceding example inserted to demonstrate the outcome:

$$\$2,929,976 = \frac{\$500,000}{(20\% - 3\%)} - \$800,000^*(4.4\% - 3\%)$$

The resulting equity value of approximately $2.9 million can be added to the $800,000 of interest-bearing debt to yield the fair market value of invested capital of $3.7 million. In the WACC block format in Exhibit 9.10, this yields weightings of 21.4% and 78.6% and a resulting WACC of 16.6%. This computation reflects the result that could have been achieved by the iterative process previously shown in this chapter, had it performed additional iterations and not rounded numbers.

To confirm these results, a long-term growth rate of 3% is subtracted from the WACC of 16.6% to yield the capitalization rate of 13.6%. Capitalizing the NFC_{IC} by 13.6% generates the values and debt equity percentages shown in Exhibit 9.11, which produce similar debt–equity ratios used to derive the WACC (one or two additional iterations would produce the same ratios).

EXHIBIT 9.10 Computation of WACC

Component	*Net Rate*	*Ratio*	*Contribution to WACC*
Debt @ Borrowing Rate (1 – t)	4.4%	21.4%	0.9%
Equity	20.0%	78.6%	15.7%
WACC Applicable to Invested Capital			16.6%

EXHIBIT 9.11 Single-Period Capitalization Method to Confirm Validity of WACC Weights

Net cash flow available to invested capital	$500,000	
WACC capitalization rate (16.6% − 3.0%)	13.6%	
Fair market value of invested capital	$3,700,000	100%
Less: Interest-bearing debt	$800,000	21.6%
Indicated fair market value of equity	$2,900,000	78.4%

Thus, the shortcut formula generates consistent fair market value debt and equity weightings and eliminates the need to perform multiple iterations with the SPCM. Formulas that simplify, however, seldom eliminate the need for common sense and informed judgment. In this case, carefully review the outcome to determine if the resulting debt and equity weights appear to be consistent with the general trend and structure in that industry. Also recognize that the formula employs specific costs of debt and equity that must be appropriate for the resulting debt–equity weightings and capital structure. If, for example, the capital structure produced by the formula includes heavy financial leverage, the associated costs of the debt and equity may have to be adjusted to recognize this outcome.[3]

Common Errors in Computing Cost of Capital

In applying these cost of capital principles, several questions frequently arise where erroneous answers could lead to poor investment choices:

- As a shortcut to performing the iterative process in computing the WACC, can I use industry average debt-to-equity weightings from industry sources such as BizMiner, Integra, or RMA Annual Statement Studies?

  These industry debt-to-equity averages are most commonly derived from actual unadjusted balance sheets submitted to that industry source. Aggregating the data, however, does not eliminate the problem that the weightings are based on book values rather than market values.

---

[3] Frank C. Evans and Kelly L. Strimbu, "Debt & Equity Weightings in WACC," *CPA Expert* (Fall 1998): 4–5. Reprinted with permission from *CPA Expert*. Copyright© 1998 by American Institute of Certified Public Accountants, Inc.

The private company financial statements used to generate the averages probably reflect typical attempts by owners to minimize income taxes or achieve other objectives. Any such strategy could change the book value of equity versus its market value, which is primarily a function of anticipated future cash flows. Thus these sources should not be used because they do not reflect market values.

Industry averages typically reflect historical rates of return computed based on accounting information. Because investments are future oriented, use of historical rates to reflect investor choices can cause serious distortions to value. To illustrate, assume two returns on equity from RMA (actually, in RMA this ratio is identified as pretax income/net worth), 40% from a more profitable industry and 10% from a less profitable one. Computing value from these rates using a single-period capitalization computation, assuming a return of $1,000,000, yields these results:

$$\frac{\$1,000,000}{40\%} = \$2,500,000$$

$$\frac{\$1,000,000}{10\%} = \$10,000,000$$

Note that the use of the higher 40% rate of return from the more profitable industry produced the lower value while the lower rate of return from the less profitable industry produced the higher value. This demonstrates the potential distortion to value that can result from using historical measures of earnings compared to dubious book values. As explained in Chapter 2, valid rates are derived by comparing current cash investments at market value against the future cash returns received – dividends and/or capital appreciation – on those investments. The resulting rates reflect a price paid at market value compared to an actual cash return.

As discussed in the previous two chapters, one source of market-based rates of return is *Valuation Handbook: U.S. Industry Cost of Capital*, published by Duff & Phelps, LLC. This annual publication, which is heavily influenced by large-cap companies, contains industry financial information related to revenues, profitability, equity returns, ratios, capital structure, cost of equity, and weighted average cost of capital based on market values rather than book values.

- How much influence should the target company's capital structure – whether it has more or less financial leverage – have on the value of the company?

The target's existing capital structure should not materially influence its investment value to the buyer. Buyers have alternative sources of financing operations, and capital is usually an enabler, rather than a creator, of value. Since strategic buyers bring capital to the transaction, the target's capital structure is seldom of great importance to the buyer. If the target is illiquid or has excessive debt, these weaknesses could reduce its stand-alone fair market value. Conversely, if the target carries low-cost financing that could be assumed by the buyer, this could increase its value. Aggressive buyers also may look to the assets owned by the company as a source of collateral to finance their acquisition, although this is a financing rather than valuation consideration.

▪ Should buyers use their own company's cost of capital or hurdle rate in evaluating a target rather than computing an appropriate WACC for the target?

Wise buyers and sellers enter into a transaction knowing both the fair market value of the target on a stand-alone basis and the approximate investment value to each potential strategic buyer. Determining the fair market value requires computation of the target's WACC to calculate what the company is worth to its present owners as a stand-alone business.

To determine the investment value to a strategic buyer after adjusting the forecasted earnings or net cash flow to reflect consideration of synergies, begin with the buyer's cost of capital. From this rate, which reflects all of the buyer's strengths, adjustments should be made, taking into account the risk profile of the target. For example, a large company with a WACC of 12% may look at three different targets with varying levels of risk and apply WACCs to them of 14%, 16%, and 18% to reflect their varying levels of risk to that buyer, given its overall WACC of 12%. In short, the role of the WACC is to provide a rate of return that is appropriate to the perceived investment risk, not to reflect the buyer's risk profile or cost of capital.

The acquirer that uses the same hurdle rate in assessing the value of every acquisition implicitly assumes that each carries the same level of risk, which is seldom true. A single rate will tend to undervalue safer investments that merit a lower rate and overvalue riskier investments that require a higher rate.

In addition, a word of caution should be noted when using WACC. The standard WACC calculation discussed above assumes both a fixed capital structure with static costs of equity and debt capital. While WACC and its underlying assumptions are widely accepted and used in the market, the reality is that WACC is rarely constant. In instances where a capital structure is expected to change, it is more correct to employ an iterative process that reflects changes in the capital structure as the level of debt decreases (or increases).

Investments bring substantial differences in their levels of risk. To maximize value, buyers and sellers must be able to identify and quantify risk. In merger and acquisition, this is done primarily through application of the income approach, where risk is expressed through a cost of capital.

There is a substantial body of financial theory available to quantify the costs of debt and equity capital sources and to deal with them on a combined basis through a WACC. When these procedures are applied properly, risk can be measured and, in the process, managed to maximize returns.

CHAPTER 10

Market Approach: Using Guideline Public Companies and M&A Transactions

Although market multiples are widely quoted as a source for determining value for merger and acquisition (M&A), they are often misused. With this introduction, we are not discouraging the use of multiples – in fact, value is most often communicated in M&A in terms of multiples (i.e. EBITDA and revenue multiples) – rather, we are suggesting caution when using multiples to avoid distorting value.

Because of the practical importance of multiples in M&A, this chapter reviews the fundamental steps in the process and offers suggestions and cautions along the way.

The market approach is based on the *principle of substitution*, which states that "one will pay no more for an item than the cost of acquiring an equally desirable substitute." Thus, with the market approach, value is determined based on prices that have been paid for similar items in the relevant marketplace. Expert judgment is needed for interpretations of what companies are considered to be similar and what markets are relevant. Expertise helps in choosing what multiple to use to gauge the company's performance. Knowledge is also required to properly determine whether the market multiples reflect value on a control or lack of control basis. Finally, substantial judgment is necessary to determine what multiple is appropriate for the target company; it could be the mean or median multiple derived from the range of multiples of a group of companies, or a multiple within or outside of that range.

The market approach relevant to valuation for M&A includes two primary methods: the transaction multiple method and the guideline public company method. They result from different kinds of transactions and yield different types of value, so their distinction must be clearly understood.

A variety of multiples or ratios also can be used to compute value with either method. These are described in the "Selection of Valuation Multiples" section of this chapter.

The value determined by the market approach, like the income approach, includes the value of the tangible assets used by the company in its operations. If the business owns excess operating assets or non-operating assets, these assets can be valued separately, and this value can be added to operating value to determine the value of the whole enterprise. This process is discussed in Chapter 11.

Transaction Multiple Method

The transaction multiple method (TMM) looks at the prices paid to acquire a controlling interest in a business. The buyers in these transactions often are publicly traded companies because closely held businesses usually do not reveal financial information when they make acquisitions. However, thanks to databases such as S&P Capital IQ,[1] Pratt's Stats,[2] GF Data,[3] and DoneDeals[4] there is now ample transaction data on large and middle market private companies. Meanwhile, BIZCOMPS® and IBA Market Data (as well as Pratt's Stats) provide transaction data for very small company transactions.[5] These transactions are often strategic, where the buyer is acquiring a company in the same or a similar industry in which it currently operates to achieve various synergies or other integrative benefits. Thus the price paid

---

[1] Capital IQ has extensive market information on over 60,000 public companies and over 2 million private firms worldwide (www.marketintelligence.spglobal.com).

[2] In 2017, Pratt's Stats™ contained data on sales of over 27,300 privately held companies with a median selling price of $400,000 and an average selling price of approximately $37.2 million (www.bvresources.com).

[3] GF Data Resources reports contain detailed valuation, volume, and leverage data on private equity–sponsored transactions in the $10–$250 million value range (www.gfdata.com).

[4] DoneDeals provides approximately 7,000 sales transactions for private and public mid-market companies with sales prices ranging between $1 million and $250 million, half of which being under $10 million (www.valusource.com).

[5] In 2017, BIZCOMPS contained data on sales of over 12,650 privately held companies with a median selling price of $167,000 and an average selling price of $345,000 (www.bizcomps.com or www.bvresources.com or www.valusource.com). Meanwhile, IBA Market Data contained data on sales of over 37,000 small privately held businesses mostly generating revenues under $1 million (www.valusource.com).

often reflects investment value to that specific buyer rather than fair market value, which assumes a financial buyer.

For the transaction method to yield an appropriate indication of value, the transactional data must relate to companies that are reasonably similar to the target being valued. In addition, the synergies anticipated in the acquisition of the target must be similar enough to those reflected in the transaction data to achieve a reasonable basis for comparison. Thus it is useful to have an adequate number of strategic transactions that generate a range of multiples that can be analyzed. When working with strategic transactions, the buyer's motivations may not be fully understood. Buyers may make certain acquisitions purely for defensive reasons – to keep a major competitor out of a market. Similarly, the price paid for a target may seem unusually high in comparison with its potential benefits, but that acquisition may position the buyer to make incremental profits elsewhere. And prices and corresponding multiples may increase dramatically during an industry consolidation and decrease just as quickly. Again, strategic transactions must be analyzed carefully for this reason.

Because transaction data reflects acquisition of a controlling interest, it generates value on a control basis that is generally appropriate for direct comparison with other M&A transactions. Strategic acquisitions and resulting multiples also may reflect synergies and other benefits that are different from those available in the transaction under consideration, so caution is urged in comparison of data.

Similarly, it is wise to study an industry carefully to identify those factors that are driving M&A activity in it. These circumstances may be short-term in nature, in which case they temporarily drive up values and multiples when buyers are taking advantage of temporary opportunities. This was seen, for example, in the dramatic increase in the price of health-care practices for a period of years during the 1990s brought about by changes in managed care and other regulations. Regulations changed, however, and values quickly declined. In the 2000s, similar spikes were experienced in the funeral home business and later in insurance agencies. Thus temporary aberrations may occur that must be analyzed to assess their long-term effect on value.

A real benefit of transaction data is that it reveals information about what well-informed strategic players in an industry are doing and the prices they have paid in strategic transactions. When adequate information exists, these transactions also provide indications about selected value or risk drivers for these companies.

To illustrate application of the transaction method, assume that the target is a generic manufacturing company that came on the market at the beginning of 2017. The target's sales are approximately $300 million, with high profits by industry standards, primarily state-of-the-art manufacturing facilities, adequate raw material reserves, but only modest growth capacity as a stand-alone business. A study of the industry as of that date reveals:

- The commodity nature of products impedes company and product differentiation.
- Economies of scale create both revenue and cost synergy potential.
- A broader customer base and geographic market served to provide protection from geographic or industry downturns.
- There was a strong recent pattern of M&A activity in the industry.
- Generally low stock prices create M&A bargains.

Given these industry conditions, the transaction data in Exhibit 10.1 was gathered from a publicly available source.

When the companies involved are publicly traded, substantial information can be obtained from public sources about the nature and terms of the transactions, prices paid, and resulting multiples. The first three transactions in the exhibit were consummated; the last was an offer that ultimately was rejected by the seller.

These transactions indicate that substantial premiums – probably in the range of 40% above fair market value – were being paid by strategic buyers and private equity firms for targets in this consolidating industry. From this initial information, a thorough investigation of the buyer and the seller is

EXHIBIT 10.1 Generic Manufacturing Industry Strategic Acquisitions

Date	Buyer	Seller	Premium
11/4/2016	Megalo Manufacturing, S.A.	Reddington Holding, Inc.	51%
	1. Terms of sale: All cash		
	2. Price paid equals $195 per ton of capacity		
	3. Price paid reflects 6 times forward EBITDA		
9/2/2016	Industrie de Belgique, S.A.	Mountain Industries, Inc.	45%
	1. Terms of sale: All cash		
	2. Price paid equals $235 per ton of capacity		
	3. Price paid reflects 8 times forward EBITDA		
3/30/2017	Touchdown, Inc.	Siren Corporation	27.5%
	1. Terms of sale: Buyer's stock		
	2/27/2017	Consolidator Corporation*	Blue Industries, Inc.	43%
	1. Terms of sale: All cash		

*Latest offer rejected by Blue Industries as of 28 February 2017, with offer lapsing on 5 April 2017.

necessary to assess their circumstances, intentions, and options as of the transaction date. It should be clear, however, that buyers and sellers operating in this market would benefit substantially from this data and the details behind each of these transactions as they move forward in their negotiations.

Many of the issues discussed thus far regarding industry circumstances, company size, market position, and other competitive factors must be considered. For example, the last transaction listed was an unsuccessful offer made by Consolidator Corporation, the second largest company in the world in that industry, bidding for Blue Industries, the third largest. Whether details on a potential transaction between two companies of this size are relevant in determining the value of a much smaller target requires further analysis. This data does, however, clearly indicate pricing patterns for strategic buyers in this industry as of this approximate date.

Buyers and sellers should be particularly cautious of transaction multiples quoted by intermediaries. Intermediaries present these multiples to sellers as part of their proposal to represent the seller in the sale. Investment bankers or brokers then use the same multiples in presenting the company to prospective buyers, justifying its offering price based on these multiples. Both buyers and sellers can be misled by the seller's representations if the strategic transaction or transactions on which the multiples are based are not representative of the current market or similar enough to the target company. Without adequate similarity, the impressive multiples may not be possible. Both buyers and sellers need to recognize this potential for distortion.

Deal Structure

Another area to exercise caution when analyzing transaction multiples is how the underlying transaction is structured. Specifically, is it an asset sale or a stock sale? This topic is discussed in further detail in Chapter 15. A stock sale involves a direct transaction between the buying corporation and the selling shareholders, where the selling shareholders' stock is exchanged for value in the form of cash, stock, notes, and other possible forms of consideration. An asset sale involves a transaction between the buying corporation and the selling corporation, where the selling corporation's assets (including all or a portion of its tangible and intangible assets) are exchanged for value in the form of cash, stock, notes, and other possible forms of consideration; and then the selling corporation distributes the proceeds to the selling shareholders. That is, an asset sale involves the buyer taking on the assets of the business typically without the liabilities; in a stock sale, the liabilities go along with the assets.

In the vast majority of appraisals, it is the equity of a business that is being valued. Equity by definition includes all assets minus all liabilities. There is usually not as much potential for confusion here, except that some appraisal methods assume an asset sale; in that case, the resulting value has to be adjusted by including the assets and liabilities that are not to be transferred, in order to determine equity value.

As a general rule, the way to compare asset and stock sale values is through this formula:

Assets Transferred to Buyer − Liabilities Transferred to Buyer

= Net Assets Transferred (= Consideration Paid or Received)

+ Assets Retained by Seller − Liabilities Retained by Seller

= Seller's Equity

Typical assets retained are cash, receivables (under a certain age), bad inventory, and nonoperating assets such as company cars. Typical liabilities retained are payables and accrued expenses. Every deal is unique with respect to other obligations, such as bank debt and leases.

Guideline Public Company Method

The guideline public company (GPC) method determines value based on the price at which similar public companies are traded on public stock exchanges. As with the transaction method, value is determined through the use of multiples that compare the transaction price to some measure of operating performance or financial position. The result usually reflects value on a minority marketable basis (it could be control marketable, depending on the return used) because the guideline company shares being traded are minority interests in securities that are readily marketable. Since M&A most commonly involves acquisition of a controlling interest in a privately held company or a division of a public company, adjustments may be necessary to reflect differences in control and marketability between the guideline companies and the target. In the United States, more than 15,000 public companies are required to report electronically with the U.S. Securities and Exchange Commission (SEC). Access to this public company data is readily available through the SEC's electronic data gathering and retrieval system (EDGAR). This database includes SEC Form 10-K annual reports, SEC Form 10-Q quarterly reports, and other material disclosures. In addition, commercial electronic databases are available that summarize this information. Thus, the GPC method is widely used because of the increased convenience in gathering and analyzing the data on public companies. Nonetheless, as discussed in Chapter 8, there is a growing school of thought that the GPC method has no place in valuing private businesses, given the vast differences between public and private capital markets.

The first challenge that arises in use of the GPC method is to identify an adequate number of public companies that are similar enough to the target to provide a reasonable basis for comparison. This can be readily completed with access to various databases such as Capital IQ. For those who do not have access to such databases, EDGAR allows searches by Standard Industry Classification (SIC) code and North American Industry Classification System (NAICS) code, and commercial databases allow for searching and screening the data through use of many other parameters, such as sales volume or income level. These online sources also provide convenient summaries of this data that permit users to survey companies quickly and conveniently based on operational or performance criteria. Thus, if the initial search generates 25 potential guideline companies, a review of this summary data often can eliminate a substantial number of potential companies that fail to meet subsequent tests for appropriateness. Once the population of guideline companies is reduced to 10 or 12, further analysis can be made with the goal of optimally having about 4 to 7 companies to serve as proxy for the market.

Depending on the characteristics of the target, many searches will be less successful. Because of the target's size, industry, or product line, very few or no guideline companies may be available for comparison. When initial searches do not generate an adequate list of guideline companies for comparison, the criteria of the search can be broadened to additional NAICS or SIC codes or to a broader definition of the industry. Such a decision, however, always requires care and judgment because the results of the market as determined by the guideline companies must serve as a reasonable guide in assessing the target. The less similar the guideline companies are to the target, the less reliable the results will tend to be.

If the initial search based on industry parameters identifies an adequate population of potential guideline companies, further selection criteria must be employed to determine which ones are most similar to the target. Many different criteria can be used, but these are commonly recognized:

- *Size.* Usually based on sales volume.
- *Products or services.* When the guideline companies have multiple product or service lines, these and the sales volumes of each must be compared with those of the target for similarity.
- *Markets served.* The markets of many industries are divided into segments determined by geographic considerations, customers, products or services, or technology, each of which could affect the suitability of a company to serve as a guideline company.

- *Financial performance.* Differences here often reflect distinctions in product lines, quality, or markets served, all of which should be considered in comparing the target to the guideline companies.

With these criteria in mind, larger well-known public companies, particularly conglomerates, are seldom appropriate guideline companies. Their size, breadth of products, extensive markets, and financial strength usually make them a poor basis for comparison with a middle-market company. If such comparisons are made, be particularly sensitive to the resulting multiples and the weight that comparison is given in the overall determination of value.

Just as the target company's financial statements may require adjustment for nonoperating or nonrecurring items, the financial statements of guideline companies may need to be adjusted. The objective in either case is to produce financial statements that provide the most accurate indication of the true economic performance of the entity. Adjustments also may be necessary if one or more of the guideline companies employ accounting methods that are different from those of the target.

Once guideline companies have been selected and operating multiples for them have been chosen and computed, an appropriate multiple to apply to the target must be determined. Begin this process by reviewing those competitive factors that most influence risk and value in that industry. With these factors in mind, look at the range of multiples of the guideline companies used in your analysis. Assume, for example, that the multiple you have chosen is the well-known price to earnings (P/E) ratio. Look at the range of the P/E ratios of the guideline companies. In assessing this range, consider the performance of each of the companies and the strengths and weaknesses each possesses. From this analysis, identify what characteristics and performance the market is rewarding with high multiples and what factors contribute to lower multiples. In the process, also begin to relate the target's operating performance, products, and other characteristics more closely to those of the guideline companies. That is, identify those guideline companies with which the target is most similar. Next, compute and analyze the mean and median guideline company multiples, the upper and lower quartiles, and the range from lowest to highest. Look further at the statistical dispersion of the guideline company multiples, noting in particular their coefficient of variation, which should provide an indication of the consistency or reliability of the data.

Next, return to those value drivers and risk drivers that appear to be most influential in the industry, and compare the target to each of the guideline companies with respect to those factors. Then compare the target to the guideline companies in terms of significant measures of financial performance, such as profit margin, asset utilization, return on assets, and liquidity.

With these qualitative and quantitative factors in mind, rank the target compared to the guideline companies in terms of each of these characteristics and overall.

Based on this comparison, assess whether the target is as strong as the average – the mean or median – of the guideline companies. If it is not, which is usually the case with smaller or middle-market–size companies compared to public guidelines, then the mean or median multiple of the guideline companies is probably too high for the target. After all, a selection of the mean or median guideline companies' multiples implies that the target possesses the approximate level of strength of the average of the companies against which it is being compared.

If the guideline companies appear on average to be stronger than the target, next compare the target to the one or two guideline companies that have the lowest multiples. It is not unusual for all of the guideline companies to be stronger than the target; in this case, the multiple chosen for the target would be outside of, or below, the range for the guideline companies. Such a result does not invalidate the use of the GPC method; on the contrary, it suggests that an investor who is considering a variety of investments, including guideline companies and the target and their respective levels of risk, would pay a lower multiple of earnings to own the target than it would pay for the stronger guideline companies.

Growth tends to be a factor that drives higher market multiples. Therefore, look carefully at both historical and forecasted growth in both revenues and earnings. More important, study carefully those factors that are causing growth to occur in the guideline companies, and carefully assess their future growth prospects. Then apply this same analysis to the target, both on a stand-alone basis and operating as a segment of the buyer.

Armed with this analysis, select an appropriate multiple for the target. It should reflect the competitive conditions that are driving risk and value in the industry and the strengths and weaknesses of the target relative to the guideline companies and their respective multiples. The multiples selected for the target also should make sense when compared to the mean, median, and range of multiples of the guideline companies.

One of the biggest benefits of using the GPC method is the opportunity it provides to thoroughly analyze companies operating in that industry to determine what drives their value. In the process of performing this analysis, usually one develops a much better insight into those strategies that have created strength and success in companies as well as those characteristics that hamper companies and create problems or weaknesses. These conclusions should reconcile with the analysis of the industry and those competitive factors that most influence value in the industry. Armed with this insight, much of the mystery that sometimes surrounds the market approach is eliminated and value is much easier to understand and quantify.

Selection of Valuation Multiples

Many different market multiples are used. Some are quite popular and have been widely accepted in a specific industry while some practitioners use the same one or two multiples in every appraisal that they do.

We suggest care in this selection because multiples of different levels of operating performance or financial position may disclose different information about the target company. Market data and company performance may allow use of only certain multiples. For example, in technology or emerging industries, where many guideline companies are in the development stage or relatively new, revenues may be the only operating measure for which a multiple can be determined because many of the companies do not generate profits. However, so much of a company's ultimate performance is determined by what happens below the revenue line with expenses that revenue may not provide an accurate picture of performance or value.

As Chapter 6 explains, in M&A analysts are considering an acquisition of a controlling interest in the target, and most commonly they do not want the analysis to include distortions that could be caused by the target's current capital structure. The same concerns apply when employing the market approach, so an invested capital model is generally preferred over directly valuing equity. Therefore, the numerator in the multiple should be the market value of invested capital (MVIC) rather than stock price, where MVIC is the sum of all common and preferred stock and interest-bearing debt in a business enterprise, excluding cash.

Correspondingly, when the numerator indicates a value of debt and equity, the denominator must also. (This will be explained in the next section, "Market Multiples Commonly Used.") If common stock is being valued using invested capital multiples, the value of senior securities (e.g. interest-bearing debt and preferred stock) must be subtracted from the resulting MVIC to arrive at the indicated value of the company's equity.

The time periods for which the multiples or ratios apply also must be considered carefully. The objective should be for the time period of the guideline company multiples to be approximately the same as that of the target. Typical time periods include the latest fiscal year, most recent 12 months, forecasted future 12 months, or an average of some number of historical years. If the ratio involves a balance sheet measure, such as equity or assets, it is often of the latest available balance sheet date.

Because guideline companies have different fiscal year-ends, variations in the timing of this data are common. It is wise, however, to consider carefully the effect, if any, of these variations, particularly when operating in cyclical or, to a lesser extent, seasonal industries. In certain cases, variations in dates by as little as one quarter can create material differences.

Also be sensitive to general fluctuations in market levels, particularly in volatile industries or in periods of volatile market activity. Stock prices and their resulting multiples can change dramatically in a short period of time. This fact again suggests a need for careful assessment of overall market trends and changes in the guideline company stock prices and multiples over time.

Finally, when using the transaction method, extreme care must be taken when there are changes in the economic cycle. For example, given the higher valuations and greater access to financing that existed in 2005 through 2007, transaction data from that time period was irrelevant during the recession that began in 2008. Even if data from transactions during such a downturn is available, the transactions may be distressed sales that do not provide an accurate picture of a healthy company's value. In some cases, though, transactions that occurred during the recession in 2001 may generate data that was more relevant during the recession that took hold in 2008.

Commonly Used Market Multiples

Although a variety of market multiples appear in financial literature, only a few receive wide recognition and application. While there may be variation in the application of those listed next, these are the multiples that are most commonly used to determine value for M&A.

- *P/E.* Price/earnings is one of the most widely used multiples in the public markets. The price of common stock is the numerator, and income after taxes on a per-share basis is the denominator.[6] This multiple is appropriate for most profitable companies with a stable capital structure that is consistent with the capital structure of the selected guideline companies. This equity multiple will produce an equity value directly. Since the P/E is based on after-tax income, the multiple will be much higher than the revenue multiple and somewhat higher than the EBIT and EBITDA multiples mentioned below.
- *MVIC/R.* Market value of invested capital/revenues, another popular multiple, assumes a homogeneous industry where the revenues can reasonably be expected to produce a consistent quantity of earnings or cash flow. It may also be useful in certain industries, such as the restaurant industry, to eliminate any discrepancies in the definition of earnings between the subject and among the guideline companies, which may arise in using earnings multiples. Although revenue multiples often

---

[6] This may also be calculated as market value of equity divided by net income after taxes.

reflect price in the numerator, it is more appropriate to reflect MVIC in the numerator. Reflecting price in the numerator produces confusing results because price is a measure of equity and the denominator is a return to debt and equity. Revenue is a measure of operating results that comes before interest expense in the income statement.

- *MVIC/EBIT or MVIC/EBITDA.* Market value of invested capital/EBIT (earnings before interest and taxes) and EBITDA (earnings before interest, taxes, depreciation, and amortization) are widely used in the M&A community. These returns include the interest expense return to the debt holder, so the numerator must be the aggregate market price of the equity and debt. Multiples of EBIT or EBITDA frequently are quoted without substantiation, particularly by sellers or their intermediaries. For this reason, these multiples should always be challenged to identify their source, if any, and how they were derived. While the source commonly is based on little more than rumor or speculation about unsubstantiated prices paid in an industry, the multiples sometimes are based on a single, strategic transaction that may reflect unique synergies to that buyer, synergies that may not be relevant in any other transaction. Also, when an investment banker or business appraiser states that a company is worth the commonly quoted 5× EBITDA, there is a key underlying assumption that those earnings will continue into the future. A higher multiple is a forecast of higher expected growth. When developed correctly, these multiples can provide substantial insight into both investment value and fair market value. The key is to ensure that they are supported by proper calculations of transactions that are appropriate for comparison.

Both EBIT and EBITDA are what the company would have earned if not for obligations to its creditors and the tax authorities. Both multiples are pretax and predebt and thus reflect a level of earnings available for debt service, stockholders, and, in the case of EBITDA, capital expenditures (assuming depreciation and amortization on average reflect the required level of capital expenditures). As such, they measure earnings at a level that captures solely the company's underlying operating performance. Therefore, it does not matter if the company being valued has a significantly different capital structure or tax position as compared to the guideline companies from which the multiples are being derived (one of the significant weaknesses of the P/E multiple).

EBIT multiples are useful where differences in accounting for noncash charges (e.g. depreciation) are not significant. EBITDA multiples are particularly favored to eliminate differences in depreciation policies and get closer to a company's underlying performance. However, caution should be exercised in using either of these multiples in terms of how they are derived, whether they reflect proper economic adjustments, and whether they properly reflect future growth potential.

There are several limitations to be aware of when using these multiples as an indication of value. By definition, they ignore interest and other expenses that can account for a material portion of a company's cash outflow. In addition, they ignore cash outlays for capital expenditures and changes in working capital, and thus may not be realistic. That is, these multiples ultimately overstate value in times of working capital growth and significant capital improvements. Furthermore, EBITDA says nothing about the quality of earnings and ignores distinctions in the quality of cash flow resulting from differing accounting policies. Despite their shortcomings, however, both multiples can be legitimate indicators of value.

- *P/CF.* Price/cash flow, where cash flow is most commonly gross cash flow, is net income plus depreciation and amortization (and depletion in some industries), not net cash flow. Net cash flow is not selected because it may be difficult to estimate the net cash flow for each of the public guideline companies. (Remember, net cash flow components should be shown in amounts necessary to fund anticipated operational needs, not simply those that occurred historically.)
- *P/BV.* Price/book value, where book value equals stockholders' equity on the balance sheet (which is not a measure of value). This multiple used to be popular in M&A valuation in the banking industry. Although commonly quoted, it is seldom a reliable measure of performance or value because it does not involve an accurate measure of the company's performance or financial position.

Other multiples may be computed, but the ones just listed are seen most often. Some multiples have become particularly popular in certain industries. When these are encountered, they should be evaluated carefully to determine if they do provide an accurate indication of value. Exhibits 10.2 through 10.5 provide illustrations of how various multiples of seven public companies in the food distribution industry can be computed and displayed for analysis.

In reviewing the data in the exhibits, consider the points made in the previous discussion about how to select an appropriate multiple for the target from the guideline company data. Consider first which multiple or multiples would provide the best indication of value for the target, including whether multiples of stock price (equity) or invested capital should be used. Look at the range of the multiples and the resulting mean and median multiples. If necessary, adjust for any outliers. For example, the book value multiple in Exhibit 10.5 for Sysco is an outlier that may need to be omitted from the sample. Also, consider looking at the data in terms of quartiles, where the first quartile represents the 25th percentile, the second quartile is the median, and the third quartile represents the 75th percentile. Each of the guideline companies presented should have been evaluated carefully for similarity to the target in terms of size, products, markets served, operations, and financial attributes. In this case, given the size of most of these

EXHIBIT 10.2 Calculations of Market Values of Equity and Invested Capital

Guideline Company	Ticker	12/30/2016 Stock Share Price		Common Shares Outstanding		Market Value of Equity		Market Value of Debt		Market Value of Invested Capital
AMCON Distributing Co.	DIT	$115.30	*	688,680	=	$79,404,804	+	$13,099,100	=	$92,503,904
Core-Mark Holding Co., Inc.	CORE	$43.07	*	46,400,000	=	$1,998,448,000	+	$385,600,000	=	$2,384,048,000
G. Willi-Food International Ltd.	WILC	$5.77	*	12,707,580	=	$73,322,737	+	$0	=	$73,322,737
SpartanNash Company	SPTN	$39.54	*	37,591,000	=	$1,486,348,140	+	$431,099,000	=	$1,917,447,140
SUPERVALU Inc.	SVU	$32.69	*	37,857,140	=	$1,237,549,907	+	$2,550,000,000	=	$3,787,549,907
Sysco Corp.	SYY	$55.37	*	550,372,070	=	$30,474,101,516	+	$8,370,579,000	=	$38,844,680,516
United Natural Foods, Inc.	UNFI	$47.72	*	50,599,000	=	$2,414,584,280	+	$597,580,000	=	$3,012,164,280

EXHIBIT 10.3 Equity Basis

Price/Earnings Ratios of Guideline Companies for the Most Recent 12 Months

Guideline Company	Ticker	Market Value of Equity (Price)		Latest 12 Months Net Income		Price/ Earnings Multiple
AMCON Distributing Co.	DIT	$79,404,804	/	$5,671,520	=	14.00
Core-Mark Holding Co., Inc.	CORE	$1,998,448,000	/	$54,200,000	=	36.87
G. Willi-Food International Ltd.	WILC	$73,322,737	/	$2,819,580	=	26.00
SpartanNash Company	SPTN	$1,486,348,140	/	$56,828,000	=	26.16
SUPERVALU Inc.	SVU	$1,237,549,907	/	$103,000,000	=	12.02
Sysco Corp.	SYY	$30,474,101,516	/	$1,031,857,000	=	29.53
United Natural Foods, Inc.	UNFI	$2,414,584,280	/	$124,852,000	=	19.34
Central 50% – First Quartile						16.67
Central 50% – Third Quartile						27.84
Mean (Average)						23.42
Median (Second Quartile)						26.00

Price/Earnings Ratios of Guideline Companies for a Simple Average of the Most Recent Five Years

Guideline Company	Ticker	Market Value of Equity (Price)		5-Year Average Net Income		Price/ Earnings Multiple
AMCON Distributing Co.	DIT	$79,404,804	/	$6,105,542	=	13.01
Core-Mark Holding Co., Inc.	CORE	$1,998,448,000	/	$33,940,000	=	58.88
G. Willi-Food International Ltd.	WILC	$73,322,737	/	$4,439,574	=	16.52
SpartanNash Company	SPTN	$1,486,348,140	/	$30,810,400	=	48.24
SUPERVALU Inc.	SVU	$1,237,549,907	/	($390,800,000)	=	NM
Sysco Corp.	SYY	$30,474,101,516	/	$936,388,000	=	32.54
United Natural Foods, Inc.	UNFI	$2,414,584,280	/	$117,835,600	=	20.49
Central 50% – First Quartile						17.51
Central 50% – Third Quartile						44.32
Mean (Average)						31.61
Median (Second Quartile)						26.52

EXHIBIT 10.4 Invested Capital Basis

MVIC/EBIT Ratios of Guideline Companies for the Most Recent 12 Months

Guideline Company	Market Value of Invested Capital		Latest 12 Months EBIT		MVIC/EBIT Multiple
AMCON Distributing Co.	$92,503,904	/	$10,415,350	=	8.88
Core-Mark Holding Co., Inc.	$2,384,048,000	/	$90,300,000	=	26.40
G. Willi-Food International Ltd.	$73,322,737	/	$5,881,050	=	12.47
SpartanNash Company	$1,917,447,140	/	$147,842,000	=	12.97
SUPERVALU Inc.	$3,787,549,907	/	$460,000,000	=	8.23
Sysco Corp.	$38,844,680,516	/	$2,212,608,000	=	17.56
United Natural Foods, Inc.	$3,012,164,280	/	$228,487,000	=	13.18
Central 50% – First Quartile					10.67
Central 50% – Third Quartile					15.37
Mean (Average)					14.24
Median (Second Quartile)					12.97

MVIC/EBITDA Ratios of Guideline Companies for the Most Recent 12 Months

Guideline Company	Market Value of Invested Capital		Latest 12 Months EBITDA		MVIC/ EBITDA Multiple
AMCON Distributing Co.	$92,503,904	/	$12,537,500	=	7.38
Core-Mark Holding Co., Inc.	$2,384,048,000	/	$133,200,000	=	17.90
G. Willi-Food International Ltd.	$73,322,737	/	$6,858,500	=	10.69
SpartanNash Company	$1,917,447,140	/	$227,025,000	=	8.45
SUPERVALU Inc.	$3,787,549,907	/	$734,000,000	=	5.16
Sysco Corp.	$38,844,680,516	/	$3,000,977,000	=	12.94
United Natural Foods, Inc.	$3,012,164,280	/	$304,004,000	=	9.91
Central 50% – First Quartile					7.91
Central 50% – Third Quartile					11.82
Mean (Average)					10.35
Median (Second Quartile)					9.91

EXHIBIT 10.5 Equity and Invested Capital Basis

Price/Book Value Ratios of Guideline Companies for Most Recent Balance Sheet Date

Guideline Company	Market Value of Equity (Price)		Most Recent Book Value Per Share		Stock Price/ Book Value Multiple
AMCON Distributing Co.	$79,404,804	/	$66,696,240	=	1.19
Core-Mark Holding Co., Inc.	$1,998,448,000	/	$529,800,000	=	3.77
G. Willi-Food International Ltd.	$73,322,737	/	$101,591,150	=	0.72
SpartanNash Company	$1,486,348,140	/	$825,407,000	=	1.80
SUPERVALU Inc.	$1,237,549,907	/	($253,000,000)	=	NM
Sysco Corp.	$30,474,101,516	/	$2,554,944,000	=	11.93
United Natural Foods, Inc.	$2,414,584,280	/	$1,552,487,000	=	1.56
Central 50% – First Quartile					1.28
Central 50% – Third Quartile					3.28
Mean (Average)					3.49
Median (Second Quartile)					1.68

MVIC/Revenue Ratios of Guideline Companies for the Most Recent 12 Months

Guideline Company	Market Value of Invested Capital		Latest 12 Months Revenue Per Share		MVIC/ Revenue Multiple
AMCON Distributing Co.	$92,503,904	/	$902,921,200	=	0.10
Core-Mark Holding Co., Inc.	$2,384,048,000	/	$11,507,400,000	=	0.21
G. Willi-Food International Ltd.	$73,322,737	/	$76,439,930	=	0.96
SpartanNash Company	$1,917,447,140	/	$7,734,600,000	=	0.25
SUPERVALU Inc.	$3,787,549,907	/	$17,086,000,000	=	0.22
Sysco Corp.	$38,844,680,516	/	$53,076,604,000	=	0.73
United Natural Foods, Inc.	$3,012,164,280	/	$8,672,001,000	=	0.35
Central 50% – First Quartile					0.21
Central 50% – Third Quartile					0.54
Mean (Average)					0.40
Median (Second Quartile)					0.25

companies, an analysis using these multiples is more applicable to valuing a very large food distributor, such as Ken's Foods, as opposed to a smaller one, such as Pastene. The multiples of those companies that appear to be most similar to the target then should be reviewed relative to the overall range of multiples and the mean and median. The strengths and weaknesses of the target also should be compared with the guideline companies in assessing a multiple that would be appropriate for the target.

In selecting the multiple for the target, the goal is to choose a number that accurately positions the target relative to these alternative investment choices. If the target is approximately equivalent to the average of these choices, a multiple near the mean or median would be appropriate. Conversely, if the target is weaker than all of the choices, the multiple chosen for it should reflect this fact.

Remember that the multiples generated by the GPC method reflect prices paid by minority owners for marketable securities. If the multiples derived from this data are then used to determine the value of a controlling interest in a closely held company, which is usually the case, adjustments may be necessary to reflect differences, if any, in the degree of control and marketability of the interest in the target being acquired. When the multiple is applied to a control return for the target, a control, marketable value results.

This chapter began with a caution that the market approach produces multiples that often are applied incorrectly in estimating the value of a business. Caution is necessary because many times this data is misinterpreted. The market approach can, however, provide substantial information about prices and trends within an industry as of the appraisal date. The transaction method, which most likely generates a control, marketable value to a strategic buyer, often reveals prices that well-informed buyers are willing to pay for targets in their industry. The GPC method can reveal fair market value on a control or minority, marketable basis, reflecting the price paid by financial buyers. Successful use of both methods requires that adequate transactions in companies sufficiently similar to the target are available to constitute a market and that adequate data about those transactions can be obtained to permit a thorough analysis. In the process of gathering and analyzing this information, much useful information can be learned about what drives risk and value in that industry and in those companies. This information can be very helpful in assessing the target. The review of the market data should complement the competitive analysis of the target that has already been completed in the valuation process. Although the market approach must be used carefully to generate accurate estimates of value, it can be most illuminating and its use is strongly encouraged.

CHAPTER 11

Asset Approach

So far, discussion has heavily emphasized the value that can be created through strategic acquisitions. As a result of the synergies created by the combination of two companies, revenues may be enhanced, expenses may be reduced, and the companies can take advantage of other benefits that working together provides. The advantage is quantified by comparing the present value of the combined returns to those on a stand-alone basis, recognizing how risk changes in the process.

Not all targets are evaluated this way, however. Buyers sometimes make acquisitions primarily to achieve control of the assets owned by the target. Asset value also may be important in capital-intensive industries or in acquisitions where valuable nonoperating assets can be sold after the purchase of the company to recover some of the acquisition cost. Some targets are underperforming and generate little or no return. This absence of a return on a stand-alone basis means that the company's operations are generating no net cash flow and, therefore, no general intangible value. In the absence of general intangible value, the company's value on a stand-alone basis is derived from a hypothetical sale of its assets.

Thus the primary circumstances where the asset approach (sometimes referred to as the *cost approach*) would be used to value a business for merger and acquisition are when the buyer's primary goal is to acquire specific tangible or intangible assets or the target's value is limited to the total of specific tangible assets because its operations fail to generate adequate intangible value.

The asset approach may be applied by opportunistic buyers who look for owners who must sell under adverse circumstances. One classic example of this is the family business that is heavily reliant on a key individual – often the founder – who has become incapacitated or left the company and cannot be replaced. This unfortunate circumstance does not always occur in a quick or unexpected fashion. Owners may wait too long to groom successors or have unrealistic expectations about their children's ability or a reluctance to replace them. As time passes and the chosen successors are unavailable or prove to be incompetent, the chief executive officer may experience declining energy or health. Without this leadership, performance may drop suddenly, customers begin to lose faith and look elsewhere, and the company's intangible value quickly diminishes or disappears altogether.

Shrewd buyers, sometimes known as bottom fishers, look for these situations, particularly when they possess the key attributes that the target has just lost. In this case, on a stand-alone basis, the target frequently possesses only tangible asset value, and the owners must sell at a relatively low price.

This same result – little or no general intangible value – may occur in industries that are rapidly consolidating or those where excess capacity exists. The consolidation often is driven by economies of scale, new technologies, or changes in selling or distribution procedures that render smaller companies uncompetitive on a stand-alone basis. In these circumstances, even when a company operates at its maximum efficiency and serves its customers well, the business may possess no general intangible value – goodwill – because changing competitive conditions have eliminated its ability to compete as a stand-alone.

These conditions are common in business, particularly when management is not proactive in adjusting to changing competitive circumstances. Wise investors routinely monitor industry and company conditions to assess their ability to compete in the long term. When competitive circumstances put them at a disadvantage, they change operations or liquidate and seek investments that provide a better return. Failure to do this commonly results in a sale price based on asset value.

Book Value versus Market Value

Book value and *net book value* are accounting terms, which unfortunately include the word *value*. Book value, however, is rarely an indication of market value because it typically reflects the net undepreciated historical cost of assets as determined by accounting procedures. There is no attempt in the depreciation process to report assets at what they are actually worth, so it is typically unwise to assume that specific assets are worth the amount at which they are carried on the company's books. The market value of an asset is dependent on many factors, including the market of available substitutes, technological changes, and inflation. While some assets, such as vehicles, tend to decline rapidly in market value, others, such as real estate, often appreciate. For this reason, where asset values are a material influence on the outcome of a business valuation, it is generally advisable to have appraisals on the major assets involved.

Premises of Value

Asset or cost methods are conducted under either a *going-concern* or a *liquidation* premise. The going-concern premise assumes that the business will continue operating and the assets are appraised at their value "in use." Conversely, if it is assumed that the operations of the business will cease and a liquidation will occur, a liquidation premise is appropriate. Under the liquidation premise with an orderly liquidation value assumption, the assets are valued at the proceeds they can generate in a sale that includes a reasonable amount of time that allows the items to be sold piece by piece in pursuit of higher prices. Under a forced liquidation value assumption, the assets are valued under a forced sale circumstance, such as at an auction. Under either assumption, the costs involved to liquidate the business must be considered and subtracted in determining the net proceeds.

Use of the Asset Approach to Value Noncontrolling Interests

When the acquisition or sale of a noncontrolling (or minority) interest is considered, using the asset approach to determine value may be inappropriate. Because this approach determines value based on the hypothetical sale of the underlying assets, implicit is the assumption that the interest being appraised possesses the authority to cause a sale of those assets. Unless a legal agreement provides to the contrary, minority ownership interests generally cannot cause assets to be sold or the cash proceeds to be paid to the owners unless the controlling owner agrees. For the same reason, it is typically not appropriate to conclude that a pro rata portion of excess cash or other nonoperating assets is available to the minority shareholder, particularly if a control shareholder is present. The control shareholder can determine, first, if the assets are sold and, second, if the proceeds are to be distributed to shareholders.

Nonetheless, there are exceptions to avoidance of the asset approach when appraising a noncontrolling interest. In such instances, both a discount for lack of marketability and a discount for lack of control, discussed in Chapter 12, will likely be applicable.

One exception is in the valuation of holding companies. When the purpose of such an entity is to hold assets for appreciation, the return generated by the assets often is inadequate to produce an appropriate value under an income or market approach. These conditions commonly make the asset approach more appropriate because it is the assets owned by this type of business that attract the buyers in this marketplace.

Another exception is when some companies are in the midst of an economic or industry downturn. For example, the construction industry is often more adversely impacted by recessions than most, such that the indication of value from the expected future cash flow can be materially lower than that from the asset approach. In such instances, when considering both the willing buyer and the willing seller under the fair market value standard, the asset approach may be more appropriate. The adjusted book value, discussed next, would be applied where the tangible assets and working capital are marked to market and intangible assets, such as order backlog, would be added to determine equity value for that construction company.

Adjusted Book Value Method

Whether determining fair market value or liquidation value, the common procedure under an asset approach is to adjust the company's balance sheet accounts from book values based on accounting computations to market value. Doing so includes adding assets not on the balance sheet and deleting any on the balance sheet that lack market value. The adjustments to specific assets involve consideration of the next factors.

Cash

Cash generally does not require adjustment. The most common exception occurs when the cash position is either excessive or deficient.

Accounts Receivable

The relevant question to consider is whether 100% of the receivables are collectible. If not, the uncollectibles should be removed, based on these primary considerations:

- The company's history of collections as a percentage of total receivables
- A review of the aging of receivables
- The industry's ratio of bad debts to total receivables
- The company's credit-granting policies
- The state of the economy
- The status and outlook for the company's industry
- The status and outlook for the company's dominant customers, if any
- The status and outlook for the primary industry of the company's customers
- Whether the company delays commissions or other benefits to sales-people, manufacturers' representatives, or other sales agents pending collection of the receivables from the sales; if so, that portion is an expense that will reduce the asset value of the trade receivables.

Inventory

Depending on the industry – retail, wholesale, or manufacturing – the composition of a company's inventory will vary. In most instances it will be comprised of one or more of these categories:

- *Raw materials.* Materials purchased for use in production of the product but that have not yet been used in the manufacturing process. It could be valued under last in, first out (LIFO), first in, first out (FIFO), or average cost and may need to be adjusted to reflect shrinkage, obsolescence, or similar factors.
- *Work in progress.* Products or services that ultimately will be sold and on which process has begun but is not yet completed. The value should be equal to the accumulated cost as of the balance sheet date for raw materials, plus direct labor and applicable overhead. If any interruption in operations is anticipated, this inventory probably has a very low sale value.
- *Finished goods.* Assuming there is no reason to question the marketability of these completed products, value should be equal to total cost of production or cost to replace, without provision for profit.

Differences in inventory cost flow methods, LIFO, FIFO, or average cost frequently cause material effects on the income statement and the balance sheet and must be adjusted. When a company uses LIFO,[1] the notes to its financial statements provide the amount of the LIFO inventory reserve. If the company's statements do not have accompanying notes and it uses LIFO (a rare situation), the company's accountant should be able to provide the necessary information for adjusting the balance sheet to a FIFO basis. During periods of inflation, the FIFO inventory method records earlier, lower inventory costs on the income statement, which reduces cost of goods sold and increases gross profit and taxable income. This procedure leaves the more recent higher costs – those that most closely approximate current market value – in inventory on the balance sheet. Thus, the FIFO method tends to overstate income but produce a more realistic inventory. Conversely, the LIFO method charges the later, more inflated costs into cost of goods sold, which reduces gross profit and taxable income and produces a more realistic measure of income. Last in, first out leaves the earlier inventory costs – which are generally below current market value during a period of inflation – on the balance sheet, which leads to an unrealistically low inventory balance.

---

[1] LIFO is applicable only to companies reporting under U.S. Generally Accepted Accounting Principles (GAAP). LIFO is not permissible under International Financial Reporting Standards (IFRS).

The magnitude of the potential distortion depends on both the level of inflation and the rate of a company's inventory turnover. It is generally not advisable to compare a target company that uses a one-cost flow method for inventory to other companies before making necessary adjustments for differences created by these inventory accounting methods. Also note that adjustments to both the balance sheet and the income statement may require tax adjustments as well. Such adjustments can be accomplished either by creating a current liability, called deferred income tax, or by netting the tax against the increased value of the inventory on the balance sheet. Adjustments to the income statement should be tax affected as well.

Exhibit 11.1 illustrates a conversion from LIFO to FIFO inventory accounting when a company had a LIFO reserve of $335,000 at the beginning of the period and of $440,000 at the end of the period. The resulting increase in profit would be shown on the income statement, and both financial statements could be adjusted for the tax effects of these changes.

Prepaid Expenses

This account generally does not require adjustment as long as the buyer can acquire the benefits of the item purchased or receive a refund for the advanced payment.

Other Assets

Look at the composition for possible adjustment. Common examples of items that may require adjustment are marketable securities, cash surrender value of life insurance, other nonoperating assets, covenants not to compete or goodwill previously purchased, and notes receivable, particularly from the selling shareholders. If these items are not used in the company's operations, they should be removed from the balance sheet. Other items

EXHIBIT 11.1 LIFO to FIFO Inventory Valuation Conversion

Line Item	LIFO Basis	LIFO Reserve	FIFO Basis
Beginning Inventory	2,000,000	335,000	2,335,000
Add: Purchases	4,000,000		4,000,000
Available for Sale	6,000,000		6,335,000
Less: Ending Inventory	−400,000	−440,000	−840,000
Cost of Goods Sold	5,600,000		5,495,000
Increase in Profit			105,000

should be converted to market value based on the benefit that they provide to the company.

Fixed Assets

When fixed assets are written up to market value, consider recognizing the tax that would be due on the increased value. Considerations include:

- The tax, if it is applied, could be netted against the written-up value or shown as a deferred tax liability.
- Nontaxable entities, such as S corporations, face different levels of taxation.
- The level of the tax to be applied, recognizing that the well-informed seller and buyer, each realizing that trapped-in capital gains affect value, may negotiate some difference between the no-tax and the full-tax positions.
- As an alternative, the tax on the trapped-in gain could be reflected through an increased lack of marketability discount. This reflects the likely buyer's recognition that the fixed asset with lower book value provides less tax shelter and creates greater eventual taxable gain.

Intangible Assets

The intangibles on the balance sheet often are based on the allocated portion of cost from an acquisition or the costs to create. In either event the objective is to adjust them to their market value from their unamortized book value. If specific intangibles, such as patents, copyrights, or trademarks, possess value, this value could be determined using an income, market, or cost approach, as explained in Chapter 18, with the intangible then listed at that amount.

On the balance sheet, goodwill or general intangible value should be removed and replaced with its market value.

Nonrecurring and Nonoperating Assets and Liabilities

This category consists of nonrecurring activities or items not expected to recur. Nonoperating assets are assets not needed to maintain the anticipated levels of business activity. Examples could include one-time receipts or payments from litigation, gains or losses on sales of assets, cash in excess of that needed to fund anticipated operations, marketable securities, income from interest or dividends received on nonoperating cash, or investments or interest paid on nonoperating debt.

When appraising a control interest, nonoperating assets usually are added to the operating enterprise value to calculate the total enterprise value. When valuing a minority interest, this value may or may not be added back, recognizing that the minority interest may or may not have access to it.

Off-Balance Sheet Assets

Capital leases should be recorded on the balance sheet. They require adjustment only if the lease terms do not reflect market conditions. Operating leases are not shown on the balance sheet but may require adjustment to the lease expense on the income statement if the lease is not carried at a market rate.

Warranty obligations are another significant type of asset (dealer) or liability (manufacturer or service provider) that will be off-balance-sheet in many companies. Discussion with management, manufacturers, and industry data sources can often assist in the quantification of these items.

Although there are usually few adjustments, the liability section of the balance sheet requires scrutiny. Common liability adjustments include:

- *Asset-related liabilities.* Liabilities related to assets that were adjusted also may require adjustment. For example, if real property was removed as an asset, any related liability (or liabilities) also may need to be removed. If later, at the total enterprise level, the value of the real property is added to the operating value (which was developed using a market-rate rent), the related debt can be netted against that real estate value.
- *Interest-bearing debt.* If the interest charged on a note payable is a fixed rate that is materially different from the market rate on the valuation date, the debt should be adjusted. This process is similar to the adjustment to determine the market value of a bond with a fixed rate of interest when market rates of interest are significantly different.
- *Accruals.* Often accruals for vacation, sick time, and unfunded pension or profit-sharing plans and the effects of exercise of employee stock options are not on the balance sheet but are obligations at the time of the valuation and should be recorded.
- *Deferred taxes.* Based on the treatment of the deferred tax due on assets written up from book to market values, a deferred tax liability may be appropriate.
- *Off-balance sheet liabilities.* Common unrecorded items, particularly in closely held companies, include guarantee or warranty obligations, pending litigation, or other disputes, such as taxes and employee claims, or environmental or other regulatory issues. These liabilities are generally assessed and quantified through discussions with management and

legal counsel. It is also useful to inquire as to whether the company has made commitments to purchase quantities of raw material from specific suppliers over a future period or made guarantees or cosigned for obligations of other companies or individuals.

Generally speaking, the adjustment to the equity section is only to bring the statement into balance by netting the adjustments to the assets and liabilities sections. Most often these adjustments are made to retained earnings. Another adjustment often made is to eliminate any treasury stock so that the statement reflects only the issued and outstanding shares.

Treatment of Nonoperating Assets or Asset Surpluses or Shortages

When the operating value of a target is determined by an application of the income approach or market approach, adjustments for the value of specific assets owned by the target may be necessary to determine the total value of the entity being appraised. This situation occurs most frequently when a target owns assets not used in its operations, has excess operating assets such as surplus cash or fixed assets, or has an asset shortage such as a deficient level of working capital. When any of these conditions is present, the operating value determined by the income or market approach probably will not reflect the effect on value of these factors, and they must then be treated as an adjustment to the preliminary determination of operating value.

In the negotiation process, either the buyer or the seller may be unwilling to have the nonoperating assets or excess assets included in the transaction. When this happens, adjustments to value for these items must be made. Depending on the circumstances, these adjustments may reflect the specific sale terms that are negotiated and the price the buyer is willing to pay under those terms rather than the specific value.

Specific Steps in Computing Adjusted Book Value

The application of the adjusted book value method under a going-concern premise is most commonly referred to as the *adjusted book value method* and involves these five steps:

1. *Beginning point.* Obtain the target's balance sheet as of the appraisal date or as recently before that date as possible. (Audited financial statements are preferable to reviewed or compiled statements, and accrual basis statements are preferable to cash basis.)

2. *Adjust line items.* Adjust each asset, liability, and equity account from book value to estimated market value.
3. *Adjust for items not on the balance sheet.* Value and add specific tangible or intangible assets and liabilities that were not listed on the balance sheet.
4. *Tax affecting.* Consider the appropriateness of tax affecting the adjustments to the balance sheet. Also consider whether any deferred taxes on the balance sheet should be eliminated.
5. *Ending point.* From the adjustments, prepare a balance sheet that reflects all items at market value. From this amount, determine the adjusted value of invested capital or equity, as appropriate.

Asset-intensive targets or companies that lack operating value because they generate inadequate returns are frequently valued by the asset or cost approach. This approach usually is appropriate only for appraisal of controlling interests that possess the authority to cause the sale that creates the cash benefit to shareholders. Whether using the adjusted book value method to determine the value of the assets in use or liquidation value to determine their worth under either orderly or forced liquidation conditions, this approach involves adjusting balance sheet accounts to market value. These adjustment procedures also are used to reflect the value of nonoperating assets or asset surpluses or shortages that may exist in companies whose operating value is determined by an income or market approach.

CHAPTER 12

Adjusting Value through Premiums and Discounts

Sit back and take a deep breath before applying a premium or discount. Although these valuation adjustments are not typically seen in an investment value setting involving synergistic buyers of entire companies, they are very applicable under the fair market value standard. And since buyers and sellers should understand the fair market value of 100% of the target company on a control basis (and the fair market value of any applicable lack of control interests that individual investors may own), they clearly benefit from an understanding of premiums and discounts. When applied, these adjustments often have a larger impact on value than any other adjustment made, so they should receive careful consideration. These adjustments are not made automatically and should not always be at a constant percentage. Care at the beginning of this process is often rewarded with time saved and a better value estimate.

This care begins with terminology because in the application of premiums and discounts, various terms, particularly minority and control, are often misused. *Control* describes an interest, whether minority or control, that possesses a material degree of control. A control interest is not always a majority interest, and a minority interest may possess control, depending on the presence or absence of rights of various ownership interests. *Minority* describes an interest, whether minority or majority, that lacks a material degree of control. Therefore, to avoid any confusion, we will use the term *noncontrolling* rather than *minority*. Ownership of less than 50% of the outstanding shares of stock does not always constitute lack of control; this could be the case if the majority interest owned nonvoting stock.

Applicability of Premiums and Discounts

Each valuation method or procedure may generate different characteristics of value. The transaction multiple method typically results in a control marketable value while the guideline public company method may generate a control or noncontrolling marketable value. The income approach can generate a control or noncontrolling value, each of which probably carries different levels of marketability, and the asset approach most commonly generates a control marketable value. Consequently, premiums and discounts must be considered for each value indicated because adjustments that are appropriate for one indicated value may not apply to another. This point is emphasized because a common error in business valuation is to assume that a discount or a premium is required based on the characteristics of the company being appraised. For example, if the target company is a closely held business in which a controlling interest is being acquired, do not automatically assume that a control premium and a discount for lack of marketability must be applied to each value determined for the company.

The correct methodology is to identify the nature of the value initially computed by each appraisal method. This value is then compared to the characteristics of the subject company to determine what adjustments, if any, are required. The applicability of adjustments for control or lack of control can be determined by answering this question for each valuation method: Was the degree of control implicit in the valuation method the same or different from the degree of control inherent in the interest being valued?

If the degrees of control are different, a premium for control or a discount for lack of control may be required. For example, the transaction multiple method implies a degree of control approximately equivalent to the degree inherent in the acquisition of a 100% interest in a business. If this data is used to appraise a comparable ownership interest, no discount or premium is required because the method produces a value that reflects a degree of control appropriate to the interest being valued. If the characteristics of the value initially determined are different from the interest being appraised, then a premium for control or a discount for lack of control may be required to determine the appropriate value.

After the issue of control versus lack of control is determined, the degree of marketability must be considered. Although the degree of marketability is distinct from the degree of control, they are related, and marketability is influenced by control. Therefore, the adjustment, if any, for the degree of marketability should be made *after* the adjustment for control. Similar to the process just applied, determine the need for an adjustment for marketability by asking this question: Is the degree of marketability that is implied in the method employed to compute the initial indication of value the same or different from the degree of marketability inherent in the interest being valued?

For example, if the guideline public company method generates an initial indication of value on a noncontrolling marketable basis and a noncontrolling interest in a closely held company is being appraised, a discount for lack of marketability is warranted. Conversely, if the transaction multiple method generates a control marketable value and the interest being appraised possesses those characteristics, no adjustment for lack of marketability would be required.

In summary, to begin the process of application of premiums and discounts, identify the nature of each value initially determined in terms of its degree of control and marketability. Then compare each result to those characteristics of the ownership interest in the target company to determine if any adjustments must be made to the initial indication of value of that method.

Application and Derivation of Premiums and Discounts

The degree of control inherent in an ownership interest can affect its degree of marketability. Therefore, control premiums or discounts for lack of control are imposed prior to adjustments for the degree of marketability. Further, these adjustments are applied in a multiplicative, rather than additive, procedure. For example, if a discount for lack of control (DLOC) of 20% and a discount for lack of marketability (DLOM) of 35% are to be applied to a control marketable value initially determined to be $10 million, these adjustments would be applied:

Control, marketable value initially determined	$10,000,000
Application of DLOC of 20%	(1–20%)
	$8,000,000
Application of DLOM of 35%	(1–35%)
Noncontrolling, marketable value	$5,200,000

Control Premiums

A control premium is imposed to reflect the increase in value that is provided through the benefits of control when the initial indication of value does not reflect this capacity. This is also referred to as a *market participant acquisition premium* (MPAP).[1]

Control premiums are derived from studies, conducted annually in the United States, of acquisitions of controlling interests in public companies as compared to their preannouncement stock trading prices (which are on

---

[1] For a thorough analysis on the application of the MPAP, see The Appraisal Foundation's Valuation for Financial Reporting (VFR) Advisory #3 on the market participant acquisition premium.

a noncontrolling basis). Since the publicly traded entities involved must report the results of the transactions to the U.S. Securities and Exchange Commission (SEC), they are available for analysis and review. Another source of empirical evidence comes from prices at which holding company interests (i.e. closed-end mutual funds, real estate investment trusts, and SEC-registered limited partnership interests) sell compared with their underlying net asset values.[2]

In valuation for M&A, it is important to note that the use of control premiums paid in other transactions should be done with extreme care by a buyer, who could risk overpaying for a company as a result. No two transactions are alike and there is a wide range of premiums.

Discount for Lack of Control

A DLOC can be derived from the control premium data; no source of data from the public security markets enables direct computation of a DLOC. The DLOC reflects the diminution in value caused by the lack of control. This discount can be applied either to a minority interest or to a majority interest that lacks some degree of control. It is applied when the initial indication of value reflects control but the ownership interest being appraised lacks control.

Discount for Lack of Marketability

The DLOM reflects the diminution in value resulting from the inability to promptly convert an ownership interest into cash.

It also results from market data, much of which is thought to provide a more accurate indication of this value adjustment than the market data used to suggest the control premiums. The most common source of DLOM percentages is restricted stock studies. Restricted stock, which is also known as letter stock or Rule 144 stock, is stock issued by a corporation that is either not registered with the SEC (and so cannot be sold into the public market) or is SEC-registered stock that is restricted from being sold into the public market. These studies, which have been conducted by various organizations over the past 40 years, have analyzed the prices paid for securities of publicly traded companies that are otherwise marketable except for a restriction that prevents their sale for a limited period of time. The restrictions prevent the securities from being traded in transactions on the open market but allow them to be sold in private transactions. The buyer in these transactions, however, is still subject to the restriction, and

---

[2] For further information on how to derive control premiums and discounts for lack of control and marketability, the reader is encouraged to refer to Shannon P. Pratt, *Business Valuation Discounts and Premiums*, 2nd ed. (Hoboken, NJ: Wiley, 2009).

therefore is willing to pay only a discounted price to acquire a security that cannot be immediately converted into cash. The holding period of the restriction varies by transaction but before 1997 typically did not exceed 24 months. Beginning in 1997, the holding period for certain restricted securities was reduced to 12 months. Beginning in 2008, this holding period was reduced to 6 months. Initial studies of this reduced restriction period indicate that the discounts for lack of marketability have declined with the shorter required holding period and increased market activity in these shares. The results of the restricted stock studies indicate a typical discount of approximately 35% during the 1990s. Thus, non-controlling ownership interests in shares of stock of publicly traded corporations, which were only temporarily restricted from being sold on the open market for a fixed period, suffered a reduction in value of about one-third due to this lack of marketability. This fact indicates the market's strong demand for liquidity and the substantial reduction in value that occurs as liquidity declines.

Application of Premiums and Discounts

A quantitative way to determine a DLOM is to use the Black–Scholes Option Pricing Model to calculate the cost of structuring a hypothetical risk-free sale through the use of put options.[3] This method, which relies on the cost of a put option as a proxy for a discount for lack of marketability, reflects the theoretical cost of ensuring that the shares may be sold at no less than their current value when liquidity is achieved. In doing so, it enables one to determine in a quantitative manner a DLOM as a check to the DLOM as estimated by the empirical studies.

Apply Discretion in the Size of the Adjustment

Although there is a natural inclination to view the market data presented as absolutes, premiums and discounts should not be applied on an on-or-off basis as if one was turning a light on or off. Instead, these adjustments should

---

[3] For further discussion on this methodology, see: (1) David B. H. Chaffe III, "Option Pricing as a Proxy for Discount for Lack of Marketability in Private Company Valuations – A Working Paper," *Business Valuation Review* 12, no. 4 (December 1993): 182–188; (2) John D. Finnerty, "An Average-Strike Put Option Model of the Marketability Discount," *The Journal of Derivatives* (Summer 2012): 53–69; (3) Z. Christopher Mercer, *Quantifying Marketability Discounts* (Memphis, TN: Peabody Publishing, 1997), pp. 403 – 414; (4) Aswath Damodaran, *Investment Valuation*, 3rd ed. (Hoboken, NJ: Wiley, 2012), pp. 683–688; (5) Frank K. Reilly and Keith C. Brown, *Investment Analysis and Portfolio Management*, 5th ed. (Fort Worth, TX: Dryden Press), pp. 347–354.

be applied like a dimmer switch that allows the light to be gradually raised or lowered depending on the circumstances. Discounts or premiums must be applied in recognition of the specific facts and circumstances, which could cause the adjustment to be smaller or larger. For example, a 40% shareholder in a company where the remaining 60% of the shares are owned by one other shareholder possesses less control and influence than would be the case if that same 40% interest shared ownership with many shareholders, none of whom owns greater than a 1% interest. Both circumstances featured a 40% ownership interest, yet the relative degree of control of these interests would be vastly different.

Furthermore, consider the influence possessed by the 2% shareholder when the other 98% of the stock is owned by a single shareholder. Then consider the influence of the 2% shareholder when the remaining 98% is held equally in two 49% ownership blocks. In this case, the 2% shareholder becomes the swing vote, which in spite of its very small ownership can wield substantial influence. These examples reinforce the need to consider the specific factors listed in Exhibit 12.1 that could affect the size of the premium or discount. Once again, appropriate application of these adjustments requires judgments that require experience and an understanding of the underlying market data.

EXHIBIT 12.1 Specific Company Factors that Can Affect the Size of Adjustments

Factors that Affect the Degree of Control

- Effect of stock ownership structure on ability of non-controlling owners to approve certain corporate actions, determine management compensation and perquisites, and set operational and strategic policy and change the course of business
- Effect of stock ownership structure on ability of non-controlling owners to influence selection of members of the board of directors
- Effect of stock ownership pattern that provides "swing vote" influence
- Level of legal protection to non-controlling shareholders in that jurisdiction
- Stock that lacks voting rights
- Ability to declare and pay cash and/or stock dividends
- History of consideration of non-controlling shareholder interest

Factors that Affect the Degree of Marketability

- Presence of restrictions on the transferability of shares of stock
- Presence of buy/sell agreement that hampers transferability of shares
- Existence of a "put" right that allows a shareholder to sell shares to the company at a previously agreed upon price if conditions of the put right are met.
- Degree of attractiveness of the block of stock
- History and intent of dividend payments that are relatively small or large
- Presence of a reasonably organized market for sales of companies in that industry
- Presence of consolidation or pressures to consolidate in that industry
- Likely population of buyers of that size interest in that industry

Control versus Lack of Control in Income-Driven Methods

In Chapter 6, adjustments to income were discussed, including those made for payments of above-market compensation to shareholders. Known as control adjustments, generally speaking, these should be made *only* when the ownership interest possesses the legal authority to implement these control adjustments. These control-type adjustments may be less significant in larger transactions because the adjustment is not material to the company's resulting income or cash flow. For smaller companies, however, control adjustments can have a substantial effect on value. It is generally inappropriate to reflect control or noncontrolling adjustments to value through application of a premium or discount. Instead, the difference in value on a control versus lack-of-control basis should be reflected through adjustments to the return – income or cash flow – rather than through application of a premium or discount. This is illustrated in Exhibit 12.2, where a company had net income before excess compensation of $5 million. In choosing to pay excess compensation of $1 million to control shareholders or their beneficiaries, an implied discount for lack of control of 20% resulted. If, however, the company had chosen to pay excess compensation of $3 million, the reduction from control value would have been 60%. Thus the magnitude of the discount is determined by the relative size of the excess compensation. When this compensation constitutes a significant portion of the company's income before compensation, major differences between the control versus lack-of-control value can result.

Because market data on control premiums and implied discount for lack of control cannot accurately reflect the variations caused by the different levels of excess compensation, in income-driven methods the differences in control versus lack of control should be computed by adjusting the return, as shown in Exhibit 12.2, rather than through imposition of a control premium to a lack-of-control value or discount for lack of control to a control value.

Fair Market Value versus Investment Value

Some of these discounts that may apply when determining the target's stand-alone fair market value may not be applicable when determining the investment value relevant to a specific acquirer. For example, the DLOM, which is appropriate for the stand-alone value of a private target, may be inappropriate for investment value when the acquirer is a public company.

Premiums and discounts can constitute the largest adjustment to value made in a business valuation. While these adjustments tend to be less prominent in valuations for M&A than they are for estate and gift-tax purposes, they still require careful consideration. This process begins by identifying the

EXHIBIT 12.2 Computation of Control and Lack-of-Control Values through Adjustment to the Return

	Lower Excess Compensation	Higher Excess Compensation
	In millions	
Net Income before Excess Compensation (control return)	$5	$5
Less: Excess Compensation[a]	−1	−3
Net Income after Excess Compensation	$4	$2
Computation of Control Value[b]	$\dfrac{\$5}{20\%} = \$25$	$\dfrac{\$5}{20\%} = \$25$
Computation of Lack of Control Value[b]	$\dfrac{\$5}{20\%} = \$25$	$\dfrac{\$2}{20\%} = \$10$
Resulting Implied Lack of Control Discount	$\dfrac{\$25 - \$20}{\$25} = 20\%$	$\dfrac{\$25 - \$10}{\$25} = 60\%$

[a]Excess compensation includes many types of control adjustments including salary, bonuses, fringe benefits, payments to favored parties, and other forms exercised by the control shareholder.
[b]Assumes use of single-period capitalization method and 20% capitalization rate.

nature of the value initially determined by each valuation method to assess whether application of a premium or a discount is appropriate. Determination of the appropriate size of the adjustment requires an understanding of the market data from which the premium and discount benchmarks are derived. These benchmarks do not constitute definitive percentage adjustments; rather, the facts and circumstances of the interest being appraised must be evaluated to determine the size of the adjustment. Ultimately, this is a professional judgment, but with background and experience, analysts can make defendable adjustments.

CHAPTER 13

Reconciling Initial Value Estimates and Determining Value Conclusion

Once an appraiser has applied one or more valuation approaches and reached an initial conclusion of value, the inevitable question is, "Is it correct?" That is, is the value that has been determined for the ownership interest reasonable and defendable based on conditions as of the valuation date and the quality and quantity of information available?

Because there are many qualitative assessments and quantitative steps leading to the initial indications of value, the review and reconciliation process should be both thorough and methodical. Business valuation involves many computations, and most of the calculations made later in the process are dependent on the accuracy of previous numbers. So accuracy is essential, and sound work habits include review of all computations.

Reaching the final value conclusion by accepting the initial estimate or by averaging the different results of several methods does not ensure a defendable conclusion. The key to a sound result is a comprehensive review that challenges the underlying assumptions, methods, information, and calculations of each process employed.

Essential Need for Broad Perspective

Begin with the basics. Review the appraisal assignment by answering these questions:

- What property or ownership interest is being appraised? Was it specific assets, an equity interest, or invested capital?
- What specific legal rights or limits are attached to this property?
- Do other ownership interests exist that possess preferential claims on this property or its returns?

- Does this ownership interest reflect control or lack of control?
- What is the degree of marketability of the ownership interest?
- What is the date of the appraisal, and did the analysis include only information about the company and its external environment that was known or knowable as of that date?
- Was the standard of value fair market value on a stand-alone basis to a financial buyer without consideration of synergies, or investment value to a strategic buyer inclusive of synergies, or both? Or was it some other standard of value?

Whenever possible, all three valuation approaches – income, market, and asset – should be considered to determine an estimate of value. One or more of these approaches may be inappropriate or less appropriate because of the nature of the assignment or of the subject company, or the quality or quantity of information that is available. As a result, it is quite common that one approach is used as the indicator of value and the others are used as a check to value. Each approach computes value based on different criteria. The income approach bases value on expected future returns, which are discounted or capitalized at a rate of return that reflects a relative level of risk. The guideline public company and transaction multiple methods of the market approach base value on prices paid for equity interests in guideline companies in public markets in the case of the former, and prices paid for guideline companies in arm's-length transactions in the case of the latter. The asset approach derives value from the underlying assets owned by the business considering a hypothetical sale. Thus, each of the approaches takes a different view of the target with each view providing a unique perspective on what drives value. Analysts should attempt to use each approach or be prepared to provide an explanation of why any approach is rejected.

Once initial values are determined, often it is helpful to step away from the details of the assignment and then return to take a fresh look at the conclusions. In reviewing the work, ask whether a reasonable, unbiased individual would reach the same conclusions of value. Examine to be sure the conclusions are not influenced by a desire for a high or low value. Consider whether the value recognizes the company's history; its competitive environment, including industry and economic conditions; its internal strengths and weaknesses; and likely future conditions. If synergies are considered, be sure they are recognized only when computing investment value, not fair market value. Evaluate whether the estimate of value considers appropriate buyer and seller knowledge of market considerations and motivations in the transactions. Ask whether both the buyer and the seller, in possession of the relevant facts, would accept the assumptions as reasonable.

In making this assessment, consider further the general applicability of each appraisal approach to this assignment. Use the summaries in Exhibit 13.1 to assess whether an approach is appropriate.

Consider the applicability of each approach in light of the competitive assessment of the company. Pay particular attention to what drives risk and value in that company and in that industry and how each approach considers these key variables. Identify any risk or value drivers that may have been

EXHIBIT 13.1 Summary of Applicability of Business Valuation Approaches

Income Approach	Market Approach[a]	Asset Approach
Company derives significant value from its operations.	An adequate number of companies are reasonably similar to the subject company.	Company owns a significant amount of tangible (fixed) assets.
Company generates a positive income or cash flow.	M&A transactions involve acquirer circumstances and targets that are reasonably similar.	Company creates little value from its operations.
Company possesses significant intangible value.	There is adequate data available about the companies used for comparative purposes.	Company's balance sheet includes most of its tangible assets.
Company's risk can be quantified accurately through a rate of return.	Companies generate multiples that provide a reasonable indication of market conditions and prices as of the valuation date.	It is possible to obtain accurate appraisals of the company's tangible assets.
Company's future performance can be reasonably estimated through a forecast.	Subject company is large enough to be compared to the companies used in the market approach.	Ownership interest being appraised possesses control or access to the underlying asset value.
Company has distinctive products, services, or processes that might indicate intangible value	Company is sufficiently profitable to make earnings multiples meaningful.	Company depends heavily on competitive contract bids, and there is no consistent or predicable customer base.

[a]This discussion of the market approach refers only to applications of the guideline public company and transaction multiple methods.

overlooked or not given appropriate consideration by an approach and the resulting effect of this on any of the values determined.

When the value conclusion clashes with the rule of thumb for that industry, determine the reason. Doing so will provide guidance as to whether the value opinion needs to change (less likely) or why the rule of thumb does not work for this specific appraisal (more likely). Also take into account whether rules of thumb are commonly employed in that industry and whether they have been considered. Because rules of thumb are often simplistic generalizations that fail to adequately address factors unique to a company, they should not be used as the sole method of estimating value. If, however, they are widely recognized in that industry, they should at least be computed as a reasonableness check against the primary approaches to value. Industry participants frequently refer to these metrics, so it is wise for the appraisal to consider and discuss their applicability and reasonableness.

In application of the income or market approaches, evaluate any adjustments made to the return employed and whether these adjustments were reasonable and appropriate. In doing so, again recognize that synergies should be considered only in computing investment value. Further, recognize that the income and market approaches, which determine value based on a measure of the company's performance, are heavily dependent on the reasonableness of that performance estimate. So the performance should be reviewed once again in light of the company's competitive environment. To achieve a rigorous review of the work, employ these critiques – income, market, and asset approach reviews – to the results of each approach, considering the matters in an unbiased manner.

Income Approach Review

The income approach is often used in business valuation for M&A because of its theoretical strengths and flexibility. Investors recognize the theoretical soundness of basing value on future returns discounted at a rate that reflects their relative level of risk. In addition to being grounded in sound theory, the income approach easily accommodates computation of fair market value or investment value, using an equity or invested capital model on a control or lack-of-control basis with consideration of the appropriate degree of marketability. It can employ historical or forecasted returns and can measure the return as various amounts of income or cash flow.

For the income approach to be appropriate, the company's value should be heavily influenced by its income or cash flow. This is usually the case for profitable operating businesses, and this approach may not be appropriate for companies that generate low returns. As such, the review should focus on the two key variables used to compute value: the return (e.g. cash flows or earnings) and the rate of return (e.g. discount rate).

For a comprehensive review of the value determined by the income approach, *objectively* assess these areas:

Fair Market Value versus Investment Value

- The return and rate of return chosen to compute the company's fair market value should reflect its operating performance and risk profile as a stand-alone company.
- The investment value should consider the effects of synergies on return. The rate of return should reflect the acquiring company's risk profile and resulting cost of capital, adjusted for the risk profile of the target company.

Invested Capital versus Equity

- Consider that valuation for M&A usually employs the invested capital model to prevent financing considerations from influencing operating value. Proper application requires appropriate and consistent use of invested capital returns and rates of return.
- In use of the invested capital model, look for potential distortions to the company's weighted average cost of capital (WACC) caused by extremes in the company's degree of financial leverage. Consider whether market conditions would permit that capital structure and what debt and equity costs would be appropriate for that degree of leverage.
- Recognize that the debt and equity weights in the WACC computation should be made based on market values rather than book values, which may require use of the iterative process or the shortcut formula in the computation of the WACC.

Measurement of Return

- Consider the appropriateness of the return stream chosen for the assignment. Net cash flow to invested capital generally provides the most precise measure of cash return to capital providers, and it is the return for which the most reliable rates of return are available. Other measures of return are generally less accurate, are more susceptible to manipulation, and usually must rely on less defendable rates of return.
- Consider the company's past operating performance and why it generated that performance in assessing the likelihood of it achieving its forecasted future performance.
- Consider the likelihood of achieving the forecast, given economic and industry conditions and the company's competitive position in light of its strategic advantages and disadvantages.

- Review any normalization adjustments made for nonoperating and non-recurring items of income and expense, recognizing that the objective in making the adjustments is to present the most accurate possible portrayal of the company's future operating performance. Also review any adjustments to income for above- or below-market compensation paid in any form to owners or their beneficiaries. Generally speaking, these adjustments are usually appropriate only when appraising a controlling ownership interest that possesses the authority to change this compensation.
- In reviewing the company's forecasted volume, consider pricing and unit volumes, by products and product lines, given economic and industry conditions.
- Given forecasted economic and industry conditions, consider the reasonableness of forecasted expenses and resulting profit margins.
- Review the company's tax attributes as of the valuation date and the reasonableness of estimated future tax rates, given its legal and tax status and the tax jurisdictions in which it operates.
- Review for reasonableness the forecasted level of change in working capital and investment in fixed assets. Where possible, review forecasted turnover ratios of accounts receivable, accounts payable, inventory, and fixed assets as part of this assessment, and compare this to both historical performance and industry standards.
- In choosing the long-term growth rate for use in the single-period capitalization method or the terminal value in the DCF method, consider:
  - The long-term economic and industry outlook.
  - The company's current competitive condition and the likely duration of its competitive advantages and disadvantages.
  - The company's profits, management capabilities, and sources of financing to fund that pace of growth.
  - Remember that choice of a growth rate above the forecasted industry growth rate implies that the company will be able to gain market share indefinitely.
- If the DCF method is employed, assess the reasonableness of the length of the forecast period, which should be long enough to reflect all anticipated material changes in cash flows and should achieve a stabilized return in the final forecast year that is considered to be sustainable in the long term.
- When the potential exists for substantial variation in the company's future return, consider the use of probability analysis (see Chapter 6) to reflect the effect of this variation on value.

Choice of Rate of Return

- Check for the compatibility of the rate with the return used to measure performance. Common areas where the return or the rate of return are misapplied include:
  - Equity versus invested capital elements
  - Pretax versus after-tax returns
  - Net cash flow versus net income
- Consider the appropriateness of the methodology in arriving at the equity discount rate:
  - The capital asset pricing model (CAPM) is typically not appropriate in the appraisal of a lower middle market closely held company because its underlying assumptions seldom apply to such companies.
  - The modified capital asset pricing model (MCAPM) overcomes many of these limitations when a beta for the target company can be derived from an appropriate list of guideline companies, and specific-company risk is factored in. When the guideline public company method is used within the market approach, MCAPM may work in the income approach.
  - The build-up method, with its assumption of a beta of 1, is generally most appropriate to appraise a lower middle market closely held company, particularly businesses where the guideline public company method was rejected, given the addition of a specific-company risk premium that includes any industry-related risk.
- Consider whether the size premium recognized is appropriate for the subject company.
- Consider whether the discount rate accurately reflects risk within the industry, either through choice of the beta or the specific company risk premium.
- Consider whether the discount rate reflects specific company risk factors recognized in the competitive analysis. This rate also should reflect the primary risk drivers and value drivers influencing the company's performance and the company's relative level of strategic advantages and disadvantages.

Single-Period Capitalization Method

- Consider that for this method to be appropriate, the single-period return chosen should accurately represent the company's expected long-term annual performance.

- Consider also that this method assumes that return will grow at a constant rate into perpetuity and that this long-term growth rate must be reasonable, given the company's competitive position and long-term economic and industry conditions.

Control versus Lack-of-Control Value

- Consider that in an income approach, the major factor that determines the difference in value on a control versus lack-of-control basis is the choice of the return stream.
- Generally speaking, normalization adjustments for above-market compensation in any form paid to owner employees or their beneficiaries should not be made when valuing interests that lack the authority to institute these changes.
- The distinction between control and lack-of-control value may be less clear when above-market compensation is not paid and the return to the controlling and minority shareholders is approximately the same. However, this is likely to be reflected in the application of any appropriate premiums or discounts.
- Recognize the limitations in the accuracy and appropriateness of employing control premiums or minority interest discounts. Also recognize the theoretical limitations of data from which these adjustments are derived.

Degree of Marketability

- Recognize that controlling ownership interests generally possess substantially more marketability than minority interests and that discounts for lack of marketability for controlling interests, when applicable, are typically in the range of 5 to 15%. This range often reflects the time and transaction costs required for the buyer to resell that controlling interest, but application of this is arguable.
- Recognize that minority interests in closely held companies are highly unmarketable and subject to discounts that are typically at least 25 to 40%.
- Recognize that the degree of control or marketability can be influenced by numerous factors unique to the subject company and that the resulting discounts or premiums will vary in size depending on these factors.

Other Adjustments to Value

- Consider that nonoperating items of value excluded in the computation of the company's operating value may have to be added to operating enterprise value to compute the total value of the enterprise.

- Consider that the value of nonoperating assets may not be added back in the computation of the value of a noncontrolling interest that lacks the authority to liquidate these assets. Conversely, the presence of substantial liquid nonoperating assets could improve the liquidity and safety of a noncontrolling interest; when that occurs, the discount rate should reflect this financial characteristic. This is also the case where the business owns a substantial amount of real estate, which is typically characterized as being a less risky asset than an equity interest in a private company.

Market Approach Review

Values determined by the market approach also require careful review. Because the market approach primarily determines value as a multiple of some measure of operating performance or financial position (e.g. EBITDA, net income, or revenues), these two variables – the performance measure and the multiple – require close scrutiny in assessing the accuracy of the results of this method.

In reviewing the accuracy and reasonableness of the market approach and the multiples chosen for the target:

- Consider how similar the guideline public companies are to the subject company in terms of these factors:
  - Size
  - Products or services, and their breadth
  - Markets and customers
  - Competition
  - Management depth
  - Financial performance
  - Financial leverage and liquidity
  - Access to capital
  - Customer concentration
  - Vendor or supplier reliance
  - Technology and research and development capability
  - Quality and capacity of physical plant
  - Accuracy of financial information and internal controls
- Review whether the multiples for the guideline companies in the current year are consistent with longer-term trends, or if the market appears to be abnormally high or low as of the valuation date.
- Consider whether the anticipated future conditions are similar to the past and what the likelihood is that any differences are reflected accurately in the multiples of the guideline companies for the current period.

- Consider how the target company compares to the guideline companies in terms of major performance characteristics, including:
  - Growth
  - Profitability
  - Efficiency in asset utilization
  - Financial leverage and coverage
  - Liquidity
- Consider the range (often a central 50%), mean, and median multiples of the guideline companies, to which of the guidelines the target is most and least similar, and whether the target company is stronger or weaker than all of the guidelines, and why.
- When applying transaction data from other M&A, take into account what was included in each transaction. While data from public company multiples involves stock transactions, data from private transactions, particularly smaller ones, is often asset sales. If the transaction is an asset sale and stock is being valued, adjustments must be made for those transactions. In some cases, this will involve adding back all current assets and subtracting out current liabilities. In others, it may involve adding back all current assets with the exception of inventory. In the end, if the transaction is an asset sale and you are valuing stock, that transaction needs to reconcile to a stock value.
- Consider the timing of the transactions being used as a benchmark. For example, given the higher valuations and greater access to financing that existed in 2007, transaction data from that time period is likely to be irrelevant to a company being valued in the beginning of 2009, when a recession was in full swing. In a recession, even if data from more recent transactions is available, the transactions may be distressed sales that do not provide an accurate representation of a healthy company's value.

Asset Approach Review

Because the asset approach does not adequately recognize the profitability of a business, it is frequently inappropriate in the appraisal of profitable companies. This method is used most often in the appraisal of asset-intensive companies or underperforming businesses that do not generate an adequate return on capital employed.

In assessing the results of the asset approach:

- Consider whether the value determined is under a going-concern premise or a premise of liquidation. The liquidation premise assumes the company will cease operations, which generally renders use of the income or the market approach to be unreasonable.

- Consider whether the interest being appraised possesses the legal authority to execute a sale of assets. Because noncontrolling interests typically lack this capacity, the asset approach is seldom appropriate to appraise a minority interest of an operating company.
- Consider whether the company's value is derived primarily from ownership of its assets rather than from the results of its operations. This condition would support use of the asset approach.
- Consider the quality and reliability of the asset appraisals or other means under which the net asset value was determined. Although an asset approach may be an appropriate choice, its reliability is dependent on accurate asset valuations.
- Consider the intangible assets owned by the company. If they are not identified and valued, the asset approach will likely result in an understatement of value.
- Consider whether any of the target company's assets are carried on its balance sheet at a low tax basis, which could subject a buyer to a potential built-in gains tax on a subsequent sale.

Some Quick Checks to Make When Values from the Income Approach and the Market Approach Disagree

The market approach generally should produce a value that supports the results from the income approach. When they disagree, consider these issues:

- If appraising a control interest, as is most common in valuations for M&A, check to see that the results of both methods reflect this fact. Do the approaches use substantially different measures of return on a control basis? If one approach computes value based on a minority return and applies a control premium, while the other reflects control through the use of a control return, what differences or distortions do these techniques cause?
- While the income approach generally uses a forecast, the market approach typically computes value as a multiple of a historical return. If the historical and forecasted returns are substantially different, determine why this difference occurs and which more accurately portrays the company's potential as of the valuation date. The other computation may require further adjustment.
- The market approach most commonly employs a multiple of the operating performance of a single period, such as earnings per share or EBITDA. Because this multiple is the reciprocal of a capitalization

(continued)

(continued)

rate that is applied to the return of a single period, convert the multiple to a capitalization rate and add back the estimated long-term growth rate to compute the implied discount rate. Compare this rate to that used in the income approach after allowing for differences in the return used (e.g. income versus cash flow, pretax versus after-tax income, etc.). Where differences occur, consider adjustments to the multiple or rate that appears to be less reasonable or is based on less reliable data.

- The transaction multiple method, depending on the character of each transaction, typically generates investment value on a control basis. In assessing this, first review whether the strategic transaction(s) provides a realistic indication of the market for the subject company. Also compare this to the investment value on a control basis computed through the income approach, looking to see which computation provides a greater degree of confidence and why their results differ.

- When the guideline public company method is used, look at the range of multiples as well as the mean and median multiples of the guidelines. Again allowing for differences in the return stream used, compute the implied capitalization rate and discount rate generated by these multiples. Next, consider the reasonableness of these rates compared against the discount rates and long-term growth rates employed in the income approach. This comparison should highlight the implied short-term growth rate included in the market multiples.

- Look at the multiple chosen for the target company and its resulting equivalent discount rate and growth rate for that return stream. Assess the reasonableness of these rates in light of the conclusion from the income approach. When inconsistencies occur, one may need to reassess the selection of a multiple for the target company.

Value Reconciliation and Conclusion

After the results of each procedure have been thoroughly reviewed, the final estimate of value must be determined. When more than one approach has been employed, the results can be averaged, but this is not recommended. Computing a simple average implies that each method was equally appropriate to the assignment or that each produced an equally reliable result.

Although this could happen, it is more likely that one of the procedures more accurately portrays and quantifies the key risk and value drivers present and generates a more defendable estimate of value. When this occurs, the methods may be weighted either mathematically or subjectively. The reconciliation form presented in Exhibit 13.2 provides a convenient way to present results for review and consideration. Ultimately, the choice of mathematical or subjective weightings, the amount of the weightings, and the final opinion of value is a professional judgment based on a solid understanding of the company following a thorough qualitative and quantitative assessment. If this were not the case, software programs could be more effectively employed and business valuation would be greatly simplified. The process, however, is too complex to be reduced to a formula or program.

Exhibit 13.2 illustrates the reconciliation process when initial values were determined by the DCF, guideline public company, and transaction multiple methods. In reviewing each of the methods to determine a final opinion of fair market value, the appraiser concluded that the DCF method generated a value on which a high degree of confidence could be placed. The forecasted return appeared to be achievable based on the company's historical experience, competitive strengths and weaknesses, and industry conditions. The net cash flow to invested capital return, adjusted to reflect control through the add-back of above-market compensation paid to owners, appeared to provide an accurate indication of the company's earning capacity. The rate of return was developed using sound methodology and was able to accurately reflect the major risk drivers and value drivers present in the company.

The guideline public company method used a return to minority shareholders without consideration of excess compensation and employed a 30% control premium to convert from a minority to control estimate of fair market value. The appraiser had a reasonable level of confidence that the guideline companies provided an accurate indication of market prices from which to determine an appropriate multiple for the target company. Due to the lack of confidence in the 30% control premium, the results of this method were given only a 20% weighting in the final computation of value. (If above-market compensation is paid, normally it would be added back to income to generate a control return from which control value could be computed directly through use of the guideline public company method, thus avoiding the need for application and defense of a control premium.)

The transaction multiple method looked at several strategic transactions that the appraiser concluded represented investment value to a specific buyer. These transactions did, however, provide an indication of what well-informed buyers in that industry were willing to pay for controlling interests in strategic transactions, and therefore they were recognized but given very little weight.

EXHIBIT 13.2 Reconciliation of Indicated Values and Application of Discounts and Premiums Appropriate to the Final Opinion of Value

Valuation Method	Indicated by Method (Preadjustments)			Adjustments for Differences in Degree of		Adjusted		Weight	Weighted Component Value
	Interest Being Valued	Value	Basis	Control	Market-ability	Fair Market Value	Basis		
Discounted Cash Flow Method	100%	$36,000,000	Control, as if freely traded	None	None	$36,000,000	Control, marketable	70%	$25,200,000
Guideline Public Company Method	100%	$35,000,000	Minority, as if freely traded	25% premium	None	$43,750,000	Control, marketable	20%	$8,750,000
Transaction Multiple Method	100%	$44,000,000	Control, as if freely traded	None	None	$44,000,000	Control, marketable	10%	$4,400,000
Fair Market Value of a 100% Closely Held Interest on an Operating Control, Marketable Basis									$38,350,000
Plus: Non-operating Assets									$1,500,000
Fair Market Value of a 100% Closely Held Interest on a Control, Marketable Basis									$39,850,000
Divided by: 2,000,000 Issued and Outstanding Shares									2,000,000
Fair Market Value per Share on a Control, Marketable Basis									$19.93

Checks to Value

Checks to value are performed once indications to value are determined based on the various approaches to valuation. The conclusion of value derived in applying one or a combination of the various valuation methods can be checked by considering:

- *Implied value multiple.* Even if the methods within the market approach are inadequate to provide an indication of value, typically resulting in that indication being derived solely by the income approach, that conclusion can be tested in terms of a multiple of revenue or some level of earnings (net income; earnings before interest and taxes; or earnings before interest, taxes, depreciation, and amortization). An assessment will have to be made in terms of where the resulting multiple falls in relation to the relevant market.
- *Rules of thumb.* Usually come in the form of some multiple of revenues or earnings. No one ever seems able to identify the specific transactions from which rules of thumb were determined, and they seldom change with economic or industry conditions. As such, they do not provide the basis for an appraisal. However, since they are often referenced in many industries in an M&A context, they should be considered as a reasonableness check to help corroborate the indicated values determined by other methods.
- *Prior transactions.* Prior transactions of the company's stock can provide an indication of value when they are at arm's-length and occurred within a reasonable amount of time of the valuation date.
- *Intangible assets.* In instances when the income and/or market approaches are used to value the company, the asset approach applying an adjusted book value method may also be suitable as a check to value. This is the most time consuming and challenging check to value as it involves an assessment of the working capital and tangible assets, plus identification and value of the intangible assets using the methods discussed in Chapter 18.
- *Book value.* In most going-concern valuations, book value – the difference between a company's total assets and total liabilities as they appear on the balance sheet – is at best a floor. Nonetheless, it may be helpful to consider the premium between the book value and the indicated fair market value. If there is little or no premium between the two, and that is not consistent with market trends, it is advisable to understand the reason or reconsider key assumptions in the analysis.
- *Justification of purchase.* Also called a leveraged buyout (LBO) analysis or a business broker method, this test assesses the adequacy of the forecasted cash flows to cover debt payments resulting from a transaction.

Debt service can be viewed as a return on the buyer's investment and therefore can be compared to returns of alternative options. A buyer uses the assets of the business (plus personal assets for smaller companies) to secure an acquisition loan and then uses the cash generated by the business to repay it. The justification-of-purchase test compares the indicated value based on projected cash flows to the required term, contingency reserve, interest rate, and down payment. If the assumptions for these four factors are reasonable, the indication of value is considered to be reasonable.

- *Private equity buyout.* Related to the justification of purchase is a check to value that considers the anticipated deal structure in a private equity buyout. An example is presented and explained in Exhibit 13.3.

Candidly Assess Valuation Capabilities

This chapter has presented a summary of risk and value drivers and the resulting reconciliation of methodologies and computations required to produce a defendable opinion of value. In considering these issues and computations, it is time for business owners or their advisors to take a cold, hard look at their appraisal knowledge and skills in assessing a potential sale or acquisition. Valuations should routinely analyze the many points reviewed in this chapter. The points summarized here should make sense, and appraisers should be comfortable with the underlying theory and computations.

Where there are gaps in knowledge or experience, candidly consider the consequences of a lack of expertise in these issues. M&A usually involves large amounts of money and long-term commitments. If business owners or their advisors are not suitably comfortable with business valuation theory and techniques as summarized in this chapter, they probably should seek professional assistance before making major decisions that carry such substantial consequences. The cost of professional assistance is generally small relative to the potential benefits: an accurate valuation followed either by completion of a successful transaction or, more important, by rejection of one that should be avoided.

Valuation Scenarios – Platform for M&A

The focus of the last seven chapters has been on measuring private company fair market value on a stand-alone basis. In valuation for M&A, this is akin to a company's intrinsic value since value is being determined based on the perceived characteristics inherent in the subject company, without regard to any buyer-specific characteristics or synergies.

EXHIBIT 13.3 Sample Private Equity Buyout Structure

		Amount	Implied Multiple
Purchase Price[a]		$63,200	
Revenue[b]		$75,200	0.84
EBITDA[b]		$8,500	7.44
MVIC/EBITDA		$63,200	7.44
EBITDA		$8,500	
Mezzanine[c]	13.4%	$8,500	1.00
Senior Debt[d]	31.6%	$20,000	2.35
Total Debt	45.1%	$28,500	3.35
Equity	54.9%	$34,700	
Sources of Funds			
Mezzanine	12.8%	$8,500	
Senior Debt	30.1%	$20,000	
Rollover Equity[e]	9.5%	$6,320	10.0%
PEG Equity[f]	47.5%	$31,540	
Total	100.0%	$66,360	
Uses of Funds			
Equity Purchase	85.7%	$56,880	
Rollover Equity[e]	9.5%	$6,320	10.0%
Purchase Price	95.2%	$63,200	
Fees[g]	4.8%	$3,160	5.0%
Total	100.0%	$66,360	

[a]Investment value as determined in Exhibit 21.2.

[b]Latest year's revenue and EBITDA, see Exhibit 21.1. The implied multiples are 0.69× revenues and 6.08× EBITDA.

[c]A mezzanine lender has agreed to provide $8.5 million, equivalent to 1× EBITDA.

[d]A bank has agreed to lend $20 million, equivalent to 2.3× EBITDA.

[e]The PEG has requested that Cavendish (the seller) invest 10% of the proceeds in the form of an equity rollover, paid for by proceeds realized in connection with the transaction. This is subordinate to the PEG's equity investment and all outside financing. As such, the seller is at risk for this amount, but has the opportunity to participate in a future sale (a "second bite at the apple").

[f]To complete the transaction, the PEG invests $20,615,000, comprised of $18,030,000 to cover its portion of the transaction acquisition plus $2,585,000 in fees.

[g]The PEG funds buyer-related fees and transaction costs, amounting to 5% of the purchase price.

In planning for a potential transaction or for general strategic planning purposes, this provides a baseline valuation from the seller's perspective and it establishes a platform to determine a range of values under several exit scenarios (discussed in Chapter 14). In other words, the seller should aim to sell at a price above stand-alone fair market value. In valuation for M&A, there is an important distinction between stand-alone fair market value and investment value. As a reminder, investment value is value to a particular buyer and therefore, by definition, there can be several investment values for one company. Just as the seller will aim to sell above fair market value, the buyer will aim to pay as much below investment value as possible, thereby minimizing what it pays for expected synergies and adding to shareholder value rather than diminishing it.[1]

As Warren Buffett famously said, "Price is what you pay, value is what you get." Price typically ends up being somewhere between fair market value and investment value if both buyer and seller have been represented by qualified M&A or valuation advisors. In addition, timing, personal dynamics, company positioning, market conditions, and the extent to which there is a bidding process all heavily influence where price ultimately falls in relation to value in an M&A transaction.

---

[1] Appendix 13A, written by Justin Johnson, CFA, ASA, provides a more in-depth explanation of how a disciplined and thorough valuation analysis can aid buyers in identifying successful acquisition targets.

Appendix 13A   Disciplined and Thorough Valuation Analysis Key to Avoiding Failed M&A Deals

By Justin Johnson, CFA, ASA[2]

There are many reasons companies enter into a merger or acquisition transaction. Regardless of the specific drivers, however, the common theme underlying all deals is the expectation that the combination will increase shareholder value for the acquirer. Ironically, it is estimated that well over 50% of M&A deals fail – meaning they end up destroying shareholder value instead of creating it. This surprising statistic underscores the difficulty company boards face in determining whether a deal is worth pursuing. A greater emphasis on a disciplined and thorough valuation analysis is key in helping boards in their ability to identify and avoid bad deals or to guide them in negotiating and structuring deals that may make better financial sense. This section will discuss what constitutes a disciplined and thorough valuation analysis and how such an analysis can help boards identify companies that could be successful acquisition targets.

Analysis of a Hypothetical Synergistic Deal

For our purpose, we will assume that a public company acquirer has identified a potential target. The target company operates in the same business as the acquirer and serves similar customers. The expected cost savings from the business combination may be compelling due to an overlapping distribution network of both the acquirer and the acquisition target and because production and administrative staff redundancies can be eliminated from the acquisition target. This is a classic example of a synergistic deal. Synergies refer to the ability of the acquirer to add the target company's revenue to its top line while at the same time eliminating many of the costs associated with achieving that revenue by eliminating duplicate operations and functions, thus increasing overall profit.

The first step in the valuation process is to establish the market value of the target company without regard to buyer-specific synergies. While acquirers are ultimately most interested in analyzing the valuation of the combined company, establishing the market valuation of the target on a stand-alone basis should be done first for two reasons:

---

[2] Justin Johnson, CFA, ASA, is co-CEO of Valuation Research Corporation based in San Francisco. Mr. Johnson has over 20 years of financial and valuation advisory experience providing solvency opinions, fairness opinions, and capital surplus opinions as well as considerable experience in conducting valuations for investment, financial reporting, and tax purposes.

1. To provide the buyer perspective on a baseline valuation that the board of the target company might expect to realize in the transaction.
2. To establish a reference point by which the buyer can analyze and evaluate how much additional synergy it brings to the table over and above a market level of synergy.

Establishing the Value of an Acquisition Target

There are several generally accepted approaches for establishing the value of an acquisition target (see Exhibit 13.A1 for an overview of commonly used approaches). The first two approaches are used primarily for publicly traded targets. For our purpose, we will assume the acquisition target is a private company and its value may be established using the other four approaches.

One of the most common approaches relies on the trading multiples of guideline companies in the public markets. Care is required in the selection of public companies to ensure comparability of operations, size, and/or growth prospects with the target company. Another common approach is to look at industry M&A deal multiples for similar targets. For this approach, it may be instructive to distinguish between financial sponsor deals and strategic deals. Strategic acquirers can and often do pay higher multiples for targets due to acquirer-specific synergies. This approach yields a control/synergistic level of value. Value indications for these approaches should be based on applying observed market multiples to the target's stand-alone earnings before interest, tax, depreciation and amortization (EBITDA) (or other financial metrics that may be more appropriate) without factoring in any buyer-specific synergies.

If a reliable long-term forecast is available for the target company, the financial advisor will often use a discounted cash flow (DCF) analysis to establish value. It is important to keep in mind, however, that such an analysis is only as good as the underlying financial forecasts used to perform the DCF model. For this reason, a DCF analysis may be given less weight and may even be omitted in some instances. If the financial advisor does choose to conduct a DCF analysis, caution must be used in relying upon the financial projections prepared by the target company. One pitfall would be to take at face value any forecast that appears overly optimistic about future performance relative to historical performance. Careful due diligence should be conducted on such a forecast to determine if it is reliable. In some instances, a "haircut" may be applied to the forecast to offset the optimistic nature of the long-term plan while in other instances the financial advisor may develop a more reasonable set of projections by looking at the historical performance of the target as well as industry norms. In any event, the financial forecast should not factor in any buyer-specific synergies.

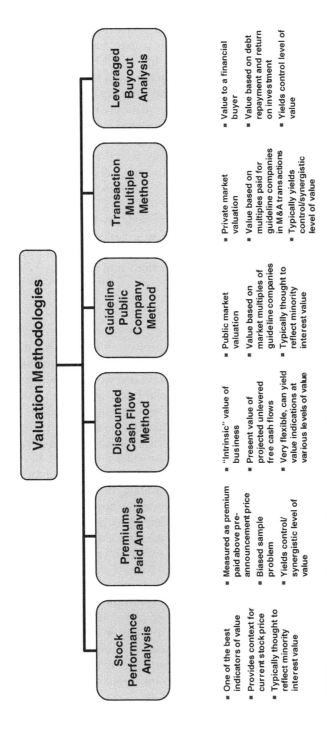

EXHIBIT 13.A1 Common Valuation Methodologies in M&A

Last, if the target company is likely to attract financial buyers, then it would also be prudent to value the company using a leveraged buyout (LBO) analysis. This approach values the target by establishing what a financial buyer would be willing to pay for the company given the financing structure it may implement. In addition to its equity investment, a financial buyer will likely seek to use debt to finance the acquisition in order to enhance equity returns. If a company is underperforming relative to the industry, the LBO model may also include some assumptions about reorganization to better align the target company's performance with the overall industry. The financial sponsor may also seek to use the target company as a platform from which to make add-on acquisitions to increase EBITDA and realize value through multiple expansion at exit.

Once all approaches have been performed, the financial advisor will triangulate the various pricing indications to establish an overall baseline valuation range for the target. This analysis provides a useful benchmark to the acquirer in determining a preliminary offer value.

Establishing Value for the Acquirer

The next phase of the valuation analysis involves assessing what the value of the acquirer will be pro forma for the acquisition. This analysis is different than the market valuation analysis because we are now conducting a review from the perspective of a particular buyer and what the value of the acquisition is to that specific buyer (i.e. investment or synergistic value). This value may be different for each potential buyer in the market, with the most highly synergistic buyer able to offer the highest purchase price (by definition, investment value is value to a particular buyer).

In performing this valuation analysis, there are a number of factors that need to be carefully analyzed before determining the viability of the deal. If it is viable, then we determine how much the buyer can afford to pay for the target and still increase shareholder value. Some of these factors include the amount of expected synergies, the costs associated with realizing those synergies, the amount and type of purchase consideration, and the trading multiples for the acquirer's stock. We will address each of these factors in turn.

Money spent on outside advisors who perform due diligence on the target to estimate the potential synergies of a deal is usually money well spent. Management should be careful in relying on its own estimates of synergies. In many cases, the amount of synergies cannot be estimated with precision and may be a wide range. Because of difficulties in identifying and estimating potential synergies, it is recommended that management run a sensitivity analysis to assess the impact of the transaction on the acquirer's stock price. This is best performed in a sensitivity table that varies both the amount of assumed synergies and the amount of purchase consideration, which provides the board with a visual tool to understand how much it makes sense to pay at varying levels of synergy. With this analysis, the acquirer should keep in mind that for many deals the amount of synergies actually realized is lower than projected. In addition, it may take longer than expected to realize those synergies and the associated one-time costs might be higher than expected. From the buyer's perspective, a good deal is one that is accretive to the acquirer's stock price even at the low end of the range of expected synergies. An even better deal is one that still increases shareholder value despite synergies below the low end of the estimated range. Conversely, deals that are only accretive at or near the maximum amount of projected synergies will likely end up destroying shareholder value. The same logic applies to the estimated one-time costs necessary to integrate the target's operation into the acquirer's and achieve synergies. Similar to the synergies themselves, these one-time costs may also be difficult to estimate with precision and their range may be wide and a sensitivity analysis around this assumption may also be required. The idea behind the sensitivity analysis is to look at the financial impact of the transaction on a conservative basis. For example, if the scenario analysis shows that a deal increases shareholder value even if (a) actual synergies realized are at the low end of expectations, (b) one-time costs incurred to realize those synergies are at the high end of the range, and (c) the purchase consideration is reasonable relative to the market valuation of the target company, then the deal will likely end up beneficial from the acquirer's standpoint.

Considerations of Other Impacts on Value

It is also important to analyze the impact of the type of purchase consideration on value. How will the acquisition be financed? The purchase price can be financed with available cash, proceeds from newly incurred debt, stock, or a combination of these. Use of debt will create a drag on future earnings in the form of interest expense. Interest expense is effectively another cost of realizing the transaction synergies that must be considered. If acceptable to the seller, using stock consideration may be advantageous to the buyer. But if stock is used, placing selling restrictions on the shares until after the expiration of any transition services agreement is advisable, so as to incentivize the sellers to ensure a smooth transition and to reduce risk for any transition issues. While the sellers must wait until they can convert their shares to cash, they will benefit in the run-up in the value of the stock assuming that transaction synergies are realized as planned.

Another factor that needs to be considered is the valuation multiple of the acquiring company. If historically it has been somewhat volatile, it may be advisable to run a sensitivity analysis on the pro forma value of the stock, assuming a range of valuation multiples for the acquirer that are consistent with its recent trading history. The lower the valuation multiple, the lower the increase in value from transaction synergies.

There may also be other factors that need to be analyzed. For example, one assumption underlying most deals where the acquisition rationale is cost synergies is that the target's revenue will survive the acquisition without any loss of customers or decrease in the level of business from any given customer. However, in many acquisitions this does not prove to be the case. The acquirer will need to evaluate whether incentives will need to be put in place with those at the target who have key customer relationships or directly with customers to ensure revenue is preserved and relationships transfer. This will be an additional cost that will be an offset to the synergies to be realized.

Having established both the fair market value of the target and the investment value of the target to the specific buyer, the acquirer is in a good position to negotiate with the seller. A buyer will typically be willing to pay up to the market level of synergies. The buyer should be careful paying for synergies beyond that point.

No board of directors goes into a deal with the intent to destroy value and yet that is what often ends up happening. In many instances, a greater emphasis on a disciplined and thorough valuation analysis as outlined above can make the difference in helping a board of directors in its ability to distinguish a good deal from a bad one.

Specialty Issues

CHAPTER 14

Exit Planning[1]

The foundational premise of this book is that private companies are investments, and accordingly, their owners must continually plan to build, protect, and harvest this portion of their wealth. We explained in great detail in prior chapters how to accurately measure private company value, but this knowledge may provide little or no benefit unless owners can successfully harvest this wealth.

Commonly called *exit planning*, few owners or advisors recognize the breadth of what this harvesting process entails or how critical this planning is for most owners to succeed in achieving their private company goals.

To appreciate the odds against a successful exit, consider first external market challenges. As mentioned in the opening paragraphs of this book, merger and acquisition (M&A) advisors disqualify roughly 65% to 75% of prospective sellers and, according to a U.S. Chamber of Commerce Study, only 20% of the businesses that are for sale will successfully transfer hands to another owner. This implies that only 5% to 7% of companies actually get sold.

Although less commonly recognized, internal company and owner circumstances commonly create even larger impediments to a successful exit. Owners frequently are conflicted over issues and goals surrounding their exit. Beyond a sale of their company, they seldom recognize the range of exit options from which they have to choose. And just because an owner wants to make a change does not mean he or the company is immediately ready to execute that change successfully.

Before we explain how to plan an exit through a proven six-step process that was developed by John Leonetti of Pinnacle Equity Solutions, let us

---

[1] The authors gratefully acknowledge the input of several exit planning concepts described in this chapter from John Leonetti, founder and CEO of Pinnacle Equity Solutions, Inc.

examine why exiting a private company investment is unique and difficult. Armed with this realization of the high risks and major rewards involved, owners should be more willing and able to plan effectively.

Why Is Exit Planning So Difficult?

For private company owners who have built significant value in their businesses, preparing an exit plan seems like an obvious step that most would be eager to take. Yet this seldom happens. Although comprehensive statistics are not available, many practitioners who deal with private company owners would conclude that relatively few achieve their major goals in exiting their company. This begs the question: Why is exit planning so difficult?

The answer begins with the realization that the exit decision is usually highly complex, and this challenge is made even more difficult because most owners and their advisors see this decision as primarily financial. The decision about whether to exit a company, and, if so, how, typically involves four distinct but related considerations. Each may require careful planning and present obstacles to achieving the owner's desired result. In addition, as needs and goals are identified, some likely will conflict with others, causing owners to have to compromise. As the years pass, an owner's life circumstances, and thus his needs and goals, change. In the meantime, business conditions change as well. So what may be a sound plan in one year under one set of circumstances may prove unworkable at a different time. When a company has multiple owners, these variables often multiply, making identification of a strategy that fits everyone's needs even more difficult.

Sound planning clearly begins with recognition of the primary issues involved so that owners can identify their needs and goals and set priorities in accordance with them. The four issues owners must address in planning to exit include:

1. *Strategic business issues.* The conditions of a company will clearly affect its value, its relative level of attractiveness to other potential owners, and what the company needs to succeed going forward. Many companies may need several years of pre-exit preparation to enable any sort of exit to be feasible. The size of the company, its dependence on key executives or customers, and general economic and industry conditions all can have a major impact on exit strategy and timing.

   Thus the first component of the owner's exit decision centers on a strategic assessment of the company and what must be done to it to enable successful transition. For some owners, this assessment is particularly difficult because it requires an evaluation of their leadership and performance, identification of any shortcomings or gaps in their skill set and management team, and consideration of how the company they are accustomed to leading must change.

2. *Financial issues.* For many, if not most, owners, an exit can have a major effect on their wealth, annual income, or cash flow, the riskiness of their overall portfolio of investments, and the liquidity of their investments. The exit plan may involve the owner leaving the company and having no continuing stream of income from it, or staying with the company in some capacity with a commensurate level of compensation and benefits continuing from the business.

Before an exit, many private company owners have much or virtually all of their wealth concentrated in their single private company investment. Depending on the magnitude of that wealth, the other investments the owner may have, and the owner's age, this may constitute anything from a sound to a highly risky investment strategy. Also, depending on the owner's age, lifestyle, standard of living, and tolerance for risk, the exit plan he chooses may entail making major or minor changes in his income and overall financial security.

Private company exit plans frequently involve transaction structures that include contingent compensation in future years or assumption of buyer debt. These decisions can also have a material effect on the owner's income and risk profile. Just ask any owner who sold a company in a transaction that involved an earn-out that was not achieved or an owner who financed the sale of his business to a buyer and several years later had to foreclose on the loan and assume control of what had by then become a crippled company.

3. *Professional or career issues.* Many private company owners struggle to distinguish between their ownership or investment in their company and their *employment* in their company. As owners consider exit planning, they may choose to end their employment in the company but continue in some capacity as an owner, or end their ownership in the company but continue in some capacity as an employee.

For many owners, building their company was one of the major events and achievements in their life, and they may want to continue their involvement in it. Owners may consider a change in duties or responsibilities, but their desire to work may actually be the most important priority in their overall exit plan. Consequently, assessment of an owner's professional goals and objectives is a critical step in the exit process. In doing so, he must assess what kind of work he wants to do and not do, how much he wants to work, and for approximately how long he intends to work. In addition, he must assess whether he can and wants to work with or for others and the compensation he would require for whatever level of work he does.

It is easy for some owners to underestimate the importance of their work and what work matters most to them. For example, some owners want to shed administrative duties or the responsibility of being the boss while others may want most to remain in control. Making these decisions often requires significant introspection and perhaps recognition by an owner that he is no longer able to perform certain roles in the company.

4. *Personal issues.* In addition to strategic, financial, and professional concerns, private company owners commonly have personal issues that have a substantial bearing on their exit decision. Some of these relate to their individual circumstances while others involve people who are important to them.

On an individual basis, the decision to exit a company may be driven by the owner's age or health, interests outside of the company, his personal stature and identity that he sees coming from his position with the company, and the long-term legacy of the company itself. Owners who have put much of their life effort into building a business will identify with it and may experience a significant sense of loss in any type of exit from the company. They need to explore these personal issues to identify what is most important to them to ensure that their exit plan includes accommodating these needs.

Private company owners frequently have other people in their lives – most commonly family members, employees, or fellow owners – whose circumstances (e.g. income and financial security) would be materially impacted by an exit decision. Some might lose their jobs or see their employment status and compensation change dramatically if an exit occurs. Depending on the way the exit is structured, other people's status as owners of the company could change, and they could view these changes as either a positive or a negative. Private company owners must identify those stakeholders who are of most concern, assess how the various exit choices would affect them, and then weigh this against their various other priorities.

Once these four issues in the exit decision – strategic, financial, professional, and personal – are identified, they must be prioritized. That is, owners need to identify the most important financial and nonfinancial needs and goals related to the exit decisions. While some of the goals may make sound financial sense, others may not. For many owners, a successful exit decision cannot be measured strictly in dollars and cents. As addressed later in this chapter in Step 2 of the six-step exit planning process, owner readiness is defined in terms of both financial and mental readiness. Some of the owners' goals may reduce their income or wealth but give them peace of mind. This is clearly how the decision about a private company investment differs so much from the typical decision to sell public company stock.

While the former is most commonly an intensely personal decision, the latter is purely financial.

Identifying a sound exit plan that accommodates these four issues is a major challenge for individuals who own 100% of their company. When a private company has multiple owners, each will have his own needs and goals, and when owners have differences in age, wealth, liquidity, appetite for risk, desire to work, and standard of living, deriving an exit plan that meets their mutual needs can be a significant challenge.

The lesson here is that exit planning is essential for sound, private-company owner decisions because these decisions entail an unusually complex combination of strategic, financial, professional, and personal issues. There is a distinct advantage to recognizing these issues and establishing priorities well in advance of any intended exit date. Particularly when there are multiple owners involved, the added time should enable the greatest flexibility to accommodate conflicting needs and goals.

What Makes Planning for Your Private Company Investment Unique?

Standard investment theory, which applies most practically to publicly traded companies, urges portfolio diversification, sufficient liquidity, and continual risk-versus-return analysis, particularly over time as life circumstances, needs, and goals change. Accordingly, most business owners engage a personal financial advisor to assist them to achieve these goals. A private company investment, however, is all too often excluded from this analysis because the financial advisor has little or no information about what this investment is worth, the annual cash flow return it generates, its level of risk, or what legal restrictions or other factors affect its liquidity. All too often, an owner's privately held business is not given sufficient (or any) consideration in the overall personal financial plan. While this lack of information should be alarming, it becomes more so when we consider three characteristics that commonly accompany a private company investment.

1. *It is typically the owner's largest investment.* That is, most owners of private companies have a greater portion of their wealth tied up in their business than anywhere else. Although this concentration may be appropriate but somewhat risky for a 35-year-old who is just building his wealth, it is much more risky for the 50-year-old and could seriously threaten the financial security of the 65-year-old. Investment theory strongly encourages portfolio diversification as people near retirement, but many if not most private company owners fail to consider this in their financial plan.

2. *The owner's private company investment is the riskiest security in his portfolio,* assuming he owns a typical blend of public company stocks and bonds. As Chapter 8 explains in detail, the private company's small size, relatively limited management, lack of access to capital, and reliance on key customers, among other factors, creates a risk profile that typically demands a net cash flow return on equity of at least 20%. So private company owners commonly have their wealth concentrated in a single, relatively risky asset.

3. *The owner's private company investment is his least liquid investment for several reasons.* There is no public exchange where this stock can quickly be sold. This limitation is often made worse by the fact that most companies are not ready for sale on short notice and typically take about a year to sell, if they can be sold at all. In addition, it is often quite expensive (transaction fees, accounting fees, legal fees, etc.) and time-consuming to sell a private company. As we will see below, the psychological separation of an owner from his business is also a large issue that adds to the challenges of illiquidity.

Private companies often are heavily dependent on key owners and/or executives who possess unique knowledge, contacts, or skills that materially contribute to the company's success. Although these factors reflect positively on the owner's contribution to the company, they can be a negative in the exit planning process. Buyers would generally be reluctant to acquire a company whose performance is highly dependent on the owner and a few key people unless it is certain that those people will stay with the company at least for a specified period of time after a sale. This can lead to the sad circumstance of the owner planning to sell his business and retire in five years only to find himself four and half years into this process realizing that he can get a good price for the company only by agreeing to work for three more years after the sale. Had he realized this five years earlier, he could have begun to work on building a management team that is available to replace him when the future sale takes place.

One or more other factors are commonly present that complicate any exit plan. The first is stock transfer restrictions in the company's bylaws or shareholder agreements. These commonly exist to prevent unwanted individuals or entities from obtaining an ownership interest in the company. Although such provisions provide protection, they can sharply limit or virtually eliminate a shareholder's ability to sell his stock. These restrictions alone make annual review of bylaws and shareholder agreements in a private company an absolute necessity.

When there are multiple shareholders in a private company, shareholder restrictions can be further complicated by the needs and goals of the other shareholders. Some may oppose any change in ownership or lack the financial means to acquire any shares offered for sale. Others may oppose the company acquiring shares through a recapitalization and may use an individual shareholder's desire to sell stock to extract a lower price or other concessions from him. Other shareholders may have no involvement in the company or even no knowledge of it or of their investment.

Timing a private company sale can also be a challenge. The shareholder who wants to leave in three or five years may find that, when that date finally arrives, the company or industry conditions have weakened substantially, greatly reducing the sale price. Others who are ready to sell may find that they face restrictions from supplier agreements or demands from customers that make exiting difficult except under adverse price and terms.

> The exit planning process cannot be approached solely from a financial perspective. Assessing an owner's mental readiness to exit is as, if not more, important.

Clearly, the sale of stock in a private company is very different from calling a broker to sell shares in Amazon, Google, IBM, or ExxonMobil. Business owners must understand their company's value, the risk and returns that accompany that investment, and the unique characteristics that complicate transfer of any private company investment. Armed with this knowledge, owners can include their private company investment in their overall portfolio and personal financial planning to achieve appropriate levels of diversification and liquidity.

Why Should Exit Planning for Your Private Company Begin Now?

The prior sections explain the unique complexities of exit planning for a private company and its owner(s). And while most owners do not recognize all of these complexities, they generally are also reluctant to deal with the uncertainty of change in their private company, which is a major part of their life. Unless an emergency occurs, owners usually conclude that it is easier to put off addressing these issues to a future time, so the years go by with no exit plan.

For many owners, this think-about-it-later exit planning strategy often leads to one of the three *D*s in disaster exit planning: divorce, disability, or death. Each of these events, which most commonly strike a private company owner unexpectedly, can materially reduce the company's value as well as the owner's exit alternatives. Divorce often leaves an owner emotionally wounded and in need of cash for an equitable distribution settlement at a time when he is least able to give the company the attention it needs.

Disability can be to the owner's health or to the company's health, either of which can decrease the company's value and eliminate one or more exit options. Death often leaves the company without its leader or visionary, and this gap can hurt relations with customers and suppliers and cripple operations. In addition, unless proper estate planning is in place, the company may have to be sold to generate the cash to pay estate taxes that are due.

Planning in advance is essential because, as has been discussed, one or more factors commonly prevent immediate execution of most exit options. Whether it is building a successor management team, preparing the company for a sale, or waiting for better market conditions before exiting, delays commonly occur. A soundly drawn exit plan recognizes these timing issues to minimize unwanted delays and fit an owner's timing preferences.

Advanced planning also accommodates the changes in an owner's needs and goals that occur over time due to age, health, outside interests, desire to work, or other factors. This is particularly important when the company has multiple owners because each will want to get out under favorable circumstances, and there must be a market for the shares of any exiting owner.

As the discussion about exit planning that follows emphasizes, an effective plan typically requires a team of professionals from several disciplines and a quarterback to lead the process. Most of the professionals involved tend to focus on their specific tasks and are often reactive in nature. That is, they will do what they are asked to do when they are asked to do it. Thus it is up to the owner's exit planning quarterback to see to it that an effective plan is developed and that each service provider works to achieve the owner's priority goals.

While five or ten years is a long period to plan most activities, it is the time frame required for effective planning to exit a private company. The complexities of the process, the reality that needs and goals change over time, continually changing business conditions, and the varying circumstances that multiple owners bring to an investment create a compelling case to plan well in advance. Ultimately, the owner should consider the exit as an entrepreneurial opportunity to control the narrative and significantly boost business value.

Exit Planning Process

An exit plan is a written outline of an owner's business exit strategy that addresses the strategic, financial, professional, and personal issues that have been described. It also identifies and quantifies the accounting, business, insurance, legal, tax, and valuation issues involved in transitioning a private company. Although the sale of a company is an event, the exit plan is a process. Exit planning is something that is done over time and may, but does not necessarily, include selling the business. The exit plan is built around the personal objectives of the business owner. As such, it is something that should be completed by the business owner, with the help of a team of outside advisors, regardless of that owner's age and current position, and regardless of the company's stage in its business life cycle. A successful transition will require a thoughtful and coherent exit plan. This is a planning (and execution) process that requires active participation from the owner because the owner needs to have well-defined goals as well as a firm understanding of the options for transition that are available. The planning (and execution) process is not something that can be delegated to another professional. As described below, active owner participation is critical to a successful plan being developed and implemented properly.

The owner's exit plan should also be a part of a company's strategic plan because it will directly impact how the business will grow. For business owners, along with death and taxes, it is inevitable that they will have to transfer their business at some point in the future. It is best to be prepared for that inevitable transfer with the plan of doing so on the business owners' terms. As stated at the outset of this book, sellers may sell under adverse conditions or accept too low a price due to lack of preparation or knowledge. There are broader consequences. Business owners may be forced to exit under adverse conditions and may not be in the position to choose the most advantageous exit due to lack of planning, thereby not only negatively impacting themselves, but also their business, employees, family, and even community.

It is crucial for business owners to assemble and lead a team of experts who can work together and who understand the various exit options and have experience guiding owners in the direction that best aligns with the owner's personal and business goals. This team[2] ideally includes an accountant, business appraiser, estate attorney, insurance advisor, M&A advisor, personal financial planner, and tax attorney, with only one of these professional advisors acting as exit planning quarterback. Each advisor brings an area of expertise necessary to make the exit plan successful. No one advisor understands all the factors and has all the answers, but each must have experience in the exit planning process. Each type of advisor has specific strengths and weaknesses and different motivations. Owners who are engaged in the exit planning process should focus on how well their team is functioning together to meet the owner's goals. While the quarterback can organize and facilitate the flow of information, owners still need to be

---

[2] There is overlap with the advisory team for an M&A transaction discussed in Chapter 4. However, the business owner should ensure that each member of this team has specific exit planning experience.

diligent that the team is collaborating and functioning properly and that no one advisor's ego or other shortcomings disrupt the planning and/or execution process. Ultimately, the motivations and goals of the owner, not the advisors, must direct the exit plan. The role of the exit planning quarterback is to set the exit plan according to the business owner's goals and coordinate the process with each of the advisors.

This chapter has presented the importance of exit planning as well as why and how exit planning can be such a challenge for owners. However, there is a process that can be followed to bring some clarity to an otherwise potentially very confusing and complex exercise. This process has been around for a decade and has been used by thousands of owners and professional advisors in designing their exit plans.

Exit planning can be described as a six-step process to be discussed throughout the remainder of this chapter:[3]

1. Plan the exit by setting the owner's exit goals.
2. Determine the owner's financial and mental readiness.
3. Identify the type of exiting owner.
4. Learn and choose the most applicable exit option.
5. Understand the range of values a business can have and the one applicable to the chosen exit option.
6. Execute the exit strategy plan to reach the business owner's goals and protect his wealth.

Step 1: Setting Exit Goals

The process for establishing an exit plan begins with setting the owners' exit goals. This allows the owners to identify, clarify, and prioritize objectives while maintaining control of the process. This goal-setting process is unique to each business owner. It involves the integration of business-level planning and reflects the owners' circumstances and needs with financial, professional, and personal goals to answer these questions:

> *Exit*: What do you want to achieve with your business exit?
> *Succession*: How will your business run without you?
> *Legacy*: Where do you want your wealth to go, and what would you like your business to be?

---

[3] This six-step process is sourced from John M. Leonetti, *Exiting Your Business, Protecting Your Wealth* (Hoboken, NJ: Wiley, 2008). The reader is encouraged to read this book and visit www.exitingyourbusiness.com and www.pinnacleequitysolutions.com for more in-depth guidance on the exit planning process.

The answers to these questions reflect the preferences of each individual owner. It is critical that the owner be an active part of the goal-setting process and that a sufficient amount of time is spent thinking through a number of potential scenarios for the future. Goal clarity is the key. Once an owner is clear on what he wants to see happen in the future, the planning process is ready to move to the next step. But getting clear on the future of a privately held business is a significant challenge for a majority of owners. The challenge lies in the fact that rarely will an owner be able to choose a direction that works well for every stakeholder in the business. As a result, owners are often conflicted with various parties' interests in determining the best way to move forward with the personal and business planning.

For example, one owner may want to get the most money he can out of the business, diversify personally, and keep working. If this includes a sale to an outside party, it may come at the cost of giving up control of the company and changing the culture of the business. Long-term, loyal employees may resent this action even though it works for the owner's personal and professional goals. Another owner may prefer to diversify his wealth and give back to the employees, transfer to the management team, or transfer to family members. These internal transfers may not allow the owner to meet his personal financial goals and most likely leaves the owner personally liable for debts as well as the success of the business going forward. As will be seen later, each of these alternatives has its own exit option, covered in Step 4 of the exit planning process, and each option has its pros and cons. Understanding the various options and weighing the impact to the owner, and others, of each option is at the heart of gaining the clarity of goals that the owner needs to take action and move the planning and execution forward.

Further, when a private company has multiple owners, the exit planning may reveal conflicting or incompatible goals. Such differences do not make either owner wrong in a judgmental sense; but having multiple owners in a business adds to the complexity mentioned above, requiring more consideration to get to goal clarity and alignment of various ownership parties. Sometimes when owner goals differ enough, the best solution may be for one to exit this business and invest elsewhere. A great benefit of exit planning is identification of such differences at the earliest possible time to provide the best chance to resolve them effectively.

Business owners must work with their team of advisors to put together a written plan that:

- Identifies and prioritizes financial and nonfinancial goals.
- Establishes a business, professional, and personal strategy to achieve the goals.
- Sets a time frame.
- Lists post-exit activities.

Doing this involves consideration of many questions; a sample of them includes:

- When you consider exiting this business, what do you currently think you want to accomplish with your exit?
- Where do you see yourself in 20/10/5/2 years?
- How important is it to you to leave a legacy to your employees and/or family members?
- Whom do you want to own and/or run your business after your exit?
- Whom have you identified as your key employees, and what role would you like to see them have as you plan your exit and after?
- If there are family members involved in the business, what do you see as their role in the future?
- Do you know how much your business is worth and that it can have different values under different circumstances?
- What portion of your wealth is tied to your business?
- What is your risk tolerance?
- What kinds of activities (business or nonbusiness) do you see yourself involved in after you have exited your business?

These are just a few of the personal and business considerations business owners should be making in setting exit goals. These goals must be prioritized and put in print to guide the adjustments needed to be made to the business. At the outset of the exit planning process, the exit goals will be impacted by both the financial and the mental readiness of the business owner.

Step 2: Owner Readiness

Many business owners tend to subordinate their personal needs to the needs of the business. In the process of doing so, owners tend to reinvest profits into their businesses and also tend to allow their businesses to monopolize their time, often ahead of time spent with family and recreation. As a result, owners become fully invested in their companies, both financially and personally.

To simplify the process of planning an exit, and to expand on the goal-setting process in Step 1, owners can measure their financial and mental readiness to determine how prepared they are for an exit today. Using this simplified process, owners can calibrate their current situation and begin to think through what needs to be done next in their exit planning. Again, exit planning is a process, not a transaction. And knowing where you stand today, both financially and mentally, is a very helpful step toward knowing how and when you may be able to reach the goals stated in Step 1. This Step 2 helps determine their financial and mental readiness to exit.

From a *financial readiness* perspective (i.e. an owner's personal wealth position), business owners will either depend on the proceeds (which can be continuing to earn income or cash received from a sale) that will come from the exit to meet long-term goals (lower financial readiness), or they will not (higher financial readiness). With the help of the exit planning team, the owners' current level of wealth, diversification, risk tolerance, sources of income, expenses that are run through the business, expected post-exit lifestyle, and need for survivor benefits for spouse and children must be identified so that decisions on the business wealth can be made in the proper context.

For owners with a lower financial readiness, there is a gap between their current wealth position and the asset base required to satisfy their future financial goals. What this means is that there is not enough money held outside of the business to support the owner's personal lifestyle. And this is very easy to understand as growing, successful businesses often require reinvestment of profits, rather than having owners distribute this cash personally. This gap represents the amount of liquidity that owners will need to get out of the business to satisfy their post-exit expenses and their desire to provide for future generations. Generally speaking, owners with lower financial readiness will have fewer exit options and will require more extensive planning. They will have to consider a combination of (1) growing the business to meet their goals; (2) executing a partial exit soon in order to diversify while still maintaining control of the business; (3) selling out and continuing to work for the new owner; and (4) reducing expected expenses following their exit. For owners with higher financial readiness, there are considerably more exit options available.

From a *mental readiness* perspective (i.e. an owner's attachment to the business), business owners may be ready to get out, have a good idea of how to fill time outside the business, and/or perceive an exit as a healthy and natural next step in life (higher mental readiness). Alternatively, they may be heavily involved in the day-to-day operations of the business, have strong emotional or sentimental attachment to the business, have few or no hobbies outside running the business, see the business as a job rather than an investment, and/or subconsciously resist steps necessary to plan an exit. The business may simply be their identity (lower mental readiness). Whatever their mental readiness may be, the business owner may want to consider investing in a coach for themselves or joining a peer-CEO group like Vistage.

As is demonstrated in the survey data in the next section, a majority – 84% – of American privately held business owners have a low mental readiness to exit their companies. This is an interesting statistic to consider when combined with the data previously provided on the aging Baby Boomer owners.

With the owner's personal goals for the business exit established, and his financial and mental readiness determined, he and his advisors can begin to define the type of exiting owner he is and proceed with the rest of the exit plan.

Step 3: Type of Exiting Owner

Step 3 involves an owner identifying with the type of exiting owner he most resembles. There are four general types of exiting owners, determined by each owner's financial and mental readiness to exit. Establishing which type of exiting owner one is helps identify the exit options that are most likely suitable for the owner to begin to build an exit plan.

"Rich and ready to go" owners are characterized as having both high financial and high mental readiness. They are ready to go and can afford to choose their exit. Their personal involvement is not critical to the daily operations of the business, they have limited emotional or sentimental attachment to the business, they have sufficient wealth outside the equity interest in the company to sustain their lifestyle, and usually estate tax issues need to be incorporated with the exit.

"Well-off but choose to work" owners have high financial but low mental readiness. These owners can afford to leave but do not know what else they would do without running the business. From a mental readiness perspective, their personal involvement is probably critical to the daily operations of the business, they enjoy work, and are prone to have emotional attachment to the business. Financially, like the "rich and ready to go" owner, they have sufficient wealth, including sources of income outside the business, and may be facing estate tax issues. These owners may be considering a controlled and phased exit from the business.

"Stay and grow" owners are characterized as having both low financial and low mental readiness to exit. They are not ready to stop working and have not yet accumulated sufficient personal wealth to sustain their post-exit lifestyle. As illustrated in the next section, the majority of U.S. business owners today are stay-and-grow owners. They are interested in focusing the growth of the business on an exit in the distant future and would like to save for the future in a tax-efficient manner.

"Get me out" owners have low financial but high mental readiness. They want out immediately for the most money possible. These owners have limited options, the only one of which may be to sell their business. They are not prepared financially for the business exit and may have maintained their lifestyle by living out of the business, but are still highly motivated to stop working, at least in the current business.

EXHIBIT 14.1 Exit Quadrant Chart

Any given business owner may not fit perfectly into any one of these four types but may favor one and have qualities of another. The exit quadrant chart in Exhibit 14.1 incorporates Steps 2 and 3 of the exit planning process and helps show where an owner may fall in regard to both financial and mental readiness.

To increase the ability of business owners to measure their readiness for an exit, an online software-survey tool was created to help owners take this measurement. Over the course of three years of surveying business owners, more than 1,500 surveys were completed. The survey tool is named the Business Exit Readiness Index – referred to as the BERI report – and is shown in Exhibit 14.2.

These survey results are a view into American business owners' general readiness for their exit. These survey results serve the purpose of helping owners who have a low mental readiness see that they are truly not alone if they are feeling like they are not ready to transition out of the business they started (or bought) and built.

Further, a closer look at the survey results illustrates not only a low mental readiness, but that a majority also have a low financial readiness for an exit today. As stated above, these stay-and-grow owners represent the readiness of a majority of owners today. And, given this fact, the question for many owners becomes not only "How can I save more money outside of the business to secure my personal financial/retirement planning?," but also "How attached do I feel to my business and how is this preventing me from objectively planning for the largest financial asset that I own?"

In fact, the name *exit planning* does not necessarily serve the business owner market well because it suggests, intuitively, that an exit is time to go. However, as mentioned a number of times throughout this chapter, the exit planning process is actually a long-term process designed to assist business

EXHIBIT 14.2 Business Exit Readiness Index

owners, over a period of time, with their planning for an *eventual* exit. Truth be told, by the time an owner is ready to go there is really not a lot of time to make changes that are often needed for a successful transition. The results of this BERI survey should help owners to see that they are not alone in their financial and mental readiness and that they should work on their exit plans over a longer period of time to have a successful personal and business transition.

Step 4: Exit Options

Upon completion of Steps 1, 2, and 3 business owners are engaged in the exit planning process, have thought about their personal and business goals, and know their financial and mental readiness for an exit. Now the process moves toward understanding the options that are available to transition the company and to most closely align with the goals set in Step 1. A complete exit strategy plan will examine all the pros and cons of the exit options available to determine which one is the best fit for helping a business owner achieve his overall goals. This is where the owner will realize that selling the business may not be the only or best option for an exit. As illustrated in Exhibit 14.3, there are many exit options. Recognizing that most privately

EXHIBIT 14.3 20 Exit Options

Carve-outs	Liquidation (selective, orderly, or forced)
Debt refinancing	Recapitalization
Divestitures	Sale to employees (ESOP)
Dual-class recapitalizations	Sale to family
Gift to charity	Sale to management (MBO)
Gift to employees	Sale to management and outside investor
Gift to family	Sale to a third party
Initial public offering	Share repurchasing
Joint ventures	Spin-offs
Leveraged recapitalizations	Strategic alliances

held businesses will not experience an initial public offering (IPO) and are not interested in liquidating the company, we focus on the five most common exit alternatives for a going-concern business: sale, recapitalization, employee stock ownership plan (ESOP), management buyout, and gifting.

Sale to a Third Party

The sale of a business to a third party is the most intuitive and easiest to understand of the exit options. Many business owners are aware of companies in their industry selling to a larger competitor (or investor) and some owners will even have a sense of the multiple at which companies in their industry are often valued. This option requires understanding the basic components of a sale transaction in order to be better prepared for the potential sale. The benefits of M&A were discussed in Chapter 1, and the M&A market and planning process were discussed in Chapter 4.

This option is generally the most effective means to immediately realize shareholder wealth, given that it involves building value and selling at the highest price. Owners typically receive highest value but possibly lose their job, give up strategic and financial control of business, realize none of the business's future value, and are subject to taxes and fees.[4] The value that exiting owners will receive for the sale of the business is simply whatever the market will bear (i.e. what a buyer will pay). As mentioned at the outset of this chapter, M&A advisors disqualify roughly 65% to 75% of prospective sellers, implying that other exit options for those businesses may make more sense. Also, as the BERI statistics illustrate, less than two in 10 business owners today have a mental readiness that indicates that they are a candidate for a sale of their company.

---

[4] For a select few companies, an initial public offering may be an alternative exit to a sale.

Business owners are well-served in knowing that there are many actions that can be taken, years in advance of a sale transaction, to increase the value of the business and make the company more transferable in the future. This book's title – *Valuation for M&A* – suggests this very fact.

Private Equity Group Recapitalization

The combination of increasing legislation on public companies, availability of inexpensive debt financing, more cash available for investment, aging Baby Boomer business owners, and a growing economy has led to a surge in the number of private equity investors. In 2017, PitchBook Data, Inc. reported that there were 13,039 active private equity groups (PEGs) worldwide, 6,434 of which were headquartered in the United States. These firms backed 64,471 companies worldwide, including 30,682 in the United States. Initially, PEGs focused on the middle, upper middle, and large-cap markets. With increasing valuations for larger companies and overall growth in the number of PEGs, PEGs have moved downstream to the lower middle market, buying small to grow big. PEGs are now doing deals as small as $5–10 million if the company has a unique selling proposition, has growth potential, is profitable, and has a good management team. As a result of these trends, PEG recapitalization has become a more viable exit option for the business owner.

A recapitalization transaction is when owners sell a controlling stake in the business to a PEG, take some cash out of those proceeds, and likely continue to run the business at an operational level. The PEG provides funding and management expertise to help grow the business. The funding may provide capital for growth that could not otherwise be achieved with only an owner's capital base or to finance an acquisition. The selling owner receives value (i.e. is paid) exclusive of any possible synergies but maintains a stake in the future value of the company and continues to work under an employment agreement. This is typically an option for owners with both low financial and mental readiness for an exit (i.e. stay-and-grow owners).

While the PEG option looks very good on paper, many owners will struggle with this alternative because privately held business owners often are not interested in having partners in their business (worse yet, becoming someone else's employee). These owners should consider the statistics that highlight the growing force that private equity is in the marketplace today and learn about how PEG transactions have evolved over time to accommodate a variety of needs and concerns of the privately held business owner.

Employee Stock Ownership Plan

An ESOP is an internal transfer of ownership involving the sale of all or, more often, a portion of the company's equity to an employee benefit trust. An

ESOP trust – the vehicle that is created to purchase the company's shares – is a qualified retirement plan with vesting schedules, contribution limits, and other requirements under the Employee Retirement Income Security Act. ESOPs have been around for over 40 years and have been an ideal tool for thousands of business owners to design their exit plans, offering an internal transaction as opposed to a sale or a PEG transaction.

An ESOP provides an internal market for the company's stock, offers diversification for owners, rewards long-term employees with ownership opportunities, incentivizes employees to increase productivity, provides a qualified retirement plan, and affords substantial tax benefits for company and its owners. In addition, owners can maintain control, keep their job/salary/reasonable perquisites, and participate in the company's future value because of the ESOP's flexibility. The ESOP can be an option for three of the four types of exiting owner. Overall, the ESOP is an attractive option for owners who are looking to cash in part of their equity (via a tax-free rollover for added liquidity[5]), may not be ready to retire, and want to leave a legacy for their employees. Owners looking to get out quickly may not be interested in an ESOP.

Overall, an ESOP is a very flexible tool, but has a certain amount of complexity to it. Experienced exit planning professionals, as well as those who represent ESOPs exclusively, can help to clarify this complexity for owners to see whether an ESOP is a viable option to help those owners meet their personal and business goals.

Management Buyout

A management buyout (MBO) is another exit strategy involving an internal transfer of ownership. However, in this case, ownership is sold directly to the company's existing management team (and, perhaps some co-owners and/or family members). Four benefits of this exit option are:

1. A controlled exit can occur over many years, providing a flexible deal structure and tax situation.
2. Value is maintained through the continuity of business operations.
3. The transaction does not require an outside party.
4. It rewards the team that helped grow the business.

Drawbacks include:

1. Lack of employee liquidity to purchase the business.
2. Changes in relationship from employer/employee to business partners.

---

[5] For C corporations under Internal Revenue Code Section 1042.

3. Business will likely need to serve as collateral.
4. Negotiating with the people who work for the owner.

The MBO is typically an option for owners with high financial and low mental readiness for an exit (i.e. those who are well off but choose to work). MBOs can be a challenge for owners who want to shift the risk of business ownership to a buyer/PEG with financial backing, allowing that owner a pay-day for their years or even decades of effort. That said, there are many owners whose desire is to reward the very employees who helped that owner achieve the success that they hold today. MBOs require a high degree of engineering between the owner and management team, thus requiring an experienced team of professionals for the execution. A complete exit planning process will include the financial and nonfinancial pros and cons of an MBO for an owner's exit planning.

Gifting

Gifting strategies involve transferring ownership to family members or employees. Gifting strategies can be, and often are, used in combination with other strategies, such as ESOPs and MBOs, to transfer additional amounts of company stock to employees, heirs, or charities. In most cases, these programs do not include any cash flow back to the business owners. However, certain transactions allow for income streams back to exiting owners as well as current-year tax deductions that financially reward exiting owners for the assets that have been gifted away.

If contemplated, gifting should be done early in the exit process, ideally long before a sale (if any) of the company, so that when value increases, that growth is outside the owner's estate. If the timing is not right to sell the company (e.g. during a downturn or when it does not fit in with the owner's near-term goals), it may be a good time to do some estate planning and gift shares. Gifting is more an issue of a legacy than an exit or succession, unless of course family is involved in the business and is part of the leadership team that is expected to come into future ownership. Gifting is therefore typically an option for owners with a high level of financial readiness but is neutral to owners' mental readiness for an exit (i.e. owners who are either well off but choose to work or are rich and ready to go).

Although it is not an option most business owners want to think about, and is outside the scope of this book, liquidation is an option that in some cases might have to be considered. When a business is consistently under-performing and management has refused to alter poor practices, or if there is no one to buy the business, liquidation may be the best way to preserve value. Failure to take advice to liquidate voluntarily and in an orderly manner may sometimes lead to bankruptcy.

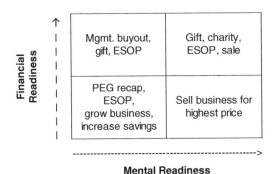

EXHIBIT 14.4 Exit Options Chart

Each of these exit options, illustrated in Exhibit 14.4, has a different value associated with it. It is important to understand the concept that a business does not have one value; rather, it has a range of values. The next section explains how there can be different values for the same business.

Step 5: Range of Values

Valuation is a central part of the exit planning process. A business is often an owner's most valuable asset. As such, commonly for owners with low financial readiness, their financial security depends on maximizing value (and minimizing taxes) and converting that asset's value to cash. Owners and their advisors must know the current range of values of the business to determine how financial objectives can be met. When looking at the overall portfolio of assets, owners can readily obtain the current value of their marketable securities and real estate holdings. However, they cannot get a handle on their personal net worth without understanding how much their illiquid business is worth.

The value of a business depends on the premise and standard of value (introduced in Chapter 1), and these are determined based on the purpose and perspective of the exit plan. Throughout this book, we allude to the fact that value is a range concept and not an exact number. Many business owners do not know the value of their company, nor do they understand how that value can change. Consequently, they are unlikely to realize that each exit option has a different value associated with it.

In order to examine the financial outcome from analyzing each of the exit options, business owners must understand the range of values that exists for the business. This concept of a range from an M&A perspective was raised in Appendix 13A as it relates to synergies gained

EXHIBIT 14.5 Continuum of Value

Liquidation Value		Fair Market Value (FMV)		Investment Value
$15,000	$19,000	$31,000	$35,000	$41,000

Liquidation → Gift → ESOP → MBO → PEG Recap → Strategic Buyers

	EBIT	Implied Value
Book Value[a]		$15,000
FMV of Minority Interest[b]	$6,900	$19,000
FMV of Controlling Interest[c]	$7,650	$31,000
Investment Value – Horizontal Integration[d]	$8,650	$35,000
Investment Value – Vertical Integration[e]	$10,150	$41,000

[a]Cavendish's book value at the Valuation Date (Year 5) for liquidation purposes. We assume no additional adjustments to book value. See Exhibit 21.3 in Chapter 21.
[b]Fair market value of a minority interest for gifting purposes. This assumes that FMV is based on a 4 times EBIT multiple and discounted for lack of marketability by 30%. Because a minority interest is being valued, adjustments for excess compensation are not made. EBIT is sourced from Exhibit 21.1.
[c]Fair market value of a controlling interest, potentially for a PEG recapitalization. This also assumes that FMV is based on a 4 times EBIT multiple. EBIT is adjusted for excess compensation of $750 (see Exhibit 21.7) and no DLOM is applicable.
[d]Investment value to a strategic buyer seeking horizontal integration. Adjusted EBIT of $7,650 is further adjusted for reduced expenses, resulting in a $1,000 increase in EBIT. For purposes of this example, a 4 times EBIT multiple is paid, but investment value often reflects a higher multiple (lower discount rate) than FMV.
[e]Investment value to a strategic buyer seeking vertical integration. Adjusted EBIT is further adjusted for increased revenues as well as reduced expenses, resulting in an additional $1,500 increase in EBIT.

from a transaction. In exit planning, the range concept is considerably broader. Business appraisers restrict the use of their appraisals to a specific purpose for good reason. A conclusion of value is directly impacted by the purpose and underlying standard of value. Each company's range of value can be observed in the form of a continuum. As illustrated in Exhibit 14.5, which applies data from our case study presented in Chapter 21, this range can be significant.

On the very low end of the continuum of value is liquidation value. For a going concern, on the lower end of the fair market value range is the straight financial buyer who discounts expected future cash flow of the company, assuming only organic growth at the company's (typically higher) cost of capital. This starts with the minority shareholder who has minimal liquidity and who has no control over management of the company, including controlling owner discretionary expenses. Therefore, discounts for lack of control and for lack of marketability, as explained in Chapter 12, are typically appropriate. This is fair market value applicable to the gifting and ESOP options.

The value continuum then moves to the controlling shareholder who has control over management and has the ability to sell the company if he so chooses. Discounts for lack of control are no longer applicable, and discounts for lack of marketability are either minimized or not applicable. This is fair market value applicable to the sale to a financial buyer and is therefore often applicable to the MBO option.

The continuum then continues toward investment value involving synergies, where there may be a portfolio buyer who brings overhead efficiency to the table by eliminating some of the company's operating expenses and is looking to the company as a platform to expand into a particular market. Next is the strategic buyer seeking horizontal integration – where a company dominates a market at the same stage of the production process by monopolizing resources at that stage – by decreasing costs through the combination of operations. At the top is the strategic buyer seeking vertical integration – where a company has control over several of the production and/or distribution steps involved in the creation of its product or service – to increase revenues by leveraging other businesses. The option of a sale to a third party can be at several different levels. Part of the exit plan is recognizing which buyer would find the company most appealing.

As introduced in Chapter 3, value drivers reflect the company's strengths that enable it to both minimize risk and maximize net cash flow returns. They include synergies expected from M&A, industry position, growth trends, quality and reputation of the business, cash flow and profitability, customer relationships, geographic expansion possibilities, brand name, technology, intellectual property, and assembled workforce, among others. To understand the ranges of value at the upper end of the continuum, owners must have a solid grasp of these value drivers.

Step 6: Execution of Exit Plan

This final step in the exit planning process is all about getting a plan completed. After measuring an owner's goals, determining their readiness, and identifying what type of owner they most closely resemble, the process includes an evaluation of the exit options as well as an understanding that value is a range concept and owners will, essentially, receive the value of the exit option that they choose. Now, in Step 6, the focus is on structuring a transaction, reviewing the tax implications of certain structures, drafting the legal agreements needed to execute a plan, and assembling the right advisory team to assist with the (ongoing) planning and execution of the exit.

EXHIBIT 14.6 Preserve, Protect, and Increase Value

Preserve Value	Protect Value	Increase Value
S Corporation	Review insurance	Grow revenues
ESOP	Legal audit	Reduce expenses
CRT	Eliminate personal guarantees	Diversify customers
	Separate real estate	Solid management
		Groom successor

An integral part of the exit planning process, as it pertains to valuation, is to preserve value by minimizing taxes, protect value from creditors, and increase value through value drivers. As outlined in Exhibit 14.6, value can be preserved by converting the business to an S corporation, setting up an ESOP, or establishing a charitable remainder trust (CRT), among others. Value can be protected by reviewing insurance policies, conducting a periodic legal audit, removing personal guarantees, separating the real estate from the operations, and setting up multiple entities, to name a few. Value can be increased by growing cash flows and reducing risks associated with those cash flows. Growing cash flows can be achieved by increasing revenues and eliminating discretionary expenditures. Reducing risks to cash flows can be achieved by solidifying and diversifying the customer base, building a solid management team, and grooming a successor. Critical to the process is the ability to present to potential buyers the history of the business and management's strategy for future growth. Getting the company's financial statements in order, coupled with a documentation of management's strategy to grow the business, adds credibility to the story of the business. Periodically obtaining an independent appraisal of the business serves several purposes, including identifying value drivers specific to the business and establishing an objective estimate of value for planning purposes. This is all part of execution.

A significant portion of the exit planning process is understanding, building, and realizing value in the business. To realize value, effective execution of the exit plan is required.

Execution entails coordination and planning involving deal structuring, taxes, estate planning, legal agreements, and much more. It is a step-by-step process that can take a number of years of transferring value, then management, and finally control. Considerations include market conditions and market timing, maximization of value versus associated risks, external versus internal factors, strategic business factors, sentimental attachment to the business, psychological measures of success, and potential for a family member to manage the business.

Ensuring that there is a competent and professional advisory team in place is essential for a smooth and successful exit. Early implementation and periodically revisiting the exit plan will better help define the business owners' timetable and eventual success of their exit.

The vast majority of business owners looking to sell their companies fail to do so within three years of setting out in the process. These owners will be in a much better position to sell at an optimal price in the future if they have an exit plan to initiate alternative plans in the meantime. To begin to understand what an optimal price would be, one must learn the fundamentals of valuing a business covered in the previous eight chapters.

CHAPTER 15

Art of the Deal[1]

The preceding chapters have emphasized the essential need for managers and shareholders to understand value to operate a company successfully and to make sound estimates of value. In the merger and acquisition (M&A) world, however, much of the real action takes place *after* stand-alone fair market value and investment value have been determined. Structuring and negotiating a transaction – doing a deal – is the next step in the M&A process. This chapter describes the process of negotiating a deal from both the buyer's and the seller's viewpoint. Although every transaction is different and each may present unique demands, needs, or circumstances, the concepts and principles presented here provide excellent guidelines to help buyers and sellers reach their ultimate goal: successfully negotiate and close the transaction.

Unique Negotiation Challenges

A broad range of knowledge and skills is required to accomplish this task. Negotiators in M&A should be skillful communicators – in listening, speaking, and writing – must understand value, and should possess a reasonable knowledge of the tax code and accounting principles. As discussed in Chapter 4, the M&A team should include legal, tax, and valuation specialists, one of whom also may serve as the negotiator. Buyers and sellers who fail to recognize the need for this breadth of knowledge frequently negotiate the wrong price or terms of sale.

In considering these transaction issues, it may be helpful to review the discussion in Chapter 4 in the sections Sales Strategy and Process and Acquisition Strategy and Process.

---

[1] The authors gratefully acknowledge the contributions to this chapter made by Michael J. Eggers, ASA, CBA, CPA, ABV, of American Business Appraisers, San Francisco, California; email: mje@abasf.com.

Sellers sometimes feel that as the owner or chief executive officer (CEO) of their company, they understand the business better than anyone else and, as a result, are best qualified to negotiate the sale. Similarly, CEOs or controlling shareholders of the buying company may conclude that their authority best equips them to negotiate the ideal price and terms of sale. While sellers and buyers may possess extensive knowledge and the authority to approve or reject the deal, they must recognize that a negotiation is a process in which they have a role. The key is to understand the role that each member of the negotiating team should play and then have each member stick to that function.

Interpersonal and communication skills are emphasized because the deal-making process frequently plunges buyers and sellers into intense negotiations that will determine the course of a company's operations for a long time. The negotiations may affect numerous careers, where people will work and what they will do, and people's personal fortunes are often hanging in the balance. And with so much at stake, the key negotiators are usually strangers to each other and often rely on M&A team members whom they hardly know.

With these circumstances in mind, qualified advisors should be in position to engage in an initial exchange of thoughts about value and *their* – as opposed to *their client's* – justification for their value opinion. As dispassionate professionals, they should be able to advance toward an acceptable range of value for the start of future negotiations or recognize that they are probably too far apart to pursue the deal. The advisors should understand that in these discussions, it is their value recommendations that are being presented, not their client's sale or purchase offer. This process protects the client, who is the ultimate decision maker, from making any commitment to price or terms, but enables each side to get a good sense of the other's expectations and negotiating style.

It also enables the buyer and sellers to avoid the urge to rush into discussions of price. *Price is not value.* Price can be affected dramatically by the deal terms, including:

- The amount of cash exchanged at closing
- Deal structure – stock sale/purchase versus asset sale/purchase
- Terms of sale – cash versus stock versus some combination
- Treatment of personal goodwill
- Presence of a covenant not to compete
- Employment or consulting contract for seller
- Seller financing and/or presence of collateral and security agreements

In the early negotiation stages, seek agreement on other essential but less confrontational issues, such as plans for the future of the business and the role of the seller or other key people after the sale. In this preliminary stage of negotiation, the seller's nonfinancial or personal concerns also can be identified and assessed by both sides. In the process, the operational capability of the new venture can be evaluated. In resolving these initial issues, buyers and sellers are simultaneously developing a level of trust and negotiating process that will assist both with the more difficult issue of price. At a later stage, differences in price may appear to be smaller, and both sides will have built momentum toward resolving the inevitable gap that will exist.

When it is time to discuss price, remember the dictum "Seller's price, buyer's terms." Given the array of techniques available to structure transactions, buyers often can develop an offer that both fits the budget and makes the seller want to sell. Typically, if the buyer can meet or approach the seller's price, the seller often will be flexible as to how consideration is paid.

Deal Structure: Stock versus Assets

Sellers are wise to recognize that when experienced buyers evaluate a potential acquisition, they carefully assess its risk. One of the first and most important risk assessments is the consideration of whether to purchase the stock of the target from the shareholders or all or selected corporate assets from the corporation.

Although most of the well-publicized acquisitions of public companies are stock transactions, in the middle market, both stock and asset sales are common. Buyers and sellers should be aware of the advantages that each structure provides. Too often, parties on one side of a transaction will insist on only one possible structure without considering creative ways to close the deal with a different structure. Typically, the advantages that a given structure provides to one side create corresponding disadvantages for the other side. Therefore, both sides are wise to recognize the consequences that the structure creates as they form their negotiating strategy. In general, sellers prefer stock sales, which provide the advantage of having taxation occur only at one level. Conversely, buyers typically prefer an asset acquisition, where they receive a stepped-up tax basis in the assets acquired and reduce their risk by acquiring only identified assets and liabilities. Because the circumstances of each transaction vary, each side should seriously evaluate both transaction structures to identify and quantify the pros and cons involved, particularly the risk and net after-tax cash flow consequences, to ultimately negotiate the best possible deal. An overview of the advantages and disadvantages when the transaction is structured as a stock sale and as an asset sale is presented next and summarized in Exhibit 15.1.

EXHIBIT 15.1 Stock versus Asset Transaction Buyer/Seller Comparison Chart

STOCK TRANSACTION

	ADVANTAGES	DISADVANTAGES

BUYER	1. Some stock transactions (e.g. a tax-free exchange of stock) are not taxable, whereas *all* asset transactions are taxable.
	2. Often less time-consuming and costly than an asset transaction.
		1. No basis step-up to buyer (unless Section 338 is elected).
		2. Thus the buyer pays with after-tax dollars.
		3. If individual buys, financing is outside the Company.
		4. Tax attributes generally carry over, but
		  a. NOLs are lost if over 50% ownership change,
		  b. otherwise only part of NOL is usable annually, and
		  c. consolidated return limits (CRCOs and SRLYs).
		5. Contracts continue in force (good or bad).
		6. Unwanted assets, liabilities, and contingencies, but buyer may seek to be indemnified against any undisclosed liabilities.

SELLER	1. Buyer takes the corporation's business subject to all its liabilities. 2. Seller wants lower long-term capital gains. 3. No need to liquidate after purchase. 4. Some stock sales may qualify for ESOP or reorganization treatment. 5. All assets are sold, so there is no need to get rid of unwanted items.	1. Seller's warranties and guarantees are broader. 2. If seller finances, collateralization is more difficult. 3. It is more difficult for the seller to hold back some assets. 4. If there are NOLs, they cannot be used to offset other income.

EXHIBIT 15.1 (*Continued*)

ASSET TRANSACTION

	ADVANTAGES	DISADVANTAGES
BUYER	1. Tax basis of assets acquired is fair market value. 2. Price paid is deducted, amortized, or depreciated. 3. Buyer can choose the business form. 4. Selected assets are bought and liabilities assumed. 5. More debt and equity structuring flexibility. 6. Less exposure to seller's contingent liabilities.	1. Buyer typically cannot use seller's tax accounting methods (disadvantage if assets on books are worth more than fair market value). 2. Buyer may want to keep certain contract rights. 3. May get a step-down in basis if there is a bargain purchase. 4. C and triangular reorganizations may limit basis step-up. 5. Built-in capital gains (BIG) tax for certain S corporations.
SELLER	1. Less warranty exposure obligation to the buyer. 2. If no *BIG* tax, buyer gets more flexibility often with little tax cost to seller. 3. Easier to retain selected assets. 4. Seller may keep some tangible or intangible assets. 5. Gives the buyer greater flexibility in structuring the deal.	1. For a C corporation or a recently converted S corporation, the issue of double taxation is often a major problem. 2. If corporation is a C or S, with *BIG* tax exposure, double tax cuts for seller. 3. Buyer may underpay for unwanted assets. 4. Contract rights may not be easily transferred.

Stock Transaction

Generally speaking, in a stock transaction, all of the tangible and intangible assets and all of the liabilities, including unknown and contingent liabilities from current or prior acts of the seller and its agents, are acquired by the buyer. These include the unknown skeletons in the closet that buyers fear so much.

SELLER'S VIEWPOINT Sellers, in general, strongly prefer a stock sale because as long as the stock was held for more than one year, shareholders only pay tax once, at the personal level on the difference between the sale price and their cost basis in the stock. This tax is computed at long-term capital gains tax rates, which are generally more favorable than ordinary income tax rates. In negotiations, sellers may attempt to allocate as much of the proceeds as possible to the stock sale and the least amount possible to consulting contracts or covenants not to compete because they are taxed as ordinary income versus the lower capital gains tax rate on the stock sale.

Because the seller receives this tax advantage and this structure creates tax and other disadvantages for the buyer, the seller typically must accept a lower sale price in a stock deal. In addition, a stock deal causes buyers to accept all known, unknown, and contingent liabilities of the company, which can substantially increase their risk. As a result, buyers frequently demand extensive representation and warranties as part of the sale agreement to protect them from unknown potential liabilities that may accompany any acquisition of stock.

Thus, sellers should identify and, wherever possible, make any necessary changes to minimize the risks to which the buyer may be exposed in acquiring the seller's company. By taking these steps, the seller may make a stock deal sufficiently less risky to a potential buyer so the transaction can be structured as a stock purchase.

Because stock deals are so unattractive to buyers, sellers frequently find far fewer buyers willing to purchase stock. Where minority shareholders exist, sellers usually must obtain their approval, which may require separate negotiations with them.

RISK MANAGEMENT THROUGH INSURANCE Insurance is often a practical tool to assist in risk reduction. Liability insurance, known as tail coverage, usually can be acquired at a reasonable marginal cost to the buyer, and structured as an additional rider on the buyer's existing policy. If the buyer requires that the seller purchase this insurance, the premium likely will be much higher as a separate new policy. This is a good example of something the buyer can provide to the transaction at a lower cost than the seller for the same benefit. Deal price can be affected and benefit provided to both buyer and seller.

BUYER'S VIEWPOINT A major disadvantage in a stock acquisition for the buyer is assumption of the target company's fixed assets at their existing tax basis, which is often after substantial depreciation already has been deducted. Thus, the buyer is able to write off far less of the acquisition cost, although some special tax elections may be available to avoid this consequence.

To reduce the charge against earnings, some public company acquirers may prefer that more of the cost be classified as general intangible value subject to amortization rather than shorter-term depreciation. This reflects the fact that public companies are frequently more focused on earnings while private company buyers generally aim to minimize taxes.

In addition to the unfavorable tax consequences to a buyer of a stock purchase, this structure also creates added potential risks for the buyer. With the stock purchase, the buyer acquires all of the target company's liabilities. The buyer's principal concerns are contingent liabilities, underfunded retirement plans, and potential product liability claims from current or prior acts of the seller or its agents. The potential for loss from these liabilities often creates a more extensive due diligence process for the buyer, who must search much more carefully for these liabilities. The buyer also may be constrained by the seller's unwillingness or inability to provide warranties and representations that the buyer desires.

In a stock acquisition where less than 100% of the stock is acquired, buyers must contend with minority shareholders who may file dissenting shareholder actions. Because of all of these negative consequences for buyers, they typically can negotiate a much better price and sale terms with a stock transaction.

Stock transactions provide some benefits to the buyer, although they carry substantial disadvantages. Because the corporate structure has not changed, the corporation's contracts, credit agreements, and labor agreements tend to remain in place unless they are specifically voided or subject to approval as if assigned when there is a material change of shareholders. Having these agreements in place may ease the acquisition and integration process for the buyer. The buyer also acquires any favorable tax attributes of the seller, such as ordinary or capital loss carryforwards. Buyers may be able to elect Internal Revenue Code Section 338 provisions, which allow for a stepped-up basis in the stock, which they can offset with tax attributes acquired or through payment of a tax. As part of the negotiation process, buyers may attempt to allocate as much of the sale price as possible to consulting contracts or covenants not to compete because these are generally tax deductible to the buyer.

COLLARS AND PACKAGING ADJUSTMENTS When a buyer purchases stock, he or she acquires the company's current position. That is, the seller's working capital, defined as current assets less current liabilities, is part of the value of the company. When the price is negotiated to be effective as of a future closing date, the current position is often guaranteed by the seller to be within a range, say 10%, of the agreed value at the closing date.

For example, Sellco has had an average working capital balance of $10 million for the last two years. This normalized working capital amount is an agreed part of the value exchanged in a purchase of all of the outstanding common shares of Sellco. As part of the definitive agreement, a 10% collar is negotiated that states that if the working capital is less than $9 million, a dollar-for-dollar reduction in the purchase price will result. Similarly, if working capital is more than $11 million, a dollar-for-dollar additional consideration will be paid.

Asset Transaction

In a transaction structured as the sale and purchase of assets, only those tangible and intangible assets and liabilities specifically listed in the purchase agreement are transferred. Buyers tend to favor this structure because they can specifically exclude assumption of all or selected liabilities; it typically works to the disadvantage of the seller.

Generally, sellers retain cash, receivables, and payables in an asset transaction. Any of a seller's debt assumed by the buyer amounts to an increase in the purchase price for the buyer and represents additional consideration paid to the seller. Early in the negotiating process, both parties should identify any assets that are not intended to be part of the transaction so that these may be excluded from those assets listed in the definitive agreement. When elements of working capital are excluded from the transaction, buyers must consider the short and intermediate cash flow and financing needs of the new operation when it starts without the seller's cash, receivables, and payables.

Seller's Viewpoint

The major disadvantage to the seller of an asset sale is that the *proceeds are taxed twice* for a C corporation, first at the corporate level on the asset sale and second at the individual shareholder level when the corporation is liquidated and the proceeds are distributed to the shareholders.

The seller may face additional, onerous tax consequences in the form of recapture of depreciation deductions, which must be classified as ordinary income to the corporation at the time of sale. The corporation also must immediately recognize any amount paid for goodwill as a capital gain. This double taxation of asset sale proceeds can dramatically reduce what the seller actually receives after all taxes are paid in an asset deal. On the plus side, because buyers strongly favor an asset purchase, they are generally more willing to pay a higher price for this type of deal.

Because an asset sale involves only the transfer of specifically identified assets and liabilities, this form of transaction leaves the seller responsible for any remaining liabilities that were not part of the sale. These liabilities commonly include contingent liabilities, accrued retirement fund contributions, accrued employee benefits, lease obligations, and ongoing litigation costs. The seller also may face one-time fees and taxes associated with the transfer of the assets, such as real estate transfer taxes. In an asset sale where the sellers intend to continue to operate the business that remains, the sale of the assets may temporarily disrupt operations as the assets are removed and the business adjusts to their absence.

Sellers usually face fewer representations and warranties with an asset sale because buyers are able to identify more accurately exactly what is involved in the transaction. When all or only specific assets are being purchased, the buyer has no need to extend due diligence to a review of the sellers' bylaws, corporate minutes, financial statements, credit agreements, and so on. Sellers should resist such attempts, which are appropriate only in a stock sale. Where minority shareholders exist, asset transactions also generally reduce legal actions from dissenting shareholders that could take place in a stock sale.

Buyer's Viewpoint

With an asset acquisition, the buyer achieves the major tax advantage of being able to carry the assets purchased at their current fair market value. This stepped-up basis allows the buyer to depreciate much of the acquisition cost. In addition, any amount of the purchase price in excess of the fair market value of the tangible assets that was paid for specific intangible assets, such as patents or copyrights and general goodwill, generally may be written off for income tax purposes.

Buyers also benefit in an asset acquisition by acquiring only those liabilities that are specifically identified as part of the sale. Thus they avoid contingent and unknown liabilities.

In an asset sale, buyers also can avoid acquiring risky assets. Most commonly risky assets include real estate that may carry environmental hazards and uncollectable receivables or unsalable inventory. Buyers also can determine the entity that acquires and owns the assets, which may create tax planning and risk management opportunities.

In return for these benefits, buyers usually must pay a substantially higher price to purchase assets than if stock were purchased. The higher price recognizes both the benefits provided to the buyer and the substantial tax disadvantages created for the seller. Asset acquisitions frequently create problems for buyers, although these are usually offset by the benefits that have been described. In acquiring assets rather than the stock, technically speaking, the buyer fails to acquire the target's employees, customers, or contracts. Although the buyer may have preferred to avoid certain employees or contracts, he or she may have difficulty negotiating with other employees, labor unions, and customers. The company's relations with suppliers, including credit arrangements and its relations with banks and lessors, also must be established. In addition, buyers may be unable to use some of the target's licenses or permits that provided it with certain advantages. However, with an asset transaction, the buyer can selectively rehire desired employees and may have the opportunity to selectively continue the most advantageous contracts.

By buying assets, the buyer also cannot carry over any favorable tax attributes owned by the seller and typically loses the seller's unemployment compensation and worker's compensation insurance ratings.

Section 338 Election

In the United States, tax law allows in certain instances both buyer and seller to treat a transaction as a stock sale for legal purposes, but treat the sale as an asset transaction for tax purposes. Specifically, the buyer is legally buying stock, but is treated as though they bought assets, while the seller is legally selling stock, but is treated as though they sold assets. The Section 338(h)(10) election is where the seller recognizes the taxable income resulting from the sale of the assets. The Section 338(g) election is where the buyer recognizes the taxable income resulting from the sale of the assets. Both types of Section 338 elections require that the buyer is an S or C corporation and it acquires at least 80% of the target company's stock.

Allocation of the Purchase Price

If the transaction is structured as an asset sale and purchase, one of the very first things both buyer and seller should do is prepare a preliminary purchase price allocation, even if the purchase price is not yet fully developed or determined. The purpose of the draft allocation is to encourage both sides to consider the concepts and taxation of the planned transaction. Form 8594, which is required by the U.S. Internal Revenue Service, is an excellent tool to start these discussions. Too frequently, parties reach agreement on price, terms, financing, and even discuss the concept of purchase price allocation without confronting the related tax consequences.

Misunderstanding the purchase price allocation has often been the source of a failed transaction and hard feelings at the end of deal negotiations. Therefore, Form 8594 should be completed on a tentative and preliminary basis on acceptance of the letter of intent. It will help to ensure that both sides appreciate the tax consequences of each asset allocation decision and how each ultimately affects the buyer's net after-tax cash cost and the seller's net after-tax proceeds from the sale. Purchase price allocation considerations from a financial reporting perspective are discussed in Chapter 17.

Transaction structure is complicated. Those provisions that benefit one side tend to work to the disadvantage of the other side. Therefore, both sides constantly must focus on the risks that each transaction structure provides and avoids. Equally important, each side must constantly focus on both the buyer's net after-tax cost and the seller's net after-tax proceeds from the deal. The final terms of a stock transaction may involve a significantly lower price but increased proceeds to the seller and/or reduced risk to the buyer. Creativity in the deal structure is essential to work out the most mutually advantageous transaction. When both parties are aware of the tax consequences to the other of the terms of sale, they can negotiate a transaction that minimizes the overall tax consequences and works to their mutual benefit.

Terms of Sale: Cash versus Stock

In large acquisitions by public companies, the buyer frequently pays for the target with stock rather than cash. These terms of sale can have a substantial effect on both the risk and the return of the parties to the transaction. While cash sales tend to be rather simple and straightforward, transactions paid for in the buyer's stock of either a publicly or a privately held company may be more complex and require careful examination.

When cash is paid, the buyer's shareholders bear the entire risk of the transaction. Sellers' risk in a cash transaction is straightforward: All they must determine is if they are getting the highest possible price and whether they can generate a higher return by continuing to hold the stock.

When the seller receives payment in the form of stock, he or she must recognize that this currency carries far more risk and volatility than cash. Also, in a sale for stock, the seller shares in the buyer's risk of success in the transaction. When the buyer is a public company, this risk begins with the immediate threat that the market will react negatively to the announcement, causing the stock price – the seller's proceeds – to diminish in value. Furthermore, public company shares received as consideration probably will be restricted from subsequent sale for a fixed period under U.S. Securities and Exchange Commission Rule 144.

As a result, when payment in stock is offered, sellers must carefully assess the quality and marketability of the currency they are receiving to determine the attractiveness of the offer; that is, sellers must exercise careful due diligence on the buyer's stock. At a minimum, sellers should obtain answers to these questions about the acquirer's stock:

- What is the condition and growth potential of the acquirer's industry?
- What is the acquirer's historical performance and future prospects?
- How is the acquirer's stock priced relative to these prospects, and how is it expected to change in the next year?
- What restrictions, if any, prevent or delay sale of any shares of the stock received?
- What is the typical trading activity in the acquirer's stock, and does it provide an adequate market for the new shareholders should they wish to sell their shares?

Since the selling shareholders will lack control of the acquirer's stock, the most influence they typically exert on the buyer's postacquisition policies and performance is through their votes if they hold a minority seat on the buyer's board of directors. Buyers sometimes can negotiate this position, but they must recognize that their minority seat may provide little more satisfaction than the ability to dissent in votes on policies approved by the majority of the buyer's board.

Because the seller knows so much about the company the acquirer wants to buy, the seller should make use of this knowledge. When paid in the acquirer's stock, the seller assumes the same risk as the buyer for the success of the acquisition. Thus, if the seller suspects that the buyer has been too optimistic in forecasts of revenue or expense synergies or the timing to achieve them, the seller will share with the buyer any failure to create this value.

Transactions structured as stock sales often receive the benefit of favorable tax treatment under certain circumstances. Under U.S. tax laws in effect as of the date of this publication, when sellers exchange their stock for stock in the acquirer and receive less than 20% of the sale proceeds in cash, the exchange portion is not currently taxed. The seller's basis in existing shares carries over to the exchanged shares, and the deferred tax does not have to be paid until the exchanged shares are eventually sold for cash.

The seller also must examine whether the offer includes a *fixed stock price* or a *fixed stock exchange ratio*. With a fixed stock price, the seller receives a quantity of shares based on the market value of the buyer's stock on a certain date divided by that established price. If there is a fixed exchange ratio, the seller will receive a fixed number of the buyer's shares for each of the seller's shares. With a fixed exchange ratio, the seller loses value if the buyer's stock price declines and benefits if the seller's stock value increases. Floors and ceilings, called collars, may be imposed to limit the parties' loss or gain. For example, if at the date of close, the price of the shares is out of the money (i.e. lower than a previously agreed price), then buyer or seller (probably both) can terminate the transaction. The stock price collar goes both ways (a price less than agreed and a price more than agreed) for fairness reasons to both buyer and seller. In the long run, temporary changes in the market value should have little effect on the transaction.

A seller also must carefully examine the rights that accompany any shares received. In addition to transfer restrictions and similar limitations, sellers should look for *bring-along (or drag along) rights*, which are similar to *change-in-control provisions*. These rights typically provide sellers with the opportunity to have the shares they have received be brought along with the acquirer's shares in a subsequent transaction that creates further gains on the sale of the acquirer's stock. These provisions provide sellers with the opportunity to profit a second time if the acquirer's stock is bought in a subsequent transaction.

The discussion thus far has assumed that the buyer is paying for the acquisition with publicly traded stock. Should the transaction currency be stock of a privately held company, the risks to the seller are even greater. With the value of the stock unknown and probably highly volatile, and the stock most likely less marketable, particularly for a minority interest, the value of a stock offer should be sharply discounted from its cash equivalent. Sellers may wish to negotiate legal provisions that provide a market for their shares. These could include a *put*, which allows them to tender their shares, either for an established price or one set through a valuation process, where the corporation must acquire the shares in accordance with the terms of the agreement. Buy/sell agreements and formal exit strategies are also options because without a mutually agreeable contracted time period within which to market the now-combined company, the sellers risk never realizing liquid or spendable cash value from the sale of their shares. Selling or exchanging private company stock for other private company stock is not a common practice and should be considered carefully before execution. Control premiums, lack-of-control discounts, and discounts for lack of marketability that relate to this topic are discussed in Chapter 12.

Sellers who are offered stock in the acquirer's company in exchange for their shares should recognize that they are taking substantial risks over the alternative of receiving an equivalent payment in cash. If the acquirer is a public company, the seller faces the immediate risk of a decline in stock value if the market reacts negatively to the acquisition. In addition, the seller is assuming all of the buyer's risk that the synergies from the acquisition can be achieved. Therefore, sellers who are offered stock by the buyer must evaluate carefully whether the buyer's stock is properly valued as of the acquisition date, the likely success of the acquisition, and the underlying marketability of the shares they receive. Unless all of these issues can be resolved favorably, sales paid for in the acquirer's stock should be avoided or should carry a substantially higher price.

Personal Goodwill

Personal goodwill (also known as "professional goodwill") refers to the value associated with the reputation, knowledge, skills, experience, training, expertise, and contacts of a key individual in a business enterprise. This is in contrast to enterprise goodwill that refers to the value associated with the overall practice entity (and therefore also known as "practice goodwill"). In certain M&A transactions, allocating a portion of the consideration to personal goodwill can provide considerable tax benefits. This is especially the case where there are a few key employees who contribute distinct value and future income stream to a C corporation. Any gain on the sale of personal goodwill is considered a capital gain, subject to lower tax rates. In addition, the acquired business does not trigger any entity-level gain on the sale of personal goodwill and the acquirer may be able to amortize the value of the personal goodwill.

Personal goodwill typically exists when a key employee has no employment or noncompete agreement, the employee's relationship with customers and/or suppliers is attached to the individual rather than the corporation, and the employee has the right to sell his/her goodwill. In the 1998 *Martin Ice Cream* case[2] in Federal Tax Court, the Court determined the following eight characteristics as necessary for personal goodwill to be present:

1. Absence of a noncompete agreement between the key employee and the company.
2. The selling company is a C corporation, and the sale is structured as an asset sale.
3. Business is dependent on a key employee's personal relationships and reputation.
4. An employee's involvement is important to the sales process.
5. Business has few, high-volume customers/suppliers.
6. Business is technical, specialized, or a professional service.
7. Business has a high proportion of intangible assets.
8. Loss of the key employee reduces the revenue and/or profits of the business.

---

[2] *Martin Ice Cream Company v. Commissioner* 110 T.C. No. 18 (1998).

Tax Court cases provide guidance for what works and what doesn't in proving the existence of personal goodwill. The following cases involved a good taxpayer outcome involving personal goodwill:

- *William Norwalk, et al. v. Commissioner*, T.C. Memo 1998-279
- *Bross Trucking, et al. v. Commissioner*, T.C. Memo 2014-107
- *Estate of Franklin Z. Adell v. Commissioner*, T.C. Memo 2014-155

However, the following cases were not favorable to the taxpayer:

- *Solomon v. Commissioner*, T.C. Memo 2008-102
- *Kennedy v. Commissioner*, T.C. Memo 2010-206
- *Cavallaro v. Commissioner*, T.C. Memo 2014-189

In order to document the existence of personal goodwill, it should be: (1) clearly identifiable in the purchase agreement, (2) agreed to by the acquiring party, and (3) valued by an independent appraiser. Personal goodwill is most often valued using a with-or-without method within the income approach, as explained in Chapter 18. This involves valuing the company assuming the key employee is no longer with the company and may be competing, and comparing the resulting value to the value of the company as is. The difference between the two scenarios represents the value of the personal goodwill. It may also be valued using a comparative transaction analysis within the market approach, where adjusted market multiples are applied to the company's expected lost revenue and/or income; or by a lost margin analysis within the income approach, which considers the potential lost incremental profit margin incurred by the company without the key employee's contributions and abilities. In the 2010 *Kennedy* decision noted above, the Tax Court rejected personal goodwill because of a lack of an independent valuation or other meaningful attempt to allocate the total transaction sales proceeds.

In conclusion, personal goodwill can provide favorable tax benefits for the parties to an M&A transaction only if it is identified in the transaction agreement and quantified by an independent and supportable valuation analysis.

Bridging the Gap

What can be done when the buyer and seller respectfully disagree about value? First, each side should reassess the pros and cons of doing the deal, including the likely effects on their shareholder value and competitive position. This analysis will help each side to focus on price and the price range over which they can negotiate a successful transaction. Next, each should look to the deal structure and the net after-tax cash cost to the buyer and net after-tax proceeds to the seller. Each should consider different possible transaction structures that may be more tax efficient to each side to help bridge the gap that separates them. For example, consider different cost allocations that may offer the seller capital gain versus ordinary income tax treatment or a structure that provides the seller with a single level of taxation versus double taxation. By concentrating on the buyer's net after-tax cost and the seller's net after-tax proceeds rather than the actual purchase price, there is usually a smaller gap to bridge. Doing this also focuses both sides on their true net cost and return.

When the transaction structure is not sufficient to close the deal, an *earn-out* should be considered. Usually defined as a percentage of some performance measure, the earn-out (also known as contingent consideration) provides an opportunity for the seller to create more value than the buyer sees in the current transaction and share in it. Earn-outs usually favor buyers who do not have to pay for benefits until they are realized. Thus earn-outs require sellers to share in the transaction risk and not be rewarded unless specific goals are achieved. The calculation of the earn-out itself is often difficult, subject to interpretation, and may lead to disputes. Some examples of earn-out terms are:

- Percentage of revenues in excess of a base amount
- Percentage of earnings before interest, taxes, depreciation, and amortization (EBITDA) when gross cash flow is most important
- Percentage of buyer net income and percentage of seller net income when competition for future capital and resources is an issue

There are numerous possible performance measures, but most important to any earn-out agreement is the definition of terms. Consider these definitional issues that could cause disagreements or confusion in an earn-out:

- What does "profit" mean?
- Is profit before or after income taxes, year-end bonuses, corporate donations, and similar deductions?
- Is profit after actual salaries and other forms of compensation, or after agreed-on or industry standard compensation levels?
- Should policies be established to limit the amount of central office overhead or other corporate charges allocated to that business unit?
- Should separate accounting for the acquired business continue to allow for comparison and earn-out calculation, or should the earn-out be based on some combination of the combined business units?
- Should the effect of a covenant not to compete or goodwill amortization from the acquisition price affect the earn-out?

Any earn-out calculation should have a detailed example in the exhibits to the definitive agreement and should include specific, verifiable definitions of terms.

During economic downturns, when earnings multiples and values typically decline, earn-outs structured to provide significant upside potential can be used to bridge the gap between sellers who see the decline as temporary and buyers looking for bargains. Other strategies for sellers include providing more seller financing (which may provide a better return than some investments in a downturn) and retaining a piece of the equity to sell at a higher value after the economy recovers.

Another tool used to bridge the gap or transfer value from buyers to sellers is the *employment agreement*. It provides a vehicle through which a buyer can make tax-deductible payments to the seller, which are taxed as ordinary income to the seller when received. Although employment agreements should reflect true market value for services rendered, they are sometimes disguised purchase-price proceeds paid on a tax-advantageous deductible basis. Both sides should evaluate cautiously what a market-based level of compensation should be to ensure that these payments are not challenged by tax authorities.

Employment agreements offer many benefits to sellers. First and foremost, they keep the seller on the payroll with this compensation, often including lucrative employee benefits, such as use of vehicles, club memberships, vacation pay, and participation in retirement programs or stock option plans. The formal employment agreement also provides a form of guarantee to the seller of continued employment and a degree of protection to the seller from unwanted termination. This type of employment agreement typically includes an established number of years and specifies that the seller cannot be terminated except for specific reasons. The agreement also often includes a provision for payment in full of a predetermined amount if both parties agree to terminate the agreement.

Employment agreements for the seller may also include an *evergreen* provision, which perpetually renews unless the buyer provides specific notice to the seller. Another possible provision in an employment agreement is an *effective termination clause*, which includes the seller's job description at the postacquisition company, including job title and identification of the supervisory position to which the seller reports. Should the buyer wish to change this reporting relationship, the buyer effectively terminates the seller, and all of the negotiated benefits for the seller immediately vest and become due and payable. The purpose of this provision is to provide sellers with a higher degree of certainty of their exact duties at the new company and the flexibility to leave under favorable terms should the circumstances change. These conditions are often important to entrepreneurs or individuals who are used to working as the senior executive in an operation and want to avoid close supervision or more regimented reporting requirements.

Events Subsequent to the Planned Transaction

As important as it is for sellers to focus on the pending transaction, the prudent seller also should consider future sale possibilities. If the buyer experiences a subsequent change in control, that is, the buyer is acquired or merged within a period – most commonly established as within 24 to 36 months from the acquisition date – additional provisions favorable to the seller may be triggered. The most common is for the seller who is receiving deferred payments to have the entire purchase price consideration be due immediately and payable on a change in control. The change-in-control provision also may provide for the original seller to share in any gain achieved by the buyer in the subsequent transaction over the seller's proceeds from the original deal.

See the Deal from the Other Side

Buyer and sellers should recognize that in a transaction where both sides are represented by reasonably experienced advisors, neither should be able to take substantial advantage of the other side unless adverse circumstances or extreme potential exist. In small and middle-market transactions, however, many participants or their advisors lack adequate training and experience, and buyer and seller circumstances can be exploited. As a result, there are frequent examples of great deals negotiated by one side or the other, although most are not well publicized.

More commonly, buyers and sellers should recognize their shared goal to structure a mutually beneficial transaction. When value is reasonably well understood and options regarding transaction structure and terms have been thoroughly explored and analyzed, the agreement that is ultimately negotiated is generally one that recognizes the mutual needs of both parties. These needs include the buyer's need to pay a price that will allow a reasonable return on investment, recognizing the risks involved, while funding the acquisition with available resources. It also will recognize the seller's desire to transfer ownership, accomplish certain personal objectives, receive fair after-tax consideration for what is sold, obtain liquidity and adequate certainty of receipt of deferred payments, and receive adequate protection should future employment be part of the transaction. Buyers and sellers must also recognize that the government's participation in the transaction in the form of tax revenues affects both parties and must be negotiated to their mutual benefit. Both sides should recognize further that businesses are usually complex operations that carry substantial uncertainties that must be identified and, within reason, provided for in the sale/purchase agreement.

With these factors in mind, both sides are strongly encouraged to consider the other's needs. While sellers will want selected nonfinancial considerations to be recognized and their financial objectives met, they must correspondingly acknowledge the buyer's risk sensitivity, competitive challenges, capital constraints, and cash flow needs.

All of this may appear to be reasonable as it is written, but objectivity is much more difficult in the heat of a negotiation. Once again, this fact emphasizes the benefits to buyers and sellers of establishing a relationship in advance of the transaction to build trust and understanding. It further emphasizes the need for sellers to begin the succession planning process years in advance of the anticipated transaction date. By doing so, the seller can better understand and provide for the buyer's needs. More important, the seller can begin to cultivate a reasonable number of likely buyers to minimize reliance on a single suitor and maximize their negotiating position and return on the sale.

The planning and search process should be a continuous one for buyers as well. The best deals are frequently companies that are not formally on the market, and identification of these opportunities is greatly enhanced by building relationships with acquisition prospects. Buyers who rely exclusively on transactions brought to them by intermediaries may experience a steady diet of overpriced targets that are being heavily promoted to many other prospective buyers as well. The complexity of the M&A process prevents most purchase or sale opportunities from happening by luck at the best possible time. Understanding value and what drives it and the mechanics of the deal process provides a much safer path to success in M&A for both buyers and sellers.

CHAPTER 16

Fairness Opinions

A fairness opinion is a qualified third-party professional's opinion as to whether the consideration offered in a change of control transaction – such as a merger, acquisition, or similar corporate transaction – either by insiders or third parties, is fair to the nonaffiliated shareholders of a company from a financial point of view. It is prepared for a fixed fee[1] for buyers and sellers, boards of directors, fiduciaries, investors, and trustees (hereinafter collectively referred to as the "Fiduciary") who are serving as an agent of the beneficiary to augment, as opposed to supplant, their decision-making process. In other words, a fairness opinion is not a substitute for the Fiduciary's deliberations and judgment, and thus is just one factor to be considered in approving a transaction.

The term *fair* does not necessarily mean the highest (lowest) or best price. It typically means that the proposed consideration falls within a range of values determined by a thorough financial and valuation analysis. However, a notable exception is when the price is above the range and the fairness opinion is being prepared for the seller.

The opinion is an impartial view of a transaction based on the expert judgment of an investment banker, business appraiser, transaction advisor, commercial banker, or accountant (hereinafter collectively referred to as the Advisor) that supports fiduciaries to the transaction in making the appropriate decision and mitigates risk by satisfying their duty of care.

While there are many similarities between a fairness opinion and a business valuation – including the underlying financial and valuation analysis, the fact that they are both valid only as of a specific point in time,

---

[1] The Advisor should not accept a contingent fee for a fairness opinion as it would suggest a lack of independence.

and the conclusion being the Advisor's judgment rather than a statement of fact – there are several major differences. In a business valuation, there typically is no actual transaction taking place; thus the appraisal is acting as a proxy to a transaction. Since the transaction is hypothetical in a business valuation, the appraiser is rendering an opinion of value; but the Advisor in a fairness opinion is *not* rendering such an opinion. Instead, the Advisor is rendering an opinion that the consideration is fair from a financial point of view. In addition, since the transaction in a business valuation is hypothetical, the buyer and seller are often hypothetical and the income, market, and/or asset approaches discussed elsewhere in this book are used by the business appraiser to determine and substantiate a specific estimate of value. In a fairness opinion, there is a transaction at hand, so the buyer and seller are known, lack of marketability is not an issue, and the value (i.e. potential transaction consideration) is tested and corroborated by applying these three valuation approaches as relevant to the particular facts and circumstances. A range of values is developed and tested applying both positive and negative outcomes that could impact value.

Fairness opinions should also not be confused with solvency opinions and capital adequacy opinions, which may also be done around certain types of transactions. A solvency opinion states that a borrower is, and will remain, solvent under the burden of additional debt. In an M&A context, it is often provided in a highly leveraged transaction to protect selling shareholders, the company's board of directors, and transaction advisors from having a transaction unravel in a potential future bankruptcy. A capital adequacy opinion involves the determination that the fair market value of a company's assets exceeds the sum of its liabilities and the par value of its capital stock.

The completion of a fairness opinion is not legally mandated in most jurisdictions. However, fairness opinions are standard practice in today's litigious environment and help to create a first line of defense by demonstrating that the Fiduciary has exercised care in the deal-making process.[2]

---

[2] In 1985, the Delaware Supreme Court held that a target firm's board breached its duty of care by approving the acquisition without "proper exercise of business judgment" (such as obtaining a fairness opinion). This case, *Smith v. Van Gorkom (Trans Union)*, 488 A.2d 858 (Del. 1985), was the first time a court held that a board of directors had breached its duty of care. While not stating that fairness opinions are required as a matter of law to support an informed business judgment, the Court has noted in many subsequent cases that obtaining a fairness opinion demonstrated that the board properly acted in making the decision to carry on with the transaction. For example, in 1996, the Court stated that obtaining a fairness opinion was a "procedural safeguard" seen as strong evidence of a fair transaction (in this case, for a going-private transaction). See *Seagraves v. Urstadt Prop. Co., Inc.*, 1996 WL 159626 (Del. Ch. 1996).

In other words, obtaining a fairness opinion acts as evidence in litigation that the Fiduciary used reasonable business judgment in making a decision on behalf of others. Furthermore, fairness opinions can play an important role in deal-making.

Why Are Fairness Opinions Obtained?

The Fiduciary should contemplate obtaining a fairness opinion when considering a number of types of transactions. Exhibit 16.1 outlines 26 examples of transactions that may prompt the need for a fairness opinion. The basic question that the fairness opinion is answering is whether consideration is fair from a financial point of view.

In 2017, Duff & Phelps published a whitepaper study of more than 3,000 publicly disclosed fairness opinions between 2006 and 2016. This study concluded that "the vast majority of fairness opinions offer valuation indications that fall within 15 percentage points on either side of a midpoint (offer price) – a clear indication of a widespread industry standard with robust methodologies and highly calibrated valuation analyses … (thus representing) a reliable way for corporate boards and executives to evaluate purchase offers."[3]

Fairness opinions are generally obtained for three reasons: to assist in the decision-making process, to mitigate risk, and to improve communication and transparency.[4,5]

- *Assists decision making.* Fairness opinions are a procedural tool that can assist the Fiduciary in their decision-making process whether to accept or reject an offer. Sensitivity or scenario analysis presented to the Fiduciary can provide context and potential implications regarding a proposed transaction that may otherwise be overlooked by parties incentivized to execute deals. For example, if a company is considering a sale to a financial buyer, scenario analysis can model what various types of strategic buyers might pay. Alternatively, if a company is early in a growth stage or has been struggling, scenario analysis can help see what might happen if the company waits a year or two to sell.

---

[3] Chris Janssen, Robert A. Bartell, A. Scott Davidson, and Yann Magnan, "In Defense of Fairness Opinions – An Empirical Review of Ten Years of Data," Duff & Phelps, LLC, March 28, 2017.

[4] Philip J. Clements and Philip W. Wisler, *The Standard & Poor's Guide to Fairness Opinions: A User's Guide for Fiduciaries* (New York: McGraw-Hill, 2005), pp. 14–15.

[5] Note: This list of factors and all other lists provided in this chapter are not intended to be all-inclusive and are not ranked in any particular order.

- *Risk mitigation.* Although any general consulting arrangement could conceivably provide similar decision-making benefits as noted above, the Advisor is providing tangible guidance to the Fiduciary alongside their independent advice. Obtaining an independent fairness opinion can also act as a legal tool that helps the Fiduciary satisfy their obligation to exercise sound business judgment. Specifically, a fairness opinion can help the Fiduciary to claim protection when faced with breach of fiduciary duty claims under a legal doctrine known as the Business Judgment Rule. This rule is a legal principle that "shields directors and officers from liability from unprofitable or harmful corporate transactions if the transactions were made in good faith, with due care, and

EXHIBIT 16.1 When May a Fairness Opinion Be Beneficial?

- Acquisitions (partial or full)
- Dissenting shareholder appraisal requirements
- Divestitures
- Employee stock ownership plan (ESOP) formation and acquisition
- Exchange offers
- Going-private transactions
- Hostile takeover contests
- Joint venture dissolution
- Joint venture formation
- Leveraged buyouts (LBOs)
- Liquidations
- Loan covenant requirements
- Management buyouts (MBOs)
- Minority shareholder buyouts
- Nonprofit entity excess benefit and private inurement avoidance
- Private placements (i.e. down-round financing)
- Recapitalizations
- Related-party transactions
- Repurchase or conversion of outstanding securities
- Restructurings
- Sales (partial or full)
- Sale of assets encumbered by a bond indenture
- Secured lender transactions (to avoid fraudulent conveyance)
- Spin-offs
- Tender offers
- Transactions where certain shareholders receive greater consideration than others

within the directors' or officers' authority."[6] Title 8, Section 141(e) of the Delaware Code states directors are "fully protected (i.e. not held liable) in relying in good faith ... upon such information, opinions, reports, or statements presented to the corporation by any of the corporation's officers or employees ... or by any other person as to matters the officers or employees ... or by any other person as to matters the member reasonably believes are within such other person's professional or expert competence."

- *Improves communication and transparency.* Fairness opinions can be shown to shareholders or external stakeholders to demonstrate and provide reassurance that the Fiduciary is exercising prudence and due care in their contemplation of a potential transaction. Fairness opinions should be obtained if there is *any* potential conflict of interest. Despite the fees associated with obtaining one, which do include a significant premium over the fees for a regular business valuation, they are much less than those involved in litigation, especially when multiple shareholders are involved. Given the fact that not only the fees, but also the time involved in obtaining a fairness opinion are considerably less than those involved in litigation, obtaining a fairness opinion in conjunction with a transaction should be viewed by the Fiduciary as an investment in essential additional advice on the transaction.

---

[6] *Black's Law Dictionary*, St. Paul MN: West Publishing Co., 2001. The Business Judgment Rule originated in 1945 in *Otis & Co. v. Pennsylvania R. Co.*, 61 F. Supp. 905 (D.C. Pa. 1945) where the Court ruled that the directors acted in good faith and thus were not liable to the shareholders even though they chose the wrong course of action. Subsequently, the board of directors' actions were protected by the Business Judgment Rule in *Unocal Corp. v. Mesa Petroleum Co.*, 493 A.2d 946 (Del. Super. 1985). In *McMullin v. Beran*, 765 A.2d 910 (Del. Supr., 2000), the Court stated that the board of directors must demonstrate that they fulfilled their "triad of fiduciary duties – loyalty, good faith, and due care" to claim protection under the Business Judgment Rule. In both *Smith v. Van Gorkom*, 488 A.2d 858 (Del. 1985) and *Revlon v. MacAndrews & Forbes Holdings*, 506 A.2d 173 (Del. 1985), the Court held that the directors failed to exercise informed business judgment and, in the former case, instead acted in a grossly negligent manner by agreeing to sell the company for too low a price, while in the latter case held the board liable even though they were not accused of acting in bad faith. Finally, a lesson in *Aronson v. Lewis*, 473 A.2d 805 (Del. 1984) was that the Business Judgment Rule may not apply to a board's actions if one or more directors may derive personal financial benefit from a transaction.

The Use of Fairness Opinions by Private Companies

Although the consumers of fairness opinions are comprised mostly of public companies, private companies have increasingly been obtaining them due largely to increased deal-related litigation. The nuances of private company ownership often involve potential conflicts of interest, making it highly prudent for the Fiduciary to obtain a fairness opinion. Private companies often contain complex capital structures, passive investors, family ownership, intercompany transactions, and/or lack independent board members. Any combination of these factors may lead to a costly litigious situation that could have been prevented or mitigated through the use of a fairness opinion. Bob Buchanan notes the following set of circumstances in which private companies obtain fairness opinions:[7]

- *Multiple Classes of Stock.* Many private companies have multiple classes of stock, each with rights different from the others (e.g. common vs. preferred), resulting in very different and often divergent interests. In contemplating a transaction, controlling shareholders and boards of directors must be careful to be fair to all parties with respect to the financial implications as they relate to those divergent interests. This also includes demonstrating that minority shareholders are getting a fair price and are being treated equitably.
- *Passive Shareholders.* Many private companies have a large number of passive shareholders (i.e. not active in the operations or management of the business). These passive shareholders will not have the same understanding of the company's business, operations, or value as the controlling shareholder, management, or board of directors. The reassurance of an outside, independent advisor could avoid or mitigate risk substantially.
- *Families.* Many private companies are owned by family groups. Others are controlled by family groups but have additional family shareholders outside the control group. Shareholders may span generational lines and hold differing outcome interests and opinions. Disputes between family members are common, especially when not all of the family members have an equal voice in management of the company.
- *Lack of Outside Board Members.* Few private companies have boards of directors comprised of many, if any, outside, independent board members. In addition, management depth and expertise are rarely sufficient to provide the expertise needed in evaluating the fairness of a transaction.

---

[7] Robert H. Buchanan, J.D., ASA, "Why Get a Fairness Opinion for a Privately Held Company?" In *Fairness Opinions in Today's Legal and Economic Environments* (Portland, OR: Business Valuation Resources, 2012).

Other considerations include when there are a large number of share-holders and where there are outside interests (such as holdings in an ESOP, in a trust, or by private equity investors). A private company that is owned in whole or in part by an employee stock ownership trust may receive an offer to merge or be acquired by an outside party, and the ESOP trustees must not only meet their fiduciary obligations to the ESOP participants, but also comply with applicable Department of Labor regulations.[8] Private company shares held by a trust may receive an offer that changes control, and the trustee needs to vote on behalf of the trust and the trust's beneficiaries. A private equity firm in the process of exiting its investment in a company in which it has a controlling interest must meet its fiduciary responsibilities to other company shareholders. Fairness opinions may also be used to satisfy requirements of debt covenants. In summary, even though private companies are not subject to the level of scrutiny facing public companies, there is always the potential of a lawsuit filed by a disgruntled shareholder.

Parties Who Prepare Fairness Opinions

The Fiduciary has a responsibility to a company's shareholders. Part of meeting that responsibility is obtaining an independent fairness opinion, which in turn involves selecting the right Advisor to do it. The Fiduciary should select the Advisor based on their qualifications and experience, and their responses to key questions such as those outlined below. When it comes to who prepares a fairness opinion in a transaction, independence in terms of the outcome of the transaction is important. This is a critical issue and one that will not go unnoticed by regulators, courts,[9] or shareholders. In fact, in 2007, the SEC approved FINRA Rule 2290, which "requires specific disclosures and procedures addressing conflicts of interest when member firms provide fairness opinions in change of control transactions." If applicable, the Advisor (typically in this case an investment bank) must disclose

---

[8] Such regulations require that the sale price is not less than fair market value and that the transaction is fair to the ESOP from a financial point of view. This is generally interpreted to mean that the transaction must be fair to the ESOP both in absolute terms (not less than fair market value) and in relative terms when compared to many financial factors that are not necessarily part of fair market value (i.e. other economic factors that may impact the ESOP to conclude that the sale offers the best return to the ESOP participants).

[9] In recent years, the Delaware Court of Chancery was exceedingly critical when perceived conflicts of interest arose in three cases between 2011 and 2014: *In re Rural Metro Corporation Stockholders Litigation*, 88 A.3d 54 (Del. Ch. 2014), *In re Del Monte Foods Company Shareholders Litigation*, 25 A.3d 813 (Del. Ch. 2011), and *In re El Paso Corp. Shareholder Litigation*, 41 A.3d 432 (Del. Ch. 2012).

whether they have had any other role related to the proposed transaction and, if so, whether they will receive any compensation that is contingent upon a close of such transaction. It is simply prudent and good practice for the Fiduciary to select an Advisor who is independent in this manner. Not doing so may leave the Fiduciary more vulnerable to lawsuits that question their judgment and decisions.

As mentioned earlier, fairness opinions are typically provided by investment bankers, business appraisers, or transaction advisors. Occasionally a commercial banker or accountant may provide them. The following is a list of factors where the independence of the Advisor would be in question:

- An investment banker or other transaction advisor who stands to earn a success fee upon the closing of the transaction
- An investment banker or other transaction advisor who structured and priced the transaction
- Any advisor who has any ownership interest in the equity or debt of the underlying company

When selecting an Advisor, the Fiduciary should not only factor in independence, but also strongly consider the Advisor's experience and expertise in providing fairness opinions. After all, the Fiduciary is relying on the Advisor's informed judgment in rendering the opinion. In doing so, the Fiduciary should ask the following questions:

- What is your firm's experience in providing fairness opinions?
- Has your firm ever been sued in connection with a fairness opinion that you prepared?[10]
- If so, how many judgments were made against you and what was the outcome?
- Do you have any potential or actual conflicts of interest with regard to the parties to the transaction?
- How often have you been involved in the negotiations of a purchase or sale of a company?
- Does your company have a fairness opinion committee? If so, please state their qualifications.

---

[10] Being sued in connection with rendering a fairness opinion should not automatically be a disqualifier when selecting an advisor. Most advisors who have been sued have significantly shored up their process, learning from the suit. If the potential advisor has been sued, the Fiduciary should probe the circumstances and inquire how that has changed the Advisor's practice.

- Please explain the review process for opinions issued by your firm.
- What is your firm's experience in the industry in which our company operates?
- What is your firm's experience with the type of transaction being contemplated by the parties?

The Advisor should also be experienced with the degree of complexity involved, which will also determine the ultimate fees charged. A sell-side transaction where cash is the total consideration is perhaps the least complex while a buy-side stock transaction with contingent consideration is more complex.

Fees, which should be fixed, vary based on factors such as the following:[11]

- Materiality of the proposed transaction
- Scope of analysis
- Turnaround time for completion
- Status of the business purchased or sold (e.g. start-up vs. mature business)
- Data quality and quantity
- Level of transaction complexity
- Form of consideration paid or received
- Breadth of distribution/reliance on findings

In the end, the Fiduciary should be comfortable in explaining to a court, if involved in a lawsuit, the parameters used in selecting the Advisor.

Components of a Fairness Opinion

A fairness opinion letter report describes the process used by the Advisor in determining that the transaction is fair from a financial point of view. It is typically delivered in the form of a brief letter, supplemented by an oral presentation by the Advisor to the Fiduciary. Behind the letter and presentation is a thorough analysis of all pertinent factors considered in rendering the opinion. Please see Appendix 16A at the end of this chapter for a sample fairness opinion letter report involving a private company buyer and seller

---

[11] Philip J. Clements and Philip W. Wisler, *The Standard & Poor's Guide to Fairness Opinions: A User's Guide for Fiduciaries* (New York: McGraw-Hill, 2005), 21.

using the facts presented in the case study in Chapter 21.[12] While there are no professional standards in the United States[13] and several other countries regarding the components of a fairness opinion, such standards have been developed in Canada.[14] In the authors' view, these standards provide a useful framework and guideline for the components of a fairness opinion by outlining the following disclosures:[15]

1. The name of the party who engaged the Advisor to perform the fairness opinion.
2. A description of the proposed transaction and the consideration being offered to the security holders (or to a group of security holders).
3. The purpose of the fairness opinion.
4. The identity and credentials of the Advisor.
5. A description of any past, present, or anticipated relationship between the Advisor and any interested party which may be relevant to the Advisor's independence for purposes of providing the fairness opinion.
6. The effective date of the fairness opinion.
7. A statement that the fairness opinion was prepared by the Advisor acting independently and objectively, or facts that might result in the possible actual or perceived lack of independence and objectivity (i.e. disclosure of any potential conflicts of interest, including any equity held by the Advisor in the subject entity).
8. A description of the relevant business, assets, or securities sufficient to allow the reader to understand the rationale of the fairness opinion

---

[12] In addition, please see the following link for an example involving a fairness opinion in the public domain prepared by Valuation Research Corporation (VRC) for Hennessy Capital Acquisition Corp. The opinion letter can be found toward the end in Annex B, with a description of the details behind the analysis prepared by company management beginning on page 161. https://www.sec.gov/Archives/edgar/data/1642453/000121390017000988/defm14a_hennessy.htm

[13] Fairness opinions are not subject to the *Uniform Standards of Professional Appraisal Practice* or any other business valuation standards in the United States. However, the Financial Industry Regulatory Authority, Inc.'s (FINRA) Rule 5150 in the United States applies to FINRA members and addresses procedures for rendering fairness opinions and requires disclosure of any conflicts of interest. In addition, the SEC issued Rule 13e-3 to set forth disclosure requirements with regard to fairness opinions in going-private transactions.

[14] Specifically, the Canadian Institute of Chartered Business Valuators (CICBV) has developed three sets of standards regarding fairness opinions: Standard No. 510 contains "Disclosure Standards and Recommendations," Standard No. 520 contains "Scope of Work Standards and Recommendations," and Standard No. 530 contains "File Documentation Standards and Recommendations."

[15] CICBV Standard No. 510, Sections 8.2 through 8.4.

and the approach and various factors influencing financial fairness that were considered.

9. A statement that the Advisor's compensation is not contingent on an action or event resulting from use of the fairness opinion or disclosure of the nature of the actual or perceived contingent consideration.

10. A description of the scope of the review conducted, including a summary of the type of information reviewed and relied upon (including discussions with company management).

11. A description of any valuation work performed or relied upon in support of the fairness opinion's conclusion.

12. A discussion of any *bona fide* offer or prior valuation or other material expert report considered by the Advisor in coming to the conclusion.

13. A statement of the key assumptions made.

14. A discussion of the factors considered to be important by the Advisor in performing the analysis.

15. An explanation of any limitation in the scope of review and of any incomplete information provided to the Advisor, including the reasons given and the potential impact on the conclusion.

16. A statement restricting the use of the fairness opinion to the persons for whom it was prepared and only for the stated purpose, followed by a statement disclaiming responsibility for losses resulting from unauthorized or improper use of the fairness opinion.

While these disclosures are essential components to a fairness opinion, identification of the standard of value, the underlying financial and valuation analyses, and the potential impact of synergies are all key to its usefulness.

A specific standard of value (e.g. fair value or fair market value) is not legally mandated in rendering fairness opinions as it is for valuations done in compliance with various financial reporting or tax requirements, or in connection with litigation. The analysis can nonetheless start by calculating the subject company's fair value as a base, and then determine various potential buyer synergies based on market data to determine a range of investment values.[16] Keeping in mind that a fairness opinion is not an exit planning or similar consulting or advisory process, there are several transaction scenarios that can be considered in determining the range of values in a fairness opinion. They include a public offering, sale to a strategic buyer, sale to a private equity firm, leveraged recapitalization, management leveraged buyout,

---

[16] An exception to this is when a fairness opinion is prepared for a transaction involving an ESOP where the parties to the transaction must follow ERISA regulations promulgated by the U.S. Department of Labor. These regulations mandate that the standard of value contemplated in a fairness opinion be fair market value.

ESOP leveraged buyout, sale to a financial buyer, break-up of the company, and orderly liquidation. Rarely, if ever, are all of these scenarios considered; the scenarios analyzed will depend on the facts and circumstances of the proposed transaction, and can be impacted by relevant case law in a given jurisdiction.

With regard to the underlying valuation analysis completed in preparing a fairness opinion, the Fiduciary should understand how the range of values was determined, how projections were used, what synergies were considered, what market data was used, and the extent to which a control premium was considered. Just as in a business valuation, the analysis involves economic and industry data, management interviews, qualitative company background, historical financial statements, projections, and past transactions of company stock. It uses this analysis to apply the income, market, and asset approaches as explained in Chapters 6 through 11 of this book to determine a range of values.[17] Specifically, the analysis provides justification for the forecasts utilized, the discount rate applied to those forecasts, the selected guideline public companies and guideline transactions, and the calculated value from each approach as it relates to the transaction consideration. In practice, unlike with a business valuation report, much of this analysis is not typically presented in the fairness opinion letter itself and remains the Advisor's property. However, it may be presented by the Advisor to the Fiduciary in a separate meeting.

When the transaction involves either the entire company or a controlling interest in the company, a control premium may be considered. However, the Advisor must take note that "a substantial premium may provide one reason to recommend a merger, but in the absence of other sound valuation information, the fact of a premium alone does not provide an adequate basis upon which to assess the fairness of an offering price."[18]

With reference to synergies, the Advisor should analyze and quantify the potential impact revenue enhancements, cost reductions, and other sources of synergy discussed in Chapter 5 may have on the range of values. Since many synergies do not materialize post-transaction as anticipated, the Advisor should exercise care if a conclusion of fairness from a financial point of view is dependent on the realization of the identified synergies.

---

[17] In the Duff & Phelps study of more than 3,000 fairness opinions studied between 2006 and 2016 cited earlier in this chapter in footnote 3, 91% of opinions included use of at least two valuation methods and 75% included use of three or more methods. The guideline public company method was used in almost all opinions analyzed, followed by the discounted cash flow method and then the transaction multiple method.

[18] *Smith v. Van Gorkom*, 488 A.2d 858 (Del. 1985).

What Fairness Opinions Are Not

While a fairness opinion is an assessment that a transaction is fair from a financial point of view, it has an otherwise limited role in terms of both other aspects of the transaction itself and its assessment of the underlying operations.

With regard to other aspects of the transaction itself, a fairness opinion does not:

- Render an opinion as to whether the highest (lowest) and best price or consideration has been offered
- Opine on the terms of the purchase and sale agreement or other legal matters pertaining to the transaction
- Represent a statement that the parties transacted fairly or in good faith
- Speak to the allocation of the transaction consideration to be received by the shareholders
- Provide guidance or an opinion on ancillary terms of the deal (e.g. lockups, termination fees, severance agreements, etc.)
- Evaluate the negotiation process leading to the proposed transaction or the business rationale of the proposed transaction
- Represent a recommendation to vote or act in a certain manner with regard to the proposed transaction (the Fiduciary determines whether the transaction is appropriate)
- Opine as to whether the transaction is fair from a legal point of view (this would be addressed in a legal opinion that is separate from the fairness opinion)
- Offer any assurances as to the legal, taxation, or accounting ramifications of the proposed transaction
- Shift responsibilities from the Fiduciary to the Advisor

There are also aspects of the operational gains from a transaction that a fairness opinion does not cover. For example, it does not opine on any technological or other benefits or synergies, nor does it affirm the strategic merit of the proposed transaction.

A fairness opinion also does not involve any kind of independent verification of information received and does not encompass any kind of inspection or appraisal of business premises or specific tangible assets/liabilities. It also does not represent any kind of audit, review, compilation, or any other kind of attestation or opinion as to the quality or accuracy of any future (or past) financial results even though it may rely on projections.

The fairness opinion is not impenetrable and does not guarantee the complete removal of risk in a transaction, nor does it provide any actual form of insurance, no matter how vigorous the due diligence supporting it may be.

Finally, a fairness opinion does not oblige the Fiduciary to accept the proposed transaction or endorse any particular decision. It is just one of several factors that the Fiduciary must consider.

Conclusion

With increased litigation following M&A transactions, coupled with increased complexity in deal structure, a fairness opinion prepared by an independent Advisor for a fixed fee is a valuable tool in the Fiduciary's decision-making process and for their demonstration of sound business judgment and due care, whether the subject company is publicly traded or privately held.

Appendix 16A   Sample Fairness Opinion Letter

March 1, 2018
Jay M. Attorney
Law Firm LLP
123 Main Street
City, Minnesota 59999

Re: Fairness Opinion Letter – Cavendish

Dear Mr. Attorney:

Jay M. Attorney, as trustee of the Lou Bertin Cavendish Trust (the "Client" or the "Trust"), has engaged Valuation Firm, Inc. ("Valuation Firm") to provide our opinion (our "Opinion") as to the fairness, from a financial point of view, of the consideration to be received by the Trust as holder of 80 percent of the outstanding capital stock of Cavendish Seafood Distributors, Inc. ("Cavendish" or the "Company"), resulting from the Proposed Transaction (as described below) as of February 2, 2018 (the "Effective Date").

Proposed Transaction

We understand Omni Food Distributors, Inc. ("Omni") has made an offer to acquire the stock of Cavendish, consisting of the following terms (the "Proposed Transaction") per the letter of intent dated February 2, 2018 (the "Agreement").

- The total consideration (purchase price) is $48 million in cash for all capital stock of Cavendish.
- It is our understanding that an Internal Revenue Code Section 338(h)(10) election will be made, such that the Proposed Transaction will be taxed as an asset deal for tax purposes.
- The purchase price assumes Cavendish will operate in a manner consistent with past practices through the closing date, and the Company will have working capital at the closing in the amount agreed upon by Cavendish and Omni based upon historical balance sheets (the "Closing Balance Sheet Calculation").
- Prior to closing, the Company would pay any unpaid accrued shareholder distributions; these amounts will not be included as accrued expenses in the Closing Balance Sheet Calculation.
- The purchase price will be adjusted up or down, dollar for dollar, by any deviations from the Closing Balance Sheet Calculation.
- The Company will be responsible for payment of tax obligations for periods prior to closing, shareholder loans, or other obligations to shareholders.

- Omni intends to negotiate postclosing employment arrangements with Lou Bertin, the Company's CEO.
- Mr. Bertin will agree to a three-year covenant not-to-compete in the amount of $600,000 to be paid in addition to the purchase price.
- There is an exclusivity period of 75 days.

Statement of Qualifications and Independence

With nearly 100 employees operating out of eight offices in the United States and two in Canada, Valuation Firm provides business and intangible asset valuations and fairness and solvency opinions for middle market and large companies. Chris Appraiser has been involved with over 2,000 business and intangible asset valuations and over 50 fairness opinions for companies in the United States and 15 other countries during his 25-year career. He holds the industry designations of accredited senior appraiser, accredited business valuator, certified business appraiser, certified valuation analyst, and international certified valuation specialist. Neither Valuation Firm nor Mr. Appraiser have any past, present, or anticipated future relationship with Cavendish or Omni aside from being engaged to prepare this fairness opinion. As such, Mr. Appraiser has prepared this fairness opinion acting independently and objectively, with no conflicts of interest.

Company Background

Cavendish is a distributor of both wild-caught and farm-raised seafood to restaurants and grocery stores in 14 central states and is considering expansion into the three Canadian prairie provinces. The Company is currently held 80% by the Trust and 20% in equal amounts by two passive investors.

Scope of Analysis

In developing our Opinion, our procedures included, but were not limited to, the following:

1. Reviewed the letter of intent dated February 2, 2018.
2. Participated in discussions with Cavendish's management team ("Management"), including Lou Bertin (CEO), Ghyslain St. Jean (COO), Michael Bertin (CFO), and John Paresseux (VP of Marketing), regarding the Company's financial condition, business, assets, earnings, expected future performance, and the Proposed Transaction.

3. Met with Management at Cavendish's offices in City, Minnesota, on February 15, 2018.
4. Reviewed the following documents:
   a. The reviewed financial statements for the fiscal years ended December 31, 2013, through December 31, 2017, for the Company;
   b. The forecast financial operating data for the fiscal years ending December 31, 2018, through December 31, 2022, for Cavendish, as prepared by Management of the Company;
   c. Other internal documents related to the financial condition of the Company provided by Management;
   d. Organization documents of Cavendish;
   e. Employment agreements with Management and Cavendish; and
   f. Other financial schedules where relevant.
5. Reviewed the schedule of allocation of consideration prepared by Management.
6. Reviewed historical trading prices of public companies deemed relevant.
7. Performed certain valuation and comparative analyses using generally accepted valuation and analytical techniques, including:
   a. Discounted cash flow analyses;
   b. Analyses of selected public company multiples deemed relevant; and
   c. Analyses of transactions deemed relevant.
8. Took into account general economic, market, and financial conditions.
9. Conducted such other analyses and considered such factors as we deemed appropriate.

Assumptions and Limiting Conditions

This Opinion is subject to certain overall assumptions and limiting conditions, many of which may have a significant influence on the conclusion, including without limitation, the following:

1. In developing our Opinion, we have relied on information provided by the Company and have performed no independent verification of the information provided.
2. We have relied on information, data, and representations obtained from public sources or provided by private sources and have performed no independent verification of the information provided.
3. We have assumed the accuracy and completeness of all information provided and assume projections and forecasts have been prepared in

good faith by Management, upon reasonable estimates that represent Company's best judgment as to future performance.

4. We have assumed the final versions of all documents reviewed by Valuation Firm in draft form conform in all material respects to the drafts reviewed.

5. We have assumed that there have been no material changes in the assets, services, financial condition, business, or prospects of the Company since the date of the most recent financial statements and other information provided to Valuation Firm.

6. We have assumed there are no liens or encumbrances, title problems, licensing violations, and hazardous materials associated with the subject assets, properties, and/or business interests being appraised. We assume no responsibility for any and all future environmental considerations and potential liabilities or for arranging engineering studies that may be required to discover them.

7. We were not retained to and we did not conduct a physical inspection of any of the properties or facilities of Cavendish, did not make any independent evaluation or appraisal of the individual assets, liabilities, or prospects of Cavendish, and were not furnished with any such evaluation or appraisal.

8. Our opinion is necessarily based on economic, market, and other conditions as in effect on, and the information made available to us as of, the date hereof. Accordingly, it is important to understand that although subsequent developments may affect our opinion, we do not have any obligation to further update, revise, or reaffirm our opinion.

9. We express no opinion on matters of a legal, regulatory, tax, or accounting nature of the Proposed Transaction or the ability of the Proposed Transaction, as set forth in the Agreement, to be consummated.

10. We have assumed the Proposed Transaction will be completed in accordance with the terms as detailed in the letter of intent dated February 2, 2018, and without any amendments thereto or any waivers of any terms or conditions thereof.

11. We have relied upon the fact that the Company has been advised by its counsel as to all legal matters with respect to the Proposed Transaction, including whether all procedures required by law to be taken in connection with the Proposed Transaction have been duly, validly, and timely taken.

12. No opinion is expressed as to whether any alternative transaction might be more favorable to holders of Cavendish's common stock than the Proposed Transaction.

Valuation Firm has not been requested to, and did not: (i) initiate any discussions with, or solicit any indications of interest from, third parties with respect to the Proposed Transaction, the assets, businesses, or operations of the Company; or (ii) advise the Company or any other party with respect to alternatives to the Proposed Transaction.

Our analysis did not take into account any potential incremental value specifically attributable to the reorganization or recapitalization subsequent to the Proposed Transaction, and we are not expressing any opinion of the price or range of prices at which the Company or interests in the Company may sell for at any time after consummation of the Proposed Transaction.

Disclosures

Valuation Firm represents to the Client as follows:

- We have not acted as a financial adviser to any party involved in the Proposed Transaction.
- Our compensation is not contingent upon any action or event resulting from use of the fairness opinion, including the successful completion of the Proposed Transaction.
- We have had no material relationships in past years or that are mutually understood to be contemplated in which any compensation was received or is intended to be received as a result of the relationship between Valuation Firm and any party to the Proposed Transaction that is the subject of this Opinion.
- Our Opinion is not intended to express an opinion as to the fairness of the amount or nature of the consideration received by any of the Company's officers, directors, or employees, or class of such persons, other than in their capacity as stockholders of the Company.

Use and Dissemination of Opinion Letter

This Opinion is being conducted solely in connection with the Proposed Transaction. This letter is intended solely for the use of the Client in (and only in) their capacity as trustees. The Client may provide a copy of this letter only to: (1) the Client's appropriate legal, accounting, and financial advisors providing services to the Client in connection with the Proposed Transaction; (2) beneficiaries of the above-referenced Trust; (3) appropriate legal, accounting, and financial advisors providing such services to the beneficiaries of the Trust; and (4) other parties who have been disclosed to Valuation Firm and consented to by Valuation Firm in advance, in writing. Further, prior to disclosing this letter to such parties, the Client shall inform each such party that he, she, or it will not disclose this letter or any portions thereof (including without limitation any conclusions as to value, the identity of Valuation Firm, its shareholders, directors, employees, consultants, contractors, affiliates, agents and representatives, or the professional associations or organizations with which they are affiliated) to any third parties.

This letter may not be disclosed, communicated, reproduced, disseminated, quoted, or referred to at any time, to any third party, other than those referenced herein, or in any manner or for any purpose whatsoever without our prior written consent.

Valuation Firm's Opinion as expressed herein is limited to the fairness, from a financial point of view, of the consideration to be received by the Trust as holder of 80% of the outstanding capital stock of Cavendish, and does not address Cavendish's underlying business decision to proceed with the Proposed Transaction. This letter is for the information of the Client in evaluating the Proposed Transaction and our opinion does not constitute a recommendation to the Client as to how he or she should vote with respect to the Proposed Transaction.

Conclusion

Subject to the foregoing, it is our opinion as of the date hereof that the consideration to be received is fair, from a financial point of view, to the Trust as holders of 80% of the outstanding capital stock of Cavendish.

Very truly yours,
VALUATION FIRM, INC.
Chris Appraiser, ASA, CBA, CM&AA, CPA/ABV, CVA, ICVS
Managing Director

CHAPTER 17

M&A and Financial Reporting[1]

Throughout this book, tools have been provided to determine and enhance company value in a merger and acquisition (M&A) context, typically in advance of a potential transaction. Over the past couple of decades, with the onset and expansion of fair value accounting, valuation has become an integral part of *post-transaction* financial reporting compliance. Specifically, in the period following a transaction, the fair value of the target company's identifiable intangible assets and goodwill is reflected on the acquiring company's balance sheet and ultimately impacts its reported earnings in subsequent periods.

This chapter provides an overview of the relevant standards and other guidance where financial reporting requirements may impact M&A activity. It starts by introducing the key principles and standards, which result in differences in assumptions and procedures as compared to the valuation concepts discussed in other parts of this book, and then introduces the types of intangible assets typically seen in purchase price allocations. It ends with a listing of additional due diligence questions pertaining to financial reporting compliance factors and a list of references for additional information. The purpose of this chapter is to provide the reader – including auditors, business owners, financial managers, transaction advisors, and valuation practitioners – with an awareness and general understanding of the financial reporting compliance factors and key valuation concepts as they relate to these factors, to be better prepared for post-M&A transaction financial reporting requirements. We provide these explanations and insights based on our experience consulting with chief financial officers and controllers immediately before or just after they have completed a transaction. Note that these

---

[1] The authors gratefully acknowledge the contribution of updating this chapter from its second edition (2010) version by Edward Hamilton, CFA, senior vice president with Valuation Research Corporation in Princeton, New Jersey; www.valuation research.com.

are financial reporting considerations, separate from any post-transaction, tax-related considerations.

U.S. GAAP and IFRS

Generally accepted accounting principles (GAAP)[2] is the language of financial reporting for businesses in the United States, and its rules are promulgated by the Financial Accounting Standards Board (FASB). Any company obtaining audited, reviewed, or compiled financial statements by an independent accountant does so in accordance with GAAP. Fair value measurements are required for GAAP financial statements. The GAAP counterpart outside the United States is primarily International Financial Reporting Standards (IFRS), and its rules are promulgated by the International Accounting Standards Board (IASB).

Over the past couple of decades, there have been substantial changes in financial reporting guidance. Many of these changes have had a direct impact on M&A transactions, which in this chapter will be referred to as business combinations, as they are referred in the FASB and IASB standards. In 2002, the FASB and the IASB issued the Norwalk Agreement, which was a memorandum of understanding between the two boards to work toward convergence of U.S. GAAP and international accounting standards. This movement had begun in 1996, when financial reporting started to move away from historical cost on company financial statements, toward fair value. Assets stated at their fair value are generally considered more useful to those relying on financial statements than when stated at historic cost.

> Given the changes in U.S. GAAP and IFRS over the past decades, financial reporting requirements have more of an impact on M&A activity than ever before.

At this point, the fair value and business combination standards are largely converged though differences remain and subsequent divergences have been introduced. Currently, there is no effort being made to converge other standards.

Virtually all developed countries, with the exception of the United States, as well as many developing countries now require use of IFRS. There is no current expectation that the United States will begin using IFRS.

These changes have impacted how deals are done worldwide. As such, a general understanding of certain accounting standards and their impact on financial reporting is necessary for management and their advisors when considering a business combination.

---

[2] GAAP, as it is referred to in this chapter, is US GAAP.

Relevant FASB and IFRS Statements

With all these changes, deal makers must be more familiar with GAAP, particularly Accounting Standards Codification (ASC) Topics 820 and 805 as well as ASC 350 and 360, than they were in the past. Outside the United States, dealmakers must be more familiar with IFRS 3 and International Accounting Standards (IAS) 36 and 38:

ASC 820 – Fair Value Measurement. Issued in September 2006, ASC 820 establishes a framework for *how* to apply fair value concepts and provides required disclosures in financial statements.

IFRS 13 – Fair Value Measurement. Issued in May 2011, and effective beginning in 2013, sets forth the principles of fair value measurement in accordance with IFRS.

ASC 805 – Business Combinations. Initially issued in June 2001, revised in December 2007 and amended by subsequent Accounting Standard Updates, ASC 805 addresses accounting for business combinations, including determination of the purchase price and identification of intangible assets.

IFRS 3 – Business Combinations. Initially issued in March 2004, revised in January 2008, and subsequently amended, IFRS 3 sets out the recognition and measurement of acquired assets and liabilities.

ASC 350 – Intangibles – Goodwill and Other. Issued in June 2001 and subsequently amended by ASU 2017-04, ASC 350 relates to impairment of goodwill and other indefinite-lived intangible assets.

ASU 2014-02 and ASU 2014 2014-18. Issued in 2014, these allow private companies to apply simplified accounting guidance for goodwill and certain intangible assets.

IAS 36 – Impairment of Assets. Initially issued in June 1998 and subsequently amended multiple times, IAS 36 requires that intangible assets are not carried at more than their recoverable amount, which is defined as the higher of an asset's "fair value less costs of disposal" and its "value in use."

IAS 38 – Intangible Assets. Initially issued in September 1998 and subsequently amended, IAS 38 provides guidance on the treatment of intangible assets.

ASC 360 – Property, Plant, and Equipment. ASC 360 includes guidance on impairment testing of long-lived assets (both tangible and intangible) with definite lives.

ASC Topics 820, 805, and 350 will be discussed in more detail later in this chapter. It is important to note that both ASC 805 and 350 have an accounting alternative for private companies that simplifies both the initial valuation of, and subsequent accounting for, intangible assets and goodwill.

As a result of the Norwalk Agreement, the FASB and the IASB began their first joint project related to the accounting for business combinations to further promote the international convergence of accounting standards. With the FASB's issuance of ASC 805 and the IASB's revisions to IFRS 3, the joint effort to improve financial reporting about business combinations and to promote the international convergence of accounting standards has advanced considerably. With regard to fair value measurement, the goal was to have converged guidance to provide consistency in its application. As a result, guidance related to fair value and business combinations is largely converged. At the time of publication of this book, convergence is no longer a priority.

Reviews by the Audit Firm

Fair value estimates are audited along with other estimates that impact reported financial statements issued in accordance with GAAP and IFRS. A valuation being completed for financial reporting purposes is a compliance process governed by the principles set forth in the aforementioned standards. Although there is no requirement for companies to hire outside and independent valuation specialists, increased scrutiny from accounting regulators, stricter auditor independence rules, Public Company Accounting Oversight Board (PCAOB) oversight, and increased scrutiny of valuation work being done for financial reporting purposes has elevated the reliance on valuation specialists in recent years. Not only do valuation specialists hired in this context need a solid foundation in business valuation, but they also will need appropriate knowledge of intangible asset valuation, the specifics of fair value measurement, the aforementioned standards, and literature published by the American Institute of Certified Public Accountants, Appraisal Foundation, International Valuation Standards Council, and others. Fair value accounting is a specialized niche in the valuation profession with a different set of practices and requirements, as compared to valuations done for tax purposes, litigation, or general, valuation-based, strategic planning. Additionally, the recently launched certified in entity and intangible valuations (CEIV) credential is rapidly gaining greater acceptance to the point of being required for professionals providing fair value–related valuations. Individuals with the credential must comply with additional documentation and other requirements.

Although the ultimate responsibility for financial statements lies with company management, the determination of fair value estimates is a combined effort between management and valuation specialists. Financial executives should therefore actively monitor the work of accountants and appraisers. In response to additional standards, focus by both the Securities and Exchange Commission (SEC) and PCAOB on the quality of audits, and PCAOB findings pertaining to the audit of fair value estimates, audit firms have increased their focus in auditing fair value measurements of both publicly traded and privately held companies. The FASB provides guidance and procedures in various Statements on Auditing Standards (SAS):

> *AU-C Section 540 – Auditing Accounting Estimates, Including Fair Value Accounting Estimates, and Related Disclosures.* Establishes the auditor's responsibility related to accounting estimates including fair value and references aspects such as controls, use of a specialist, assumptions, and prior estimates.
>
> *AU-C Section 500 – Audit Evidence.* Explains what constitutes audit evidence and the auditor's responsibility in auditing it. Included is guidance related to management's use of a specialist, including evaluating competence, capabilities, and objectivity.

ASC 820: Fair Value Measurements

ASC 820 establishes a framework for how to measure the fair value of assets and liabilities for financial reporting purposes. Prior to its issuance in 2006, there had been inconsistent guidance throughout GAAP in measuring fair value and in disclosure requirements. Its IFRS counterpart, IFRS 13, was released in May 2011 and became effective in 2013. The intent was to minimize any diversity in practice as to what represents fair value for financial reporting purposes. It established a standard of value different from the fair market value standard used for tax purposes, the fair market value and fair value standards used for litigation purposes, the fair market value and investment value standards used for strategic planning purposes, and all other standards of value. It therefore differentiates from any standard of value previously defined by the Internal Revenue Service, the courts, and general business practice.

In accordance with ASC 820, fair value is defined as "the price that would be received to sell an asset or paid to transfer a liability in an orderly transaction between market participants at the measurement date."[3] To better understand the meaning of this definition, consider these points:

- Fair value was previously thought to be an *entry price* (buy-side): what a company would pay to acquire an asset or pay to settle a liability. It is now an *exit price* (sell-side).

---

[3] ASC 820-10-20 – Glossary.

- The objective is "to estimate the price at which an orderly transaction to sell the asset or to transfer the liability would take place between market participants at the measurement date under current market conditions (that is, an exit price at the measurement date from the perspective of a market participant that holds the asset or owes the liability)."[4]
- As an exit price, fair value represents the price a company would receive if it were to sell the asset in the marketplace or paid if it were to transfer the liability. The exit price for an asset or liability is conceptually different from its transaction price (an entry price). Although exit and entry price may be identical in many situations, the transaction price is no longer presumed to represent the fair value of an asset or liability on its initial recognition.
- Consistent with the exit price concept, transaction costs are expensed, not capitalized. That is, they are not to be reflected in fair value under the theory that the next acquirer is not interested in the costs incurred to complete a prior transaction.
- An orderly transaction "assumes exposure to the market for a period before the measurement date to allow for marketing activities that are usual and customary for transactions involving such assets or liabilities; it is not a forced transaction (for example, a forced liquidation or distress sale)."[5]
- The fair value measurement assumes that the transaction occurs in the principal or most advantageous market for the asset or liability. The principal market is the market with the greatest volume and level of activity for the asset or liability. The most advantageous market is the market that maximizes the amount that would be received to sell the asset or minimizes the amount that would be paid to transfer the liability, after taking into account transaction costs and transportation costs. If there is a principal market for the asset or liability, the fair value measurement shall represent the price in that market (whether that price is directly observable or estimated using another valuation technique), even if the price in a different market is potentially more advantageous at the measurement date.[6]
- It is essential to view fair value from the point of view of market participants rather than a specific entity. That is, fair value is market based, not entity specific. Market participants[7] are unrelated parties, knowledgeable of the asset or liability given due diligence, willing and able to transact for the asset/liability. As such, there are some similarities to

---

[4] ASC 820-10-05-1B.
[5] ASC 820-10-20 – Glossary.
[6] ASC 820-10-35.
[7] ASC 820-10-20 – Glossary.

the hypothetical buyer and seller under the fair market value standard. However, one major difference is that market participants may be either financial or strategic buyers. Also, given the point of view of market participants, an asset may have a high value to a market participant but little or no value to the actual acquirer.

■ Fair value assumes highest and best use of the asset by market participants. The use must be physically possible, legally permissible, and financially feasible, and must maximize the value of the asset.[8] With regard to premise of value, reporting entities must determine whether highest and best use for an asset is as part of an asset group or on a stand-alone basis.[9]

ASC 820 stipulates a fair value hierarchy that has three levels based on the observability of the inputs.

1. Level 1 inputs are given the highest priority and represent quoted prices in active markets for identical assets or liabilities.
2. Level 2 inputs include quoted prices for similar assets or liabilities, quoted prices for identical assets or liabilities in an inactive market, directly observable inputs other than quoted prices for the asset or liability, and market inputs derived from or corroborated by observable market data.
3. Level 3 inputs are given the lowest priority and also require the highest amount of disclosure but represent the vast majority of transactions, including all transactions involving closely held businesses. Level 3 inputs are unobservable and based on the company's own assumptions about what a market participant would assume. Though unobservable, they are still estimated within a market participant framework. The vast majority of transactions, including all transactions involving closely held business, include valuations required use of Level 3 inputs.

In sum, ASC 820 provides consistent guidance throughout GAAP in fair value measurement and disclosure. For M&A, perhaps the most relevant FASB statement impacted by ASC 820 is ASC 805.

ASC 805: Business Combinations

ASC 805 addresses how companies account for M&A transactions for financial reporting purposes. The accounting requirements set forth in ASC 805

---

[8] ASC 820-10-35-10B.
[9] ASC 820-10-35-10E.

are very similar to those set forth in IFRS 3.[10] As will be discussed later, the accounting alternative for private companies allows them to omit recognition of most customer relationship and noncompetition agreement assets. M&A transactions are referred to by ASC 805 as *business combinations*, which is defined as "a transaction or other event in which an acquirer obtains control of one or more businesses. Transactions sometimes referred to as true mergers or mergers of equals also are business combinations."[11] This Topic "establishes principles and requirements for how the acquirer does each of the following: (a) recognizes and measures in its financial statements the identifiable assets acquired, the liabilities assumed and any non-controlling interest in the acquiree; (b) recognizes and measures the goodwill acquired in the business combination or a gain from a bargain purchase; and (c) determines what information to disclose to enable users of the financial statements to evaluate the nature and financial effects of the business combination."[12] It is important to note that this Statement does *not* apply to: "(a) the formation of a joint venture; (b) the acquisition of an asset or group of assets that does not constitute a business or a nonprofit entity; and (c) a combination between entities, businesses, or nonprofit activities under common control." There are limited other cases where the guidance does not apply.[13]

With regard to timing, if the initial accounting for a business combination is incomplete by the end of the reporting period in which the transaction occurs, provisional amounts are recorded and adjustments may be made for up to one year following the transaction.[14]

Among the primary goals of the predecessor to ASC 805 was to provide more information about intangible assets and to improve comparability of financial results of entities. However, while the focus of this overview is on intangible assets, ASC 805 also requires financial assets, working capital items, fixed assets, real estate, and liabilities assumed to be recognized at fair value.

---

[10] While significant progress was made in converging ASC 805 and IFRS 3 in their recent respective revisions, slight differences remain in terms of the definition of fair value, the definition of control for purposes of identifying the buyer in a business combination, the treatment of nonprofits, the measurement of noncontrolling interests, preacquisition contingencies, and contingent consideration, among others. These differences are beyond the scope of this book. The recent addition of the accounting alternative for private companies (discussed subsequently) increases the difference.

[11] 805-20-20 Glossary.

[12] ASC 805-10-05-3.

[13] ASC 805-10-05-4.

[14] ASC 805-10-25-13.

Intangible assets are defined in this Topic as "assets (not including financial assets) that lack physical substance," excluding goodwill.[15] The focus on intangible assets reflects the fact that, as we have moved from being a manufacturing-based to an intellectual property–driven economy, most of the value being created in today's economy is attributable to intangible assets. Venture capitalists, private equity groups, and hedge funds all consider intangibles as having core value and therefore view them more strategically than they had in the past.

ASC 805 requires identifiable intangible assets to be recognized and measured in an entity's financial statements. Assets that are not identifiable are captured within goodwill. The recognition criteria do not apply to intangible assets acquired in transactions other than business combinations. An intangible asset is identifiable if it arises from contractual or other legal rights (e.g. trademarks, trade names, Internet domain names, noncompete agreements, licensing agreements, franchise agreements, computer software, and patented technology) or if it is capable of being separated or divided from the acquired entity and sold, transferred, licensed, rented, or exchanged – regardless of whether there is an intent to do so (e.g. customer relationships, unpatented technology, and databases).[16] An assembled workforce is not recognized as an intangible asset apart from goodwill but still may need to be valued in conjunction with the valuation of customer relationships, order backlog, existing technology, in-process research and development, or any other asset valued using the multiperiod excess earnings method (to be discussed in Chapter 18). Consistent with the market participant concept and the definition of fair value under ASC 820, value must be ascribed to an asset even though the acquirer does not intend to use it if it is believed a market participant would do so (examples include trademarks or duplicate software). An acquirer buying a competitor may not intend to use the acquiree's trademark, but if other market participants would likely use the trademark, that trademark must be recognized and valued.

In 2014, the FASB published ASU-2014-2 and ASU-2014-18, which together simplify business combination–related accounting for private companies. ASU-2014-2 allows for amortization of goodwill and ASU-2014-18 allows nonrecognition for certain assets, namely most customer relationships and noncompetition agreements. An entity may elect ASU-2014-2 (goodwill amortization) without electing ASU-2014-18 (customer relationship and noncompete, nonrecognition). Conversely, if a company elects ASU-2014-18, it must also elect ASU-2014-2.

---

[15] ASC 805-10-20 Glossary.
[16] Ibid.

ASC 805 sets forth several examples of identifiable intangible assets in five categories:

1. *Marketing related.* Marketing-related intangible assets are those used primarily in the marketing or promotion of products or services. They include such items as trademarks, trade names, service marks, collective marks, certification marks, trade dress (unique color, shape, or package design), newspaper mastheads, Internet domain names, and noncompete agreements. Under the accounting alternative, private companies are not required to recognize noncompete agreements separately from goodwill.

2. *Customer related.* Customer-related intangible assets include items such as customer contracts and related customer relationships, noncontractual customer relationships, order or production backlog, and customer lists. For purposes of being identifiable, a customer relationship is considered to meet the contractual-legal criterion if the company has an established practice of entering into contracts, regardless of whether a contract currently exists. Under the accounting alternative, private companies are only required to recognize customer-related assets that "are capable of being sold or licensed independently from other assets of a business"[17] This omits many customer relationship assets that are included for public companies.

3. *Artistic related.* Artistic-related intangible assets meet the criteria for recognition apart from goodwill if the assets arise from contractual rights or legal rights such as those provided by copyright. They include such items as plays, operas, ballets, books, magazines, newspapers, other literary works, musical works (including compositions, song lyrics, advertising jingles), pictures and photographs, and video and audio-visual material (including motion pictures, music videos, and television programs).

4. *Contract based.* Contract-based intangible assets represent the value of rights that arise from contractual agreements. They include licensing, royalty, and standstill agreements; advertising, construction, management, service, or supply contracts; lease agreements; construction permits; franchise agreements; operating and broadcast rights; use rights (such as drilling, water, air, mineral, timber cutting, and route authorities); servicing contracts; and employment contracts.

5. *Technology based.* Technology-based intangible assets relate to innovations or technological advances. They include patented and unpatented technology, computer software and mask works, databases (including title plants), trade secrets (such as secret formulas, processes, and recipes), and in-process research and development (IPR&D).

---

[17] ASC 805-20-25-30.

> The financial executive of an acquiring company should review the different types of marketing, customer, artistic, contract, and technology-based intangible assets of the target company in advance of discussions with the company's CPA and valuation specialists.

This list is not all-inclusive, but it does provide a good framework for due diligence on a company's intangible assets prior to a transaction. Following a transaction, it sets the stage for the valuation of the acquired company's identifiable intangible assets for the purchase price allocation. Although within these five categories, the FASB identified over 30 intangible assets in this list, many rarely appear in purchase price allocations. Also, numerous other intangibles exist and may be associated with a specific acquisition. The ten that perhaps arguably appear most often in purchase price allocations include:

1. *Customer relationships.* Customer-related intangible assets refer to a customer base/listing purchased in a business combination. To the acquirer, the customer relationships represent the expected ongoing and continued business relationship, and thus future revenues. Customer relationships often represent a major component of value of a purchased business. Often confused with goodwill, customer intangibles differ from goodwill when viewed from an ASC 805 accounting framework. Historically, goodwill has been defined as expected customer patronage or as the likelihood that customers will continue to do business with a certain vendor. Within this concept of goodwill, there is an expectation that certain previously existing customers will generate some level of revenue for some period of time. In contrast, the current valuation of customers for accounting purposes reflects the analysis of specific customer relationships, whose past revenues, purchasing patterns, and identity can be ascertained by the purchaser of such customer relationships in order to determine specific revenue projections from such group. The value of the customer relationships reflects the economic benefit derived from them after consideration of changes in purchasing levels and attrition. Therefore, while the cost approach may be used in certain limited instances to value customer relationships, they are usually valued using the multiperiod excess earnings method (MPEEM) within the income approach.[18]

2. *Existing technology.* Existing technology is often embedded in products and services currently sold by the company. These products are considered technologically complete because they meet design specifications and are in or beyond the beta stage. Existing technology is

---

[18] The approaches and methods mentioned to value each of these ten intangible assets are explained in Chapter 18.

normally proprietary, which refers to unpatented and patent-pending trade secrets and know-how. In many instances, existing technology is more valuable to a business enterprise than its patents. To have value, existing technology must be used in the operations of the business, provide its owner with some competitive advantage, and be protected to prevent its use by competitors. Existing technology may produce an economic advantage in the form of lower operating or manufacturing costs or via a premium price. It raises barriers to competition through time, cost, knowledge, or proper skills, even if absolute secrecy is lacking. Finally, existing technology creates or protects market position. Given these features, the value of existing technology often lies in its income-generating capacity and therefore is typically valued using the MPEEM or the relief-from-royalty method within the income approach.

3. *In-process research and development.* IPR&D represents a research and development (R&D) project that has not yet been completed. Specifically, it is technology under development whereby the underlying technology has not reached technological feasibility, a working model of the program is not available, or all the steps of a detailed program design have not been completed. Once it comes to market, it becomes existing technology. In a business combination, assets acquired to be used in R&D activities are separately identifiable assets, and each is separately valued. IPR&D tends to be leading edge and represents technology not yet readily reproducible. Each specific IPR&D project must have been the result of activities undertaken by the acquired company, the costs of which qualified as R&D costs under ASC 730. IPR&D must be estimable with reasonable reliability, have substance such that it can result in the creation of value, be incomplete such that remaining technological or engineering risks or regulatory approvals remain, and have additional R&D costs to be incurred. IPR&D must also have anticipated economic benefit such that an acquiring company anticipates that each asset singly, or in combination with other assets of the combined entity, will be used in its postcombination R&D activities. It is important to note that, in accordance with fair value as defined by ASC 820, intended use by the acquirer is no longer considered absolute. Thus, the acquirer must consider the anticipated behavior of other market participants. The fair value is capitalized and tested for impairment until completion or discontinuation. IPR&D is typically valued using a MPEEM or relief-from-royalty method within the income approach.

4. *Lease agreements.* If a company has below-market leases for real estate or equipment, there is a cost savings that has value. The fact that a company will realize certain cost savings due to the below-market

leases, and will therefore generate an identifiable stream of benefits, lends itself to use of a discounted cash flow (DCF) method within the income approach. A lease may also be above market, in which case there is a liability.

5. *Licensing agreements.* Licensing agreements can involve one company licensing a trade name or a patent in return for royalty payments. Since the valuation of these agreements depends on the amount the license adds to a company's income stream, a MPEEM within the income approach is typically used to value licensing agreements.

6. *Noncompete agreements.* A noncompete agreement is an agreement between a buyer and a seller of a business in which the seller is restricted from competing in the same industry for a specific period of time, often within a defined geographic area. When a business is sold, the buyer often obtains a noncompete agreement from the seller, whether the seller is an individual selling the family business or a corporation divesting a subsidiary. The agreement may be included as one of the terms of the overall asset or stock sale agreement (a covenant not to compete) or it can be created and bargained for as a separate asset sold to the buyer (a noncompete agreement). A noncompete document is particularly valuable to an employer who employs individuals who have access to critical information, either through job responsibility or through social interactions with owners or high-level executives. Although the signed agreement does not guarantee protection against such disruption, it deters this type of action by forcing the employee to reconsider leaving the company. While ubiquitous in transactions and therefore in business combination–related valuations, the value of noncompetes tends to be a relatively small percentage of the total purchase consideration because the probability of a seller leaving the company and successfully competing within the standard three to five years of a noncompete is often relatively low. Also, depending on the jurisdiction, noncompetes can be difficult to enforce in court. Noncompetes are typically valued using the with-and-without method within the income approach.

7. *Order backlog.* Order backlog (also referred to as contractual backlog) represents the revenue remaining to be earned on a contractual sale. Valuing order backlog is similar to valuing any contract. There is a set of expected benefits to be received from the contract, and there are costs to be incurred to receive those benefits. The methodology to be employed in estimating the fair value of order backlog must consider each of these components. The method that best reflects these components is the MPEEM. The expected cash flow to be generated from the contractual backlog is discounted at a rate of return reflecting the risk of achieving those cash flows, which is typically less than that

for the overall business because the customers associated with order backlog have been contracted and secured.

8. *Patents.* In the United States, a patent is a government grant by action of the Patent and Trademark Office to the patentee of an exclusive right to produce, use, and sell an invention. The issuance of the patent potentially provides a legal monopoly in the area covered by the patent for the legal life of the patent. The expiration date is generally 20 years from filing. The presence of patents may allow a company to enjoy a premium margin on sales of its products as well as potential cost savings. This could be due to the ability to charge a premium price or the ability to experience a cost savings that can be tied to the proprietary intellectual property. A patent's value is dependent on factors such as its age, the status of the underlying invention, the industry in which it operates, its utility, and any blocking patents, among others. There are several ways to value a patent, but the most common for financial reporting purposes is the relief-from-royalty method within the income approach.

9. *Software.* Virtually all companies have software, but value is not separately ascribed to software in all business combinations. Value is ascribed to software that is currently sold in the market either via license, software as a service (SaaS), or incorporation into a service/product offering. Like existing technology, software is viewed as proprietary. As such, it is used in the operations of the business, provides its owner with some competitive advantage, and may be treated as a secret by requiring restrictive covenants with employees, keeping knowledge segmented, maintaining file and document controls, and so on. In general, proprietary software or technology produces an economic advantage in the form of lower service, operating, or manufacturing costs. It raises some barriers to competition through time, cost, knowledge, or proper skills, even if absolute secrecy is lacking. Finally, it creates or protects a strong market position. Given these features, the value of software lies in its income-generating capacity. It is therefore typically valued using the relief-from-royalty method within the income approach. An exception to this would be software used for internal operations that does not directly contribute to revenue/income. In this case, it would likely be valued using a replacement cost method within the cost approach.

10. *Trademarks or trade names.* A trademark, as defined in the Trademark Act of 1946, "includes any word, name, symbol or device or any combination thereof adopted and used by a manufacturer or merchant to identify his goods and distinguish them from those manufactured by others." A trademark serves three basic functions: It identifies the product; it guarantees a certain level of quality; and it acts as a public

relations tool that provides a marketing function. Trademark value comes from the extent to which these three functions are served. As such, the value of a trademark lies in its ability to command a premium price, market share, and/or royalties in the marketplace. In that case, a competitor is prevented from sharing the profits accruing to the trademark owner who has invested the time and expense in cultivating the trademark. Registered trademarks are protected as long as they are actively used and are protected against infringement. A trade name is the name of a business, association, or other organization used to identify it. It is a type of marketing intangible that may or may not be the same as the trademark used to identify the company's products, such as Microsoft, which represents both. A trade name does not have the legal protection afforded to a trademark. It cannot be registered at the federal level unless it is also a trademark, and its ownership is governed by common or state law. Both trademarks and trade names can have either long or indefinite lives and are typically valued using a relief-from-royalty method within the income approach.

There are several other aspects of ASC 805 of which those involved in a business combination should be aware, but which are beyond the scope of this book and require a review of the Topic itself and related literature. Some other highlights, not all-inclusive and not previously mentioned, are summarized next.

- *Acquisition method.* In accordance with the acquisition method (formerly known as the purchase method), the acquirer measures and recognizes the assets, liabilities, and noncontrolling interest of the acquiree, as a whole, as of the acquisition date. Four procedures are required in applying the acquisition method: (1) identify the acquirer; (2) determine the acquisition date; (3) recognize and measure the identifiable assets acquired, the liabilities assumed, and any noncontrolling interest in the acquiree; and (4) recognize and measure goodwill or a gain from a bargain purchase.[19]
- *Disclosure requirements.* There is a lengthy list of disclosure requirements as outlined in ASC 805-10-50.
- *Transaction costs.* Consistent with ASC 820, transaction costs are not included in the fair value of the business acquired. Instead, they are expensed as incurred rather than capitalized.
- *Anticipated restructuring costs.* These costs are no longer booked as assets but are expensed in the period incurred.

---

[19] ASC 805-10-05-4.

- *Contingent consideration.* The fair value of an earn-out is included in the purchase price. After acquisition, earn-outs are updated to fair value periodically and when new information is available. They are remeasured through earnings rather than the historic practice of remeasuring with an offset to goodwill. As such, they are subject to mark-to-market accounting, increasing the potential for post-deal earnings volatility. If the value of the earn-out is underestimated, the acquirer will take a charge to income, thus reducing earnings. Conversely, if overestimated, the acquirer will realize a credit to income, thus increasing earnings.
- *Bargain purchases.* If the fair value of net assets acquired exceeds the sum of purchase consideration, the excess is recorded as a gain on the income statement. This represents a significant change from past practice where the excess was allocated as a pro-rata reduction to the value of tangible and intangible assets.
- *Partial acquisitions.* When ownership control is obtained in a partial acquisition, the full fair value of all assets and liabilities is recorded on the consolidated balance sheets.
- *Equity securities.* The fair value of equity securities issued as consideration is now measured at the closing date of the transaction rather than at the agreement date.
- *Contingent assets and liabilities.* Preacquisition contingent assets or liabilities (e.g. an open lawsuit or environmental hazard) of the target are recognized at fair value as of the transaction date.

ASC 805 and its IFRS 3 counterpart have created several implications on the timing, cost, and structures of business combinations. ASC 805 resulted in an increase in the number and types of assets (and liabilities) that must be measured at fair value. Acquirers will need to consider engaging audit and valuation personnel as part of their acquisition team both during the due diligence process and after the deal closes.

In closing, to demonstrate a very basic purchase price allocation under ASC 805, assume that Cavendish Seafood Distributors acquired Benno Foods for $25 million, and did not elect the accounting alternative. Benno Foods had $11 million in working capital and $4 million in fixed assets, leaving $10 million to be allocated to identifiable intangible assets and goodwill. A valuation specialist was hired to determine the fair value of the intangibles and established, upon reviewing the several possible intangible assets within the above-mentioned five categories of intangible assets with company management, that Benno Foods had a trade name, customer relationships, and a noncompete agreement. After completing the valuation, the valuation specialist determined that the fair value of the trade name was

$2 million, the fair value of the customer relationships was $3.5 million, and the fair value of the noncompete agreements was $500,000. The residual $4 million was booked to goodwill, subject to periodic impairment testing under ASC 350.

ASC 350: Goodwill and Other Intangible Assets

The requirement to allocate the purchase price following a business combination under ASC 805 will create valuation issues not only at the time of the transaction but also after. If the fair values of any assets on the financials are suspected to have dropped below their carrying (book) value after the transaction is closed, they will be subject to an impairment test under either ASC 350-20 or ASC 350-30. Using the previous example, if the business of Benno Foods becomes a separate reporting unit within Cavendish Seafood Distributors, and it is determined that its fair value has declined in the year since it was acquired, the $4 million in goodwill may be impaired and partially or completely written down. Although the impact will be after the transaction closes, the potential for future impairment must be contemplated if the transaction does not work out as expected.

The accounting alternative for private companies introduced in ASU-2014-2 allows for simplified treatment of goodwill. Under the Alternative, a company amortizes goodwill over a period of 10 years or less. Additionally, the impairment test may occur at the entity or company level or at the disaggregated reporting unit level. "Goodwill of an entity (or a reporting unit) shall be tested for impairment if an event occurs or circumstances change that indicate that the fair value of the entity (or the reporting unit) may be below its carrying amount (a triggering event)."[20] If the carrying value of the entity or reporting unit is greater than the fair value, goodwill is impaired, or written down, by the amount of this excess. The test should be performed if there is a triggering event that causes belief the fair value may be less than the carrying value. Examples include a deterioration in general economic or industry conditions, increases in costs, or entity-specific considerations such as loss of key customers or management.

In contrast to the accounting alternative, under ASC 350-20, purchased goodwill and certain intangible assets are not presumed to be wasting assets; they remain on the balance sheet (i.e. not amortized) and are assumed to have indefinite useful lives to be tested at least annually for

---

[20] ASC 350-20-35-67.

impairment. Intangible assets that have finite useful lives will continue to be amortized over their useful lives. So in the case of Benno Foods, the trademark may be amortized over 20 years,[21] the customer relationships may be amortized over 8 years, and the noncompete over 4 years. Finite-lived assets carried on the books at more than the recoverable amount are considered impaired.

The impairment test requires both initial and periodic (typically annual or if there is a triggering event) fair value appraisals. Fair value is estimated by either an independent third party or an individual internal to the company. Currently, and since the publication of ASU 2017-04, if the carrying value of the entity or reporting unit is greater than the fair value, goodwill is impaired, or written down, by the amount of this excess. Historically, and allowed until 2020, there was a Step 2 where, similar to the process that occurs at acquisition, the fair value of all assets was estimated in order to imply a new value of goodwill. The difference between the book value of goodwill and the implied fair value is the impairment amount.

If there is no impairment to goodwill in a given year, a company will not book goodwill impairment in that period. If there is impairment, any goodwill impairment losses are recognized as an expense in the income statement and the value is adjusted on the balance sheet.[22]

Fair value under ASC 820 is based on value to a market participant, rather than a particular entity. Therefore, even if an asset has no value to the acquiring company, it is recorded on its balance sheet if there is value to a market participant which may subsequently be subject to impairment. In practice, however, the actions of the acquiring company are often deemed indicative of those of a market participant.

Incorporating ASC 805 into the Due Diligence Process

Given the increasing pervasiveness of fair value accounting, an indication of its impact on the acquirer post-transaction may be beneficial during due diligence process. This will provide an understanding of potential earnings accretion or dilution, balance sheet composition, and residual goodwill.

---

[21] Note: The assumed useful lives determined herein are provided simply for illustrative purposes. Determination of an applicable useful life for an asset is fact and circumstance specific. For example, a trademark may have a finite useful life of 5, 10, 20, or some other number of years; or it may be deemed to have an indefinite life.
[22] In GAAP, under ASC 350-20, impairment charges are recorded directly against the asset. Under IFRS, impairment charges are recorded in a contra account to the asset.

As part of the due diligence process, the acquirer should consider these questions as they relate to financial reporting requirements:

- Are there procedures in place to gather information needed to comply with ASC 805 and 820?
- If a private company, will the company elect the accounting alternative? Are there any downsides to doing so?
- Will valuation specialists be hired to help identify and value the assets acquired? If so, are there procedures in place to assess their qualifications both in terms of business valuations and in valuations for financial reporting purposes?
  - Have they been lined up on an appropriate time frame?
  - Have there been discussions with them regarding expected timing, scope, and report format?
  - Has a long-term forecast been prepared beyond just a one-year budget? What is the resulting internal rate of return, and how might that correspond with a market participant's expected rate of return on those cash flows?
- Has there been a review of the main categories of assets and liabilities?
- With regard to working capital, what is the impact of bringing accounts receivable and inventory to fair value?
- With regard to fixed assets, is it acceptable to assume that book value approximates fair value or does a fixed asset appraiser need to be hired?
- With regard to liabilities, have liability measurements taken into account the credit of the borrower? Is it necessary to hire an actuary to review the target's pension plans? How will deferred tax assets and deferred tax liabilities be estimated?
- To what extent will a preliminary valuation of the intangible assets be done to estimate the impact on the acquirer's financial statements?
- What are the target company's identifiable intangible assets? Does the estimate of their respective fair values make sense in light of the potential purchase price?
- Does the company have a business plan that encompasses intellectual property?
- Does the company pay or receive any royalties relating to intellectual property?
- Has the company purchased or sold any intangible assets or intellectual property in the past?
- Are there intangible assets that are of no value to the acquirer but which will be valued in accordance with the market participant concept? What is the resulting impact?

- With regard to the assembled workforce, can the company provide a listing of its workforce, including title, date of hire, salary, and benefits? What is involved in hiring replacements? How long does it take the workforce at different levels to become fully productive?
- Can the company provide a list of its customers over the previous five (or more) years, including the revenues by customer by year?
- Can the company estimate the probability a key person will leave if he or she was not to sign a noncompete agreement, and the resulting impact to revenues and profits whether the person competes or not?
- What percentage of the company's revenues is impacted by its trademarks? Its existing technology? Its patents?
- How many in-process research and development projects are there?
- Is there IPR&D that will have to be capitalized and be subject to periodic impairment testing until completion? If so, if the project fails, how will that impact the target's financials? If so, and if the project succeeds, how will the resulting amortization impact the target's financials?
- How will the useful lives of the identifiable intangible assets impact future financial statements in terms of amortization?
- Is there potential for a large amount of goodwill, such that there is a higher risk of an impairment charge under ASC 350 in future years?
- Alternatively, is there a potential for negative goodwill such that a gain will be recorded on the income statement?
- How will the audit firm handle the review of the ASC 805 analysis? Will it have an internal group of valuation specialists reviewing the work, will it engage outside valuation specialists, or will audit team members review the work themselves? How much time in advance of the audit will be needed to complete this process?
- With regard to contingent liabilities, what is the impact of open lawsuits or environmental liabilities?
- What is the probability of the earn-out being achieved?
- What will the impact of the earn-out be on expected future earnings since it is to be remeasured through earnings in subsequent years?
- Since transaction costs are not capitalized and are instead expensed, how will that impact the company's earnings for the year?
- Will the business combination be accretive to earnings? If not, how long will it take to get back to current earnings?
- Has a plan been established to integrate the target's accounting system with that of the acquirer?
- Are you familiar with postacquisition disclosure requirements?
- Has consideration been given to the fact that restructuring activities are no longer accrued in purchase accounting and instead dilute postdeal earnings?
- Has an understanding of the tax impact of the transaction been obtained?

Some of these questions will be of more concern to larger companies with audited financial statements. But, it is important for the financial and accounting team of any acquiring firm that has financial statements prepared in accordance with U.S. GAAP or IFRS standards to consider each of these questions.

Without an assessment of the fair value implications resulting from a business combination, acquirers may be taken aback by the financial reporting consequences. This chapter has provided an overview of the key financial reporting standards to consider. The next chapter introduces the most common techniques used to value intangible assets as part of a purchase price allocation. The reader is encouraged to review the literature included in the References section for more information.

References

The standards can be retrieved from www.fasb.org and www.ifrs.org. A bibliography of books providing additional information on fair value accounting and the valuation of intangible assets follows.

AICPA Accounting & Valuation Guide, *Assets Acquired to Be Used in Research and Development Activities* (New York: American Institute of Certified Public Accountants, Inc., 2013).

Appraisal Foundation – Best Practices Series:

- *The Identification of Contributory Assets and Calculation of Economic Rents*, 2010.
- *The Valuation of Customer-Related Assets*, 2016.
- *The Measurement and Application of Market Participant Acquisition Premiums*, 2017.
- *Valuation of Contingent Consideration*, 2018.

King, Alfred M., *Executive's Guide to Fair Value: Profiting from the New Valuation Rules* (Hoboken, NJ: Wiley, 2008).

Mard, Michael J., James R. Hitchner, and Steven D. Hyden, *Valuation for Financial Reporting: Fair Value, Business Combinations, Intangible Assets, Goodwill, and Impairment Analysis* (Hoboken, NJ: Wiley, 2010).

Mard, Michael J., Steven D. Hyden, and Edward W. Trott, *Business Combinations with SFAS 141R, 157, and 160: A Guide to Financial Reporting* (Hoboken, NJ: Wiley, 2009).

Pellegrino, Michael, *BVR's Guide to Intellectual Property Valuation, 2nd ed.* (Portland, OR: Business Valuation Resources, 2012).

Razgaitis, Richard, *Valuation and Dealmaking of Technology-Based Intellectual Property* (Hoboken, NJ: Wiley, 2009).

Reilly, Robert F., and Robert P. Schweihs, *Guide to Intangible Asset Valuation*, (New York: American Institute of Certified Public Accountants, Inc., 2013).

Smith, Gordon V., and Susan M. Richey, *Trademark Valuation: A Tool for Brand Management* (Hoboken, NJ: Wiley, 2013).

Smith, Gordon V., and Russell L. Parr, *Intellectual Property: Valuation, Exploitation, and Infringement Damages* (Hoboken, NJ: Wiley, 2005).

Smith, Gordon V., and Russell L. Parr, *Valuation of Intellectual Property and Intangible Assets*, 3rd ed. (Hoboken, NJ: Wiley, 2004).

Zyla, Mark L., *Fair Value Measurements: Practical Guidance and Implementation*, 3rd ed. (Hoboken, NJ: Wiley, 2018).

CHAPTER 18

Intangible Asset Valuation

Although the U.S. economy has shifted from a production base to a knowledge base, where intangible assets comprise approximately 87% of the S&P 500 market value,[1] financial reporting has only begun to address this momentous change. As discussed in Chapter 17, ASC 805 and IFRS 3 require that the purchase price following a business combination be allocated to all the tangible and intangible assets acquired, resulting in the fair value of an acquired company's intangible assets to be booked on the balance sheet of the acquiror. However, all the value created through a company's internally developed intangibles does not find its way to its balance sheet.

The purpose of this chapter is to provide a basic understanding of how intangible assets are valued. (For a more in-depth explanation of intangible asset valuation techniques, see the References section in Chapter 17.) An awareness of intangible asset valuation methods introduced in this chapter will provide the reader with the tangible benefit of being better prepared for the postmerger and acquisition (M&A) transaction financial reporting compliance requirements discussed in Chapter 17. In addition, it will provide the reader with the intangible benefit of beginning to focus on the value of a company's intangible assets and the means by which these assets are put to work to create, build, and maximize company value, as discussed in Chapter 2. The better you can identify and understand a company's intangible assets, the closer you are to that company's true value.

---

[1] As determined through independent research conducted by Ned Davis Research, Inc. and commissioned by Ocean Tomo in 2015. This represents a complete inversion from the late 1970s, when approximately 20% of a public company's value (based on the Standard & Poor's 500) was derived from its intangible assets. Over the past 40 years intangible assets as a percentage of S&P 500 market value was 17% in 1975, 32% in 1985, 68% in 1995, 80% in 2005, and 87% in 2015.

Approaches to Valuing Intangible Assets

Just as in business valuation, no single method exists for determining the fair value of intangible assets. However, there does exist a generally accepted theoretical foundation to the process of valuing these assets revolving around the three generally accepted valuation approaches throughout all appraisal disciplines: the income approach, the asset approach, and the market approach. The three generally accepted valuation approaches are intended to reflect the respective economic (income), utility (asset), and comparative (market) characteristics of the subject asset.

Income Approach

The income approach is based on the economic principle of anticipation (i.e. the expected economic income to be earned). It measures the value of an intangible asset based on the expected stream of monetary benefits attributable to it over its remaining useful life. Generally, the present value of the income stream to be generated over the intangible asset's remaining economic life is determined. Doing this involves an analysis of financial information and input from financial, marketing, and operations personnel to develop the future income stream attributable to the asset. The three fundamental components of the income approach include a projection of economic income, an estimation of the time period to project economic income, and the selection of appropriate risk-adjusted discount and capitalization rates. Given these components, economic income (i.e. cash flows, net income, or royalty savings) is converted into a present value equivalent through discounting. The fair value of the asset is the sum of the discounted future income. This approach assumes that the income derived from the particular intangible asset will, to a large extent, control its value. The approach can be most useful if the subject intangible asset is or has the potential to become an income-producing property. It is weakened if there is not sufficient data to adequately support estimates of economic income, capital charges (if any), and the selection of the appropriate discount or capitalization rate.

Among the more common methods to value intangible assets within the income approach are the discounted cash flow method (DCF), the multiperiod excess earnings method, the relief-from-royalty method, and the differential value method. The DCF was described in Chapter 7; the other methods are described later in this chapter. It is important to note that these are not the only methods used within the income approach to valuing intangibles. They are, in the authors' experience, the most widely used for financial reporting purposes. Other methods include the profit split method, the yield capitalization method, and the direct capitalization method.

The income approach is often most appropriate for the valuation of these intangible assets: contracts, customer relationships, existing technology, in-process research and development, licenses and royalty agreements, noncompete agreements, order backlog, patents, certain software, and trademarks.

Asset Approach

The asset approach is based on the economic principles of substitution and price equilibrium, stressing the utility characteristics of the asset. A prudent investor would pay no more for an asset than the amount necessary to replace it. Reproduction cost contemplates the construction (or purchase) of an exact replica of the subject intangible asset. Replacement cost contemplates the cost to recreate the utility of the subject intangible asset, but in a form or appearance that may be different from an exact replica of the actual intangible assets being valued. The asset approach is most useful as a value indicator when the components of the asset are relatively new and reasonably reflect the highest and best use of the subject asset. This approach is often used to estimate the value of a special-purpose asset, where there may be little potential for sale or lease in the marketplace.

The asset approach is not as comprehensive as the income and market approaches when it comes to valuing most other intangible assets. Many of the important factors that drive value are not directly reflected in this approach and must be considered apart from it. Specifically, the asset approach does not directly incorporate information about the amount of economic benefits associated with the assets. These benefits are driven by demand for the product or service and the profits that can be generated. Information about the trend of the economic benefits, the duration over which the economic benefits will be enjoyed, and the risk associated with receiving the expected economic benefits are all not directly factored into the asset approach model.[2]

Perhaps the most widely used method within the asset approach to value intangibles, to be described later in this chapter, is the replacement cost method. An example of the application of this method is presented in Exhibit 18.4 by way of valuing an assembled workforce. It is important to note that for certain other intangible assets that may be valued using this method, such as internally developed software, one of the biggest challenges is to determine external (economic) obsolescence and/or internal (functional, technological, and physical) obsolescence.

The asset approach is most appropriate for the valuation of these intangible assets: assembled workforces, corporate practices and procedures, distribution networks, customer relationships (in certain instances when not a company's primary income-generating intangible asset) and software (internal use).

---

[2] Gordon V. Smith and Russell L. Parr, *Valuation of Intellectual Property and Intangible Assets, 3rd ed.* (Hoboken, NJ: Wiley, 2000), 213.

Market Approach

The market approach is based on the related economic principles of competition and equilibrium. It is the approach that most closely reflects quoted market prices, highest on the hierarchy of value under ASC 820. The fundamental assumption within the market approach is that other buyers of comparable assets were willing, had knowledge of all relevant facts, and consummated a deal that was fair and, therefore, represented fair value at that time and for that asset.

The market approach arrives at an indication of value by comparing the intangible assets being appraised to comparable (i.e. guideline) pieces of property that have been recently acquired in arm's-length transactions. The market data is then adjusted for any significant differences, to the extent known, between the comparable properties and the intangible assets being valued. A major benefit of the market approach is its simple application when a truly comparable transaction is available. This situation is most commonly found when the acquired asset is widely marketed to third parties. The market approach is weakened if the selected comparable transactions are not comparable to the subject asset on or about the valuation date.

To properly conduct a market approach, the appraiser needs to identify arm's-length transactions of similar assets, disclosure of pricing information, and reasonable knowledge of the relevant facts known to the transacting parties. In general, although intangible assets are marketable and occasionally sold apart from a business, there often exists little or no comparable transactional data. This is because these assets and properties are created over time and are designed to service the needs of a particular business entity. As such, valuations involving intangible assets lean toward the income and asset approaches; application of the market approach is rare for intangible assets.

However, market-based inputs are used in determining appropriate royalty rates for the intangible assets being valued by way of a relief-from-royalty method within the income approach (e.g. trademarks, patents, and certain types of technology). In addition, it may be appropriate for the valuation of intangibles such as liquor licenses or franchises.

Key Components to Intangible Asset Valuation

Before describing the most common methods within these three approaches to value intangible assets, it is important to understand six key components within the income approach in determining the cash flows attributable to specific intangible asset being valued. These components, which are fundamental to the application of the multiperiod excess earnings method to be described later, include remaining useful life, revenues related to the particular intangible, expenses related to the particular intangible, contributory asset charges, an applicable discount rate, and a tax amortization benefit.

Remaining Useful Life

One of the first steps in the valuation of intangible assets when applying the income approach is to establish a remaining useful life. This is a divergence from traditional business valuation where, assuming a going concern, the life of a business enterprise is automatically assumed to be indefinite. Determination of remaining useful life is both the most difficult aspect of valuing an intangible asset and one of the most important drivers of its value. The longer the remaining useful life, the higher the value. The useful life for intangible assets is typically discrete (i.e. over a finite period of time) but may, for certain assets, be indefinite (i.e. over a long period of time, not specifically identifiable, but not necessarily infinite).

When valuing an intangible asset, remaining useful life is determined based on the expected time the asset will contribute to the estimated future cash flows of the company, and may or may not coincide with how long the asset is amortized under generally accepted accounting principles (GAAP). Considerations made in determining useful life[3] include expected use of the asset by the entity, expected useful life of any comparable asset, and any legal or contractual provisions that may limit or extend the asset's useful life. The effects of obsolescence, demand, competition, and other economic factors (such as the stability of the industry, known technological advances, legislative action that results in an uncertain or changing regulatory environment, and expected changes in distribution channels) must also be taken into account.

As an example, the valuation of customer relationships often requires the estimation of future cash flows over an expected remaining useful life. The way in which customers survive over time (i.e. the asset's survivor curve) is important in determining how the future income from, and thus the value of, this income-producing asset declines. For customer-related intangibles, an attrition analysis is typically the means to estimate the remaining economic life. The retention and attrition rates associated with customer renewals are used to estimate the asset's turnover rate and, hence, its survivor curve. To estimate the retention rate associated with a company's customer relationships, the change in composition of the customer relationships over a defined period of time (say, five years) is examined to determine an attrition rate.

---

[3] ASC 350-20, ¶11 and IAS 38 ¶90.

For a patent, the statutory life in the United States is 20 years from the date on which the inventors filed with the United States Patent and Trademark Office, with certain exceptions. For valuation purposes, this does not necessarily mean that the remaining useful life of the patent is to be determined based on the amount remaining in its statutory life. For example, the average effective patent life for pharmaceuticals is 11.5 years.[4] Overall, for patents and other technology-based intangibles, a life-cycle analysis (remaining life based on expected future financial viability), as opposed to attrition analysis, is typically the means to estimate the remaining economic life. The other key factor to consider is how long the company can exploit the underlying technology covered by the patent. More often than not, this is less than the statutory life.

> In valuing a business under a going-concern premise, the underlying assumption is that it is expected to have an indefinite life. However, for most intangible assets, the life is finite. As a result, determining an intangible asset's useful life is one of the most important drivers of its value.

Trademarks, however, do not have a defined statutory life and are often valued assuming an indefinite useful life, similar to a business. However, consideration must be given to changes in market preferences and long-term sustainability of the subject trademark in determining whether the useful life should be indefinite, long term, or short term.

Other considerations in determining remaining useful life include company management's expectations as to the expected future use of the asset and any legal or contractual provisions that either may limit the useful life or may enable renewal or extension of its legal or contractual life. Economic factors, including demand, competition, obsolescence, technological developments, distribution channels, and regulations, must also be considered. Overall, consistent with ASC 820, special consideration must be given to market participant expectations (i.e. the considerations must be market based, not entity specific).

In terms of accounting amortization, the intangible asset is typically amortized over its useful life on a straight-line basis but ultimately depending on the pattern in which the economic benefits of that intangible are used up. If its useful life is determined to be indefinite, it may be subject to periodic impairment testing rather than amortized.

---

[4] Pharmaceutical Research and Manufacturers of America, *Pharmaceutical Industry Profile 2009* (March 2009): 39; www.phrma.org.

Revenues

Once the remaining useful life is established, the next step in determining projected cash flows attributable to the intangible asset being valued is to determine the portion of forecasted company revenues attributable to that asset. Using the valuation of customer relationships as an example, this may be done by first analyzing the revenues generated, for example, by the company's top 20 of 1,000 total customers who make up 80% of its revenues in the most recent 12 months ending on the valuation date. For each subsequent year, the results from the remaining useful life (attrition) analysis of, say, five years are applied to these revenues, showing a steady decline over time. Due to the fact that revenues associated with the existing customer relationships cease, it is important to note that the cash flow analysis applicable to existing customers reflects forecasts for a finite period. However, even though the useful life is deemed to be five years in this case, the forecast may continue on for several additional years to reflect the fact that the decline is not straight line but exponential to account for the smoothing out of customer relationships over time. Typically, a cash flow analysis reflects a residual (terminal) factor to capture value attributable to a business beyond a finite forecast period. Since customer relationships have a limited life, however, a forecast only for the applicable years is completed.

Expenses

Once the expected future revenues attributable to the specific intangible asset being valued are determined, we can move forward to the next level of the cash flow projections. For customer relationships, all expenses are determined based on the company's projected customer-related expenses, both direct operating expenses and general and administrative expenses. Since these expenses include sales and marketing expenses associated with generating new accounts, and the premise of the valuation of the existing customer relationships is that we are not valuing any new customers acquired after the valuation date, the overall operating expenses must be adjusted to ensure that no sales and marketing expenses associated with new clients are included. This leads to an increase in profit margin relative to the overall business enterprise.

In a purchase price allocation, if certain intangible assets (e.g. a trademark) are valued, it is necessary to recognize the contribution of that trademark to the profitability of the customer relationship. To do so, one must include a royalty charge based on the royalty rate applied in the valuation of the trademark. These concepts are illustrated in Exhibit 18.1.

EXHIBIT 18.1 Multi period Excess Earnings Method – Valuation of Customer Relationships

	20x1	20x2	20x3	20x4	20x5	20x6	20x7
All Current and Future Customers	$50,000,000	$55,000,000	$59,400,000	$63,600,000	$68,000,000	$70,700,000	$73,500,000
Beginning Customer Relationships Revenue	$50,000,000	$46,428,571	$41,387,755	$36,894,227	$32,888,568	$29,317,810	$26,134,733
Annual Growth Factor of 4%							
Customer Relationship Revenue After Growth	$50,000,000	$48,285,714	$43,043,265	$38,369,997	$34,204,111	$30,490,522	$27,180,122
Annual Attrition Rate (assuming a 7-year remaining useful life)	7.14%	14.29%	14.29%	14.29%	14.29%	14.29%	14.29%
% Remaining	96.43%	92.86%	79.59%	68.22%	58.48%	50.12%	42.96%
Current Customer Relationships Revenue	$46,428,571	$41,387,755	$36,894,227	$32,888,568	$29,317,810	$26,134,733	$23,297,248
Operating Margin	11.0%	11.8%	12.5%	13.5%	13.7%	13.7%	13.7%
Add: Sales & Marketing Expense on New Accounts	1.0%	1.0%	1.0%	1.0%	1.0%	1.0%	1.0%
Adjusted Operating Margin	12.0%	12.8%	13.5%	14.5%	14.7%	14.7%	14.7%
Operating Income	$5,571,429	$5,305,158	$4,965,193	$4,776,082	$4,302,820	$3,835,656	$3,419,214
Less: Return on Trademark @ 1.5%	$696,429	$620,816	$553,413	$493,329	$439,767	$392,021	$349,459
Pretax Income	$4,875,000	$4,684,341	$4,411,779	$4,282,754	$3,863,053	$3,443,635	$3,069,755
Less: Provision for Income Taxes @ 27%	$1,316,250	$1,264,772	$1,191,180	$1,156,343	$1,043,024	$929,782	$828,834
Net Income	$3,558,750	$3,419,569	$3,220,599	$3,126,410	$2,820,028	$2,513,854	$2,240,921

EXHIBIT 18.1 *(Continued)*

Less: Return on Working Capital	$188,036	$167,620	$149,422	$133,199	$118,737	$105,846	$94,354
Less: Return on Fixed Assets	$136,036	$121,266	$108,100	$96,364	$85,901	$76,575	$68,261
Less: Return on Non-compete Agreements	$614,714	$547,974	$488,480	$435,445	$388,168		
Less: Return on Assembled Workforce	$860,321	$766,915	$683,650	$609,425	$543,259	$484,277	$431,698
Total Return on Contributory Assets	$1,799,107	$1,603,776	$1,429,651	$1,274,432	$1,136,065	$666,697	$594,313
Cash Flow Attributable to the Customer Relationships	$1,759,643	$1,815,794	$1,790,948	$1,851,978	$1,683,963	$1,847,157	$1,646,608
Present Value of Cash Flows @ 14% Discount Rate	$1,648,057	$1,491,795	$1,290,686	$1,170,763	$933,815	$898,519	$702,601
PV Cash Flows Before Amortization Benefit (Years 1-7)	$8,136,235						
PV Cash Flows Before Amortization Benefit (beyond Year 7)	$2,167,466						
Sum of Present Value of Cash Flows Before Amortization Benefit	$10,303,701						
Plus: Tax Amortization Benefit	$1,379,092						
Indicated Fair Value of the Customer Relationships	**$11,700,000**						

Contributory Asset Charges

The projected net income is then reduced by the return on the underlying contributory assets, whose employment predicates the operations of the business, to determine the cash flows attributable to the customer relationships. These contributory assets may include working capital, fixed assets, contracts, and assembled workforce, among others. This represents a capital charge or economic rent adjustment and "is intended to ensure that, when economic income is analyzed on an enterprise level, there is a fair return on the investment of all the assets that are used or used up in the production of the income associated with the subject intangible."[5] The rate of return calculation varies for each asset category. Working capital levels may be determined based on management's forecasts, as long as they are deemed to be consistent with those of a market participant. Fixed asset levels may be set at the level of the company's fixed asset requirement relative to its total revenues. In contrast, the contracts and assembled workforce levels may be set at their respective fair values relative to the company's total revenues in each given year. The returns on contributory assets are typically expressed as a percentage of the revenue stream.

In general, returns on each of the contributory assets are selected in light of current costs of funds, the type of asset, and their respective acceptance as collateral for debt-financing purposes. A specific rate is calculated in part based on a typical mix of debt and equity financing. By reflecting returns on contributory assets in valuation calculations, an allowance is made for fair returns on the assets that are required to realize the related revenues. This represents a proxy for a royalty charge for use of these assets.

Once the returns on these contributory assets are determined, they are subtracted from the projected pretax or net income to provide for a fair return on the working capital, tangible assets, and intangible assets that are used in the creation of income associated with the intangible asset being valued and to ultimately determine the cash flow attributable to that intangible.

Applicable Discount Rate

Since the various methods within the income approach involve estimating the expected future net cash flows attributable to the subject intangible asset, those future income streams must be discounted to their present value. This discount factor should reflect both the business and financial risks of an investment in the intangible asset, as well as an assessment of its relation to the company's overall weighted average cost of capital (WACC). As discussed

---

[5] Robert F. Reilly and Robert P. Schweihs, *Valuing Intangible Assets* (New York: McGraw-Hill, 1999), 177.

in Chapters 8 and 9, the determination of the required rate of return is thus predicated on risk assessment. The higher the risk, the higher the required rate of return and the lower the value. An investor will expect a higher rate of return on a stock than on a Treasury bond or bank certificate of deposit. For assets, the discount rate increases as we move down the balance sheet from working capital to intangible assets. Examples of factors that contribute to risk in valuing a given intangible asset include the characteristics of the company owning that asset, the revenue-generating potential of the intangible, the market for that asset, and the holding period for that asset, among other characteristics. For international transactions, political and economic risks specific to the particular country, as well as the ability to expatriate earnings, must also be considered when determining an applicable discount rate.

Given that the economic benefit associated with a company's customer relationships is directly impacted by the company's overall operating structure (including its profitability), the risks associated with an investment in this type of an asset are typically tied to the overall risk, as measured by the company's WACC. The same could be said for trademarks. However, especially with regard to customer relationships, there are instances where the risk might be considered to be higher than that of the overall business and could, for example, be tied to the implied discount rate of the company's intangibles as determined in a weighted average return on assets (WARA) calculation.[6]

The discount rate applicable for many intangibles may be higher than the company's WACC while for others it may be lower. With order backlog, for example, the applicable discount rate may be materially lower than the WACC because the risk associated with collecting revenue from the portion of customers who have already been contracted and secured is lower than that of the overall company. On the other end of the spectrum, with existing technology or, even more, with in-process research and development (IPR&D), the applicable discount rate may be materially higher than the WACC. The risks associated with an investment in a company's technology are greater than those with the company itself because of the unknown nature of the rapidly changing competitive forces. Proprietary technology is often considered the most valuable asset of a business. It is also often considered the most risky, after IPR&D, because the technology can be inadvertently divulged or independently developed by another and the exclusivity of the technology may be lost. The risk associated with the IPR&D is highest because there is a risk that a project will not be completed, or may not be accepted by the market, and that the corresponding projected revenues and profits will not be realized.

---

[6] WARA reflects the return on the asset (left-hand) side of the balance sheet, as compared to WACC, which reflects the return on the capital (right-hand) side.

> Assets within a business have different risk and return characteristics. The discount rate should reflect the risk associated with the income attributable to the intangible asset being valued. Although the discount rate applicable to a company's trademark or its customer relationship is often tied to its cost of capital (WACC), the discount rate associated with its in-process research and development is often considerably higher, while that associated with its order backlog is often lower.

Tax Amortization Benefit

In the United States, Internal Revenue Code (IRC) Section 197(a) provides for the tax amortization of certain intangible assets over a 15-year period.[7] Since intangible assets are often valued on an after-tax basis, this amortization benefit should be included in countries where it is applicable in the forecast of cash flows to reflect the incremental value provided by this tax deduction to any given intangible asset that is amortizable for tax purposes. As such, the amortization is added back to cash flow, given its tax shield benefit.

At first glance, one might assume that this is the case only in an asset purchase, as the intangible assets generally are not amortizable for tax purposes in a stock purchase. However, for financial reporting purposes, the tax amortization benefit is included in the valuation of the intangibles in a stock transaction under the assumption that each individual asset could be sold separately. Essentially, the value of the asset is the same regardless of deal structure. A stock purchase will result in a deferred tax liability to offset the missing tax benefit.

The formula for the tax amortization benefit is:

$$PV_{CF} * (n/(n - ((PV(k, n, -1) * (1 - k)\,{}^\wedge\,0.5) * t)) - 1)$$

where:

$$PV_{CF} = \text{Present value of cash flows from the asset}$$
$$n = \text{Amortization period}$$
$$k = \text{Discount rate}$$

$PV(k, n, -1) *$
$(1 - k)\,{}^\wedge\,0.5 = $ Present value of a \$1 annuity over the amortization period, at the given discount rate. This is raised to the 0.5 to reflect use of midyear convention, which is explained further in Chapter 8.

$$t = \text{tax rate}$$

---

[7] Although this is generally the rule for intangible assets, there are exceptions. For example, IRC Section 167 provides for the tax amortization of software of three years.

In calculating the tax amortization benefit in the next three exhibits, we assume a 15-year life, a 14% discount rate, and a 27% tax rate.

All six of these factors – remaining useful life, revenues, expenses, contributory asset charges, discount rate, and tax amortization benefit – play a key role in applying perhaps the most widely used method to value an intangible asset – the multiperiod excess earnings method.

Intangible Asset Valuation Methods

Within the three approaches to value intangible assets, there are several methods. In purchase price allocation studies following a business combination, the methods most commonly used are the multiperiod excess earnings method, the relief-from-royalty method, the differential value method, and the replacement cost method.

Multi period Excess Earnings Method

The multiperiod excess earnings method (MPEEM) is an income approach–based method in that it estimates the value of an intangible based on the expected future economic income attributable to that asset. It is very similar to the discounted cash flow analysis (or DCF) within business valuation. Like the DCF, the MPEEM is based on the premise that the value of an asset can be determined by forecasting the future financial performance of that asset and identifying the surplus cash that it generates. The assessment of such future cash flows requires that the risks associated with an asset be analyzed and that such risk be reflected in calculating the present value of those future cash flows. In essence, the MPEEM attempts to measure what a buyer would be willing to pay currently for the future cash-generating potential of the subject intangible asset. However, it differs in many ways in that it spans over a finite (versus indefinite) period, most often includes only a portion of the company's revenues and corresponding expenses, is adjusted for contributory asset charges, and, in certain instances, is subject to a tax amortization benefit. Essentially, the MPEEM isolates the cash flow attributable to a particular intangible asset by identifying, and deducting, portions of the total cash flow that are attributable to other assets. It is most commonly used to value the primary income-generating intangible asset of a business enterprise (e.g. customer relationships or existing technology).

The value of the intangible asset determined by the MPEEM is the sum of the present value of the projected debt-free net cash flow, in excess of returns on contributory assets over the life of that asset. As seen in the example presented in Exhibit 18.1, for customer relationships, fair value can be established in eight steps:

Step 1. Estimate the first forecast year of expected customer revenues (the base year times the growth [shrinkage] rate in revenues).

Step 2. Estimate the expected customer revenues over a finite forecast period (expected customer revenues in the finite forecast period times the survivor curve decay rate determined by an attrition analysis).

Step 3. Determine the forecasted after-tax profits over the finite forecast period (by estimating cost of goods sold and operating assets required to generate the revenue associated with the customer relationships [i.e. excluding any expenses involved in generating new customers]).

Step 4. Determine the net cash flow from the subject customer (step 3 minus the contributory asset charges due to a fair return on tangible and intangible assets).

Step 5. Estimate the company's risk-adjusted cost of capital.

Step 6. Estimate the discount rate applicable to the overall intangible assets and the specific intangible asset being valued, making sure the discount rate reconciles to the WARA and WACC.

Step 7. Discount the forecasted net cash flows by this applicable discount rate.

Step 8. Add an applicable tax amortization benefit.

The MPEEM can be displayed in this simplified version:

Projected Revenue
Less: Total Expenses (cost of goods sold and operating expenses)
Equals: Operating Income
Less: Return on Assets Subject to a Royalty Rate (e.g. trademarks)
Equals: Pretax Income
Less: Taxes
Equals: After-Tax Income
Less: Return on Contributory Assets
Times: Present Value Factor
Equals: Present Value of Cash Flows
Plus: Tax Amortization Benefit
Equals: Indicated Fair Value of Subject Intangible Asset

Relief-from-Royalty Method

The relief-from-royalty method (RFRM) is an income approach–based method that assumes that an intangible asset is valuable because the owner of the asset avoids the cost of licensing that asset. Under the RFRM, an estimate is made as to the appropriate royalty income that would be negotiated in an arm's-length transaction if the subject intangible asset were licensed from an independent third party. The royalty savings are then calculated by multiplying a royalty rate, expressed as a percentage of revenues (or net operating income), times a determined royalty base (i.e. the applicable level of future revenues or net operating income). This method represents an appropriate and generally accepted methodology for determining the value of an intangible asset and is often applicable in valuing trademarks, patents, existing technology, and software, among others. It assumes that a company would be willing to pay for the right to use an established asset in the sale of similar products that it would not otherwise enjoy were it not the owner of the assets.

In determining an appropriate royalty rate, a sample of guideline, arm's-length royalty, or license agreements are analyzed. The license agreements selected should represent transactions that reflect similar risk and return investment characteristics that make them comparable to the subject intangible. The risk-and-return investment characteristics may include industry conditions, barriers to entry, the ability to generate an expected level of economic earnings for the owner or licensee, the age of the intangible, potential for expansion and exploitation, the degree of consumer recognition, timeliness, technological risk, use specificity, geographic coverage of the intangible, and so on. Based on an assessment of the risk-and-return investment factors of the subject trademark as compared to the guideline transactions, a fair royalty rate is estimated for that trademark. This royalty base is then multiplied by the royalty rate to determine the company's royalty savings and then adjusted for any ongoing legal or administrative maintenance expenses.

Royalty savings are determined on an after-tax basis, because, if the owner of the intangible asset did not own the asset and had to pay royalties for its use, these royalty payments would be deductible for income tax purposes.

The RFRM can be applied for both finite and indefinite-lived assets. When applied for an indefinite-lived asset, such as some trademarks, a growth-in-perpetuity method is used (similar to a typical DCF model in valuing a business enterprise) to estimate the residual value of the royalty savings beyond the forecast period. In applying the growth-in-perpetuity method, the value of the perpetuity at the end of the forecast is equal to the royalty savings in the final year of the forecast period adjusted for growth and then divided by the capitalization rate. Finally, an applicable tax amortization benefit is added to determine fair value of the asset.

As with any intangible asset, the discount factor, which is used to determine the present value of the future income streams attributable to the subject intangible, should reflect both the business and the financial risks of an investment in that intangible. The determination of the required rate of return is thus predicated on risk assessment. For a trademark, the discount rate may be in line with the company's overall discount rate. For existing technology, a premium over the company's overall discount rate may be warranted. An example applying the RFRM in valuing a trademark assuming a five-year finite life is presented in Exhibit 18.2.

Differential Value Method

The differential value method (DVM) is an income approach–based method that values an asset by comparing the present value of cash flows over a defined period of time with the asset to the present value of cash flows over the same period without the asset. The DVM is often used to value assets for which it is difficult to assign a direct revenue/income stream but that contribute to the generation of revenue and income. The DVM is performed in one of two ways:

1. A with-or-without analysis, also known as an income increment/cost decrement analysis, where the value of the subject intangible (often a covenant not to compete or a franchise agreement) is the probability-weighted difference between the present value of the cash flows over a defined period when estimated assuming all assets are in place, as compared to all assets except the subject intangible are in place.
2. A Greenfield analysis, where the value of the subject intangible (typically a Federal Communications Commission [FCC] broadcast license or cable franchise rights) is valued using cash flow projections that assume the only asset of the business that is owned is the subject intangible, and all other assets are acquired, internally developed, or leased.

The most common intangible asset seen in purchase price allocations that is valued using the DVM is the covenant not to compete. In applying the DVM to value noncompete agreements, differing assumptions are used to determine two sets of projected cash flows of the business, one with the noncompete in place and the other without the noncompete in place. Estimates of value are determined based on the two varying cash flow models to determine the impact on the cash flows of the business on a comparative basis. The cash flows are forecasted out over the useful life of the noncompete, which can either be its term or some period beyond its term if warranted by the expected economic impact on the business. The difference between the two values represents the fair value of the noncompete. An example of this is reflected in Exhibit 18.3.

For purposes of this description, the company's current business operations (i.e. base case, with the noncompete agreement in place)

EXHIBIT 18.2 Relief-from-Royalty Method – Valuation of a Trademark

	20x1	20x2	20x3	20x4	20x5
Calculation of Royalty Savings:					
Revenues Covered by Trademark	$50,000,000	$55,000,000	$59,400,000	$63,600,000	$68,000,000
Times: Royalty Rate	1.5%	1.5%	1.5%	1.5%	1.5%
Royalty Savings	$750,000	$825,000	$891,000	$954,000	$1,020,000
Less: Maintenance Charge	$50,000	$50,000	$50,000	$50,000	$50,000
Pre-Tax Royalties after Maintenance Charge	$700,000	$775,000	$841,000	$904,000	$970,000
Provision for Income Taxes at 35%	$189,000	$209,250	$227,070	$244,080	$261,900
Net Royalty Savings	$511,000	$565,750	$613,930	$659,920	$708,100
Present Value of Net Royalty Savings at 14%	$478,595	$464,801	$442,442	$417,181	$392,666
Present Value of Net Royalty Savings	$2,195,685				
Tax Amortization Benefit	$293,880				
Indicated Fair Value of Trademark	$2,500,000				

EXHIBIT 18.3 Differential Value Method – Valuation of a Noncompete Agreement

Multiple-Scenario DVM	Scenario 1: Present Value of Cash Flows WITH Agreement	Scenario 2: Present Value of Cash Flows WITHOUT Agreement	Present Value of Lost Cash Flow	Probability of Competition	Weighted Value
Competition Begins in Year 1	$15,322,536	$3,781,503	$11,541,033	10%	$1,154,103
Competition Begins in Year 2	$15,322,536	$5,156,105	$10,166,431	10%	$1,016,643
Competition Begins in Year 3	$15,322,536	$8,009,981	$7,312,554	10%	$731,255
Competition Begins in Year 4	$15,322,536	$11,194,072	$4,128,464	20%	$825,693
Competition Begins in Year 5	$16,799,349	$14,055,674	$2,743,676	20%	$548,735
Competition Begins in Year 6	$19,559,732	$17,064,191	$2,495,540	20%	$499,108
No Competition			$0	10%	$0
Present Value of Cash Flow Protected					$4,775,538
Tax Amortization Benefit					$639,179
Indicated Fair Value of Non compete Agreement					**$5,400,000**

348

will be referred to as Scenario 1 and the company's operations without the noncompete in place will be referred to as Scenario 2 (i.e. with competition). Further assume that the term of the noncompete is five years, but the economic impact is expected to continue an additional year. In Scenario 1, the cash flows used are typically the same as those forecasted to be realized by the company as a whole. Therefore, typically the only difference between application of the DCF analysis for the entire business as compared to Scenario 1 is that Scenario 1 reflects the company's cash flows over, in this example, a finite six-year period.

Scenario 2 estimates the impact that competition from key employees (or the nonexistence of the noncompete) would have on the company's revenues, expenses, resulting cash flows, and, ultimately, the value of the company. The two most material factors to consider are: (1) the expected revenues to be lost in each year over the forecast period (four years in our example), and (2) the probability of competition in each of the six years. Other factors to consider include the mix of fixed versus variable expenses, the potential in salary savings if the key person were not on the payroll, changes in capital expenditure needs with lower revenues, and an overall assessment of the risk differential. In determining the probability of competition, one must consider the existence of factors such as proprietary know-how, trade secrets, and entrepreneurial tendencies within the company, as well as the presence of an earn-out payment due to the key employees.

Replacement Cost Method

The replacement cost method (RCM) is an asset approach–based method that values an asset by estimating the current costs necessary to create a similar asset. It is the method most frequently used to implement the asset approach for the assembled workforce intangible asset. The costs to replace an assembled workforce include the costs to recruit, hire, and train a replacement workforce.

The underlying theory of the RCM is that by purchasing an operating business, the company avoids the expense and time necessary to recruit and train personnel if it had been acquired without the existing staff. The value of the assembled staff includes management experience and technical know-how of certain employees. Factors to consider include the availability of replacement personnel, degree of specialization of people in the organization, salary and fringe benefits, other compensation, search fees and expenses, and nonproductive time during a training period. The training expenses per employee vary depending on the complexity or sophistication of the employee's duties. These expenses include payment of wages, salaries, and fringe benefits for the time an employee is unproductive. An example applying the RCM in valuing an assembled workforce is presented in Exhibit 18.4.

Training costs are based on the productivity of a typical new hire and the estimated time that will elapse before the employee reaches full productivity. For all employees, some level of productivity is expected on the date of hire, as the assumption is made that all personnel have the initial basic skills and experience; otherwise they would not have assumed the position. Any initial and temporary shortfall in productivity is attributable to the employee's need to adapt to the procedures and circumstances of the position. Generally speaking, unproductive time is greatest when the person is first hired and normally diminishes to near zero within six months. Since it is assumed that any unproductive time initially present will diminish to zero on a straight-line (linear) basis, over the above time period, it is also implied that the productive time will increase on a straight-line basis, correspondingly over the above period, and will ultimately reach 100% by the end of the training (unproductive or not 100% productive) period. Consistent with the previous discussion, to account for the unproductive time, the employee group is then assigned an initial block of unproductive time that encompasses all the unproductive time over a determined number of months. For example, it can be assumed that, on average, the company's employees are 50% productive during this training period.

> The four most widely used methods to value intangible assets are the multiperiod excess earnings method, the relief-from-royalty method, the differential value method, and the replacement cost method.

Applying these training-period factors to the average annual salaries, which include fringe benefits, for the entire workforce yields the average training cost associated with each employee. Again, multiplying this cost by the number of personnel in the employee group provides the total cost of training. Adding the total cost of recruitment to this amount yields the total cost of replacement per employee. By multiplying the number of employees by the average total cost of replacement per employee, the total replacement cost of the company's assembled workforce is estimated.

Nuances within this method must be considered. For example, replacement cost may assume a workforce that has different characteristics from the one currently in place. If applicable, the RCM must reflect a scenario where the current workforce in place that consists of older, highly compensated employees may be replaced with younger, equally skilled, lower-paid employees. In addition, an opportunity cost may be considered to reflect any forgone cash flows during the time it takes to create the asset as compared to the cash flows that would be realized if that asset was held by the company.

EXHIBIT 18.4 Replacement Cost Method – Valuation of an Assembled Workforce

EMPLOYEE CATEGORIES	Recruiting Expenses			Training Expenses		
	Quantity	Estimated Recruiting	TOTAL	Average Annual Employee Costs	# of Months Until Fully Productive	TOTAL
CEO/Founder	1	$210,000	$210,000	$700,000	18	$525,000
Upper Management	18	$90,000	$1,620,000	$360,000	6	$1,620,000
Middle Management	78	$22,500	$1,755,000	$150,000	3	$1,462,500
Staff/Support	205	$4,500	$922,500	$50,000	1	$427,083
	302		$4,507,500			$4,034,583

Indicated Fair Value of Assembled Workforce   **$8,540,000**

Conclusion

Intangible assets comprise the bulk of a company's value, yet that value is not reflected in its financial statements. In fact, that value is not readily seen or measured. Yet shareholders and managers must gain an understanding of that value in their strategic planning. An integral part of value creation, which drives strategic planning and thus creates focus and direction, is to understand and build value of a company's intangible assets. This chapter introduced four of the most commonly used methods to value intangibles, but there are several others. The reader is encouraged to check the References section at the end of Chapter 17 to gain a better understanding of these methods. Shareholders, managers, and advisors only partially comprehend and build company value if they are not giving adequate focus to the value of their company's intangible assets.

CHAPTER 19

Measuring and Managing Value in High-Tech Start-Ups

Few investors emerge unshaken from the market rollercoaster of bear markets, especially the one we experienced back in 2008–2009. Yet the ride can be even more unsettling for shareholders and managers in nonpublic, high-tech start-ups, where the stock price is unknown and the assets owned are almost entirely intangible. This is why the forward-looking entrepreneur makes business valuation the centerpiece of rigorous annual strategic planning.

This chapter explains the unique challenges of measuring and managing value in high-tech start-ups to maximize shareholder value. In valuing a high-tech start-up company, one must first understand the differences as compared to established businesses, assess the company's strategic position, identify its stage of development as defined in terms of operational development, ascertain its stage of development as defined in terms of financing and required rates of return, and consider its path toward either a sale or an initial public offering (IPO).

Why Appraisals of High-Tech Start-Ups Are Essential

Appraisals are valuable, and necessary, in a number of areas and situations involving high-tech start-ups. Granting employee stock options as a form of incentive compensation is a common trigger for a valuation. When a start-up company lacks adequate capital to pay competitive wages, stock options are often the lure used to attract qualified personnel; the effectiveness of the options is dependent on the state of the economy and the markets. A valuation is fundamental to properly estimating the fair market value of the options as of the date of issue and to preparing for possible future review by the U.S. Securities and Exchange Commission or similar agency in other countries.

In the United States, start-up companies with complex capital structures (i.e. companies that are typically venture backed and have gone through one or more rounds of financing, resulting in the issuance of preferred stock) typically obtain independent valuations to be in compliance with certain tax and financial reporting requirements. When employee stock options are issued, the grant price is set to equal the underlying common stock's fair market value at the time of issuance to avoid excess compensation expense. For tax purposes, Internal Revenue Code section 409A states that deferrals of compensation under a nonqualified deferred compensation plan for all taxable years are includable in gross income to the extent not subject to a substantial risk of forfeiture and not previously included in gross income. Compensation is deferrable on stock options that are issued at an exercise price greater than or equal to the fair market value of the stock on the grant date. For financial reporting purposes, Accounting Standards Codification Topic 718 (ASC 718) relates to the treatment of accounting transactions in which an entity exchanges equity instruments for goods or services. For purposes of determining the cost of equity-based compensation, ASC 718 requires the use of fair value for most transactions. After the fair value as of the grant date of the equity compensation is determined, the cost is recognized over the period during which an employee is required to provide services in exchange for the award.

A start-up's early stage, when it often requires capital, may also be the best time for estate planning. The confident entrepreneur will gift shares in the start-up phase in anticipation that value will increase in later years. A valuation in connection with the gifting of shares is required by the Internal Revenue Service, and the gifting of shares in a start-up phase is likely to have the most advantageous tax treatment.

Like any company, a start-up may become involved in litigation issues, such as shareholder disputes, marital dissolution of one of its shareholders, infringements of intellectual property, and contract disputes. The start-up may also consider hiring an appraiser in connection with the formation of a buy–sell agreement or the purchase of key-person life insurance.

Perhaps the most compelling situation is the key role the valuation process can play in achieving the company's primary financial goal: maximizing shareholder value. For many high-tech start-ups, maximizing shareholder value often means building a project (e.g. a technology, a drug, etc.) and convincing a buyer or the markets that the project has unique potential and substantial value. Annual strategic planning with a focus on value and value propositions can enable shareholders and management to chart the optimum direction for the company. With valuation at the center of the planning process, management can continually assess the company's strategic position and value as a stand-alone business versus its increased value through a sale or IPO.

Key Differences in High-Tech Start-Ups

Development-stage companies typically have a limited track record, little or no revenues, and no operating profits. High-tech start-ups share these characteristics but often with a higher level of uncertainty because they are operating in new or emerging markets or in industries lacking traditional business models and performance benchmarks. Further heightening the uncertainty is the fact that a company may be developing new products that are experimental or completely unknown to their potential customer base or the market at large.

Because a start-up's success is so closely tied to the time and cost involved in product development, production, and marketing, forecasts must be accurate and detailed. Reluctance to set and address key forecast parameters rigorously, including prices, volume, costs, and capital investments at each development stage, is frequently the first step toward miscalculating the company's true performance and ultimately its value.

Continual technological changes and short product life cycles challenge accurate forecasting and contribute to the volatility of value. As will be discussed, these issues necessitate careful attention to competitive factors to identify the company's strategic advantages and disadvantages, which ultimately determine the rates of return or multiples that are chosen to compute value.

Tangible asset holdings and the size of the company's asset base are less important in a technology company. When technology is the primary asset, most or all of the value in the company comes from intangibles, including intellectual property and human capital. Such fragile and dynamic assets can quickly diminish in value, more so than property, plant, and equipment. Thus it is important to identify newly formed intellectual property and obtain adequate patents and legal protection.

Lack of adequate capital is a common constraint because initial funding, whether from entrepreneurs, angel investors, or venture capitalists, is generally made to move the company to the next development stage within a set time and cost. This critical cash burn rate imposes a discipline on the start-up to stay within forecasted cost and time deadlines, because high-tech companies generally have little or no borrowing capacity. Lack of a proven product, service, or customer base and few tangible assets mean that the start-up can at best leverage only limited debt funding, which usually carries high rates and imposes tight constraints on management. The markets have shown that investors question the business models of many high-tech companies, in particular those that continue to reflect losses, especially when they lack a clear plan to develop and commercialize the underlying technology or product.

Value Management Begins with Competitive Analysis

Traditionally, investors look at significant financial measures – including sales and sales growth, operating margins, asset efficiency, and cash flow – as a basis for their decision making. These measures, however, reflect results rather than causes. For a more robust valuation, the focus must identify what creates the cash flow and therein the value. This is done through external and internal assessment of the company's strategic position – the competitive analysis.

These same principles apply to high-tech companies. Although managers may focus on industry-specific metrics, such as sales dollars per customer or website hits per advertising dollar, the emphasis in a fast-paced market must tilt toward the company's ability to create new or improved products or services and to build its competitive position and cash flow.

External Analysis

For start-ups, this analysis begins with the external or industry analysis, which is often difficult because competitors are frequently small divisions of large corporations or are relatively unknown. As a new technology emerges, there is often substantial uncertainty about its application – in what markets, for what products, and when. For example, numerous software companies lurch from one application of their technology to another as competing or collateral applications emerge and their target market changes in the process. Customers emerge and disappear rapidly as distribution channels redefine the end user of the technology.

Sales growth prospects can change rapidly as the technology develops and its resulting products and customers are identified. Value fluctuates accordingly. This uncertainty spurs the high-return demands of venture capitalists during the early funding rounds of a new technology. Without more reliable information about a company's potential products, customers, and competitors, the resulting higher risk requires higher rates of return.

Customer concentrations frequently occur in emerging markets, where lack of information or inadequate marketing or distribution capabilities preclude start-ups from full access to all potential customers in the marketplace. The typical start-up, particularly in the early stages, lacks one or more core competencies in production, marketing, sales and distribution, or finance that prevent it from capitalizing on the value of its technology. Companies that recognize these limitations and acquire the needed competencies can change their value dramatically as they move their technology from concept, to products, to customers, to cash flow.

This progression also emphasizes the potential distinction between a start-up's stand-alone fair market value, which could be low, and its potentially much higher value to strategic buyers. Such buyers often have means to move a technology to the cash flow stage much more quickly, efficiently, and successfully than a start-up. Thus management must continually identify the missing capabilities that stand as barriers to success. Doing this includes ongoing revisions in the time and cost to bring a product to market, which can precipitate major swings in value as the company's technology develops or fails to develop. Setbacks or delays may leave a company particularly vulnerable on a stand-alone basis when its burn rate and borrowing limitations threaten its viability. Therefore, exit strategies, including positioning the company for merger partners or strategic buyers, must also be part of the start-up's ongoing strategic planning.

Internal Analysis

Most important in the internal analysis is continual examination of how the technology will lead and lend itself to products or services and ultimately to cash flows. This analysis begins with a review of the business plan and forecast, particularly an assessment of the financial investment required to complete and perfect the product. The competitive advantages that support the forecasted volume, pricing, and margins must be carefully scrutinized. Uncertainties may require adjustments to the forecast – either in dollars or timing delays – or thorough application of probability analysis to quantify possible outcomes.

Because key people are usually essential in a development-stage business, particular attention must be paid to both management and technical personnel. Executives are often scientists with little management expertise or experience, and gaps may exist in sales and marketing, production, or finance. While competence in these functional areas may be less critical in earlier stages, the management team in place must have or develop the required professional background and experience to advance the company to growth and, typically, a liquidity event. Gaps in capabilities do not doom a company. They do, however, create limits and frequently signal the need for an exit strategy that positions the business for its next growth stage.

Most start-ups offer stock options to attract and keep key people, and these options can have a significant effect on value per share. Management should also recognize how stock option value is computed for nonpublic shares of stock. The well-known Black–Scholes Option Pricing Model (BSOPM) generally overstates the value of private company stock options due to their lack of liquidity, so consideration should be given to applying a discount for lack of marketability, as discussed in Chapter 12.

> Maximizing shareholder value in a high-tech start-up company often means building a project (e.g. a technology, a drug, etc.) and convincing a buyer or the markets that the project has unique potential and substantial value

Emphasis on Planning

While many established businesses survive and even thrive with little formal strategic planning, the start-up has a much greater need for this discipline. A comprehensive plan focuses management attention on markets and customers and the products needed to serve them. It can also result in a more efficient use of cash, which will decrease the amount of funding required, ultimately resulting in an increase in investor returns.

Lack of a cohesive plan, or a plan with major gaps, usually suggests weaknesses or lack of expertise in key functional areas. Consequently, it is difficult, if not impossible, to develop realistic forecasts of the capabilities, costs, and time needed to move the company out of the development stage and to maturity. The result – uncertain goals, lack of clear direction, and little or no focus on future cash flows – means increased risk and decreased value. Where strategic disadvantages exist or essential capabilities cannot be acquired, the plan logically should move the company toward alternative strategies, including sale to a strategic buyer, sale to a private equity group, merger, or even liquidation to minimize losses.

Stages of Development

Once the key differences in high-tech companies are understood and the company's competitive position is analyzed, its relevant stage of operational development must be established. This is an essential part of valuing a start-up company. Determination of a company's stage of development will aid in settling on which method or combination of methods is most appropriate to value that company and helps in assessing the underlying risk in achieving its growth plans and eventual sale or public offering.

In 2013, the American Institute of Certified Public Accountants (AICPA) published the second edition of a Practice Aid titled *Valuation of Privately-Held-Company Equity Securities Issued as Compensation,* to provide valuation and disclosure guidance and best practices pertaining to the issuance of privately held equity securities issued as compensation. The practice aid lays out six stages of development,[1] defined in terms of operational development rather than financing:

---

[1] AICPA Task Force, *Valuation of Privately-Held-Company Equity Securities Issued as Compensation* (2013), pp. 15–16.

A *Stage 1* company has no product revenue to date and limited expense history and, typically, an incomplete management team with an idea, plan, and possibly some initial product development. Typically, seed capital, or first-round financing, is provided during this stage by friends and family, angels, or venture capital firms focusing on early-stage enterprises, and the securities issued to those investors are occasionally in the form of common stock but are more commonly in the form of preferred stock.

A *Stage 2* company has no product revenue but substantive expense history, as product development is under way and business challenges are thought to be understood. Usually a second or third round of financing occurs during this stage. Typical investors are venture capital firms, which may provide additional management or board of directors' expertise. The typical securities issued to those investors are usually in the form of preferred stock.

A *Stage 3* company has made significant progress in product development; key development milestones have been met (e.g. hiring of a management team); and development is near completion (e.g. alpha and beta testing), but often there is no product revenue. Generally, later rounds of financing occur during this stage. Typical investors are venture capital firms and strategic business partners. The securities usually issued to those investors are in the form of preferred stock.

A *Stage 4* company has met additional key development milestones (e.g. first customer orders or first revenue shipments) and has some product revenue, but is often still operating at a loss. Typically, mezzanine rounds of financing occur during this stage. Also, it is frequently in this stage that discussions would start with investment banks for an IPO.

A *Stage 5* company has product revenue and has recently achieved breakthrough measures of financial success such as operating profitability or break-even or positive cash flows. A liquidity event of some sort, such as an IPO or a sale of the enterprise, could occur in this stage. The form of securities issued is typically all common stock, with any outstanding preferred converting to common upon an IPO (and perhaps also upon other liquidity events).[2]

A *Stage 6* company has an established financial history of profitable operations or generation of positive cash flows. Some companies may remain private for a substantial period in this stage. An IPO could also occur during this stage.

---

[2] The actual stages during which liquidity events occur or discussions with investment bankers for an IPO take place depend on several factors. Those factors include, for example, the state of the economy, investor sentiment, and the state of the IPO market.

Once the company's stage of development is defined in terms of its operations, it can then be determined in terms of financing.

Risk and Discount Rates

The Practice Aid also provides guidance related to rates of return required by investors in companies of various stages of development.[3] That guidance classifies four stages of development,[4] outlined next, as they relate to required rates of return rather than in terms of operational development. This aids in determining an appropriate discount rate for the company being valued.

1. Start-up stage investments typically are made in enterprises that are less than a year old. The venture funding at this stage (i.e. seed capital) is typically provided by individual venture capitalists (e.g. angel investors). This funding is to be used substantially for product development, prototype testing, and test marketing. The rates of return for investments at this stage are in the range of 50% to 70%.[5]

2. First-stage or early-development investments are made in enterprises that have developed prototypes that appear viable and for which further technical risk is deemed minimal, although commercial risk may be significant. Smaller venture capitalists often provide funding at this stage for basic product development. The rates of return for investments at this stage are in the range of 40% to 60%.

3. Enterprises in the second, or expansion, stage usually have shipped some product to consumers (including beta versions). Larger venture capitalists often provide funding at this stage for revenue growth, product or service marketing, and distribution. The rates of return for investments at this stage are in the range of 35% to 50%.

4. Bridge/IPO-stage financing covers such activities as pilot plant construction, production design, and production testing, as well as bridge financing in anticipation of a later IPO. The rates of return for investments at this stage are in the range of 25% to 35%.

---

[3] AICPA Task Force, *Valuation of Privately-Held Company Equity Securities Issued as Compensation (2013)*, 148.

[4] The stages of development are described in two publications: James L. Plummer, *QED Report on Venture Capital Financial Analysis* (Palo Alto, CA: QED Research, 1987), pp. 1-11–1-14, and William A. Sahlman and Daniel R. Scherlis, "A Method for Valuing High-Risk, Long-Term, Investments: The Venture Capital Method," *Harvard Business Review* (August 12, 2003), pp. 6–7.

[5] Rates of return determined in ibid.

Due to the fact that for every success there are several failures, these rates of return are ultimately not achieved on every investment by venture capitalists but are applied to compensate for the company's expected performance shortfall relative to the forecast. In addition, discount rates are higher for start-ups because of a higher degree of uncertainty in receiving any future cash flows and a longer time frame in receiving them if they are generated. With an understanding of the company background – including an analysis of its external and internal environments, its stage of development, and consequently its risk characteristics – one can move into the actual valuation of the company.

Start-Ups and Traditional Valuation Methods

As emphasized in Chapter 2, to focus on value, investors must be able to measure it; so valuation should be an integral part of strategic planning. A valuation analysis quantifies the risk and return consequences – the change in value – of each external and internal competitive factor. This process creates the roadmap for management to increase cash flows while minimizing risk to maximize shareholder value. The traditional income, market, and asset approaches, discussed in Chapters 6 through 11, apply in valuing start-ups. However, there are different considerations when applying these approaches to start-ups.

Income Approach

As discussed in Chapter 7, the income approach measures the value of a business based on the expected stream of monetary benefits attributable to the subject company. There are two methods within the income approach – the single-period capitalization method and the discounted cash flow method – the difference being a forecast of one year versus several years.

The single-period capitalization method (SPCM) is almost never appropriate in the appraisal of start-up companies, particularly high-tech businesses. The start-up company's income or cash flow, if any, is hardly ever representative of long-term potential, and successful start-ups experience very rapid growth, after which increased competition or new technology slows growth to a more normal rate. The capitalization process cannot accurately capture these changes.

The discounted cash flow (DCF) method is far more effective because it reflects the expected future growth in terms of revenues, earnings, and ultimately cash flows. The main benefit of a DCF – carefully thought out projections of future expected returns – is also its biggest detriment. This disadvantage, the reliability of those projections, is exacerbated with start-up companies. Start-ups are often characterized as having never generated positive cash flow, having limited or no financial history, and/or being in such a unique space that there are no guideline companies from which to draw reasonable comparisons. As such, some practitioners argue that, because the forecasted cash flows are highly speculative since the underlying technologies are unproven or the products are undeveloped, this method is marginalized in valuing start-ups. The reality is that all valuation methods are more speculative for start-ups than for established companies, but the fundamentals of valuation remain the same. Specifically, revenue growth must be estimated, initial losses must be understood, a sustainable operating margin once the company reaches relative stability must be projected, reinvestment to generate growth must be assessed, the relevant number of years to forecast until the company reaches stability must be established, a terminal value typically based on a sale or IPO must be estimated, and an expected rate of return must be determined. As Aswath Damodaran notes:

> The valuation of a firm with negative earnings, high growth, and limited information will always have estimation error.... The error in the valuation is not always a reflection of the quality of the valuation model, or the analyst using it, but of the underlying real uncertainty about the future prospects of the firm. This uncertainty is a fact of life when it comes to investing in these [start-up] firms. In a valuation, we attempt to grapple with this uncertainty and make our best estimates about the future. Note that those who disdain valuation models for their potential errors end up using far cruder approaches, such as comparing price-sales ratios across firms. The difference, as we see it, is that they choose to sweep the uncertainties under the rug and act as if they do not exist.... Even if a valuation is imprecise, it provides a powerful tool to answer the question of what has to occur for the current market price of a firm to be justified. Investors can then decide whether they are comfortable with these assumptions, and make their decisions on buying and selling stock.[6]

The source of value for a start-up company comes entirely from expected future growth. Since there is little to no history with which to work, the forecasts are subject to considerable uncertainty. Just as in any valuation, the appraiser needs to work closely with management in

---

[6] Aswath Damodaran, *Investment Valuation: Tools and Techniques for Determining the Value of Any Asset,* 3rd ed. (Hoboken, NJ: Wiley, 2012), 661–662.

developing forecasts. If a business plan is in place, the appraiser must review it and discuss any changes to the assumptions since it was written. By the very nature of a start-up company, projections can become outdated very quickly due to rapid changes and developments. Also keep in mind that forecasts can be overly optimistic because they are often used to secure financing. This must be dealt with through the discount rate, as discussed in the preceding section of this chapter, and/or probability-weighting forecasted cash flows.

The application of a DCF can be done using the traditional two-stage model or a three-stage model, as described in Chapter 7. In a two-stage model, value is calculated based on the sum of the present value of forecasted earnings over several (typically five) years and the present value of the terminal value. The terminal value is often determined based on either a multiple of some level of earnings or cash flows[7] and typically reflects the majority of a start-up's value. In a three-stage model, an interim level of growth is estimated over an additional period (possibly the next five years), after which the terminal value is computed. Either way, reasonable financial projections are essential to the process in light of management's capabilities, market potential, the technology, and the industry.

In the end, the income approach, using a DCF analysis, is an effective way to value a start-up company. In its application of a forecast of expected future cash flows, the DCF can reflect variations in the company's return as it moves through development stages. It also conveniently accommodates sensitivity and probability analysis.[8]

Market Approach – Guideline Companies

The market approach arrives at an indication of value by comparing the company being appraised to guideline publicly traded companies or to guideline businesses which have been recently acquired in arm's-length transactions.

Market multiples are often used in valuing start-up companies because they are relatively simple to understand, market based, and easy to apply. The fundamental problem with using multiples for start-ups is that they impose a static application to a very volatile situation. As explained in Chapter 10, market multiples can be obtained either from public companies (i.e. a guideline public company method) or from acquired companies

---

[7] When done in this manner, many practitioners feel that the income approach becomes more of a hybrid of the income and market approaches.

[8] However, it is important to note that this applies to valuing the company as a whole. If just the common stock of a company with a complex capital structure (i.e. one with preferred stock) is being valued, one or more of the equity allocation methods discussed toward the latter part of this chapter must be applied.

(i.e. a transaction multiple method). Generally speaking, the results from the former are marketable, minority indications of value, since the source is multiples of liquid, noncontrolling interests in public companies. The results from the latter are typically either marketable or nonmarketable controlling indications of value, since the source generally reflects multiples of entire companies that were acquired.

> An essential part of valuing a high-tech start-up is to determine its relevant stage of development in terms of its operations along the six stages, from having no product revenue to having an established financial history, and its financing and resulting required rates of return along the four stages from seed capital to IPO.

The traditional price-to-earnings (P/E) multiple is rarely applicable in valuing start-ups, and even earnings before interest and taxes (EBIT) and earnings before interest, taxes, depreciation, and amortization (EBITDA) multiples are seldom applicable. Instead, multiples of revenue are commonly seen, largely because start-ups often have no earnings to which a multiple can be applied. To be effective, there must be relative homogeneity in the operations of the market sample to the company being valued. In certain industries, for example, the mix of service versus product revenues is an important consideration in determining the comparability of revenue multiples.

Given the basic fact that so much can happen in a company below the revenue line, a multiple of some level of earnings is preferable as a supplement to a revenue multiple. One such multiple is earnings before interest, taxes, research and development, because certain start-ups incur high levels of research and development (R&D) expenses. There also may be some very industry-specific multiples. For example, a multiple of the number of subscribers enrolled by an Internet company may be a good indicator of value.

As emphasized in Chapter 10, when analyzing public company multiples in general, it is important to note that there can be a significant disparity between public companies and closely held businesses. Those companies that attract public investment typically enjoy above-average revenue growth, both current and projected, and far greater access to capital. Start-ups are unlikely to be as advanced in the development of their particular product or service compared to a company that has been able to go public.

The challenges in applying the SPCM are the same when applying earnings multiples to valuing start-ups. The earnings multiple also cannot accurately capture anticipated changes in growth from initial very rapid growth to a slowdown in growth rates with the onset of increased competition. Thus a multiple of 100 times earnings for a high-tech start-up is probably based on unrealistically low earnings in comparison with the company's future earnings potential, and short-term versus long-term growth expectations are very different. The resulting value seldom makes sense.

Multiples that have been derived from strategic transactions may suffer from the two factors just described. Furthermore, strategic transactions often reflect synergies that only a specific buyer could achieve. Similar distortions occur when multiples are derived from industry leaders. For a start-up business to derive multiples based on the performance of Amazon or Google is to attribute to that start-up the size, growth, customer base, and brand recognition of these highly successful businesses when the start-up possesses few, if any, of these strengths.

When market multiples are used to value start-ups, one must remember to factor in any equity infusion that would be necessary to generate the future revenues and earnings. It may also be necessary to discount the indication of value resulting from those future multiples back to present value, since the analysis is using a future indication of value to determine value today.

In summary, because market multiples, such as multiples of revenues or various levels of earnings, are so widely quoted in valuing start-ups, they can be employed, but with appropriate precautions.

Market Approach – Prior Transactions

Consideration of prior transactions involving company stock is another method within the market approach. For start-up companies, this typically encompasses an analysis of recent arm's-length rounds of financing using an option pricing method to infer the total equity value of the company at the issuance of the preferred shares. This is often referred to as the backsolve method, in which the equity value is solved for in an iterative manner such that the implied value of the preferred shares is equal to the per-share issuance price. The value of the preferred shares in the option pricing method consists of the combined value of their liquidation preference and common share value above the liquidation preference. Since the option pricing method appreciates the rights and preferences of each equity class, the implied value of the common shares is less than the preferred shares.

Asset Approach

As described in Chapter 11, the asset approach is a general way of determining a value indication of a business's assets and/or equity interest using one or more methods based directly on the value of the assets of the business, less liabilities. It is the least relevant approach to value a start-up company due largely to the fact that virtually all of a start-up's assets are intangible, which are hard to identify and value and are not recorded on the balance sheet.

If applicable to a start-up, the asset approach might be used when a company has significant cash balances and/or marketable intellectual property (e.g. patents) but has not achieved any meaningful milestones, or in liquidation scenarios.

Alternative Valuation Techniques

Although the traditional valuation approaches apply in valuing start-ups, alternative techniques are often appropriate. These techniques include Monte Carlo simulation (MCS) and real options analysis (ROA).

MCS, discussed in Chapter 6, is a probabilistic technique that can be used in conjunction with a DCF analysis.[9] It is useful in determining the probability of different DCF value outcomes and can illustrate how different combinations of values impact various DCF value outcomes. This technique allows one to identify key assumptions and a range of likely values for those key assumptions with a known distribution (e.g. standard normal), and to develop confidence intervals for the resulting value.

As an illustration, while one might assume that increased competitive threats heighten risk and may therefore reduce value, the increased probability that a given technology is successfully developed by a start-up after one year, which is picked up in MCS, results in a higher value that more than offsets any potential decrease in value attributable to increased competitive threats. A DCF results in one value from a range of best guesses within a given scenario. MCS considers all possible combinations of input variables and generates a probability distribution describing the possible outcomes for each input variable. The result is a calculation of value that includes both a most likely outcome and a series of reasonably probable but less likely outcomes. In summary, MCS provides a more thorough analysis of the possible outcomes than does a standard DCF or sensitivity analysis.

Investors can employ another tool to manage risk in a highly speculative environment. A traditional DCF cannot accurately reflect the ability of investors or venture capitalists to make follow-on investments (e.g. a right of first refusal to invest in a later stage of financing assumes certain characteristics similar to a call option on a company's stock). ROA, also described in Chapter 6, uses option pricing methodologies to account for the buyer's ability to wait, compile, and analyze newly available competitive data and

---

[9] As well as forecasting liquidity events and other purposes.

then decide to buy equity at a later date. The merit of using ROA lies in the right (option) to proceed or abandon a given investment. At expiration, a call option is worth the stock price less the exercise price. Prior to expiration, a call option is worth the stock price less the present value of the strike price after both prices are adjusted for the riskiness of the option. Each of the option pricing models is based on the volatility of the underlying stock price, the difference between the current stock price and the strike price, and the length of time until expiration. Therefore, as uncertainty increases, real options actually increase in value as they help investors manage risk.

QED Survey of Valuation Methods Used by Venture Capitalists

Although the traditional valuation methods are applicable in valuing high-tech start-up companies, venture capitalists (VCs) often rely on variations of these methods. In 1987, QED Research published the *QED Report on Venture Capital Financial Analysis*.[10] Although it is dated, this study is still widely referenced as it provides tremendous insight and clarity into how financial analysis has been done by venture capitalists, including how they value start-up companies.

The factors to evaluate new venture prospects introduced earlier in this chapter are determined by analyzing the business plan and conducting site visits and interviews. Once these factors are considered, the valuation process can begin. QED presented four alternative valuation methods used in the VC community:

1. Conventional VC valuation method (VC method)
2. First Chicago method (FCM)
3. Fundamental method
4. Revenue multipliers

Conventional VC Valuation Method

The VC method is a residual valuation method that considers only one scenario at two points in time: the current date and the future cash-out date. It also requires assumptions on the compounded annual revenue growth rate to the liquidity event and margins at that time. This method follows the formula calculated in Exhibit 19.1. In this example, revenue is assumed to be

---

[10] James L. Plummer, *QED Report on Venture Capital Financial Analysis* (Palo Alto, CA: QED Research, 1987). This section is sourced from Section 2, "Summary of Valuation Methods Used by Venture Capitalists."

EXHIBIT 19.1 Conventional VC Valuation Method

Present Value of Company	$\dfrac{R * (1+g)^{\wedge}n * a * P}{(1+r)^{\wedge}n}$
R = revenue	$2,500,000
g = growth	40%
a = after-tax profit margin at liquidity	14%
P = expected P/E ratio at liquidity	19
n = number of years to liquidity	5
r = discount rate	40%
Indicated fair market value of equity	**$6,700,000**
Amount of required capital	$4,000,000
Minimum percentage ownership requirement	59.7%

$2.5 million and grow at an average compounded annual rate of 40% over the five-year holding period, at which time the VC exits through a company IPO. With an after-tax profit margin of 14%, an assumed P/E multiple of 19,[11] and a discount rate of 40%, the indicated fair market value of the company and its equity (assuming no interest-bearing debt) is $6.7 million.

In this and the remaining three valuation methods (unless otherwise indicated), we make the simplifying assumptions of only one VC investor, one round of financing, one class of preferred stock, a company at the second stage of development, a compound annual growth rate, constant margins, and no adjustments for net operating loss carryforwards.

First Chicago Method

The FCM[12] initially follows the techniques of the VC method and then probability-weights three outcome scenarios: success, sideways survival, and failure. This method requires the analyst to consider potential alternative outcomes rather than relying on an oversimplified revenue or earnings multiple. In practice today, these concepts are applied by way of a probability-weighted expected return method, discussed later in this chapter.

Nonetheless, this method is intuitive and relatively easy to replicate. Exhibit 19.2 illustrates how value is calculated under the FCM. A value

---

[11] Alternatively, other multiples (i.e. revenue or other levels of earnings) may be used.
[12] As noted in the QED Report on pages 2–7, the FCM is described at length in Stanley C. Golder, "Structuring and Pricing the Financing," and in Stanley A. Pratt and Jane Morris, *Guide to Venture Capital* (Wellesley, MA: Venture Economics, 1986).

EXHIBIT 19.2 First Chicago Method

		Success	Sideways Survival	Failure
(1)	Revenue growth rate[a]	50%	20%	0%
(2)	Revenue level after 3 years	$8,437,500	$4,320,000	$2,500,000
(3)	Revenue level after 5 years	$18,984,375	$6,220,800	
(4)	Revenue level after 7 years		$8,957,952	
(5)	After-tax profit margin and earnings at liquidity	18% $3,417,188	9% $806,216	
(6)	Price/Earnings ratio at liquidity	20	10	
(7)	Company value at liquidity[b]	$68,343,750	$8,062,157	$900,000
(8)	Present value of company[c]	$12,707,456	$764,813	$327,988
(9)	Probability of each scenario	50%	40%	10%
(10)	Expected company PV at each scenario	$6,353,728	$305,925	$32,799
(11)	Indicated fair market value of equity		**$6,700,000**	
(12)	Minimum percent ownership requirement[d]		**59.7%**	

[a]Revenue base of $2,500,000. Assumes the same revenue growth rate per year for each scenario.
[b]Value at liquidity is determined as Earnings × P/E for the Success and Sideways Survival Scenarios. For the Failure Scenario, it is assumed that the Company never becomes profitable and is liquidated for $900,000 after 3 years.
[c]A 40% discount rate is assumed. A time factor of 7 years is assumed for the Success Scenario, 5 for the Sideways Survival Scenario, and 3 for the Failure Scenario.
[d]Represents the VC's initial investment ($4,000,000 in this example) as a percentage of value.

of $6.7 million is calculated for a profitable start-up company generating $2.5 million in revenues, which recently closed a round of financing raising $4 million. Rows 1, 5, 6, and 9 are inputs; the remaining rows are formulas.

In the Success Scenario, revenue is assumed to grow at an annual rate of 50% over the five-year holding period to nearly $19 million, at which time the VC exits through an IPO. With an after-tax profit margin of 18%, the company's earnings are approximately $3.4 million. Applying an assumed P/E multiple of 20, the market capitalization of the company's equity is $68.3 million at the point of cash-out. Assuming a 40% discount rate, the present value of the company after the five-year holding period is $12.7 million.

In the Sideways Survival Scenario, revenue is assumed to grow at a considerably lower annual rate of 20% over a longer seven-year holding period to nearly $9 million, at which time the VC exits through a sale to a competitor due to lower revenue growth and profit margins. Therefore, the VC's investment survives, but the company does not survive as a separate entity. Employing an after-tax profit margin of 9%, the company's earnings are approximately $800,000. Applying an assumed P/E multiple of 10, the market capitalization of the company's equity is $8 million at the point of cash-out. The present value of the company after the seven-year holding period is approximately $765,000, assuming a 40% discount rate.

In the Failure Scenario, revenue never grows beyond the $2.5 million that existed when the VC invested the $4 million. After three years, the VC decides to pull the plug and reinvest the money in companies with greater potential. The VC is able to sell the company's assets and dissolve it for an assumed $900,000. The present value of the company under this scenario after the three-year holding period is approximately $328,000, assuming a 40% discount rate.

Company value is then calculated in lines 9 through 11, with the VC assigning probabilities to each scenario and multiplying them by the present value of the company under each scenario, resulting in a value of $6.7 million. Finally, line 12 shows that given an investment of $4 million and the resulting value of $6.7 million, the VC's minimum percentage required ownership is 59.7%, calculated by dividing the $4 million required by the calculated value of $6.7 million.

The FCM allows for analyzing several what-if scenarios. However, it is important to keep in mind that the example presented assumes a growth rate in revenues, constant margins, and the same discount rate. It also assumes that the VC is willing to make an investment decision based on the expected values obtained from the results of this method.[13] In many instances, the analyst would need to vary these assumptions. In practice, the analyst would consider a range of scenarios that are appropriate for the opportunity under consideration.

Fundamental Method

The fundamental method resembles the DCF, discussed earlier in this chapter and in more detail in Chapter 7, using a discounted future earnings analysis. Rather than focusing on the assumed date of liquidity, as is the case with the previous two methods, this method considers several years into the future, both before and after a liquidity event.

---

[13] See Plummer, *QED Report on Venture Capital Financial Analysis*, chapter 6, for more details on the treatment of risk tolerance in the FCM as well as its use in estimating the effect of liquidation preferences and warrants on the value of a deal.

EXHIBIT 19.3 Fundamental Method

Year	Revenue[a]	Revenue Growth	Net Margin	Net Income	PV Factor[b]	PV of Net Income
1	$3,750,000	50%	18.0%	$675,000	0.7143	$482,153
2	$5,625,000	50%	18.0%	$1,012,500	0.5102	$516,578
3	$8,437,500	50%	18.0%	$1,518,750	0.3644	$553,433
4	$12,656,250	50%	18.0%	$2,278,125	0.2603	$592,996
5	$18,984,375	50%	18.0%	$3,417,188	0.1859	$635,255
6	$26,578,125	40%	17.0%	$4,518,281	0.1328	$600,028
7	$34,551,563	30%	16.0%	$5,528,250	0.0949	$524,631
8	$41,461,875	20%	15.0%	$6,219,281	0.0678	$421,667
9	$47,681,156	15%	14.0%	$6,675,362	0.0484	$323,088
10	$52,449,272	10%	14.0%	$7,342,898	0.0346	$254,064
Terminal value[c]				$52,449,272	0.0346	$1,814,745

Indicated fair market value of equity	**$6,700,000**

[a]Revenue for the latest 12 months is $2,500,000.
[b]The present value factor is based on a discount rate of 40% using end-of-year convention.
[c]The terminal value is calculated as Year 10 earnings divided by a capitalization rate of 14%, and discounting it at the end of Year 10 applying the 40% discount rate. The 14% capitalization rate is calculated assuming that the discount rate is at a mature stage of 18% and the long-term sustainable growth rate is 4%.

Like the FCM, this method is intuitive and relatively easy to replicate, with simplifying assumptions as presented herein. Exhibit 19.3 illustrates how value is calculated under the fundamental method.

One may argue that the forecasting required to apply this method is highly speculative. The reality is that any method used to value a start-up company is highly speculative and fraught with uncertainty. Forecasting an exit several years in the future is equally speculative, given the inability to predict economic cycles, market activity, and IPO opportunities several years in the future. The benefit of this method is that it requires thinking through factors such as revenue growth, inevitable deceleration in revenue growth, and different levels of profitability as the company moves through its life cycle. These factors require consideration of market share and market penetration. Although not illustrated in our example, this method can also show the impact of additional start-up losses until the company's position stabilizes. For earlier-stage companies expecting substantial losses over the next few years, this method may serve only as a check to value.

Revenue Multipliers

As indicated by its name, a revenue multiplier is a factor that is multiplied by the company's revenue (generally on an accrual, not a cash, basis). Revenue can either be for the next 12 months (leading) or the current fiscal year (trailing). Just as in the valuation of any business, the revenue multiple may be based on a sample of guideline public companies or guideline transactions. Revenue multipliers are often used for companies in the early stages of development for which little or no profit has been realized. They suffer from the same weaknesses as well in terms of not accounting for differences in profit margins, requirements for capital expenditures and working capital, R&D time and intensity, and marketing and production lead time. Nonetheless, they are an extremely simple and quick method to apply as checks to value derived by other methods.

A Probability-Weighted Scenario Method to Value Start-Ups

The QED survey illustrated that there are several methods used by VCs in valuing start-up companies. It also demonstrated that VCs often use multiple methods. This fact, coupled with the application of traditional valuation approaches, suggests that multiple valuation methods should be applied in valuing start-ups and weighted according to their outcome probability and relevance to the company being valued, based on a particular company's stage of development and other characteristics.

Traditional probability analysis calls for identification of likely outcomes (e.g. optimistic, most likely, and pessimistic) and then weighing the likelihood that each will occur. Of course, these outcomes depend on the company's ability to achieve key metrics – most commonly targeted revenues, operating margins, capital reinvestments, and, ultimately, net cash flow. Therefore, each of these metrics can be included in the analysis as a variable to create a grid or spreadsheet of potential outcomes.

In valuation for M&A, especially in situations where the company has no outside investors, the valuation of a high-tech start-up company should take into account all approaches, treating them as indicators of value under different possible scenarios, and probability weight them according to expectations as of the date of value. Specifically, a probability-weighted scenario method (PWSM) should be used to value high-tech start-up companies (i.e. total invested capital – methods to allocate the equity so that the common stock portion can be valued are introduced in the next section of this chapter). A variation of the FCM used by VCs and introduced earlier in this chapter can be applied, coupled with the application of the probability-weighted expected return method used to allocate equity value and introduced in the next section.

A PWSM that considers several outcome scenarios is an effective way to value a high-tech start-up company. This method allows for consideration of different exits at different times in terms of a sale or IPO, a stay-private scenario where a long-term forecast is used to determine an indication of value, and a liquidation scenario if the business model does not materialize.

As has been discussed at great length, there are many considerations to be made in valuing a high-tech start-up. A PWSM can capture many of these considerations. Such a method consists of four primary scenarios and multiple secondary scenarios. The four primary scenarios are:

1. Sale to a third party (market approach)
2. Go public (market approach)
3. Stay private (income approach)
4. Liquidation (asset approach)

Secondary scenarios involve multiple possibilities within the primary scenarios (i.e. sale or IPO at different dates and values). Probabilities are assigned to each of these scenarios to conclude on a value. By way of illustration,[14] let us assume we are valuing Ahdkee Technology, Inc., a company that began operations four years ago, generated its first revenues two years later, but is not expected to generate a profit until next year. We will assume that, after in-depth analysis of its current position in the market and stage of development, the company had seven likely scenarios:

Sale in Year 2. A sale of Ahdkee at a $70 million valuation in Year 2 – 10% probability.

Sale in Year 3. A sale of Ahdkee at a $100 million valuation in Year 3 – 20% probability.

Sale in Year 4. A sale of Ahdkee at a $150 million valuation in Year 4 – 20% probability.

IPO in Year 3. An IPO of Ahdkee at a $180 million valuation in Year 3 – 10% probability.

IPO in Year 4. An IPO of Ahdkee at a $250 million valuation in Year 4 – 15% probability.

---

[14] This case study is independent of any other examples in the book. Its purpose is to illustrate the mechanics of a PWSM, not to review application of other valuation methods covered. Therefore, several assumptions will be stated rather than calculated. For example, the results of the DCF analysis will be stated without showing the underlying forecasts and discount rate derivation.

EXHIBIT 19.4 Probability-Weighted Scenario Method to Value High-Tech Start-Ups

(000's)	Indicated Value of Invested Capital	Discount Factor (40%)	Present Value of Invested Capital
Scenario 1: Sale in Year 2	$70,000	0.5102	$35,714
Scenario 2: Sale in Year 3	$100,000	0.3644	$36,440
Scenario 3: Sale in Year 4	$150,000	0.2603	$39,045
Scenario 4: IPO in Year 3	$180,000	0.3644	$65,592
Scenario 5: IPO in Year 4	$250,000	0.2603	$65,075
Scenario 6: Stay Private	$50,000	1.0000	$50,000
Scenario 7: Liquidation in Year 3	$1,000	0.3644	$364

	Present Value of Invested Capital	Probability	Probability-Weighted Value of Invested Capital
Scenario 1: Sale in Year 2	$35,714	10%	$3,571
Scenario 2: Sale in Year 3	$36,440	20%	$7,288
Scenario 3: Sale in Year 4	$39,045	20%	$7,809
Scenario 4: IPO in Year 3	$65,592	10%	$6,559
Scenario 5: IPO in Year 4	$65,075	15%	$9,761
Scenario 6: Stay Private	$50,000	20%	$10,000
Scenario 7: Liquidation in Year 3	$364	5%	$18
Fair Market Value			**$45,000**

> *Stay private.* No market transaction occurs and Ahdkee continues to pursue its business plan. Its value in this scenario is $50 million based on a DCF analysis – 20% probability.
>
> *Liquidation.* Ahdkee does not successfully adapt to the rapidly evolving technological and competitive environment and fails. Its value in this scenario is $1 million – 5% probability.

As can be seen in this example and as illustrated in Exhibit 19.4, the four primary scenarios are considered, along with multiple scenarios for potential sale and IPO of the company. Factors considered in assigning probabilities include:

■ There is a 75% probability of a successful IPO or sale of Ahdkee occurring sometime between Years 2 and 4, a 20% probability that it will continue in its current form if a successful liquidity event does not occur, and a slight chance (5%) of business failure.

- A successful IPO (25%) is believed to be less likely than a sale of the company (50%).

To test the value expectations for each of the three sale scenarios, the transaction method within the market approach to value, explained in Chapter 10, is used. It involves four steps:

1. *Selection of appropriate transactions.* The relied-on transactions are those of companies in similar lines of business as Ahdkee and/or having other characteristics that are similar (including selling their products to similar clients). A total of 30 relevant transactions were identified.
2. *Analysis of the selected transactions.* The average revenue multiple was 3.4, and the median was 2.6. The lowest observed multiple was 0.1, and the highest was 22.4. The first quartile of the observed transactions reflected a revenue multiple of 0.9 and the third quartile a revenue multiple of 3.5. Only revenue multiples were used since Ahdkee has not yet generated profits, and it may not generate a sufficient level of earnings to justify a meaningful earnings multiple.
3. *Review of implied revenue multiples for each scenario.* For Scenario 1, the implied revenue multiple of 1.46 (using forecasted Year 2 revenues applicable to that scenario) falls at the lower end of the observed range, between the observed first quartile of 0.9 and the median of 2.6. For Scenario 2, the implied revenue multiple is 1.74 (using forecasted Year 3 revenues). For Scenario 3, the implied revenue multiple increases to 2.17 (using forecasted Year 4 revenues). Revenues are forecasted to grow 20% per year between Years 1 and 4.
4. *Determination of reasonableness.* The range of transaction values as estimated by Ahdkee management appears reasonable based on this analysis.

To test the values for each of the two IPO scenarios, the guideline public company method within the market approach to value, also covered in Chapter 10, is used. It also involves four steps:

1. *Selection of appropriate guideline public companies.* The relied-on public companies are those of companies in similar lines of business as Ahdkee and/or having other characteristics that are similar (including selling their products to similar clients). A total of eight relevant transactions were identified.
2. *Analysis of the selected public companies.* The average revenue multiple was 4.0, and the median was 3.6. The lowest observed multiple was 1.9,

and the highest was 5.5. The first quartile of the observed transactions reflected a revenue multiple of 2.5 and the third quartile a revenue multiple of 4.5.

3. *Review of implied revenue multiples for each scenario.* For Scenario 4, the implied revenue multiple of 3.13 (using forecasted Year 2 revenues applicable to that scenario) falls at the lower end of the observed range, between the observed first quartile of 2.5 and the median of 3.6. For Scenario 5, the implied revenue multiple is 3.62 (using forecasted Year 3 revenues), at the 3.6 median of the guideline company sample.

4. *Determination of reasonableness.* The range of IPO values as estimated by Ahdkee management appears reasonable based on this analysis.

Alternatively, in certain situations – for example, in the pharmaceutical industry – the values for the IPO scenarios can be tested using actual IPO data in the subject industry. If a sufficient number of IPOs can be examined, a range of premoney valuations can be observed and compared to the assumed IPO values for Ahdkee. In addition, premoney valuations of similar companies completing IPOs in recent years relative to the fully diluted postmoney valuations at the time of their last round of financing (i.e. a step-up) can be observed. Finally, the number of days between the last round of financing and the IPO for the identified companies can be compared to the number of days between the closing of Ahdkee's latest round and the IPO scenarios being considered.

In the event that neither an IPO nor a sale of Ahdkee occurs (i.e. no market transaction), management believes that the company will continue to pursue its business plan. This Stay Private Scenario is analyzed by way of a DCF analysis, explained in Chapter 7, and results in a fair market value of $50 million.

The Liquidation Scenario considers the probability that Ahdkee is not successful at adapting to the rapidly evolving technological and competitive landscape after three years, despite its recent generation of revenues, and that it burns through its cash, is unsuccessful in raising additional capital, and ultimately fails. It is able to sell its fixed assets at an orderly liquidation value of $200,000 and its patents and other intellectual property for $800,000, resulting in a liquidation value of $1 million.

Given that Ahdkee has been shipping product and generating revenues for two years, the company is deemed to be in the second stage or expansion where, as indicated in the earlier Risk and Discount Rates section, appropriate discount rates are in the range of 35% to 50%. Based on various company-specific factors, 40% is deemed applicable to Ahdkee and is used to discount the various scenarios to present value to determine the company's fair market value.

EXHIBIT 19.5 Check to Value – Conventional VC Valuation Method

Present Value of Company	$\dfrac{R * (1+g)^n * a * P}{(1+r)^n}$		
R = revenue	$25,000,000	$25,000,000	$25,000,000
g = growth	20%	20%	20%
a = after-tax profit margin at liquidity	12%	14%	17%
P = expected P/E ratio at liquidity	20	20	20
n = number of years to liquidity	2	3	4
r = discount rate	40%	40%	40%
Indicated fair market value of equity	$44,100,000	$44,100,000	$45,900,000

The result of this analysis, as illustrated in Exhibit 19.4, yields a fair market value of $45 million.

Checks to value are performed once value is determined using this PWSM. Since it is so widely used in the VC community and is relatively easy to apply, the conventional VC method, illustrated in Exhibit 19.5, can be used to see if the parameters it requires (in this case, profit margin and P/E multiple[15]) to solve for the resulting value ($45 million in this case) are reasonable. In addition, a revenue multiple or, for later-stage start-ups, multiples of various levels of earnings can also be applied. Balancing out the results of these checks to value, one can assess the reasonableness of the conclusion of value of the start-up company.

Equity Allocation Methods

The valuation methods discussed thus far in this chapter have applied to the valuation of the start-up company as a whole. Often the valuation of the company's common stock is required. This arises in many of the situations introduced at the outset of this chapter. For example, valuations needed in connection with shares being gifted, employee stock options being granted, or certain litigation situations all require that a valuation goes beyond the start-up company's overall value, specifically to its common stock value.

When a company has a complex capital structure consisting of multiple classes of stock with differing rights and claims on its equity, additional analysis is required. Although there are many ways to value both the

---

[15] Compared to the 30 companies sold and the 8 public companies analyzed.

common and preferred stock in such situations, two equity allocation methods – the probability-weighted expected return method (PWERM) and the option-pricing method (OPM) – are used most often to allocate the total equity value of a company to the components of its capital structure, and thus assign a value to its common stock.

Under the PWERM, an analysis of future values of a company is performed for several likely liquidity scenarios. Those scenarios may include a strategic sale or merger, an IPO, the dissolution of the company in which the preferred shares receive all of the proceeds and the common shares are worthless, as well as the company's private enterprise value, assuming the absence of a liquidity event. The value of the common stock is determined for each scenario at the time of each future liquidity event and discounted back to the present using a risk-adjusted discount rate. The present values of the common stock under each scenario are then weighted based on the probability of each occurring to determine an indication of the value of the common stock. This method is generally considered appropriate to use when there are several distinct liquidity scenarios.[16]

In brief, a PWERM analysis consists of five steps:[17]

1. Identify the most likely liquidity events for the company, including when they are expected to occur, the probability of each occurring, and the equity values of the company for each. Scenarios considered can be broken down into the four categories (i.e. sale, IPO, stay private, or liquidation) listed in the preceding paragraph.
2. Determine the value of the common stock[18] for, and as of, each of the liquidity events considered.
3. Determine the present value of the common stock for each liquidity scenario.
4. Apply the probabilities assigned to each scenario to the present value of the common stock for each scenario to determine the probability-weighted value as of the valuation date.
5. Perform a check-to-value analysis to determine the reasonableness of the value of the common stock and the assumptions relied on.

The OPM treats common stock and preferred stock as call options on the equity value of the subject company. Essentially, the common stock is treated

---

[16] AICPA Task Force, *Valuation of Privately-Held Company Equity Securities Issued as Compensation* (2013), 58–61.

[17] Francis D. Mainville, "Using the Probability-Weighted Return Methodology to Value Common Stock," *Valuation Strategies* 12, no. 3 (January–February 2009): 15. The reader is encouraged to read this article for an in-depth explanation of the PWERM, with detailed examples of its application.

[18] This can also be used to value other classes of stock.

as a call option that gives the owner a right, but not an obligation, to buy the underlying enterprise at a predetermined or exercise price. The method is sensitive to certain key assumptions, such as volatility,[19] that are not easily forecasted for a privately held company. The OPM may be appropriate when the ranges of likely liquidity scenarios for common stockholders cannot be reduced to several likely ones. Additionally, it is appropriate when a liquidity event is not anticipated in the near future, as the method recognizes that common stock may have little or no value if the subject were to be sold in its entirety on the valuation date, but has a claim on future values of the company in excess of the senior claims of the preferred stock.[20]

In short, an OPM analysis consists of six steps:[21]

1. Calculate the values at which the company's preferred stock liquidation preferences are met as well as the value at which options on the common stock would be exercised.[22] These values or breakpoints are relied on in step 3 (exercise prices) and step 4 to calculate the percentage of the increases in the company's equity value due to each class of stock.
2. Determine the percentage of the increase in the company's value due to each class of stock. These percentages are used in step 4 to allocate the value of the options to each class of stock.
3. Calculate the value of the call options with exercise prices equal to the breakpoints identified in step 1 using an option-pricing model such as the BSOPM.
4. Determine the value of each class of stock based on the values of the call options just calculated and the claims that each class of stock has on those values.
5. Apply a discount for lack of marketability to the unadjusted value of the common stock to determine its fair value.
6. Perform a check-to-value analysis to determine the reasonableness of the value of the common stock and the assumptions relied on.

When valuations are needed for high-tech start-ups for purposes other than a sale, IPO, or raising an additional round of financing, the valuation

---

[19] The standard deviation of future expected returns on the equity of a company.

[20] AICPA Task Force, *Valuation of Privately-Held Company Equity Securities Issued as Compensation* (2013), 61–65.

[21] Francis D. Mainville, "Using the Option Pricing Methodology to Value Common Stock," p. 18. The reader is encouraged to read this article for an in-depth explanation of the OPM, with detailed examples of its application.

[22] More complex capital structures may require the calculation of additional breakpoints, including the value at which preferred shares convert to common if the preferred is either nonparticipating or has a maximum participation amount, and so on.

of a company's common stock alone is often required. The PWERM is most appropriate when there are several possible scenarios for liquidity events in the future, including a possible sale of the company, and their timing and valuation parameters can reasonably be estimated. The OPM is most appropriate when a round of financing recently closed or when the range of possible liquidity scenarios for common stockholders cannot be reduced to several likely scenarios. Other equity allocation methods are available but less frequently applied in practice.

Conclusion

High-tech start-ups rank among the most risky possible private company investments while offering potentially high returns. The key to making wise investments in such businesses is to base choices on sound methodology. This discipline begins with strategic analysis of the company's internal and external environment to identify strengths and weaknesses. Rigorous business planning with continual updates is essential to monitor progress and assess the continually changing likelihood of future success. The valuation of high-tech start-ups is a very complex process with substantial subjectivity. Making the correct assumptions presents a significant challenge. Nonetheless, assumptions must be made in order to value them and ultimately decide on a course of action. A probability-weighted scenario method should be applied in valuing a start-up company to assess the myriad factors that impact its value. With the methods presented in this chapter, much of the mystery that surrounds the valuation of start-up companies is revealed, and substantial rewards can be enjoyed.

CHAPTER 20

Cross-Border M&A[1]

A s with traditional merger and acquisition, there are numerous factors affecting the success of a cross-border transaction. However, cross-border activities add a significant level of complexity that must be carefully considered and evaluated. In today's globalized marketplace, cross-border activities are becoming much more common, even in middle-market transactions. It is not unusual to find a privately held company that now has operating subsidiaries or divisions located in several countries. In many cases, it is a necessity for competitive advantage, maintenance of customer relationships with multinational entities, and even survival.

There are inherent risks in not properly managing the cross-border process and there are great opportunities if it is conducted effectively. This chapter largely focuses on the strategic buy side of transactions since the majority of the decisions are directed from this perspective. On the sell side, it is likely that an investment banker will be involved to facilitate that role. Nonetheless, certain sell-side aspects are covered in the latter part of this chapter.

Strategic Buy-Side Considerations

Enhancing shareholder value and growing the target company in keeping with the overall corporate strategic plan are two key components in selecting acquisition targets. The strategic plan must assess a wide variety of issues and concerns to make the business case for the acquisition as well as determining key value drivers. When the process is undertaken, wise strategists establish a projected timeline covering all key components necessary to complete a transaction successfully. Doing this may involve locating available company talent to begin assembling the various teams required, mobilizing the task

---

[1] The authors gratefully acknowledge the contribution of this chapter written by Sid M. Shaver, CPA, CM&AA, Senior Managing Director of B&V Capital Advisors, Houston, Texas; www.bvcapitaladvisors.com.

EXHIBIT 20.1 Cross-Border Mergers and Acquisitions Major Challenges

- Accounting differences
- Agreement on valuation
- Crony capitalism
- Cultural fit
- Currency fluctuations
- Debt availability in a given market
- Economic conditions
- Entity structure and governance
- Financial reporting
- Financing
- Governmental and regulatory compliance
- Integration post-acquisition
- Legal (common vs. civil vs. religious vs. mixed law)
- Measuring exposure to country-specific factors
- Securities transferability
- Tax laws

force, and scheduling the milestones for measuring the activity. Cross-border transactions have several key challenges, as presented in Exhibit 20.1 and covered in more depth throughout this chapter, that require careful attention.

Products and Services

Initially, products and services must be evaluated to determine if there is a fit, an opportunity for growth, and the potential for shareholder value accretion. In conducting an analysis of this type, consideration must be given to the availability of bundling these products with existing products, expansion of the customer base, cross-selling opportunities, and the overall quality of the products, especially in the case of manufactured goods.

The customer base, its strength, the depth of its market, and whether it carries brand recognition into other markets must be closely examined. Along with this, it is vital to determine whether the market is largely local, receptive to additional products, growing or shrinking, as well as the economic condition of the local market.

Scalability is a key consideration in evaluating the areas and is a significant focal point. For instance, will there be an opportunity to share or reduce costs, access customers, improve capacity utilization at existing facilities to achieve perceived synergies, or have significant increases in revenue or earnings because of existing relationships?

Product competiveness, market share, technological advances, and general market position are key considerations.

Assembling the Team

When considering cross-border transactions, a significant aspect is selecting the right team to conduct the business strategy, negotiations, due diligence, financial, legal, engineering, geopolitical, labor, and cultural fit analysis.

Business strategy analysis will necessarily include a number of team members mentioned earlier in the feasibility stage to determine if the opportunity is worth pursuit. Business prospects will be evaluated and consideration given to their inherent strengths and weaknesses to determine which areas present the greatest opportunities or challenges to overcome.

Selecting the appropriate negotiation team is vital to even begin the process. This team needs to be well-versed in the company's market, its culture, reputation, decision makers, and the potential valuation parameters.

A complete understanding of cultural aspects and formalities with respect to personal styles and customs must be thoroughly investigated and understood. Negotiations likely will be conducted differently depending on regional customs, including timeline considerations. Beyond the negotiations, the team must include local legal experts who can navigate the acquiring company through statutory noticing requirements, local disclosure issues, and the general nature of typical transactions, including governmental involvement and any required approvals. Disclosures are often required in various countries that may or may not be considered normal to the acquirer and may have an impact on the transaction structure and the manner in which negotiations are conducted, including confidentiality concerns.

Both local and company legal teams must work in conjunction to understand the business environment and any obstacles that might develop with the business practices employed in certain regions. Foreign Corrupt Practices Act provisions, which address accounting transparency requirements and bribery of foreign officials, must be taken into consideration for U.S.-based companies considering cross-border acquisitions as well as for U.S.-based acquisitions with foreign operating subsidiaries. Additionally, directors and officers' legal liabilities in connection with a cross-border transaction need to be considered and evaluated. Expertise in financial, tax, currency, labor laws, government regulations, and entity formation is vital to building a comprehensive team.

Taking these issues separately, each requires a unique discipline fully versed in the requirements for a successful transaction.

Financing, for instance, can prove to be particularly troublesome in cross-border transactions. Issues associated with raising capital and perfecting title and liens can certainly present unusual challenges. Due to legal structures either present or not present, lenders, investors, or capital providers must have some assurance that funds invested have some degree of protection. Extremely creative structures or encumbrance of other more attractive assets may be required to accomplish acquisition financing. Any contingencies with respect to financing can contribute to costly delays in closing transactions. The plan for financing a cross-border transaction needs to be considered well in advance unless resources are readily available for such purposes and exist as a key component in the existing strategic growth plan.

Taxation Issues

Tax matters often have a significant impact on the ultimate success of a transaction. Understanding the tax structure and ability to repatriate funds subject to tax are important considerations. Many countries have strict policies regarding corporate tax withholding and may restrict the free flow of funds in or out of a country. Some tax issues concern treaty-related provisions that must be thoroughly understood relative to a contemplated transaction. Transfer pricing – the exchange rate for goods between related companies – can have serious tax consequences. Tax authorities worldwide are keenly concerned with the pricing and methods used for cross-border transactions.

With respect to currency, a key consideration is to determine the relative strength of currencies and exchange rates and any impact these may have on future business within or out of a country, product pricing implications, competitiveness, and stability of the region's financial base. The carrying value of an asset post-acquisition can be significantly impacted by a valuation change or adjustment in a currency. Determining the denomination with which transactions are conducted is an important element.

Labor Matters

Labor laws and customs can be vastly different in various countries or regions of countries. Gaining a complete understanding of labor laws is essential to being able to succeed. There can be tremendous differences associated with an acquisition in a developed versus an emerging economic region. Along with labor issues, there may be requirements to invest in infrastructure, to hire a certain percentage of local people, and to train and educate local people to perform jobs. Social taxes and other requirements may be unique or require special attention. Reductions in workforce or other situations that arise may require a completely different approach and governmental involvement.

Acquisition Entity

Corporate or entity formation to acquire a target may be entirely different as to structure, governance requirements, formalities, and disclosure. It is imperative to locate sophisticated talent knowledgeable in all aspects of entity formation.

Geopolitical Issues

Consideration of political issues is essential to careful analysis of a merger, acquisition, business combination, or joint venture with cross-border implications. Political, economic, and safety issues each merit review and evaluation. Many countries face ongoing turmoil, with frequent changes in political power, resulting in changes in orientation toward business, sometimes with drastic consequences. One must understand where control exists, how political power is exercised, and the stability of the host government. Historically, countries have had revolutions, coups, and industrial nationalization, all of which will likely continue to persist. In gathering this data, stability is relative, and often only a near-term evaluation is realistic. Current political events can also impact or derail a planned transaction.

Existing economic realities in certain areas may impact political decisions and must be examined closely for political policy changes.

Safety and security risks are also a concern and impact the ease of movement of people, products, and materials into or out of regions. Evaluating the region to determine the acceptance of foreign ownership or retaliation against it are key risk considerations. Companies that are well-versed in cross-border transactions often employ security experts to provide much of the data on regions and geopolitical risk assessments as a part of the proposed transaction analysis.

Transaction Valuation Issues

In preparation for an acquisition, the target company's overall preliminary valuation range must be calculated. During this process, it is especially important in a cross-border transaction to analyze the relative strengths of currencies. The strength of a currency often impacts the amount a company is willing to pay. An acquirer with a strong currency will be able to pay less; conversely, it becomes much more expensive if the acquirer's currency is weak relative to that of the target. The valuation process may require translating financial reports from one currency to another for comparative purposes. An analysis of operating cash flow, demand for capital expenditures, expected synergies, cost of funds, growth assumptions, and inherent risks will be required to formulate a preliminary range of values for the target.

The relative strengths of currencies can have a profound impact on postclosing assumptions made in the valuation stage. Depending on the status of an existing currency, the postclosing elements of a transaction, including earn-out provisions and seller-financed notes, can be materially affected should a currency fluctuate substantially.

In analyzing the company for transaction valuation purposes, historical capital expenditures will be reviewed. The need for improved equipment and facilities needed to support planned growth must be factored into the model as well as financing assumptions relative to acquiring these assets.

Perceived synergies will be considered to determine if there will be improved earnings resulting from duplications or overlaps in job functions, cost reductions resulting from improved buying power, or distribution channels the buyer may enjoy.

Depending on the acquirer's financial circumstances, an acquisition may be funded in a number of ways, including issuing stock, borrowing from traditional sources, partnering with other financing sources, using available cash, or having the seller carry a portion of the purchase price either through notes or an earn-out contingency. Acquirers generally have a targeted cost of capital and an expected rate of return to be achieved from the acquisition. Financial modeling will be done at this stage to select the most appropriate acquisition terms and structure designed to achieve the lowest cost of capital and the highest expected rate of return on capital employed.

These factors will all be taken into account in creating a discounted cash flow analysis resulting from the acquisition along with an anticipated terminal value at some proposed exit point to determine the overall effective rate of return that is projected to be generated. Other valuation methods discussed throughout this book may also be employed.

CURRENCY CONVERSION CONSIDERATION   To account for currency fluctuations for discounted cash flow analytical purposes and overall valuation issues, the International Fisher Effect may be applied to equalize or create parity among currencies. The theory behind this application is based on underlying interest rate parity and implies that the expected change in currency exchange is determined by the equivalent differences in the interest rates present in each country at the time. The difference in rates is generally attributable to future or forward rates and the current or spot rate of the currencies. Theoretically, the country with the higher interest rate would be more susceptible to inflation, and its currency would tend to depreciate over time relative to that of the other country in a lower-inflation environment. The interest rate parity theory tends to perform better when used for acquisitions occurring in developed countries where relative stability exists between the given currencies. Inflation or the potential for inflation can be a factor when determining whether to use the spot rate or future expected rate and factoring in inflation expectations. These factors are taken into account in establishing currency exchange rates between various countries as well as balance-of-trade and other circumstantial considerations.

Acquirers may choose to protect themselves from exposures related to currency risk by hedging it. By hedging, they effectively stabilize fluctuations by transferring risk to others willing to invest or take a position in the target country's currency. Conceptually it operates much like insurance against fluctuations and volatility in the underlying currency with an acceptable cost relative to the exposure. A hedge can be accomplished by trading over-the-counter forward currencies, purchasing futures options, or using exchange-traded futures. The Chicago Mercantile Exchange is a leading exchange for currency trading, operating with electronic trading on an around-the-clock basis. Most significant quoting services like Bloomberg or Reuters have readily available information for real-time quotes.

In actual practice, published currency exchange rates are used to convert historical balance sheet information at varying points in time from the target's rate to that of the acquirer's. Historical income statement conversions are often calculated using average annual currency exchange rates. Historical cash flow conversions generally are calculated using a combination of currency exchange rates for conversion based on the categorical elements and timing of financial events. Future projected financials will be predicated on existing exchange rates adjusted for anticipated inflation or deflation resulting from economic reports. Additionally, information related to future country and global financial expectations can be found in studies published by the International Monetary Fund (IMF). This excerpt from the IMF's website is related to the reports relevant for this analysis:

> The World Economic Outlook (WEO) database contains selected macroeconomic data series from the statistical appendix of the World Economic Outlook report, which presents the IMF staff's analysis and projections of economic developments at the global level, in major country groups and in many individual countries. The WEO is released in April and September/October each year. Use this database to find data on national accounts, inflation, unemployment rates, balance of payments, fiscal indicators, trade for countries and country groups (aggregates), and commodity prices whose data are reported by the IMF.[2]

INTERNATIONAL COST OF CAPITAL Similar to the currency conversion issue is the consideration for the international cost of capital. It has long been known that investment risk will vary from country to country based on political, regulatory, and economic conditions. Although this variance between the United States and England is minimal, it can be substantial between the United States and developing nations. Adjusting the rate of return for this country-risk factor may not be precise, but even an approximate adjustment assists in the development of a rate of return applicable to a given country.

---

[2] IMF: www.imf.org.

Next we present an overview of the international cost of capital adjustment methods, together with sources of more specific information. Before starting, it must be noted that the currency of the cost of capital must be matched to the currency of the forecasted cash flow when estimating foreign cost of capital. In addition to equity, size, and company-specific risk factors included in a company's cost of capital as described in Chapter 8, an assessment must be made of a company's exposure to country risk. This approach adds an additional risk component to the rate of return developed for investments in the United States through the capital asset pricing model (CAPM) or the build-up method. The procedure used by many practitioners is to obtain the country-risk component from the *International Country Risk Guide Annual.*[3]

To convert CAPM to a country-specific format, one needs a risk-free proxy for the country, a beta specific to the country, and a country-specific equity risk premium. The risk-free rate for each country used to develop the country-specific equity risk premium is often selected from the income return on each country's long-term government bond, as provided by the IMF. The country-specific beta is estimated by comparing the volatility of a country-specific index to the volatility of the world market comprised of the index of various countries – for example, the Standard & Poor's 500 for the U.S. index. To a varying degree, from country to country, this process is limited by the availability of data over a historical period long enough to make the equity risk premium sufficiently reliable.

It is not recommended that this process be attempted from the limited data and description contained in this book. For more information on this process, contact Wiley or Duff & Phelps[4] to obtain a copy of the *International Valuation Handbook – Guide to Cost of Capital.* This guide provides country-level country risk premia, relative volatility factors, and equity risk premia, which can be used to estimate country-level cost of equity globally, for up to 188 countries. Another source is Professor Aswath Damodaran's website,[5] which has a wealth of financial data including risk premiums for other markets based on the country ratings assigned by Moody's. MSCI[6] provides a broad array of index information and in-depth research relative to global investment initiatives that could be helpful in the cross-border acquisition analysis phase.

---

[3] Published annually in October, the *International Country Risk Guide Annual* compiles every analysis published for each of 140 countries during the previous 12-month period, www.prsgroup.com.
[4] www.wiley.com or www.duffandphelps.com.
[5] www.damodaran.com.
[6] www.msci.com.

Simply adding a country risk component to a cost of capital is a less complex process than the country-specific conversion of the CAPM. If a rate of return for an investment in another country is needed, obtain the details from each of the sources just listed (and perhaps others that may become known) before deciding on the best procedure for the country-specific investment under consideration. Be careful in assessing the risk adjustment component; it may already be present to a degree. In particular with emerging countries, it is reflected in their risk-free rate of return. Furthermore with emerging countries, the risk premium may not be as high as expected simply because the markets do not support a high premium. Also note that currency risk does not typically require a separate premium in the international cost of capital since it is captured in the spot and forward currency exchange rates. When considering this adjustment, to avoid the potential for overestimating the risk, consider using Standard & Poor's Investment Advisory Services or Moody's Investor Services to determine the sovereign bond spread correlated with U.S. Treasury bonds.

Another potential financial risk that merits adjustment consideration in the CAPM is the underlying default or credit risk, including steadily increasing debt costs in emerging countries experiencing rapid development. While this risk can be monitored, it can be regional or provincial as well as country-wide.

Selection of a tax rate to apply against earnings in the discounted cash flow model will likely be that of the target and where the income is earned. Yet if profits are intended to be repatriated to the acquirer, consideration should be given to the effects of taxes paid in the foreign country offset by deductions in the acquirer's country and effective tax rate.

Once these considerations have been discussed and rates selected, the next step in valuation modeling is to test the theoretical valuations versus the target's future expectations in order to further refine the valuation model.

When possible, the acquisition team should meet with the seller's management team to evaluate business growth prospects. Assumptions must be made as to probable growth rates of revenues and earnings based on these discussions to build a properly constructed model. Assumptions made by the seller's management team are a key component to understanding the opportunity and its potential for enhanced future value and the final valuation used for the definitive purchase agreement.

Mitigating risks in an acquisition is always a consideration. Certain risks, if known, may cause an adjustment in valuation based on the potential contingent outcome. Other risks may not be easily quantifiable and will require careful structuring techniques that may involve a view to longer time frame for the entire price to be paid. Deferring a portion of the cash purchase may be necessary until the risk is known, understood, quantifiable, or no longer exists. The potential for charge-backs will be a consideration for material adverse events, should they arise.

Once the analytical process is complete and a valuation range is established, the negotiation team can begin discussions. Valuation can be a hotly contested area, and the negotiation team needs to be fully prepared to support and defend its analysis. As with any transaction of this type, multiple scenarios need to be considered along with creative solutions to bridge valuation gaps between the acquirer and the target.

Preliminary Negotiations Ensue

After the business case is made, valuation ranges are established, and board approval is granted to move forward, typically somewhere in this process a confidential nonbinding or minimally binding memorandum of understanding or letter of intent is signed outlining the general terms of the proposed transaction, earmarked deadlines, and contingent language for unforeseen matters that may arise. Often investment banking professionals representing the respective parties are involved in formulating and negotiating the terms outlined in these documents. Investment bankers act as intermediaries and can assist in bridging some of the cultural issues present in different negotiating styles. After an agreement to move forward is reached, formal due diligence commences.

Due Diligence

Proper due diligence in cross-border transactions can be extremely tedious, difficult, and quite expensive. The due diligence team must do significant preplanning to ensure that issues of significance are covered and understood, how they will be communicated, and how the process will be coordinated. Many of these matters will have been identified as issues in the business case strategic planning phase, but at this point it becomes essential to analyze and test assumptions by directly reviewing documents, interviewing personnel, and conducting a detailed analysis of customers, vendors, and products.

Generally, due diligence in any transaction is a fact-finding project to gain clarity and understanding or to identify issues not readily apparent.

The due diligence team may include experts in legal, financial, operations, engineering, sales and marketing, human resources, taxation, and information technology. The book *Due Diligence for Global Deal Making* provides a comprehensive guide to techniques utilized in these categories for cross-border transactions.[7]

Legal experts will be analyzing corporate records, shareholder minutes, contracts, obligations, titles, structure, leases, pending legal matters, closed claims, contingent claims, and matters related to sales or transactions with other countries of relevance and compliance with existing laws. A significant part of the legal due diligence may relate to intellectual property for products or processes and protections that may or may not be in place. Consideration may be given to the transfer of intellectual property by the acquirer and protections that may be needed. The legal team may review issues related to product warranty policies, product liability coverage, and insurance policies. Other areas may involve labor union contracts, which may be jointly reviewed by legal and human resources personnel.

In conducting financial due diligence, the team will be evaluating accounting records, systems employed in recording transactions, the method used to account for transactions, and calculating actual cash flows of the business, assumptions made in the financial reporting process, and the quality of personnel involved in the financial reporting process. Often financial statements will require reformatting or repositioning accounts to better match those of the acquirer to determine the presentation and quality of the combined companies. Along with this, translation may be required, financial account titling may be in a different language, a different vernacular may be used as a description, and, of course, currencies may be reflected differently, requiring calculations at various times to account for currency fluctuations. It is advisable to discuss reports, management letters, and financial reporting issues with the outside accounting firm.

If the company is a manufacturer, a significant amount of time will be devoted to analyzing the costing methods used to calculate inventory balances and the corresponding amounts applied to cost of goods sold used in determining the business gross margin. Time and attention will be spent on accounting policies related to cut off and closing dates for recording sales, accounts receivable, inventory, and accounts payable activities. The financial due diligence team will evaluate and analyze cash management processes, customer and vendor terms, and business practices related to accounts receivable collections and accounts payable payment cycles.

Operations and engineering team members are interested in the manufacturing and distribution processes, equipment and facility quality, production and engineering talent, as well as quality of manufactured

---

[7] Arthur H. Rosenbloom, ed., *Due Diligence for Global Deal Making* (New York: Bloomberg Press, 2002).

goods. Quality control certifications such as ISO[8] 9000 or 9001 will be reviewed as well as production and quality control documents, safety manuals, safety records, and other pertinent documents. Efficiency in operations will be analyzed, along with scrap percentages and inventory, production, and supervisory controls. Systems used to operate the plant and equipment (referred to as SCADA, for supervisory control and data acquisition) will be compared to current state-of-the-art systems to determine whether the technology employed is advanced or needs to be upgraded. Other experts used may include metallurgists to examine the quality and grades of materials used in the process, cost estimators familiar with calculating and formulating appropriate labor and overhead rates, and efficiency experts to evaluate processes in place. Machining experts are often involved to determine if regular maintenance has been performed, the life of existing equipment, and any required repairs.

Facilities will require evaluation as to adequacy, safety, and available capacity. If strategic plans require or anticipate significant growth, it is vital that the equipment and facilities are capable of supporting it.

Members of the sales and marketing team will evaluate the customers, customer concentration, geographic regions, opportunities for cross-selling other products into the existing customer base, expansion of products to other regions or other customer bases, market or product overlaps, and existing sales and marketing methods employed. Product branding and reputation are a consideration as well as product pricing and market position. It must also be determined whether the company is a high-end or low-cost provider and the extent to which the combined companies will have a philosophical business fit.

This team will evaluate these products versus those of competitors, calculate overall market size and demand, determine relative market share, and estimate the available market share that can be attained. Customers will be analyzed based on buying patterns, relative financial strength, and tenure with the company.

Sales team members will be focused on sales literature, distribution, ability to bundle other products, sales methods employed, commission or noncommission sales, sales call reporting systems, inside and outside sales, support, service and warranty policies. Both the marketing and sales teams will evaluate the website delivery systems, messages conveyed, and customers' use of the website for product information and order placement. Distribution channels, warehouses, and other methods of product delivery will also be considered and evaluated.

---

[8] The International Organization for Standardization (www.iso.org) is designed for equalizing and standardizing business processes worldwide.

Other factors to consider might include product labeling, trademarks, product claims, advertising programs, industry involvement, trade association memberships, and overall product integration with existing products.

Human resources is concerned with policies related to employee pay; benefits; labor laws; disclosure issues; documentation; compliance with labor statutes; and governmental requirements related to training, educating, and retention of employees. A significant function of human resources will be to evaluate the cultural fit, language barriers, acceptance or adherence to new policies and procedures, work schedules, and overall attitude of the employee base relative to a business combination of the type contemplated. A study conducted by Professors Rajesh Chakrabarti, Narayanan Jayaraman, and Swasti Gupta-Makherjee discussed cultural differences in cross-border transactions and the impact they played from a historical perspective in the ultimate success of transactions.[9]

A key component to a successful outcome is directly related to the employee base being receptive to new owners, particularly if it is no longer owned domestically.

Taxation covers a broad range of matters, including accounting methods for tax filings, taxation in a foreign jurisdiction, repatriation of funds, foreign tax credits, state and local taxes, transactions between the acquirer and target postclosing related to transfer pricing issues, mandated government withholding, and employment and social taxes.

Given the scope of these areas, the tax team will require experts in many areas, including the regions in which the target company operates, the domestic region where the acquirer resides, and overlapping jurisdictions. A complete compilation of all tax filing requirements, taxes, tax treaties, foreign tax credits, entity taxation in various forms, and other matters is a necessity.

As part of this process, compliance with tax statutes must be reviewed as well as the prevailing attitude toward tax reporting and payment of taxes present in the target company.

Included in the process is determining the most tax-efficient methods for the acquisition as well as post-acquisition tax planning and filing requirements. There also may be various tax incentives that are attractive and require that certain formalities be observed or documented.

Information technology (IT) is vital in today's global market. Members of the IT team will analyze operating software, applications, hardware, intellectual property, licenses, compliance with licenses, provisions, and transferability of licenses. Distribution and protection of information are key

---

[9] Rajesh Chakrabarti, Narayanan Jayaraman, and Swasti Gupta-Mukherjee, "Mars-Venus Marriages: Culture and Cross-Border M&A," November 21, 2005. Available at SSRN: http://ssrn.com/abstract=869307.

components in this area, as is the security of the systems. Policies and procedures for redundant systems, backup, off-premises storage, software versions, and related matters are of key concern. Integration of the existing systems to the acquirers or installation of compatible systems may be required. IT is chiefly concerned with maintaining an uninterrupted flow of information to the acquirer postacquisition.

Once satisfactory due diligence has been completed, ongoing formal negotiations continue, including preparation of documents, clarification of points, and determination of transaction type (e.g. stock versus asset). Due diligence is designed to find hidden risks and, in doing so, highlights those that would be assumed in a corporate stock purchase, that would likely not be an issue in an asset purchase, where certain obligations are excluded. Essential business reasons may exist to acquire the stock – for example, difficult-to-obtain existing contracts, permits or licenses that are not easily transferable. In those cases, certain historical risks may be set aside, excluded, or retained as seller obligations. Outstanding issues are brought to a close, and an understanding is reached either to move forward or discontinue the process. Resolution issues related to the controlling document language, controlling legal authority, controlling currency for transaction proceeds, and other matters are clarified.

The acquiring entity's integration team fine-tunes the plan for postacquisition to best ensure a seamless business combination. Relevant personnel of the target and acquirer may at this point begin the collaboration effort necessary to get the key components in place. Plans will be established for data transfer, name changes, employee reports, banking relationship, cash management, invoicing, preparation of closing schedules and balance sheet, contract transfers, and other matters necessary to be completed postclosing.

During this stage, critical regulatory filings and approvals may be required. Depending on the jurisdiction, this process may result in a potential delay. The possibility exists that the acquisition as proposed will not be approved for any number of reasons. For instance, the U.S. Congress passed the Foreign Investment and National Security Act of 2007, which closely monitors and scrutinizes foreign investment in U.S. companies, particularly those in sensitive business areas involving technology, shipping ports, energy, or other areas affecting infrastructure. For its part, the European Union (EU) requires companies either in or considering doing business in Europe to gain approval for mergers to ensure it does not result in market dominance or unfair competitive practices. The governing body in the EU is referred to as the Directorate General for Competition.[10] Likewise, the United States has antitrust laws and may require Hart–Scott–Rodino Act filings to determine if the proposed acquisition results in an anticompetitive market. There are certainly other laws, but these serve as representative

---

[10] http://ec.europa.eu/dgs/competition.

examples of typical required filings. With a positive response, the process moves forward.

Sell-Side Considerations

From the seller's perspective, it is critical that the acquirer actually can consummate the transaction. Part of the investment banker's process is to evaluate the historical record of the proposed acquirer in accomplishing successful cross-border acquisitions and post closing handling of business matters. The proposed acquirer should be evaluated as well with respect to potential problems with regulatory requirements, out-of-favor status with government authorities, or any other matter that might bar it from completing the transaction. Investment bankers should provide a preliminary range of value and an anticipated structure that can be analyzed for net cash proceeds and tax treatment or planning opportunities. Key considerations will involve the initial signing of a letter of intent; purchase price negotiations; the cash component; issues related to securities provided as consideration, including marketability, restrictions, or valuation; earn-out clauses; and the accounting standards or methods discussed in Chapter 18 used to perform postclosing calculations. The seller will need to have access to high-caliber tax talent to evaluate significant tax aspects of the proposed transaction.

The currency used for the acquisition and postclosing payments for notes or earn-outs can create significant changes in overall valuation, should there be a substantial change in currency valuation, and result in material alterations in the planned economics. For example, an agreed-upon purchase price was reached, with the balance of proceeds to be distributed in future periods; however, should the underlying currency decline, the seller will actually receive less economic value than anticipated. To protect against this concern, the seller may elect to hedge this currency risk, lock down the value of future proceeds, and minimize this risk.

Representations and warranties in a cross-border transaction can be particularly troublesome in determining the enforceability of provisions. As a result, the acquirer may seek to set aside or escrow larger amounts of the purchase price as a protective mechanism. Thresholds and hold-back clauses may be more severe than normal as well. Due to the nature of overall uncertainties in these transactions, representations and warranties may be quite lengthy. The seller may need legal expertise to cover the cross-border implications of these terms.

It is also possible that the closing documents will need to be translated into another language, which can add an additional layer of difficulty in constructing documents that legally mirror one another.

At the final stage, documents are signed and exchanged, funds or securities are transferred, and the process of fully integrating the entities begins.

Case Studies

PART V

Case Studies

CHAPTER 21

Merger and Acquisition Valuation Case Study – Distribution Company

The theory and procedures presented in this book are much easier to understand when they are applied in a real-world situation. This chapter presents a comprehensive case that illustrates the application of many of the concepts that have been presented. The Cavendish Seafood Distributors merger and acquisition (M&A) case involves a company created by the authors based on the many companies we have appraised. Because of our obligation to client confidentiality, all of the details here, including the guideline public companies, are fictitious, but we believe they represent the typical lower middle market M&A circumstances that buyers and sellers must be prepared to encounter. Any similarity between Cavendish Seafood Distributors or the fictitious public companies described in this case and any actual company is purely coincidental. We have also created a generic economic and industry environment as background. The case is designed to describe a reasonable procedure based on the facts and circumstances presented. They may not be appropriate for other valuations, especially when done for other purposes. That is, some of the approaches and assumptions presented in this case might be different if the valuation was done for tax, financial reporting, litigation, or another purpose. In our attempt to present a realistic scenario, some factors in the case are not completely clear and some issues remain unresolved. Information is not perfect, and assumptions and estimates must be made, which certainly reflect real-world circumstances.

The case begins at the end of the Current Year, with Cavendish facing competitive threats and the clear need for transition planning. To begin this process, Cavendish's stand-alone fair market value is determined, first using net income to invested capital as the measure of return rather than net cash flow. This is done to demonstrate the use of an income measure because this is the language that is frequently spoken by sellers and their intermediaries. The single-period capitalization method within the income approach is also employed to demonstrate its use, although for a transaction of this size, the added detail provided by the discounted cash flow (DCF) method would be preferred. Cavendish's stand-alone fair market value is also computed by the guideline public company method, and we present brief applications of the transaction multiple method and the adjusted book value method. The results of these various methods are reconciled into a final opinion of the fair market value on a stand-alone basis of Cavendish's invested capital and equity.

Although several potential buyers are introduced in the case, Omni Food Distributors emerges as the strongest strategic buyer. Various synergies are estimated, and the investment value of Cavendish's invested capital and equity to Omni is computed using the DCF method.

Throughout the case we attempt to present sufficient explanation to allow the reader to understand each step in the valuation process. Valuation at this level must employ seasoned judgment based on knowledge of general economic conditions, industry circumstances, the competitive position of the target and guideline companies, and a thorough understanding of business valuation theory. In determining value, the appraiser serves as a surrogate for the hypothetical buyer and seller in the fair market value determination and for the strategic buyer in the investment value determination. Those parties typically make estimates and assumptions based on the facts and circumstances available as of the valuation date. That is the challenge presented in valuing Cavendish.

History and Competitive Conditions

Cavendish Seafood Distributors was founded 20 years ago by entrepreneur Lou Bertin after a successful career as a restaurateur. Cavendish, which was organized as a C corporation incorporated under the laws of the state of Minnesota and named after one of Lou's favorite seaside towns in Prince Edward Island, has one class of common stock with 1 million shares outstanding, 80% of which is owned by Bertin with the remaining 20% owned in equal amounts by two passive investors. Over the past five years, Cavendish has paid cash dividends, although it cut the payment in the past year in response to its lower income and internal cash needs.

In Bertin's prior career, he had achieved substantial success as a restaurateur, owning a chain of seafood restaurants in the north-central states. Bertin, who has an MBA and always wanted to run his own business but was tired of the demands of running a restaurant chain, recognized a need for better distribution of fresh wild-caught seafood to restaurants in his home state. Beginning with close friends who were involved with the seafood processing business in Maine and British Columbia, his company has expanded to distributing both wild-caught and farm-raised fish to restaurants and grocery stores in 14 central states and has been considering expansion into the three Canadian prairie provinces.

Much of Cavendish's growth has been financed with debt, due in part to Bertin's decision to pay dividends regardless of unfavorable tax consequences. The minority shareholders wanted annual cash returns for their willingness to invest in the risky start-up business, and Bertin needed the funds to pay off loans from an earlier unsuccessful business venture. Toward this goal, over the past five years, he has also paid himself an annual compensation package that totaled about $750,000 per year while the market rate for his services in the latest year was about $250,000. Bertin's uncle, John Paresseux, was paid $100,000 annually as vice president of marketing but seldom came to work, and Cavendish suffered as a result of his absence.

In the past two years, several factors were increasingly pressuring Bertin to consider a sale of the company. His family had a history of heart problems, and in recent annual physical exams his doctor has encouraged him to slow down. He knows that his energy level and enthusiasm for the day-to-day challenges of the company are declining, and Cavendish is facing substantial increased competition from larger food distributors while the overall industry is seeing a decline in profit margins. Thus far Bertin has been able to withstand these challenges through Cavendish's niche in wild-caught and specialty seafood, which enjoy considerably higher margins than typically seen with products offered by seafood distributors. Consolidation, better financial resources, and changes in technology through the use of the Internet to conduct business, however, led Bertin to conclude that the major distributors could improve market share and increase price pressures that would erode Cavendish's margins. He also recognizes that creating and building the business was much more enjoyable for him than the management and administrative tasks that he has assumed as the company has grown.

Potential Buyers

Bertin was recently approached by a private equity fund that targets companies in diverse industries based on growth potential. In initial discussions, he was discouraged by their attention to profits and apparent desire to grow the company rapidly over the ensuing five years and then either take it public or, more likely, sell to a major food distributor. Since they had little or no experience in seafood distribution, he saw little potential for a sale to them.

An investment banker approached Bertin on behalf of Bon Repas Distributors, a privately held company that had achieved major success in the distribution of seafood throughout Canada. Looking to expand into new markets, it was considering an investment either in Cavendish or in one or more other seafood distributors in the United States. Although discussions had not advanced to the point of an offering price, Bon Repas had disclosed that its offer would be primarily stock with payments over a period of years. From his ownership of Cavendish, Bertin recognized the lack of marketability of the stock of a privately held company, particularly a noncontrolling (minority) interest. With this in mind, he broke off discussions with Bon Repas.

Ultimately, Omni Food Distributors, a food distribution conglomerate traded on the New York Stock Exchange (NYSE) and ranked in the 30% to 50% midcap range by market capitalization of firms trading on the NYSE, approached Bertin. Omni also recognized the central North American market as ripe for more growth and had begun to expand further in this market. To more quickly enter this region, it saw Cavendish as a key acquisition.

It appeared likely that Omni could also improve Cavendish's bottom line, without changing Bertin's salary, by approximately $1 million annually for each of the first four years through a combination of integration of the operations and implementation of these improvements. This would probably take 18 months, although the company's goal for completion was within 12 months of the acquisition date.

After Omni's business development executives made the initial contact with Bertin, they turned negotiations over to their investment banking firm of Merrill Goldman. To negotiate effectively, Bertin retained an experienced team of legal, tax, and valuation advisors to determine the fair market value of Cavendish as a stand-alone business, its maximum value to Omni including synergistic benefits, and a strategy to succeed in the negotiations. Bertin's team developed the information shown in Exhibits 21.1 through 21.6, which led to the determination of the fair market value of Cavendish's equity on a stand-alone basis found in Exhibits 21.7 through 21.17, and its investment value to Omni inclusive of synergistic benefits shown in Exhibits 21.18 through 21.20.

General Economic Conditions

As the negotiations were taking place, the economy appeared to be ending a long period of sustained economic growth, with most major economic indicators signaling a downturn within a couple of years. Within the food distribution industry, rising fuel prices were eroding profits.

The economy grew 2.9% last year and is forecasted to increase next year by 2.1%. Forces identified to support moderate growth in the United States include low inflation, a slow but somewhat stabilized employment outlook, and relatively stable stock prices. American consumers indicate declining confidence, but there is an increased demand in quality and healthy food.

In summary, consumer spending is moderating while inflation and interest rates have held steady at relatively low levels. Economic and employment growth have slowed but continue to be healthy. These conditions suggest a stable, moderately growing economy.

Specific Industry Conditions[1]

Wholesalers, importers, brokers, and traders carry out the distribution of seafood in the United States. As intermediaries, their livelihood depends on their knowledge of sources of supply and demand. Their role is to move product efficiently from shipper/processor to retailers, restaurants, and food-service firms.

Over the past year, some of the factors impacting seafood distributors include rising diesel fuel costs, increased airport security, and school lunch programs. Diesel fuel costs have risen 15% over the past year, cutting into the margins of seafood distributors, which have found pricing pressures challenging because these cost increases cannot be passed down to their customers. A new security law requiring screenings of all cargo transported on passenger planes may delay the loading of freight onto planes, increasing the risk of spoilage. Finally, with the beginning of a U.S. Department of Agriculture program to purchase processed Alaskan pollock for federally funded school lunch programs, increasing demand resulting from inclusion in the program is expected to lower prices, thus improving the position of processed fish to compete with other food commodities.

With regard to M&A trends, seafood product companies, processors, and wholesalers are consolidating. Large companies are advancing vertical integration strategies and expanding abroad to better compete in the global seafood industry.

Food distributors are struggling to adapt to the changing industry dynamics, forcing them to reexamine business strategies, budgets, and profit-planning processes. Consumer buying patterns and trends have changed, altering how food distributors plot their future. To keep up with retail customer demands, food distributors are redefining and transforming order, warehousing, and logistics management systems. Just-in-time delivery, time-to-market system integration, supply chain collaboration, demand forecasting, and mobile Internet access are being implemented to move merchandise efficiently and cost effectively. Distributors with truck fleets use computerized routing systems and onboard computer systems to monitor driver performance.

---

[1] Industry information sourced from First Research and IBISWorld.

Growth

Bertin expects that Cavendish, if it continues as an independent company, will achieve a 4% revenue growth rate inclusive of inflation. Given the industry conditions, this is consistent with the industry forecasts for the near to intermediate term. This rate is modest in comparison to Cavendish's 15% compound growth over the past five years. (For the sake of brevity, the case stipulates the rate of growth and certain other industry and competitive factors without providing the typical research and analysis that these drivers should require.)

Computation of the Stand-Alone Fair Market Value

Exhibits 21.1 through 21.6 present Cavendish's historic performance as well as industry average financial ratios. The adjustments to normalize Cavendish's net income to invested capital are described in the next sections.

EXHIBIT 21.1 Cavendish Seafood Distributors: Statements of Income and Retained Earnings – Five Most Recent Historical Years

($000s)	Historic -4 Year	Historic -3 Year	Historic -2 Year	Historic -1 Year	Current Year
Net Sales	$42,900	$49,300	$56,700	$65,200	$75,200
Cost of Sales	30,400	34,000	38,100	43,800	50,700
Gross Margin	12,500	15,300	18,600	21,400	24,500
Operating Expenses	5,600	7,800	10,200	12,900	16,200
Net Operating Income	6,900	7,500	8,400	8,500	8,300
Net Miscellaneous Income (Expense)	250	200	200	200	200
Gain on Land Sale	0	0	0	1,500	0
EBITDA	7,150	7,700	8,600	10,200	8,500
Depreciation Expense	900	1,100	1,400	1,400	1,600
EBIT	6,250	6,600	7,200	8,800	6,900
Interest Expense	2,000	2,100	2,100	2,100	2,300
Pretax Income	4,250	4,500	5,100	6,700	4,600
Taxes	1,500	1,600	1,800	2,350	1,600
Net Income	$2,750	$2,900	$3,300	$4,350	$3,000
Retained Earnings:					
R/E-Beginning Balance	$1,650	$3,900	$6,200	$8,500	$11,200
Less: Dividends	500	600	1,000	1,650	900
R/E-Ending Balance	$3,900	$6,200	$8,500	$11,200	$13,300

EXHIBIT 21.2 Cavendish Seafood Distributors: Income Statement, Five Most Recent Historical Years – Common Size Basis

	Historic -4 Year	Historic -3 Year	Historic -2 Year	Historic -1 Year	Current Year
Net Sales	100.0%	100.0%	100.0%	100.0%	100.0%
Cost of Sales	70.9%	69.0%	67.2%	67.2%	67.4%
Gross Margin	29.1%	31.0%	32.8%	32.8%	32.6%
Operating Expenses	13.1%	15.8%	18.0%	19.8%	21.5%
Net Operating Income	16.1%	15.2%	14.8%	13.0%	11.0%
Net Miscellaneous Income (Expense)	0.6%	0.4%	0.4%	0.3%	0.3%
Gain on Land Sale	0.0%	0.0%	0.0%	2.3%	0.0%
EBITDA	16.7%	15.6%	15.2%	15.6%	11.3%
Depreciation Expense	2.1%	2.2%	2.5%	2.1%	2.1%
EBIT	14.6%	13.4%	12.7%	13.5%	9.2%
Interest Expense	4.7%	4.3%	3.7%	3.2%	3.1%
Pretax Income	9.9%	9.1%	9.0%	10.3%	6.1%
Taxes	3.5%	3.2%	3.2%	3.6%	2.1%
Net Income	6.4%	5.9%	5.8%	6.7%	4.0%

EXHIBIT 21.3 Cavendish Seafood Distributors: Balance Sheet – As of the End of the Last Five Years

($000s)	Historic -4 Year	Historic -3 Year	Historic -2 Year	Historic -1 Year	Current Year
Assets					
Current Assets:					
Cash and Equivalents	2,250	2,500	2,850	2,100	1,650
Trade Receivable	12,400	13,100	13,900	14,950	16,300
Inventory	3,200	3,400	4,700	6,000	7,650
Total Current Assets	17,850	19,000	21,450	23,050	25,600
Property, Plant, Equip (net)	10,600	13,150	13,750	14,600	16,600
Other Assets (non-operating)	1,500	1,400	1,400	1,700	1,400
Total Assets	29,950	33,550	36,600	39,350	43,600
Liabilities					
Current Liabilities:					
Accounts Payable	7,800	7,500	8,150	8,500	9,100
Accrued Expenses	3,600	3,200	3,400	3,200	3,200
Current Portion L/T Debt	4,500	4,750	4,800	5,200	5,600
Total Current Liabilities	15,900	15,450	16,350	16,900	17,900
Long-Term Debt	8,450	10,200	10,050	9,550	10,700
Total Liabilities	24,350	25,650	26,400	26,450	28,600
Equity					
Common Stock	1,700	1,700	1,700	1,700	1,700
Retained Earnings	3,900	6,200	8,500	11,200	13,300
Shareholders' Equity	5,600	7,900	10,200	12,900	15,000
Total Liabilities & Equity	29,950	33,550	36,600	39,350	43,600

EXHIBIT 21.4 Cavendish Seafood Distributors: Balance Sheet, As of the End of the Last Five Years – Common Size Basis

	Historic -4 Year	Historic -3 Year	Historic -2 Year	Historic -1 Year	Current Year
Assets					
Current Assets:					
Cash and Equivalents	7.5%	7.5%	7.8%	5.3%	3.8%
Trade Receivable	41.4%	39.0%	38.0%	38.0%	37.4%
Inventory	10.7%	10.1%	12.8%	15.2%	17.5%
Total Current Assets	59.6%	56.6%	58.6%	58.6%	58.7%
Property, Plant, Equip (net)	35.4%	39.2%	37.6%	37.1%	38.1%
Other Assets (non-operating)	5.0%	4.2%	3.8%	4.3%	3.2%
Total Assets	100.0%	100.0%	100.0%	100.0%	100.0%
Liabilities					
Current Liabilities:					
Accounts Payable	26.0%	22.4%	22.3%	21.6%	20.9%
Accrued Expenses	12.0%	9.5%	9.3%	8.1%	7.3%
Current Portion L/T Debt	15.0%	14.2%	13.1%	13.2%	12.8%
Total Current Liabilities	53.1%	46.1%	44.7%	42.9%	41.1%
Long-Term Debt	28.2%	30.4%	27.5%	24.3%	24.5%
Total Liabilities	81.3%	76.5%	72.1%	67.2%	65.6%
Equity	0.0%	0.0%	0.0%	0.0%	0.0%
Common Stock	5.7%	5.1%	4.6%	4.3%	3.9%
Retained Earnings	13.0%	18.5%	23.2%	28.5%	30.5%
Shareholders' Equity	18.7%	23.5%	27.9%	32.8%	34.4%
Total Liabilities & Equity	100.0%	100.0%	100.0%	100.0%	100.0%

EXHIBIT 21.5 Cavendish Seafood Distributors: Statement of Cash Flows – Four Most Recent Historical Years

($000s)	Historic -3 Year	Historic -2 Year	Historic -1 Year	Current Year
Cash Flows from Operating Activities:				
Net Income (Loss)	2,900	3,300	4,350	3,000
Non-cash Expenses, Revenues, Losses and Gains Included in Income:				
Depreciation and Amortization	1,100	1,400	1,400	1,600
Gain on Land Sale	0	0	−1,500	0
(Increase) Decrease in Receivables	−700	−800	−1,050	−1,350
(Increase) Decrease in Inventories	−200	−1,300	−1,300	−1,650
(Increase) Decrease in Accounts Payable	−300	650	350	600
(Increase) Decrease in Accrued Expenses	−400	200	−200	0
Net Cash Flows from Operating Activities	2,400	3,450	2,050	2,200

(*Continued*)

EXHIBIT 21.5 (*Continued*)

($000s)	Historic -3 Year	Historic -2 Year	Historic -1 Year	Current Year
Cash Flows from Investing Activities:				
Purchase of Fixed Assets	−3,650	−2,000	−2,550	−3,600
Disposal of Fixed Assets	0	0	1,800	0
(Increase) Decrease in Other Assets	100	0	−300	300
Net Cash Flows from Investing Activities	−3,550	−2,000	−1,050	−3,300
Cash Flows from Financing Activities:				
Dividends	−600	−1,000	−1,650	−900
Increase (Decrease) in Long-Term Debt	2,000	−100	−100	1,550
Net Cash Flows from Financing Activities	1,400	−1,100	−1,750	650
Net Cash Flow Increase (Decrease)	250	350	−750	−450
Beginning of the Year Cash	2,250	2,500	2,850	2,100
End of the Year Cash	2,500	2,850	2,100	1,650

EXHIBIT 21.6 Cavendish Seafood Distributors: Financial Ratio Summary of Historical Financial Statements

	Industry Norm[a]	Historic -4 Year	Historic -3 Year	Historic -2 Year	Historic -1 Year	Current Year
Current Ratio	1.3	1.1	1.2	1.3	1.4	1.4
Quick Ratio	0.9	0.9	1.0	1.0	1.0	1.0
Sales/Receivables	6.4	3.5	3.8	4.1	4.4	4.6
Cost of Sales/Inventory	10.9	9.5	10.0	8.1	7.3	6.6
Cost of Sales/Accounts Payable	8.0	3.9	4.5	4.7	5.2	5.6
Total Debt/Total Capital	0.42	0.81	0.76	0.72	0.67	0.66
EBIT/Interest Expense	3.9	3.1	3.1	3.4	4.2	3.0
Pretax Income/Total Assets	0.12	0.14	0.13	0.14	0.17	0.11
Pretax Income/Total Equity	0.64	0.76	0.57	0.50	0.52	0.31
Sales/Net Fixed Assets	11.2	4.0	3.7	4.1	4.5	4.5
Sales/Total Assets	2.1	1.4	1.5	1.5	1.7	1.7
Sales to Working Capital	17.5	22.0	13.9	11.1	10.6	9.8

[a]The industry norm is based on the average of the five guideline public companies presented in this case for the latest fiscal year.

A qualitative assessment of Cavendish's performance as compared to that of the industry is presented in Exhibit 21.14.

Normalization Adjustment Issues

Exhibit 21.7 presents the normalization adjustments to Cavendish's income statement to yield adjusted pretax income to invested capital, also known as earnings before interest and taxes (EBIT).

EXHIBIT 21.7 Normalized Net Income for the Past Five Years: Invested Capital Basis

($000s)	Historic -4 Year	Historic -3 Year	Historic -2 Year	Historic -1 Year	Current Year
Pretax Income to Invested Capital (aka EBIT)[a]	6,250	6,600	7,200	8,800	6,900
Adjustments[b]					
Excess Officer's Compensation	600	750	800	750	750
Gain on Sale of Land	0	0	0	−1,500	0
Total Adjustments	600	750	800	−750	750
Adjusted Pretax Income to Invested Capital[a] (aka adjusted EBIT)	6,850	7,350	8,000	8,050	7,650
Normalized Pretax Income to Invested Capital[c]					8,000
Income Taxes: Federal and State, estimated at 27%[d]					2,160
Normalized Net Income Applicable to Invested Capital					5,840

[a]Invested capital reflects income before the subtraction of interest expense. As such, it is the return to debt and equity capital providers.

[b]Adjustments: The support and research related to the normalization adjustments are described in the narrative portion of the case.

[c]This amount was judgmentally selected as representative of Cavendish's long-term operating performance as of the end of the Current Year. Alternatively, the adjusted pre-tax income to invested capital of $7,650,000 in the Current Year could be increased by the anticipated long-term growth rate of 4%, which would have generated approximately the same amount.

[d]This tax rate was supplied by Cavendish's accounting firm, reflecting expected corporate federal (21% under the 2017 Tax Act) and state (7.5%) taxes. Because this computation employs the invested capital model, which is pre-debt, it does not consider the tax deductibility of interest expense. An alternative is to reduce the income tax by 27% of interest expense.

LOU BERTIN'S COMPENSATION Lou Bertin's compensation package exceeds the market rate. Cavendish's human resources expert's research indicated that the total cost of market-rate compensation paid to an arm's-length chief executive officer of a food distribution company the size of Cavendish over the past five years would have provided these savings, inclusive of payroll-related burdens:

Year	Savings
1	$600,000
2	$750,000
3	$800,000
4	$750,000
5	$750,000

JOHN PARESSEUX'S COMPENSATION Despite John Paresseux's weak performance resulting from his frequent absences, this position is required for the company's success, and the salary is appropriate for a properly qualified vice president of marketing. Thus, no adjustment is required.

MARKET RESEARCH In three of the past five years, Cavendish has spent between $200,000 and $300,000 for market research to allow the company to better understand its customer base. While some would argue that this is a nonrecurring expense that should be added back to determine normalized income, it was concluded that these costs enable the company to offer the attractive products that make it uniquely appealing to its customers. This adjustment is a judgment call and is considered to be a recurring cost because it is necessary for the company to remain competitive in the long term.

GAIN ON SALE OF LAND The company sold land in the prior year for $1.8 million that generated a gain of $1.5 million. Since this is not part of the company's ongoing income, it is subtracted as a normalization adjustment.

OTHER ASSETS Other assets include vacant land adjacent to the company and a vacation home in St. Maarten used by Bertin exclusively for personal purposes. These assets do not generate income or expenses, so no adjustment to the income statement is required. Their market value of $1.4 million can be added to the operating value to yield Cavendish's total equity value, as will be reflected in Exhibit 21.17.

Risk and Value Drivers

The factors that should influence the development of the discount and capitalization rates appropriate to Cavendish's stand-alone fair market value are described in the next sections. See Exhibits 21.8 and 21.9.

EXHIBIT 21.8 Rates Applicable to Net Income to Equity (as of the Valuation Date)

Factor	Component	Increment	Rate
	Long-Term Treasury Bond Yield[a]		3.0%
+	Equity Risk Premium $(R_m - R_f)$[b]		6.0%
=	Average Market Return for Large-Cap Stock		9.0%
+	Risk Premium for Size[c]		5.6%
=	Average Market Return Adjusted to 10th Decile Size Firm		14.6%
	Specific-Company Risk Premium:		
+	Industry Risk (larger, stronger competitors)	4.0%	
+	Financial Risk (heavy debt)	4.0%	
+	Management Risk (thin management and no succession plan)	3.0%	
+	Customer Base (strong loyalty)	−1.0%	10.0%
=	Rate of Return for Net Cash Flow to Equity[d]		24.6%
+	Convert to a Rate of Return to Net Income[e]		3.4%
=	Rate of Return for Net Income to Equity		28.0%
−	Long-Term Sustainable Growth Rate[f]		−4.0%
=	Capitalization Rate for Net Income to Equity		24.0%

[a]See explanation of the Build-up Rate in Chapter 8. This represents the yield on the 20-year U.S. Treasury Bond.

[b]The Equity Risk Premium is applied to recognize the additional risk associated with investing in large-cap publicly traded common stock (equities) instead of the risk-free 20-year U.S. Treasury Bond.

[c]The Risk Premium for Size is to recognize the additional risk associated with a company the size of the tenth decile (i.e. smallest 10%) on the New York Stock Exchange and other major markets.

[d]This is a rate of return, or discount rate, directly applicable to equity net cash flow as it is based on the return to equity investors, net of income tax to their corporation.

[e]The conversion from a rate directly applicable to net cash flow to a net income rate is made by applying the appropriate ratio of the company's net income to its cash flow on a pro forma basis.

[f]Long-term sustainable growth rate was provided in the assumptions to this case.

Note: The rate developed above is appropriate to the valuation assignment in this case. This exhibit is intended to demonstrate a process for the development of this rate, and the amounts shown are for illustration purposes only. The rate appropriate to a given valuation must consider the risks, economic and industry factors, the effective date, the size of the interest being valued, and the intended use of the appraisal.

EXHIBIT 21.9 Weighted Average Cost of Capital (WACC) and Capitalization Rate Applicable to Net Income Available to Invested Capital

Applicable Rates:			
Rate of Return applicable to Net Income (Exhibit 21.8)[a]			28.0%
Cost of Debt			6.0%
Tax Bracket			27.0%

Capital Structure (market values):[b]			
Debt			39.4%
Equity			60.6%

Computation of WACC and Conversion to Capitalization Rate			
Computation	*Net Rate*	*Ratio*	*Contribution to WACC*
Debt @ borrowing rate $(1 - t)^c$	4.4%	39.4%	1.73%
Equity Rate of Return	28.0%	60.6%	16.97%
WACC Rate of Return for Net Income to Invested Capital			19.00%
Less: Long-Term Sustainable Growth[d]			−4.00%
Capitalization Rate for Net Income to Invested Capital[e]			15.00%

[a]The rate of return applicable to net income from Exhibit 21.8 is the equity discount rate of 28%. The computation of the equity cap rate of 24% is shown in Exhibit 21.8, but is not used in this computation of WACC.

[b]The debt–equity mix is provided on a market value basis. This was achieved by employing the following formula, which is explained in Chapter 9: $E_{fmv} = (NCF_{IC} - (D (C_D - g)))/ C_E - g)$ $25,037 = [\$6,074 - (\$16,300 * (4.4\% - 4\%))] / (28\% - 4\%)$. Total invested capital: $25,037 + \$16,300 = \$41,337$ -or- 60.6% + 39.4% = 100%. The NCF_{IC} of $6,074 is derived in Exhibit 21.10 and the $16,300 ($10,700 + $5,600) is sourced from the balance sheet for the Current Year in Exhibit 21.3. In this computation, the return is net income to invested capital, rather than NCF_{IC}. To adjust for this difference, the C_E is adjusted from the 24.6% rate for net cash flow derived in Exhibit 21.8 to the 28% rate for net income in that exhibit.

[c]The borrowing rate of 6% is reduced to a 4.4% cost of debt capital as the net cost of debt is reduced by the 27% tax subsidy provided by the deductibility of interest expense.

[d]The long-term sustainable growth rate was provided in this case's narrative. It is subtracted from the discount rate to convert it to a capitalization rate.

[e]The WACC capitalization rate is applicable to net income available to invested capital (i.e. the return to equity and debt on an income basis). This amount would be equal to the net income to equity if Cavendish were debt free. Cavendish's actual interest-bearing debt will then be subtracted from invested capital value to yield equity value.

Economic Conditions

Economic and employment growth have slowed but continue to be healthy.

Industry and Competitive Considerations

Industry sales are dominated by large food distributors, some of which specialize in seafood, that have economies of scale in purchasing and marketing and benefit from the advantages of vertical integration. Independents face higher operating costs but can compete effectively by specializing in niche markets.

Financial Condition and Access to Capital

The company carries substantial debt and lacks capital for technology upgrades needed for some of its expansion plans.

Management

Lou Bertin, who is approaching the typical retirement age, is the only Cavendish employee capable of providing executive management. Marketing management is lacking, and senior management is generally thin.

Customer Base

Cavendish possesses a highly loyal customer base.

Single-Period Capitalization Computation of Stand-Alone Fair Market Value

Using the normalized net income to invested capital of $5,840,000, computed in Exhibit 21.10, and the weighted average cost of capital (WACC) and capitalization rate of 15% developed in Exhibit 21.9, the stand-alone fair market value of 100% of the equity of Cavendish on a control basis is computed to be $24,200,000, with invested capital totaling $40,500,000. This computation uses the single-period capitalization method because Cavendish's returns over the past five years have been sufficiently stable to derive a reliable estimate of the company's performance by using a return for one period. Use of this method is also supported by the choice of a long-term growth rate of 4%, which appears to be appropriate for Cavendish given economic, industry, and company conditions.

The invested capital model, which is usually employed in valuations for M&A, is used with debt and equity weightings adjusted to market values rather than book values. In this case, net income, rather than net cash flow, is chosen as the return to demonstrate its use, although net cash flow is generally preferred.

EXHIBIT 21.10 Single-Period Capitalization Method – Invested Capital Basis Converted to Equity

	Indicated Value (in thousands)
Normalized Historical Net Income to Invested Capital (Exhibit 21.7)	$5,840
Apply Long-Term Sustainable Growth to Historical Net Income (4%)	× 1.04
Normalized Forecasted Net Income to Invested Capital	$6,074
WACC Cap Rate to Net Income to Invested Capital (Exhibit 21.9)	15.00%
Indicated Value of Invested Capital (rounded)	$40,500
Less: Interest-Bearing Debt	$16,300
Stand-Alone Fair Market Value of Equity	$24,200

The rates of return have been adjusted from net cash flow to net income to prevent distortions that occur when rates and returns are mismatched.

The invested capital value of $40,500,000 derived in Exhibit 21.10 is divided by the normalized EBIT and earnings before interest, taxes, depreciation, and amortization (EBITDA) amounts for the Current Year, to yield the resulting implied multiples of EBIT and EBITDA shown in Exhibit 21.11.

Guideline Public Company Computation of Stand-Alone Fair Market Value

Using three normalized returns to invested capital for the Current Year and operating multiples, the guideline public company (GPC) method develops the stand-alone fair market value of 100% of the invested capital and equity of Cavendish. The GPC method is used because the search identified a sufficient number of publicly traded companies in the food distribution industry that were similar enough to Cavendish to determine an indication of value

EXHIBIT 21.11 Stand-Alone Fair Market Value: Implied Invested Capital Multiple of Adjusted EBIT/EBITDA

	Current Year	Implied EBIT Multiple	EBITDA Multiple
Normalized EBIT for the Current Year (Exhibit 21.7)	$7,650	5.29	
Normalized EBITDA for the Current Year	$9,250		4.38

based on the price paid for alternative investments in the public markets. Application of this method was described in Chapter 10.

The GPC method employs the invested capital model where returns to debt and equity include EBIT, EBITDA, and revenues. Since the returns are to the sum of debt and equity, these returns are compared to the market value of invested capital (MVIC), rather than the equity price per share. Based on research and analysis of the guideline companies, considering their performance and strategic strengths and weaknesses, along with industry conditions and trends, they were compared to Cavendish based on various operational performance measures. These ratios were computed for each of the guideline companies, including the mean and median for each ratio:

> MVIC to EBIT
> MVIC to EBITDA
> MVIC to Revenues

To begin the search for guideline companies, we selected the following criteria:

Guideline Public Companies

> *Industry.* SIC 5146: Seafood distributors
> *Size.* Annual sales between $7.5 million and $750 million (within a factor
>   of 10 times the size of Cavendish)
> *Type.* Minority interest transactions
> *Status.* Profitable companies, financially solvent and reasonably lever-
>   aged, that are freely and actively traded
> *Growth.* Companies whose recent historical growth rates and forecasted
>   growth rates are reasonably similar
> *Domicile.* U.S. corporations

The guideline companies[2] that were selected are:

- *Astakia Shellfish.* The largest distributor of lobsters, crabs, and other shellfish serving all of North America.
- *Cape Cod Foods.* A distributor of seafood, potatoes, apples, and cranberry products throughout the Northeast and Mid-Atlantic states.
- *Le Poisson Distributors.* A Canadian distributor of seafood serving all of eastern and central Canada as well as the northeastern and Mid-Atlantic regions of the United States.

---

[2] These are all fictional companies. As seen in Chapter 10, most publicly traded food distributors are considerably larger than Cavendish and, in practice, would at best serve as a check to value. This case illustrates a way the guideline public company method might be applied if used as an indication of value.

- *Newport Fish*. Distributor and retailer of seafood products throughout the western United States and Canada, with recent expansion to the Far East.
- *Psaria Distributors*. Distributor of seafood throughout North and South America and Europe.

From available public sources, extensive information about the five guideline public companies was gathered, including their annual reports, U.S. Securities and Exchange Commission's Forms 10-K and 10-Q, and information from various stock reporting services and industry analysts' reports. The operating performance, financial position, and cash flow of each company were analyzed. Their competitive advantages and disadvantages were considered in light of industry and economic conditions. Exhibit 21.12 summarizes each company's operating performance data.

From the data in Exhibit 21.12, operating multiples that compare the market value of invested capital to EBIT, EBITDA, and revenue are computed and presented in Exhibit 21.13, along with the resulting mean and median

EXHIBIT 21.12 Guideline Company Revenues and Operating Performance per Share

	Latest Fiscal Year	Latest Fiscal Year Revenues	MVIC/ Share	EBIT/ Share	EBITDA/ Share	Revenue/ Share
Astakia Shellfish	12/31/20x5	$144,496,000	$19.85	$1.12	$1.32	$15.27
Cape Cod Foods	9/30/20x5	$66,851,000	$5.32	$1.62	$2.83	$17.73
Le Poisson	6/30/20x5	$397,165,000	$61.05	$9.63	$11.70	$88.48
Newport Fish	6/30/20x5	$361,822,000	$13.69	$1.58	$1.93	$11.80
Psaria Distributors	12/31/20x5	$462,501,000	$28.03	$4.92	$5.73	$63.70

EXHIBIT 21.13 Guideline Company Operating Multiples

	MVIC/EBIT	MVIC/EBITDA	MVIC/Revenue
Astakia Shellfish	17.72	15.04	1.30
Cape Cod Foods	3.28	1.88	0.30
Le Poisson	6.34	5.22	0.69
Newport Fish	8.66	7.09	1.16
Psaria Distributors	5.70	4.89	0.44
Mean	8.34	6.82	0.78
Median	6.34	5.22	0.69

multiples of each operating measure. These multiples reflect investor consensus of the value of these five companies in this industry and present a foundation for selection of appropriate multiples for Cavendish based on these alternative investment choices.

Cavendish's strategic position and operating performance is compared to the guideline companies, considering the various risk factors previously discussed, including Cavendish's limited management, heavy debt, strong customer loyalty, and larger, stronger competitors. Comparison of

EXHIBIT 21.14 Comparison of Cavendish with Guideline Companies

	Discussion	Comparison to the Guideline Companies
Size	The median revenues for the five guideline companies is 5 times bigger than that for Cavendish. Cavendish is smaller than four of the five guideline companies.	Weaker
Liquidity	Cavendish's cash position has declined while its current liabilities have increased in the last year. However, Cavendish's current ratio and quick ratio have been relatively consistent and are both just above the industry average shown in Exhibit 21.6.	Average
Asset Management	Cavendish's total assets, accounts receivable, inventory, and fixed assets are all carried at substantially higher levels relative to sales as compared to any of the guideline public companies. This reflects substantial inefficiency in the utilization of all of these assets and sharply reduces the cash flow to capital providers.	Much weaker
Financial Leverage	Cavendish's debt, though decreasing steadily over the last five years as a percentage of total assets, is higher than four of the five guideline companies.	Weaker
Profitability	Cavendish's stronger profit margins compensate somewhat for the company's weaker asset utilization to generate profits similar to the guideline companies.	Average
Growth	Cavendish's 15% annual compound growth rate over the last five years is less than three of the five guideline companies, but its projected long-term growth is similar to that of the guideline companies and the industry.	Average

EXHIBIT 21.15 Calculation of Invested Capital Value of Cavendish Based on the Guideline Public Company Method

Procedure	Normalized Operating Results for the Current Year	×	Value Multiple	=	Estimated Invested Capital Value
MVIC/EBIT	7,650	×	5.25	=	40,163
MVIC/EBITDA	9,250	×	4.25	=	39,313
MVIC/Revenue	75,200	×	0.50	=	37,600

Cavendish with the guidelines on specific financial measures is presented in Exhibit 21.14.

Based on this comparison of Cavendish with the guideline public companies, the value multiples shown in Exhibit 21.15 were selected as appropriate for Cavendish when compared to the guideline companies, considering its performance and risk profile.

Estimate of Equity Value of Guideline Company Method

The market value of the company's long-term debt is subtracted in Exhibit 21.16 from the previously determined value of invested capital, to obtain an equity value, which for the market approach is rounded to $23 million.

Transaction Multiple Method Computation of Stand-Alone Fair Market Value

In the search for market data, one strategic acquisition was identified that was considered for comparative purposes. In this transaction, which occurred in the first quarter of the Current Year, Barber Food Distributors

EXHIBIT 21.16 Calculation of Equity Value of Cavendish Based on the Guideline Company Approach

Procedure	Estimated Invested Capital Value	−	Market Value of Long-Term Debt	=	Estimated Equity Value
MVIC/EBIT	40,163	−	16,300	=	23,863
MVIC/EBITDA	39,313	−	16,300	=	23,013
MVIC/Revenue	37,600	−	16,300	=	21,300
Concluded Value					23,000

purchased Scituate Poultry and Beef, which was the largest meat distributor in the country. Scituate was traded on the NASDAQ stock exchange and, in that transaction, Barber paid a 72% premium over Scituate's preacquisition stock price. This transaction, which was paid for in Barber's stock, reflected a multiple of nine times Scituate's forecasted EBITDA. Over the past 10 years, Barber has made numerous such acquisitions of food distributors, which is part of a long-term trend of consolidation in the food distribution industry. Further analysis of this transaction and others made by Barber led to the conclusion that the price paid and the resulting multiples from this transaction reflect synergies unique to Barber and do not provide a reliable basis for determination of Cavendish's fair market value. In general, it is inappropriate to attempt to establish the market based on the results of a single transaction. At best, it serves as a check to value, as discussed in Chapter 13. Procedurally, much of what was presented in Exhibits 21.12 through 21.16 would be applicable to the transaction multiple method. The differences in application between the two methods (e.g. addressing differences in deal structure when applying the transaction multiple method, a factor not applicable when applying the GPC method) were discussed in Chapter 10.

Rejection of the Adjusted Book Value Method

To consider the fair market value on a stand-alone basis of Cavendish from the perspective of the value of the assets owned by the company, an adjusted book value computation could be performed. This method, which assumes value is derived from a hypothetical sale of the specific tangible and intangible assets of the company, does not specifically recognize general intangible value that may exist as a result of the company's technology, customer base, reputation, and general goodwill factors. While general goodwill value can be computed through a computation known as the *excess earnings method*, this is typically not applicable to valuations for M&A purposes. This method is usually applied in the valuation of asset-intensive businesses or professional practices, so it will not be used to appraise Cavendish.

Summary and Conclusion of Stand-Alone Fair Market Value

The results of the valuation procedures employed to compute the fair market value of Cavendish's equity are summarized in Exhibit 21.17. After employing the various reconciliation methodologies explained in Chapter 13, the fair market value of equity is determined to be $23.5 million, including Cavendish's nonoperating assets.

EXHIBIT 21.17 Reconciliation of Indicated Stand-Alone Values and Application of Discounts/Premiums Appropriate to the Final Opinion of the Fair Market Value of Cavendish's Equity

Valuation Method	Interest Being Valued	Indicate by Method (Preadjustments)		Adjustments for Differences in Degree of		Adjusted		Weight	Weighted Component Value
		Value	Basis	Control[a]	Marketability[b]	Value	Basis		
Capitalization of Net Income to Invested Capital	100%	$24,200,000	As if freely traded	0%	7%	$22,506,000	Control marketable	60%	$13,503,600
Guideline Public Company	100%	$23,000,000	As if freely traded	0%	7%	$21,390,000	Control marketable	40%	$8,556,000
Fair Market Value of a 100% Closely Held Equity Interest on an Operating Control, Marketable Basis									$22,100,000
Plus: Non-operating Assets									$1,400,000
Fair Market Value of a 100% Closely Held Equity Interest on a Control, Marketable Basis									$23,500,000
Divided by Number of Issued and Outstanding Shares									1,000,000
Per-Share Fair Market Value of a Closely Held Share on a Control, Marketable Basis									$23.50

[a]A control premium is not considered applicable because control-based adjustments have been made to Cavendish's cash flows.
[b]The discount for lack of marketability of 7% reflects an adjustment for the time expected to sell Cavendish given the industry and the market for similar companies. However, it is important to note that there is a prevailing school of thought that no DLOM is applicable when valuing a 100% interest.

419

Computation of Investment Value

This computation of investment value will use the discounted cash flow (DCF) method and will recognize the synergies that can be achieved through this acquisition.

Risk and Value Drivers

To develop the discount rate for equity and the WACC to be used by Omni in its evaluation of Cavendish, adjustments as shown in Exhibit 21.18 have to be made to the rates developed previously in Exhibits 21.8 and 21.9 for Cavendish. Omni is a midcap-size publicly traded company, so the size adjustment for Omni is substantially less than for Cavendish. In addition, most of the specific-company risk factors for Cavendish can be eliminated when it operates as a division of Omni. In developing the company-specific risk premium for Omni, the additional risk created by the presence of competitors much larger than Cavendish is eliminated by Omni's size and market strength. However, because Omni does not possess substantial expertise or experience in the markets served by Cavendish, it imposed a 1% risk premium to reflect its movement into a less certain market. Omni's financial strength reduces the financial and management risk factors that exist with Cavendish as a stand-alone business.

While some doubt exists as to whether Cavendish's strong customer loyalty can be maintained when the company operates as a division of a conglomerate, Omni management is attracted to the very high untapped sales potential of this customer base. Cavendish lacks the expertise and resources to take full advantage of this sales potential, but Omni sees this as a substantial synergistic advantage that reduces the riskiness of this acquisition.

The discount rate to equity of 14.5% derived in Exhibit 21.18 is combined with Omni's lower cost of debt at 5%, based on the market value of Omni's debt and equity shown in Exhibit 21.19, to yield the WACC discount rate of 12% and the WACC cap rate of 8%.

It should be obvious from a comparison of Omni's WACC discount rate of 12% in Exhibit 21.19 versus Cavendish's of 19% from Exhibit 21.9 that Cavendish's operations are considered to be substantially less risky when located within the size and depth of Omni than when operating as a stand-alone company. Thus, the first factor contributing to the increase in Cavendish's investment value to Omni over its stand-alone fair market value is the reduction in risk.

EXHIBIT 21.18 Rates of Return (Discount Rate) Applicable to Net Cash Flow to Equity (as of the Valuation Date)

Symbol	Component	Increment	Rate
	Long-Term Treasury Bond Yield[a]		3.0%
+	Equity Risk Premium $(R_m - R_f)$[b]		6.0%
=	Average Market Return for Large-Cap Stock		9.0%
+	Risk Premium for Size[c]		1.0%
=	Average Market Return Adjustment for Size to Mid-Cap-Size Firm		10.0%
	Specific Company Risk Premium Adjustments:[d]		
+	Industry Risk	2.0%	
+	Financial Risk	1.5%	
+	Management Risk	0.0%	
+	Tax Uncertainty Risk[e]	1.5%	
+	Customer Base (sales potential)	−0.5%	4.5%
=	*Rate of Return for Net Cash Flow to Equity*[f]		14.5%

[a]See explanation of the Build-up Rate in Chapter 8. This represents the yield on the 20-year U.S. Treasury Bond.

[b]The Equity Risk Premium is applied to recognize the additional risk associated with investing in publicly traded common stock (equities) instead of the risk-free 20-year U.S. Treasury Bond.

[c]Empirical evidence indicates Omni's size will still justify a size premium of approximately 1%.

[d]Omni's lack of experience or expertise in this market raises its overall risk profile. Part of the synergy of Omni acquiring Cavendish is that the following risk drivers will be either eliminated or reduced: thin management and Cavendish's pre-merger heavy debt. Omni concludes that the sales potential of the underserved customer base reduces risk.

[e]Given a recent change in tax law, the Federal statutory corporate tax rate declined from 35% to 21%. Omni reflected this new 21% rate (plus applicable state tax) in its analysis to determine offering price. It has also determined that it should add a 1.5% premium to reflect uncertainty as to whether this lower rate is sustainable into perpetuity, the fact that market data used to determine inputs in its analysis were under a higher tax regime, and uncertainty in how the lower tax rates will influence M&A activity and related transaction prices.

[f]This is a rate of return or discount rate directly applicable to net cash flow as it is based on the return to investors, net of income tax to their corporations.

EXHIBIT 21.19 Weighted Average Cost of Capital (WACC) and Capitalization Rate Applicable to Net Cash Flow to Invested Capital

Applicable Rates:			
Rate of Return Applicable to Forecasted Net Cash Flow (Exhibit 21.18)[a]			14.5%
Omni's Cost of Debt			5.0%
Tax Bracket			27.0%

Capital Structure (based on Omni's Market Value):[b]			
Debt			20%
Equity			80%

Computation of WACC and Conversion to Capitalization Rate			
Component	*Net Rate*	*Ratio*[c]	*Contribution to WACC*
Debt @ Borrowing Rate $(1 - t)$[d]	3.7%	20%	0.73%
Equity	14.5%	80%	11.60%
WACC Discount Rate for Net Cash Flow to Invested Capital (rounded)			12.00%
Less: Long-Term Sustainable Growth[e]			−4.00%
Capitalization Rate for Net Cash Flow to Invested Capital[f]			8.00%

[a]The discount rate applicable to forecasted net cash flow is from Exhibit 21.18.
[b]Omni's debt–equity mix is derived from Omni's market values of debt and equity.
[c]The ratio is the equity–debt split (see note b).
[d]Omni borrows at Prime + 50 basis points. The cost of debt is calculated as 5% × $(1-27\%) = 3.7\%$.
[e]The long-term sustainable growth rate was provided in the case narrative.
[f]The WACC capitalization rate is applicable to net cash flow to invested capital; that is, the net cash flow inclusive of the returns to debt and equity.

Normalization, Synergy, and Net Cash Flow Adjustment Issues

Exhibit 21.20 shows the normalization adjustments and computation of net cash flow to invested capital forecasted for Omni's acquisition of Cavendish.

LOU BERTIN'S COMPENSATION Bertin's estimated above-market compensation of $750,000 annually will be adjusted in the same manner as it was in the valuation of the company on a stand-alone basis. Omni concluded that Cavendish's management was thin enough that market-level compensation for a chief executive officer was required. Omni further concluded that, if possible, Bertin should be retained to make use of his specialized

EXHIBIT 21.20 Investment Value of Cavendish on an Invested Capital Basis

Line Item	Year 1[a]	Year 2	Year 3	Year 4	Terminal Year
Normalized Pretax Income to Invested Capital of $7,650,000 (Exhibit 21.7) increasing at 4% annually - forecasted as a stand-alone business	7,956	8,274	8,605	8,949	9,307
Synergies					
Salary	750	750	750	750	750
Director's Fees	40	40	40	40	40
Severance Costs	−800	−800	0	0	0
Transaction Costs	−1,800	0	0	0	0
Revenue Enhancements	0	1,000	1,000	1,000	400
Economies in Cost of Sales	0	300	500	700	300
Operating Expense Reductions	200	400	400	400	100
Total Synergy Adjustments	−1,610	1,690	2,690	2,890	1,590
Adjusted Pretax Income to Invested Capital	6,346	9,964	11,295	11,839	10,897
Tax (27% Federal and state)	−1,713	−2,690	−3,050	−3,197	−2,942
Normalized Net Income to Invested Capital	4,633	7,274	8,246	8,643	7,955

(continued)

EXHIBIT 21.20 *(Continued)*

Line Item	Year 1[a]	Year 2	Year 3	Year 4	Terminal Year
Normalized Net Income to Invested Capital (Continued)	4,633	7,274	8,246	8,643	7,955
Adjustments for Net Cash Flow Applicable to Invested Capital					
Depreciation	1,800	2,400	2,000	2,000	2,000
Capital Expenditures	−6,500	−4,500	−4,000	−4,000	−2,080
Change in Working Capital	−100	−500	−550	−600	−624
Net Cash Flow to Invested Capital	−167	4,674	5,696	6,043	7,251
Capitalization Rate Applicable to Terminal Value (discount rate 12% less long-term sustainable growth rate of 4%) Divide by 8%					8.0%
Capitalized Value of the Terminal Year's Net Cash Flow to Invested Capital					90,639
11% Discount Factor with Midyear Convention (end of year in Terminal Year)	0.9449	0.8437	0.7533	0.6726	0.6355
Present Value of the Forecast Years and Capitalized Terminal Value	−158	3,943	4,290	4,064	57,601
Investment Value of Invested Capital (aggregate present values, rounded)					69,700
Less: Market Value of Interest-Bearing Debt					−16,300
Investment Value of Equity					53,400
Less: Market Value of Cavendish's Pre-merger Operating Equity (Exhibit 21.17)					−22,100
Implied Increase in Value of Cavendish's Post-merger Operating Equity (maximum investment value)					31,300

[a]The Valuation Date in this case is December 31, Current Year. This example presents a 4-year investment value benefit analysis forecast. Therefore, the first four years of the forecast period are Year 1 through Year 4.

knowledge and to assist in the transition process. In structuring this transaction, an option would be to continue to pay Bertin the above-market compensation, with this payment being a tax-deductible expense to the buyer and compensation taxed only once at the individual level to the seller. The purchase price could be reduced by this excess compensation, although the parties should consult tax and legal counsel regarding the legality of this payment arrangement.

JOHN PARESSEUX'S COMPENSATION　No adjustment is required for Paresseux's compensation. It is anticipated that he would not continue with the company after an acquisition, but a suitable replacement would be paid the same salary.

OTHER ASSETS　No adjustment to the company's return is required for other nonoperating assets, which Omni indicates it does not wish to purchase. Therefore, they are not considered part of the company's operating value, but would be added to it in computing total enterprise value of invested capital and equity.

DIRECTOR'S FEES　Cavendish incurred annual administrative costs of $40,000 related to its board of directors, which will be eliminated immediately upon sale of the company.

SEVERANCE COSTS　Omni management estimates that $800,000 in severance costs will be incurred in each of the first two years after the acquisition related to terminated employees.

TRANSACTION COSTS　Omni management estimates that legal, tax, and intermediary costs related to the acquisition of Cavendish will total $1.8 million and will be incurred at the time of the acquisition.

REVENUE ENHANCEMENTS　Taking advantage of Omni's online store that will expand into fresh, seasonal seafood as well as its diversified distribution system, Cavendish's revenue growth in Year 1 above the preacquisition forecasted annual 4% increase in pretax income to invested capital, shown on the first line of Exhibit 21.20, will raise this income $1 million per year for Years 2 through 4 and $400,000 per year thereafter. After this, Cavendish's growth should approximate the industry average annual rate of 4%.

ECONOMIES IN COST OF SALES Once capital expenditure improvements have been implemented in Year 1, cost of sales is expected to decline, as forecasted in Exhibit 21.20. Once again, in a real valuation situation, these forecasted changes would be supported by substantial detail and analysis.

OPERATING EXPENSE IMPROVEMENTS Omni will utilize more advanced on-truck refrigeration using cold-plate technology versus mechanical blower systems, thus saving on energy costs. In addition, Omni typically operates slightly above the industry norm of $500,000 in revenues per employee. With $75 million in revenues and 155 employees, Cavendish operates at $484,000 per employee. As such, Omni intends to cut at least five Cavendish employees. Combined, these changes will result in a reduction in Cavendish's operating expenses by at least $200,000 in Year 1, $400,000 in Years 2 through 4, and $100,000 thereafter.

DEPRECIATION EXPENSE Depreciation expense will follow historical trends with increases to reflect capital expenditures made in the initial years after the acquisition.

CAPITAL EXPENDITURES Omni employs the latest technology and possesses excess capacity that will be partially absorbed to meet Cavendish's initial needs. Because Lou Bertin has required, as part of the transaction, that production remain at the company's present location, substantial capital expenditures will be incurred in Years 1 and 2 to bring Cavendish's facilities to current standards.

WORKING CAPITAL Working capital is expected to increase as forecasted in Exhibit 21.20, which is consistent with Omni's current performance. Omni management did not expect to generate significant cash flows from liquidation of excess receivable and inventory balances held by Cavendish at the transaction date. For the long-term or terminal period, working capital is forecasted to grow at the anticipated long-term growth rate of 4%.

DISCOUNTED CASH FLOW METHOD COMPUTATION OF INVESTMENT VALUE TO OMNI
Using the forecasted net cash flow to invested capital that reflects the synergy and cash flow adjustments, the investment value of 100% of the invested capital and equity of Cavendish is computed to be $69,700,000 and $53,400,000, respectively, as shown in Exhibit 21.20. This is obviously considerably higher

than the fair market value of Cavendish, calculated in Exhibit 21.17, and is not what Omni would pay to acquire Cavendish, but rather what Cavendish would be worth to Omni.

Suggested Considerations to Case Conclusion

After studying this case, it is reasonable for readers to question their confidence in the reliability of the value estimate. Most readers, particularly those with more business valuation experience, may conclude that the authors underestimated or overestimated the importance of one or more competitive issues. And they may be right. Although this process is accurate when performed correctly, it is not exact.

Before any readers conclude that they are prepared to negotiate the sale or purchase of Cavendish based on the information presented, we encourage them to consider these questions:

- Are you confident that you understand the trends within the seafood distribution industry?
- What were your impressions as you toured Cavendish's facilities?
- What is your impression of employee competence and morale?
- How confident are you about Bertin's competence, motives, and future plans?
- How confident are you about your knowledge of Cavendish's "loyal customer base"?
- What about the identification and value of Cavendish's other intangible assets?
- How confident are you about the accuracy, probability of achievement, and estimated timing of each of the synergies presented?
- Thinking as the seller, how comfortable are you with Omni's intentions, and how confident are you in its ability to achieve the forecasted synergies?
- What is your assessment of how effective the integration of the two companies would be?
- Based on the facts and circumstances in this case, what are the pros and cons for structuring the transaction as an asset sale versus a stock sale and for payment in cash versus payment in stock?

These questions constitute more than inconvenient details. They are the critical qualitative variables that must be accurately quantified in the valuation process to generate a defendable indication of value and provide the basis for a sound purchase or sale decision. These are the issues that make business valuation complex. These are the issues that must be resolved within a reasonable level of accuracy for the sellers but, more important, the buyers to achieve success in a transaction. The valuation, of course, requires appropriate methodology and application. Ultimately, however, these qualitative issues must be engaged, analyzed, and quantified. You should not feel confident in your value estimate until you are certain you can provide the most informed possible answers to these questions.

The final step in the process, once buyers and sellers understand the relevant values for the company, is to make their decisions about price. That is, the buyer must decide what price and terms he or she is willing to offer for the target company to achieve strategic objectives and return on investment goals. This acquisition may be one of several the buyer is considering, and its level of risk and its fit within the buyer's overall plan may vary relative to the other choices, including simply to decline to make any acquisitions at this time. The buyer could also decide it is wise to pay well above fair market value to acquire this target, perhaps as a defensive step to prevent a competitor from entering this market, to gain market share, or to acquire a technology or customer relationship. These considerations emphasize how price is a choice, unlike value, which is a financial determination.

The seller must also decide what price and terms he or she is willing to accept to achieve financial and nonfinancial goals for investment in the company. As we have emphasized throughout this book, the sale decision for private company owners is typically complex, with financial choices being one of many factors to consider.

CHAPTER **22**

Merger and Acquisition Valuation Case Study – Professional Services Firm

In Chapter 21, we brought to life the theories and analyses discussed throughout this book by way of a case study involving the valuation of Cavendish Seafood Distribution, a fictional brick-and-mortar business. This chapter presents a comprehensive case that illustrates the application of many of this book's concepts as they apply to an increasingly growing sector of the economy, professional services firms (PSFs).

Characteristics

PSFs at their core produce intangible services as opposed to tangible end products. As such, their professional staff provide their knowledge and time to their client base, and are therefore the most important asset of these firms. The following is a list of examples of types of PSFs: accounting,[1] actuarial, advertising, appraisal, architecture,[2] brokerage, dental practices,[3] employment placement, engineering, investment banking, IT consultant, law firms,[4]

---

[1] See Robert F. Reilly and Robert P. Schweihs, *Valuing Accounting Practices* (New York: Wiley, 1997).
[2] See BVR, *What It's Worth: Architecture and Engineering Firm Value* (Portland, OR: Business Valuation Resources, LLC, 2015).
[3] See Stanley L. Pollock, *BVR's Guide to Valuing Dental Practices* (Portland, OR: Business Valuation Resources, LLC, 2011).
[4] See BVR, *What It's Worth: Law Firm Value* (Portland, OR: Business Valuation Resources, LLC, 2017).

management consulting, medical practices,[5] public relations, research, transaction advisory, and wealth management.

PSFs have the following characteristics:

- They derive revenues from personal services based on knowledge, either as a fee for service or on a contingency basis.
- They are based on relationships where business is generated by referral sources, word-of-mouth, expertise of key principals, and/or social media.
- Depending on the size of the firm and importance of key persons, owners may need to stay active for years after their company is sold and may be subject to noncompete agreements.
- Their work product is exempt from taxes in the United States. However, in most other countries, they are subject to a value-added tax (VAT), or sometimes, as in the case in Canada, referred to as a goods and services tax (GST) or harmonized sales tax (HST).
- When sold, the assets transferred to the buyer typically include equipment, furniture and fixtures, leasehold improvements, office and capital leases, supplies, identifiable intangibles, and goodwill. The seller usually keeps the cash and receivables, and pays off the debt and payables.
- There is an important distinction in goodwill between professional (individual/personal) goodwill and enterprise (practice) goodwill. Professional goodwill, which was introduced in Chapter 15, is based on an individual's reputation, knowledge, experience, training, and education. Enterprise goodwill is a company's reputation and ability to attract and retain business without dependence on an individual.

When assessing a PSF, there are a number of drivers that impact its value.[6] Exhibit 22.1 lists several value drivers and provides examples of situations that both contribute to and detract from value. In smaller firms, some of the drivers – management team, referral base, and client retention – may relate to professional goodwill, which can be difficult to measure and transfer in a merger and acquisition transaction. Despite the fact that only three of the 27 factors listed may be attributable to professional goodwill, these factors can have a significant impact on PSF value. If such factors are more prevalent, additional focus must be spent on how to minimize them in building PSF value.

---

[5] See Robert James Cimasi, *Healthcare Valuation: The Four Pillars of Healthcare Value* (Hoboken, NJ: Wiley, 2014).

[6] Keep in mind that the value we are referring to in this chapter is related to valuation for M&A. Fair market value or fair value referenced in a shareholder agreement in connection with shareholder purchases and redemptions are often lower and may include discounts for lack of marketability and/or lack of control.

EXHIBIT 22.1 Professional Services Firms' Value Drivers

Value Driver	Higher Value	Lower Value
Size	Larger firm.	Smaller firm.
Location	Urban and/or growing population.	Rural and/or declining population.
Life cycle	In the growth to mature stage.	In the late mature to decline stage.
Impact from economic cycles	An accounting firm providing tax and audit services needed despite economic conditions.	A transaction advisory firm or public relations firm that is negatively impacted by economic downturns.
Industries served	Diverse range of industries served.	Concentration of clients in one or a couple of industries impacted by economic cycles.
Services provided	Specialty knowledge (e.g. complex tax services, litigating attorneys, expert witness services, management consulting).	Commodity based (e.g. individual tax preparation, drafting of wills, 409A valuations).
Longevity	In business more than 10 years.	In business less than 5 years.
Historic growth	Proven track record of growth.	Sporadic or declining growth.
Growth potential	High and steady; in an industry serving a growing demographic.	Low or declining.
Operations	Profitable and scalable, with high realization, established procedures, best practices, and proven quality control processes.	Heavily dependent on experienced professional time, inconsistent procedures within office(s).
Management team	Several executives with a mix of technical and business development capabilities.	One or two people wearing multiple hats; older management team with weak succession plan; long working hours for key personnel; lifestyle business.
Owner work habits	Works fewer hours, delegates.	Works long hours.
Employee base	Committed and low turnover. Senior team with solid professional qualifications.	High turnover. Too top heavy or bottom heavy.
Labor supply	Strong pool of available and qualified professionals.	Market with few available professionals.

(continued)

EXHIBIT 22.1 (*Continued*)

Value Driver	Higher Value	Lower Value
Depth of personnel	Deep bench of experience.	Dependent on a key person for important segments of the business.
Referral base	Relationships dispersed among many on the management team.	Dependent on one or two key people. A firm generally reliant on referrals (i.e. because this typically implies reliance on personal goodwill).
Sources of new business	Multiple referral sources.	Few referral sources.
Recurring nature of business	"Stickiness" of client base (e.g. annual accounting attest and financial statement preparation, corporate law, ESOP valuation services, long-term public relations clients, wealth management clients).	Nonrecurring client services (e.g. litigation services, equipment appraisal).
Client characteristics	Larger firms; deeper pockets; not heavily regulated (e.g. a medical practice with a larger private pay base, an accounting or law firm with a heavy corporate base).	Smaller firms; low cash flow/profitability; subject to government reimbursement (i.e. a medical practice serving mostly Medicaid patients, an accounting or law firm with a heavy small business or individual client base).
Client concentration	Diverse client base.	One or two large clients comprising over 50% of the firm's revenues.
Client retention	Loyal and stable client base.	High level of turnover of client base.
Contractual agreements	Some or all clients tied to the subject company with contracts.	Few or no contracts in place.
Strategic relationships	Opportunities to cross-refer business to referral sources.	Unable to refer business.
Brand-name recognition	High recognition; stellar reputation; top ranking in its profession and in the industries it serves.	Not well-known or tainted reputation.

EXHIBIT 22.1 (*Continued*)

Value Driver	Higher Value	Lower Value
Cash flows	Profit margins are above industry averages; steady cash flows; recurring cash flows (e.g. established accounting firm with solid audit and tax client base).	Profit margins are below industry averages; volatile cash flows; non-recurring revenue base (e.g. law firm focusing on contingent-fee litigation cases).
Procedures	Documented procedures in place with a consistent practice of quality control.	Few or no documented procedures, inconsistent work product, poor quality control procedures.
Technological resources	State of the art; access to a high degree of information and other required technology.	Not keeping up with technological advances, including access to information.

Valuation Methods

The process of valuing PSFs is similar to valuing traditional closely held businesses such as Cavendish Seafood Distributors in the previous chapter. All three approaches to value must be considered. In most instances, because the PSF's expected future cash flows represent its primary determinant of value, the income approach is most often used to value these firms (see Chapters 7 through 9).

The market approach (Chapter 10) is often used as a determinant of value where there are a sufficient number of guideline transactions, such as with accounting firms or medical and dental practices, or where there have been past transactions in ownership interests of the firm itself. Otherwise, transaction data as well as rules of thumb[7] may serve as reasonableness tests to the value indicated by the income approach. When the market approach is applied, focus tends to be more on revenue multiples as opposed to earnings multiples, especially in the case of smaller or mid-sized PSFs with

---

[7] For example, a general rule of thumb for firms with a high degree of recurring clients, such as accounting firms, is that they trade at 1.0 times revenue or higher; while PSFs with a lower recurring client base, such as architecture firms or advertising agencies, tend to trade lower, and sometimes considerably lower, than 1.0 times revenue. When using such rules of thumb it is important to understand that in transactions, these amounts may be paid out over several years and may only be for revenue from recurring clients, meaning that the cash equivalent proceeds from a transaction can be materially lower than the rule of thumb.

compiled as opposed to audited financial statements. As a result, there is increased skepticism from potential buyers about the expenses represented on the target PSF's financial statements. Such buyers will therefore likely determine value in relation to the level of expected continuing revenues, and establish their own practices and expense structures in generating cash flow forecasts.[8]

The asset approach (Chapter 11) is rarely used as a determinant of value for PSFs given the dominance of human capital in such firms. However, one notable exception is with law firms that often do not transact for more than the adjusted book value of their net assets.[9] It is important to note in this instance that the adjusted book value may involve adding identifiable intangible assets that are not recorded on the firm's balance sheet, such as its assembled workforce, trade name, backlog, and recurring customer base.

Finally, an excess earnings method, which is a hybrid of the income and asset approaches, may be considered. In this method, excess earnings are determined by forecasting the normalized annual net income (after tax or pretax) for the company in the same manner as in the other methods within the income approach. Then, a reasonable return on the net tangible assets is subtracted from the normalized net income to determine the excess earnings. These excess earnings are then capitalized to arrive at the intangible value of the company. Once the intangible value of a company is determined, the value of the entire company can be determined by adding the value of the tangible assets to the value of the intangible assets. This method tends to be used more in a litigation context than in actual M&A transactions.

In applying the income approach, the challenge is to determine economic earnings (i.e. those generated by the business prior to bonuses, excess compensation, and perquisites). It is often not clear what portion of shareholder bonuses, for example, is a return on labor (i.e. a form of compensation) as opposed to a return on capital (i.e. shareholder/partner distribution). As such, an analysis of the firm's compensation structure, along with its billable hour expectations and practice, is an essential part of the PSF valuation process. In addition, many PSFs report their financials on a cash basis. When this is the case, adjustments are often necessary to reflect assets, such as accounts receivable, equipment, leasehold improvements, and prepaid expenses; and liabilities, such as accounts payable, accrued liabilities (often in the form of employee compensation and benefits), unearned income (often related to retainers paid for work-in-process), deferred taxes, owner retirement obligations, and/or outstanding lawsuits.

---

[8] Patrice Radogna, "Key Value Drivers in Wealth Management Firms," *Investments & Wealth Monitor* (November/December 2016): p. 37.
[9] Unless they are larger, highly profitable, and have a higher percentage of recurring revenues.

Case Study Introduction

To illustrate the valuation of a PSF in connection with M&A, we introduce Epikenon Communications, Inc., a fictitious business communications and public relations firm generating approximately $15 million in revenues and based in Boston. As explained in the first paragraph of Chapter 21, the factors presented in this case are fictitious, but are based on our experience of valuing myriad PSFs.

Epikenon was founded in 1990 by Demos Skesis and Jim Fox to provide public relations support to clients in two distinct industries – consumer products and professional services. The company's tagline is "communications, communications, communications" as demonstrated by its name, which is a derivation of the Greek word for communications. As the company developed, it expanded into servicing high-technology clients. Since its founding over 28 years ago, Epikenon has grown to 80 employees, including eight shareholders, generating approximately $15 million in annual revenues. It has offices in Boston, Austin, and Chicago currently servicing 60 clients, four of whom comprise 80% of the company's revenues. Thanks to annual valuations completed in conjunction with its shareholder agreement, the company has successfully and smoothly bought out three retiring shareholders, including both founders, and brought in all eight current shareholders.

Billing is predominantly done on an hourly basis against approved budgets. Overall, Epikenon managers and professional employees are approximately 90% billable. The average hourly billing rate is approximately $190, ranging between $120 and $350. Revenue per employee is approximately $190,000 and revenue per professional employee is approximately $230,000. Upon review of hourly rates in the public relations industry, as presented in a study completed by Gould + Partners for the PR Agency Industry, the average hourly Epikenon rate for clients is comparable to the hourly blended rate as evidenced in the study.

Potential Buyer

San Francisco–based S&J Communications has approached Epikenon with an offer to acquire the entire company. With offices in San Francisco and Seattle, S&J has built a strong reputation for providing public relations services in the high-technology sector, serving both large multinationals and rapidly growing venture-backed companies. S&J has grown to a $40 million revenue firm, but is not diversified in terms of industry served or geography. Attracted to Epikenon's industry diversification, which includes not only servicing high-technology clients, but also professional services and consumer products, coupled with its offices on the East Coast and in the Midwest, S&J has made an offer to acquire Epikenon.

Historic Financial Performance

Exhibits 22.2 through 22.7 present Epikenon's historic performance and industry average financial ratios showing the following notable factors:[10]

- Revenues have grown over the past five years from $12.7 million to $15.1 million.
- Net operating income, or EBITDA (earnings before interest, taxes, depreciation and amortization), has grown from $270,000 to $810,000, or from 2.1% of revenues to 5.4% over the past five years.
- Adjusted EBITDA has grown from $1.87 million to $2.91 million, or from 14.7% of revenues to 19.3%.
- Epikenon recently paid off all of its bank debt.
- The company's balance sheet is steady and carefully managed. Its long-term debt relates to prior shareholder buyouts.
- Epikenon's activity and profitability ratios are generally in line with industry medians while its liquidity ratio is slightly below and its solvency is better than industry levels.
- Given the company's relatively low level of debt over the past five years, its Z-score has been well above the preferred level of 2.99.

EXHIBIT 22.2   Epikenon Communications, Inc.: Income Statements, Five Most Recent Historical Years

($000s)	Historic -4 Year	Historic -3 Year	Historic -2 Year	Historic -1 Year	Current Year
Revenues	$12,700	$12,000	$13,600	$14,100	$15,100
Salaries	−8,100	−7,100	−8,300	−8,500	−9,200
Other Operating Expenses	−4,330	−4,360	−4,520	−4,820	−5,090
Net Operating Income (EBITDA)	270	540	780	780	810
Depreciation Expense	−170	−150	−130	−120	−190
EBIT	100	390	650	660	620
Interest Income	140	55	30	10	90
Interest Expense	−55	−45	−30	−30	−30
Net Income	$185	$400	$650	$640	$680

---

[10] Compare to the Financial Analysis section of Chapter 3.

EXHIBIT 22.3 Epikenon Communications, Inc.: Income Statements, Five Most Recent Historical Years – Common Size Basis

	Historic -4 Year	Historic -3 Year	Historic -2 Year	Historic -1 Year	Current Year
Revenues	100.0%	100.0%	100.0%	100.0%	100.0%
Salaries	−63.8%	−59.2%	−61.0%	−60.3%	−60.9%
Other Operating Expenses	−34.1%	−36.3%	−33.2%	−34.2%	−33.7%
Net Operating Income (EBITDA)	2.1%	4.5%	5.7%	5.5%	5.4%
Depreciation Expense	−1.3%	−1.3%	−1.0%	−0.9%	−1.3%
EBIT	0.8%	3.3%	4.8%	4.7%	4.1%
Interest Income	1.1%	0.5%	0.2%	0.1%	0.6%
Interest Expense	−0.4%	−0.4%	−0.2%	−0.2%	−0.2%
Net Income	1.5%	3.3%	4.8%	4.5%	4.5%

EXHIBIT 22.4 Epikenon Communications, Inc.: Five Most Recent Historical Years – Adjusted Earnings

($000s)	Historic -4 Year	Historic -3 Year	Historic -2 Year	Historic -1 Year	Current Year
Net Operating Income (EBITDA)	$270	$540	$780	$780	$810
Adjustments for Excess Compensation[a]	*1,600*	*1,000*	*2,000*	*1,700*	*2,100*
Adjusted EBITDA	$1,870	$1,540	$2,780	$2,480	$2,910
Adjusted EBITDA Margins	*14.7%*	*12.8%*	*20.4%*	*17.6%*	*19.3%*
Depreciation Expense	−170	−150	−130	−120	−190
Adjusted EBIT	1,700	1,390	2,650	2,360	2,720
Interest Income	140	55	30	10	90
Interest Expense	−55	−45	−30	−30	−30
Adjusted Net Income	$1,785	$1,400	$2,650	$2,340	$2,780

[a]Adjustments for excess compensation is calculated based on an analysis of the compensation for the shareholder group as compared to market data for compensation for the same positions in similar-sized public relations firms.

EXHIBIT 22.5 Epikenon Communications, Inc.: Balance Sheets

($000s)	Historic -4 Year	Historic -3 Year	Historic -2 Year	Historic -1 Year	Current Year
Assets					
Current Assets:					
Cash and Equivalents	$380	$340	$630	$280	$500
Accounts Receivable	1,130	1,200	2,210	1,780	1,740
Work-in-Process	1,400	1,400	1,270	1,460	1,200
Billable Expenses	700	550	1,180	1,670	1,520
Other Current Assets	380	370	430	430	350
Total Current Assets	3,990	3,860	5,720	5,620	5,310
Net Fixed Assets (furniture & equipment)	540	460	400	350	570
Other Assets (note receivable, investment in subsidiary, CSV on life insurance)	600	500	440	480	600
Total Assets	$5,130	$4,820	$6,560	$6,450	$6,480
Liabilities					
Current Liabilities:					
Accounts Payable	$30	$300	$600	$1,100	$1,050
Accrued Expenses	430	300	520	570	770
Unearned Revenue	1,380	1,040	2,030	1,780	1,580
Note Payable	20	580	920	300	0
Current Portion Long-Term Debt	300	230	180	150	0
Total Current Liabilities	2,160	2,450	4,250	3,900	3,400
Long-Term Debt	250	30	710	560	0
Total Liabilities	$2,410	$2,480	$4,960	$4,460	$3,400
Equity					
Paid-in-Capital	$1,120	$1,130	$1,130	$1,150	$1,190
Retained Earnings	4,200	3,750	4,270	4,540	5,350
Less: Treasury Stock	−2,600	−2,540	−3,800	−3,700	−3,460
Shareholders' Equity	2,720	2,340	1,600	1,990	3,080
Total Liabilities & Equity	$5,130	$4,820	$6,560	$6,450	$6,480

EXHIBIT 22.6 Epikenon Communications, Inc.: Balance Sheets, Five Most Recent Historical Years – Common Size Basis

	Historic -4 Year	Historic -3 Year	Historic -2 Year	Historic -1 Year	Current Year
Assets					
Current Assets:					
Cash and Equivalents	7.4%	7.1%	9.6%	4.3%	7.7%
Accounts Receivable	22.0%	24.9%	33.7%	27.6%	26.9%
Work-in-Process	27.3%	29.0%	19.4%	22.6%	18.5%
Billable Expenses	13.6%	11.4%	18.0%	25.9%	23.5%
Other Current Assets	7.4%	7.7%	6.6%	6.7%	5.4%
Total Current Assets	77.8%	80.1%	87.2%	87.1%	81.9%
Property, Plant, Equip (net)	10.5%	9.5%	6.1%	5.4%	8.8%
Other Assets	11.7%	10.4%	6.7%	7.4%	9.3%
Total Assets	100.0%	100.0%	100.0%	100.0%	100.0%
Liabilities					
Current Liabilities:					
Accounts Payable	0.6%	6.2%	9.1%	17.1%	16.2%
Accrued Expenses	8.4%	6.2%	7.9%	8.8%	11.9%
Unearned Revenue	26.9%	21.6%	30.9%	27.6%	24.4%
Note Payable	0.4%	12.0%	14.0%	4.7%	0.0%
Current Portion L/T Debt	5.8%	4.8%	2.7%	2.3%	0.0%
Total Current Liabilities	42.1%	50.8%	64.8%	60.5%	52.5%
Long-Term Debt	4.9%	0.6%	10.8%	8.7%	0.0%
Total Liabilities	47.0%	51.5%	75.6%	69.1%	52.5%
Equity					
Paid-in-Capital	21.8%	23.4%	17.2%	17.8%	18.4%
Retained Earnings	81.9%	77.8%	65.1%	70.4%	82.6%
Less: Treasury Stock	−50.7%	−52.7%	−57.9%	−57.4%	−53.4%
Shareholders' Equity	53.0%	48.5%	24.4%	30.9%	47.5%
Total Liabilities & Equity	100.0%	100.0%	100.0%	100.0%	100.0%

Future Expectations

Exhibit 22.8 presents Management's five-year forecasts, which provide the foundation for the discounted cash flow (DCF) calculations presented in Exhibit 22.10. With regard to revenue forecasts:

■ Given the nature of its client base, revenues are forecast by client classification and an estimate is made each year for business from new clients.

EXHIBIT 22.7 Epikenon Communications, Inc.: Financial Ratio Summary of Historical Financial Statements

	Type of Measure[a]	Better Indicator[b]	RMA[c]	BizMiner Median[d]	Historic -4 Year	Historic -3 Year	Historic -2 Year	Historic -1 Year	Current Year
Current Ratio	Liquidity	Higher	3.9/1.9/1.2	2.1	1.8	1.6	1.3	1.4	1.6
Receivables Turnover	Activity	Higher	18.1/8.4/6.5	9.1	11.2	10.3	8.0	7.1	8.6
Days in Receivables	Activity	Lower	20/43/56	40	32	35	46	52	43
Working Capital Turnover	Activity	Generally higher	4.2/8.2/31.2	8.7	6.9	7.4	9.4	8.8	8.3
Total Asset Turnover	Activity	Higher	4.7/2.6/2.0	3.7	2.5	2.4	2.4	2.2	2.3
Operating Margin	Profitability	Higher	8.8%	2.4%	14.7%	12.8%	20.4%	17.6%	19.3%
Return on Assets	Profitability	Higher	na	9.2%	3.6%	8.3%	9.9%	9.9%	10.5%
Times Interest Earned	Solvency	Higher	67.1/15.5/1.8	13.9	1.8	8.7	21.7	22.0	20.7
Debt Ratio	Solvency	Lower	na	25.0%	11.1%	17.4%	27.6%	15.7%	0.0%
Debt to Equity	Solvency	Generally lower	.3/1.3/2.5	31.8%	21.0%	35.9%	113.1%	50.8%	0.0%
Z-Score	Solvency	Higher	na	na	19.14	14.38	9.00	12.60	nm

[a]See Chapter 3 for an explanation of the various financial measures presented.
[b]Refers to whether a higher or lower measure is better as compared to industry peers. This column is descriptive, it is not an assessment of Epikenon's performance.
[c]RMA data is sourced from The Risk Management Association's *2016-2017 Annual Statement Studies of Financial Ratio Benchmarks* for 15 public relations agencies (NAICS 541820) with revenues between $10 and $25 million. The three ratios presented reflect the 25th percentile, median, and 75th percentile.
[d]Median data sourced from BizMiner in 2017 for 56 public relations agencies with revenues between $10 and $25 million.
na - not available, nm - not meaningful

EXHIBIT 22.8 Epikenon Communications, Inc.: Forecasted Earnings Five-Year Forecast

($000s)	Year 1	Year 2	Year 3	Year 4	Year 5
Revenues[a]	$17,701	$18,664	$19,867	$20,969	$22,334
Forecast Growth	*17.2%*	*5.4%*	*6.4%*	*5.5%*	*6.5%*
Normalized Compensation[b]	−8,460	−8,950	−9,500	−10,000	−10,670
Other Operating Expenses[c]	−5,310	−5,599	−5,960	−6,291	−6,700
Net Operating Income (EBITDA)	$3,931	$4,115	$4,407	$4,678	$4,964
Forecast EBITDA Margin	*22.2%*	*22.0%*	*22.2%*	*22.3%*	*22.2%*
Depreciation Expense[d]	−180	−190	−200	−210	−220
EBIT	$3,751	$3,925	$4,207	$4,468	$4,744
Interest Expense[e]	−7	−7	−7	−7	−7
Pretax Income	$3,744	$3,918	$4,200	$4,461	$4,737
Taxes[f]	−1,011	−1,058	−1,134	−1,205	−1,279
Net Income	$2,733	$2,860	$3,066	$3,257	$3,458

[a]Revenue projections are broken down in the following client categories based on discussions with company management and as explained in the text above. Revenue Projections:

Top Client #1	$5,459	$5,459	$5,677	$5,677	$5,904
Top Client #2	3,090	3,183	3,278	3,377	3,478
Top Clients #3 & 4	3,952	4,071	4,193	4,318	4,448
Remaining Clients	4,200	4,452	4,719	5,097	5,504
New Client Business	1,000	1,500	2,000	2,500	3,000
	$17,701	$18,664	$19,867	$20,969	$22,334

[b]Normalized compensation is based on a combination of discussions with company management and an assessment of industry compensation data.
[c]Other operating expenses are forecast to be 30% of revenues.
[d]Depreciation is based on current levels and forecast capital expenditures.
[e]Interest expense is based on the assumption that the company will borrow on average $400,000 from its line of credit currently at a rate of 3.5%, and will hold this balance for an average of six months, repaying it before year-end.
[f]Taxes are calculated at a combined federal and state corporate tax rate of 27%.

- In the current year, Top Client #1 comprised 35% of total company revenue at $5.3 million. This client renegotiates its contract with Epikenon every two years, whereby a 3% increase is forecast for Year 1 and a 4% increase is forecast for Years 3 and 5.
- In the current year, Top Client #2 comprised 20% of total company revenue at $3.0 million. This client renegotiates its contract with Epikenon every year, typically resulting in a 3% annual increase.

- The identity of Top Clients #3 and #4 tends to fluctuate based on their specific demands in a given year. Past performance indicates that their total revenues increase about 3% per year under normal economic conditions, but there is a specific project for Top Client #3 expected for Year 1. As a result, we are projecting 4% growth for Year 1 and 3% growth thereafter.
- Volume from remaining clients tends to grow anywhere from 6 to 15% annually. Based on discussions with Management on volume from remaining clients, we have projected $4.2 million in Year 1 in part due to higher backlog, 6% growth in each of Years 2 and 3, and 8% growth in each of Years 4 and 5.
- For new client business, Management has forecast $1 million for Year 1, with additional new business increasing $500,000 per year until it reaches $3 million for Year 5. This is consistent with Epikenon's efforts to mitigate its key client dependency by reducing its revenues from Top Clients 1 and 2 within five to six years to around 40% of total revenues.
- Total revenue is therefore forecast to grow 17.2% in Year 1 and between 5.4% and 6.5% in each of the subsequent four years. However, it is typically difficult for established companies to sustain organic growth of more than 2 to 5% into perpetuity due to economic cycles, competitive and other market forces, client changes, company capacity, and so on. Epikenon is subject to swings in the economy and to possible decline of work from big clients like Top Client #1 and Top Client #2. Therefore, it is reasonable to assume that Epikenon is not likely to be able to sustain into perpetuity the growth rates forecast for the discrete five-year forecast period. Given these factors, coupled with discussions with Management, we have estimated the growth rate beyond Year 5 (the fifth year of the forecast) at 3%.

Normalized compensation for the shareholder group is calculated based on an analysis of the compensation for this group as compared to market data for compensation for the same positions in similar-sized public relations agencies. Staff compensation, included in the normalized compensation, is assumed to be at market and therefore not adjusted. Other operating expenses are expected to be at 30% of revenues due to a cost reduction effort, which includes a streamlining of overhead, such as new, less expensive leases in their Boston and Chicago locations and an improved approach to their technological needs. Depreciation expense is forecast based on current levels and forecast capital expenditures. Interest expense, principal repayments, and new debt incurred net to $0 because, although the company recently paid off all its debt and does not anticipate incurring any long-term debt (interest is currently charged at 3.5%), it plans to borrow from its working capital line and pay it back within six months. Increase in net working capital (NWC) is based on the annual change in net working capital, which was computed at 18% of the annual growth in forecast revenues. This level of NWC was concluded on after a review of the company's operating cycle, the forecast growth rate in revenues, and the industry ratio of NWC as a percentage of revenues.

Risk and Value Drivers

The factors that should influence the development of the discount and capitalization rates appropriate to Epikenon's stand-alone fair market value are described in the next sections. This begins with a qualitative analysis of the value drivers for professional service firms as presented earlier in Exhibit 22.1. Quantitatively, Exhibit 22.9 is used to develop the rates.

ECONOMIC CONDITIONS. The feasibility of realizing the forecasts put forth by the company (as shown in Exhibit 22.8) is greatly affected by changes in the economic forces of the environment in which it operates. As economic conditions strengthen, corporate profits should expand, resulting in higher demand for communications, marketing, and advertising services. Further, increased popularity of social networking services and mobile media will drive demand for public relations services. This may be tempered by the fact that the economy has been growing for over eight years, since the recession officially ended, and the public relations industry is noticeably impacted by economic cycles. Overall, the ability of the company to meet its projections hinges on the overall economy and the associated expansion of corporate profits, and the need for large corporations to manage their social media presence.

INDUSTRY CONSIDERATIONS. Despite being late in an economic growth cycle, public relations agency leaders are optimistic about the outlook of the business with various industry projections over the next three years, forecasting between three and five percent annual growth. Last year's Holmes Report[11] on the public relations industry cites the ability to attract top talent, agencies' capacity to master digital media and other new communications technology, and willingness of clients to budget appropriately for public relations services as the greatest challenges facing agencies.

MANAGEMENT. The Epikenon management team is solid and has a clear strategy for the company's current and future operations, which has dictated and continues to direct the business going forward. The company has successfully and seamlessly retired three shareholders in the past seven years, with little impact on revenues and little financial strain; and top management

---

[11] www.holmesreport.com.

EXHIBIT 22.9 Rate of Return (Discount Rate) Applicable to Net Cash Flow to Equity (as of the Valuation Date)

Symbol	Component	Increment	Rate
	Long-Term Treasury Bond Yield[a]		2.6%
+	Equity Risk Premium $(R_m - R_f)$[b]		6.0%
=	Average Market Return for Large-Cap Stock		8.6%
+	Risk Premium for Size[c]		5.6%
=	Average Market Return Adjustment for Size to Mid-Cap-Size Firm		14.2%
	Specific-Company Risk Premium Adjustments:[d]		
+	Industry Risk	0.3%	
+	Financial Risk	1.5%	
+	Staffing Risk	2.0%	
+	Client Risk	4.0%	7.8%
=	***Rate of Return for Net Cash Flow to Equity***[e]		**22.0%**
−	*Rate of Return for Net Cash Flow to Equity*[e]		−3.0%
=	***Capitalization Rate***		**19.0%**

[a]See explanation of the Build-up Rate in Chapter 8. The risk-free rate of return ("Rf") is the yield that one can obtain from an investment considered to be risk-free, such as a government security. At the Valuation Date, the Rf, based on 20-year Treasury Bond rate, was 2.6%.

[b]The equity risk premium ("Rp") is the additional return that investors require for investing in a diversified portfolio of equity securities, over and above the return on a risk-free security, such as a government bond. The Rp based upon the supply-side long-horizon expected equity risk premium, as determined by Duff & Phelps data through December 31, 2016, was 5.97%.

[c]The small-company stock risk premium represents the additional return, over and above the equity risk premium, that investors require for investing in the equity of a company with a market capitalization in the 10th decile of companies (i.e. with market capitalization of less than $263 million) listed on the New York Stock Exchange ("NYSE"), the Nasdaq National Market ("NASDAQ") and the NYSE MKT (formerly the American Stock Exchange). This premium, as determined by Duff & Phelps data through December 31, 2016, was 5.59%.

[d]A specific-company risk premium is added and represents the additional return, over and above the equity and small company risk premiums, which an investor would require for investing in the equity of Epikenon. After giving consideration to all factors on a general basis, we believe that a prudent investor would analyze all of the external and internal risks, coupled with risk of realizing the forecasts, in order to determine the extent to which an Rpcs was applicable to Epikenon. Based on this analysis, we believe that a prudent investor would find an investment in Epikenon to be more risky than an investment in a "typical public company," and would require an additional premium in order to compensate for any additional investment risks. We factored this additional risk component into our calculation of the discount rate by adding a factor of 7.8% - based on an assessment of industry, financial, management, staffing, and client risk outlined above - to the cost of equity.

[e]This is a rate of return or discount rate directly applicable to equity net cash flow as it is based on the return to equity investors, net of income tax to their corporations.

continues to address succession planning issues as several key people are approaching or are in their 50s.

STAFFING. There is a focus on employee retention through increased continuing education efforts and benefits that are considered to be better than those offered by peer companies. When considering employees with more than five years with the firm, shareholder tenure with the company averages 20 years while tenure for nonshareholder management averages 14 years. There is also strong utilization of professionals, with levels around 90% as compared to industry utilization, with reported amounts typically below 85%.

CLIENT BASE. While Epikenon has excellent and long-standing client relationships, it needs to diversify its key account exposure. Its top four clients comprise between 75 and 85% of its revenues in most of the past ten years. The departure of any of these clients, especially one of the top two, which comprise 55%, would have a significant negative impact on company revenues and profitability.

Discounted Cash Flow Method

Based on the information provided above, we are now able to calculate the fair market value of Epikenon using the discounted cash flow method within the income approach. Epikenon's expected future cash flows, like those for most PSFs, represent its primary determinant of value. Given that Epikenon is expected to grow at more than just a steady state of 2 to 4% annually over the next five years, the DCF is more applicable than a single-period capitalization method as it provides a forecasting model that enables forecasting nonsteady operating patterns in the foreseeable discrete forecast period. As discussed in Chapter 7, the DCF method is based on the premise that the value of a company can be determined by forecasting its expected future cash flows and discounting those cash flows to a present value after assessing the risk in achieving those cash flows.

Using the forecasts developed above in Exhibit 22.8 and the discount rate derived in Exhibit 22.9, the fair market value of Epikenon is computed to be $15.7 million as shown in Exhibit 22.10. This is derived by taking the sum of the present value of the forecast cash flows for Year 1 through Year 5 and adding them to the capitalized value for the terminal year, which represents the value of the cash flows beyond the five-year forecast period.

Other Valuation Methods to Consider

Earlier in this chapter, we reviewed the three approaches to value as they relate to PSFs. Like most PSFs, the income approach is the most

EXHIBIT 22.10 Epikenon Communications, Inc.: Discounted Cash Flow Analysis

($000s)	Year 1	Year 2	Year 3	Year 4	Year 5	Terminal
Net Income	$2,733	$2,860	$3,066	$3,257	$3,458	
Less: Principal Repayments[a]	−400	−400	−400	−400	−400	
Plus: New Debt Incurred[a]	400	400	400	400	400	
Plus: Depreciation[b]	180	190	200	210	220	
Less: Capital Expenditures[b]	−175	−200	−200	−225	−225	
Less: Increase in Net Working Capital[c]	−468	−173	−217	−198	−246	
Net Cash Flow	$2,270	$2,677	$2,849	$3,044	$3,207	$3,303
Capitalized Value for Terminal Year ("CVTY")[d]						$17,386
Discount Factor[e]	0.9054	0.7421	0.6083	0.4986	0.4087	0.4087
Present Value of Net Cash Flows	$2,055	$1,986	$1,733	$1,518	$1,311	$7,106

Present Value of Forecast Cash Flows	$8,603
Present Value of CVTY	7,106
Indicated Fair Market Value of Equity (rounded)	**$15,700**

[a]Management has indicated that it does not intend to incur any long-term debt, but that the company will borrow on average $400,000 from its line of credit each year and will hold this balance for an average of six months, repaying it before year end.
[b]Management has forecast the expected level of capital expenditures over the next five years, and depreciation is based on current and forecast levels.
[c]Increase in working capital is equal to 18% of incremental revenue each year, consistent with the median working capital as a percentage of revenue for the public relations industry.
[d]The terminal value (CVTY) was calculated dividing the net cash flow of $3,303 as projected in the terminal value column by the capitalization rate of 19% (discount rate less the long-term growth rate).
[e]Discount factor equal to 1/[1+discount rate)^adjusted years to discount]. Years to discount (0.5, 1.5, 2.5, etc.) were calculated as the period of time between the Valuation Date and the end of each of the forecast years. A mid-year adjustment was made as annual cash flows are assumed to be received throughout the year, so that on average, cash flows would be received mid-year.

EXHIBIT 22.11 Epikenon Communications, Inc.: Single-Period Capitalization
Method

($000s)	
Normalized Net Cash Flow (based on forecast first year, Year 1, Exhibit 22.10)	$2,270
Apply Long-Term Sustainable Growth to Historical Net Cash Flow (3%)[a]	x 1.03
Cash Flow for Capitalization	$2,338
Capitalization Rate (Discount Rate determined in Exhibit 22.9, less a long-term sustainable growth rate of 3%)	19%
Indicated Fair Market Value of Equity (rounded)	**$12,300**

[a]The indicated values are $9.6 and $10.9 million at 2% and 4% long-term growth, respectively.

relevant to value Epikenon, while the market approach may be used as a reasonableness test on the results from the income approach, and the asset approach is not relevant. Within these approaches are several methods that may be considered, the most relevant of which include the following.

SINGLE PERIOD CAPITALIZATION METHOD. Within the income approach, we applied the DCF method over the capitalization method because of the company's higher growth expectations. As illustrated above in Exhibit 22.11, had we applied the capitalization method, we would have undervalued the company. While a DCF and a capitalization method may be used as two different scenarios in certain valuations, the two methods within the income approach are more often mutually exclusive. Epikenon's cash flows are expected to grow at more than 2 to 4% annually over the next five years. At 2 to 4% long-term growth, the resulting indication of value using the capitalization method would be $11.6 to $13.1 million, or $12.3 million at 3% as calculated in Exhibit 22.11 above.

TRANSACTION MULTIPLE METHOD. The market approach using M&A transaction data may also be considered. As discussed in Chapter 10, the transaction multiple method (TMM) within the market approach looks at the prices paid to acquire similar businesses and derives indications of value based on the prices at which entire companies or operating units of companies have sold. There must be a reasonable basis for selecting certain transactions or investments as a comparison to the subject company. Factors that would influence this decision include: (1) similar quantitative and qualitative data; (2) sufficient known and verifiable information on the given companies; and (3) the basis of the transactions, whether they were arm's-length or distressed sales.[12] These prices are divided by the selected companies' revenues and/or various levels of earnings to determine multiples. Multiples of revenues are most often used in valuing PSFs due in large part to how compensation is paid to shareholders and other professionals within the firm. Earnings adjusted for normalized compensation may be considered, but market data may not be sufficient to make similar adjustments to the transactions selected.

In the present case, we first searched various databases, such as Pratt's Stats and Capital IQ, for transactions involving public relations agencies over the past five years. The search resulted in insufficient data for any transactions. As a result, we expanded the search to include the past 20 years and found eight transactions with sufficient data, but all of these transactions occurred more than five years ago. We then expanded the search to include all firms engaged in some form of marketing consulting, a description broader than public relations. That search resulted in a total of 29 transactions over the past 20 years, eight of which occurred within the past five years. In analyzing this data, the following considerations were made:

- Given that this valuation is being prepared in connection with the potential sale of the company, the TMM can be one of the best indicators of the market.
- Most of the transactions involved companies similar in size to Epikenon, with only five of the 29 over $100 million in revenues and two of the 29 under $5 million in revenues.
- None of the transactions involving firms offering some level of public relations services took place in similar economic times (i.e. within the past five years).
- There was no correlation in the revenue multiples to company size, timing of the transaction, or company description.
- While all of the transactions reported sufficient information to determine a range of revenue multiples, only a fraction of them had sufficient information on EBITDA multiples.
- Due to varying compensation practices for PSFs, including firms offering marketing consulting services, there can be a significant difference in implied EBITDA multiples as seen in the results of this transaction search of 3.75× to nearly 26×.
- There was a mix of asset versus stock deals. To provide a more accurate indication of value of Epikenon's stock, adjustments should be made to the asset deals.

---

[12] American Society of Appraisers, *Business Valuation Standards,* BVS-V, Section III(B).

While the first two considerations are good reasons to apply the TMM as an indicator of value, the remaining five considerations outweigh the positives, leading to the conclusion that the results of this search were deemed to be insufficient to use as an indicator of value. Accordingly, we determined our value based on the results of our DCF analysis of $15.7 million as shown in Exhibit 22.10. This result implies a revenue multiple of 1.04 and an adjusted EBITDA multiple of 5.4 based on the current year's revenue and adjusted EBITDA. In conclusion, we have decided to use the results of our transaction analysis summarized in Exhibit 22.12 as a reasonableness check to value.

GUIDELINE PUBLIC COMPANY METHOD. In addition to the TMM, the guideline public company (GPC) method may also be considered. In review from Chapter 10, this method within the market approach looks at the multiples of public companies that are reasonably similar to the subject company, and derives relevant multiples of revenue and various levels of earnings. However, due to a significant size disparity and other factors, this method is rarely relevant when valuing most PSFs. Such is the case with Epikenon. We were able to identify four publicly traded companies that provide marketing and business communications services, including public relations to some extent. However, business communications and public relations services were only a small portion (as compared to all for Epikenon) of their service offerings. In addition, as seen below in Exhibit 22.13, three of the four guideline companies identified were considerably larger, with market values and revenues in excess of a billion dollars. The remaining company, Harte Hanks, has struggled with losses and a $15 million market value on over $400 million in revenues. As such, the GPC method serves neither as an indication of value, nor as a reasonableness check.

ADJUSTED BOOK VALUE METHOD. The balance sheet of Epikenon reflects a book value of $3,080,000 (Exhibit 22.5). To apply the adjusted book value method within the asset approach, explained in Chapter 11, the equipment would need to be appraised to its fair value on a going-concern (in-use) basis and other assets and liabilities would need to be marked to market. The result would be considerably lower than the indication of value using the DCF method of $15.7 million since most of the value of Epikenon ($12.62 million[13]) is in its intangibles. Separate valuations would need to be done on the company's customer relationships, assembled workforce, trade name, and know-how. The result may still be below actual market value because of the existence of goodwill, which would include intangible assets that cannot be measured, such as future customers. Therefore, the adjusted book value method is not an applicable method to value Epikenon.

---

[13] $15.7 million fair market value (Exhibit 22.10) – $3.08 million book value (Exhibit 22.5).

EXHIBIT 22.12 Epikenon Communications, Inc.: M&A Transaction Multiple Data

	Public Relations Firm Transactions (last 20 years)		Marketing Consulting Firm Transactions (last 20 years)		Marketing Consulting Firm Transactions (last 5 years)	
	Revenue Multiple	EBITDA Multiple	Revenue Multiple	EBITDA Multiple	Revenue Multiple	EBITDA Multiple
Minimum	0.60	6.02	0.17	3.75	0.17	3.75
First Quartile	1.17	6.39	0.92	7.86	0.28	7.64
Median	1.64	6.77	1.43	11.99	0.82	11.67
Third Quartile	1.87	13.32	2.03	14.62	0.96	17.28
Maximum	2.73	19.88	3.48	25.94	1.50	25.94
Epikenon	*1.04*	*5.40*				
Sample:						
Count	8	3	29	11	8	4
Revenue Range	$8.8 million to $151 million		$2.3 million to $403 million		$6.4 million to $140 million	
Revenue Median	$11.4 million		$25 million		$22.3 million	

450

EXHIBIT 22.13 Epikenon Communications, Inc.: Guideline Company Financial
Metrics and Multiples

($000s)	Latest Fiscal Year	Market Value of Invested Capital (MVIC)	Latest Fiscal Year Revenues	EBITDA	EBITDA Margin	MVIC/ Revenue	MVIC/ EBITDA
Harte Hanks	12/31/CY	$15,000	$404,000	($5,000)	−1.2%	0.04	n/m
MDC Partners	12/31/CY	$1,642,000	$1,421,000	$149,000	10.5%	1.16	11.0
Omnicom Group	12/31/CY	$22,604,000	$15,505,000	$2,318,000	15.0%	1.46	9.8
Interpublic Group	12/31/CY	$11,335,000	$7,859,000	$1,108,000	14.1%	1.44	10.2
Epikenon	12/31/CY	*$13,300*	*$15,100*	*$2,910*	*19.3%*	*1.04*	*5.4*

Note: To make an adequate comparison, one might consider relevant adjustments for control
and marketability as discussed in Chapter 12. *CY = Current Year*

Suggested Considerations to Case Conclusion

Before any readers conclude that they are prepared to negotiate the sale
of Epikenon to S&J Communications or to any other potential buyer based
on the information presented, we encourage them to consider the following
questions:

- In addition to the checks to value discussed above, have you reviewed
  the 27 factors in Exhibit 22.1 to ensure that you have done a sufficient
  qualitative assessment of the business?
- What was your assessment of Epikenon's management team when you
  met them to discuss the business and its future expectations?
- How concerned are you about its dependence on a few top clients?
- How confident are you that the company can improve its margins as
  much as they are forecasting?
- How assured are you that they can achieve their overall forecasts given
  where we are in the economic cycle and other factors?
- How have they performed in comparison to prior forecasts or budgets?
- Given the transaction data obtained through independent research,
  would you use it as an indicator of value or as a reasonableness check?
- Is the selected discount rate correct in light of the qualitative factors, the
  results from the market transactions, and the implied revenue multiple
  of 1.04× and EBITDA multiple of 5.4×?

- Have you run a sensitivity analysis using different discount rates and long-term growth rates?
- Should you consider a scenario analysis?
- Do you agree in using the discounted cash flow as opposed to a capitalization of cash flow, balancing the challenge of forecasting with the company's growth expectations?
- Does the resulting value properly capture the value of the company's intangible assets – especially its workforce, customer relationships, trade name, and overall goodwill?
- How do your valuation results compare to prior internal transactions and the annual company valuations?
- To what extent should you adjust the analysis to take into account potential buyer synergies?
- What is your assessment of how effective the integration of the two companies would be?
- If working with Epikenon, how would you advise on an offer where S&J uses its stock as part of the consideration to be paid, as opposed to all cash?

As with the Cavendish case in Chapter 21, these questions and others are part of the critical qualitative assessment that must be considered when valuing a company in the process of making a sound purchase or sale decision. These qualitative factors must be thoroughly vetted and quantified before you feel confident in your value estimate. Ultimately, when estimating value, the question that you are trying to answer is not simply "*What* is the value?"; it is "*Why* is the value what you are concluding on?"

Once confidence in the value estimate is achieved after adequately answering the above questions and completing a full quantitative and qualitative assessment of the subject company, as explained in the opening paragraph of this book, buyers and sellers can both win in the M&A process. The key is to understand what value is, what drives it, and how to measure it accurately to build value in a business.

About the Authors

CHRIS M. MELLEN is a managing director with Valuation Research Corporation (VRC) who leads its Boston office. Prior to joining VRC, he was president and founder of Delphi Valuation Advisors, Inc., which he sold to VRC in July 2015. He is an accredited senior appraiser (ASA), certified merger and acquisition advisor (CM&AA), certified valuation analyst (CVA), international certified valuation specialist (ICVS), and master certified business appraiser (MCBA). Chris also holds an MBA with a concentration in finance from Babson College and a bachelor of arts with a major in industrial relations and economics from McGill University. His experience includes completion or supervision of over 3,000 valuation assignments since 1989. He has performed business valuations in a wide range of industries for such purposes as strategic planning, mergers and acquisitions, tax and estate planning and compliance, financial reporting, financing, buy–sell agreements, litigation, and appraisal review. Prior to forming Delphi in 2000, he held senior-level positions in the valuation departments of two major accounting firms. In addition, Chris has served on a number of valuation-related committees, published several articles on valuation-related matters, led over 100 seminars, and provided expert testimony in court. He is the coauthor with Frank Evans of the second edition and author of the third edition of *Valuation for M&A*, and can be contacted at cmellen@valuationresearch.com or cm@delphivaluation.com.

FRANK C. EVANS is the founder of Evans and Associates Valuation Advisory Services (www.evansandassociates.net), in Pittsburgh, Pennsylvania, and a principal in American Business Appraisers.® He holds the accredited senior appraiser (ASA) and certified business appraiser (CBA) designations and held the certified public accountant accredited in business valuation (CPA/ABV) designation. With an MBA and a bachelor of arts degree in economics from the University of Pittsburgh, he performs valuations and related consultation for strategic planning, merger and acquisition, tax planning, shareholder agreements and disputes and litigation support. Frank has been an instructor for ASA, CBA, and CPA/ABV accreditation courses, served as editor of Business Appraisal Practice, and has spoken at numerous national conferences. He designed and wrote "Valuation of Companies: The Practical Aspects," a three-day seminar he has taught over 150 times throughout North America and Europe for the American Management Association. He is the coauthor with David Bishop of the first edition and coauthor with Chris Mellen of the second edition of *Valuation for M&A*, and can be contacted at fevans@evansandassociates.net.

Glossary

The following pages contain a glossary of terms used in valuation for mergers and acquisitions, as well as those referenced within this book.[1]

Adjusted Book Value – The value that results after one or more asset or liability amounts are added, deleted, or changed from their respective financial statement amounts.

Appraisal – The act or process of determining value. It is synonymous with the term *valuation.*

Asset-Based Approach – Synonymous with *cost approach.* A general way of determining a value indication of a business, business ownership interest, or security by using one or more methods based on the value of the assets of that business net of liabilities.

Benefit Stream – Any level of income, cash flow, or earnings generated by an asset, group of assets, or business enterprise. When the term is used, it should be supplemented by a definition of exactly what it means in the given valuation context.

Beta – A measure of systematic risk of a stock; the tendency of a stock's price to correlate with changes in a specific index.

Board of Advisors – A group of individuals, typically composed of technical and industry experts, who provide guidance and feedback to the company's managers and board of directors. The board of advisors does not have a fiduciary responsibility and is usually established by the senior management and the board of directors.

Board of Directors – A group of individuals, typically composed of managers, investors, and experts, who have a fiduciary responsibility for the well-being and proper guidance of a corporation. The board is elected by the shareholders.

---

[1] Unless otherwise noted, the terms referenced in this glossary are sourced from: (1) *International Glossary of Business Valuation Terms* (Business Valuation Resources, LLC, 2001); (2) Kenneth H. Marks, et al. *Middle Market M&A: Handbook for Investment Banking and Business Consulting* (Hoboken, NJ: Wiley, 2012); and (3) *Handbook of Financing Growth: Strategies, Capital Structure, and M&A Transactions,* 2nd ed. (Hoboken, NJ: Wiley, 2009).

Book Value – (1) With respect to a business enterprise, the difference between total assets (net of accumulated depreciation, depletion, and amortization) and total liabilities of a business enterprise as they appear on the balance sheet. (2) With respect to an intangible asset, the capitalized cost of an intangible asset less accumulated amortization as it appears on the books of account on the business enterprise. It is synonymous with *net book value, net worth,* and *shareholders' equity.*

Breakeven – The level of revenue in a business in which sales minus variable costs minus fixed costs equals zero.

Breakup Fee – An amount paid by a selling company to a potential buyer when the seller terminates an agreement in favor of a higher bid for the selling company.

Business Enterprise – A commercial, industrial, service, or investment entity, or a combination thereof, pursuing an economic activity.

Business Enterprise Value (BEV) – The value of the entire business enterprise (i.e. the total interest-bearing debt and equity capital of a business enterprise). It could be stated on a number of premises, including: (i) closely held; (ii) as is freely traded [such as shares in a publicly traded company on an exchange]; (iii) as a controlling interest; or (iv) as a minority interest, or some combination thereof. BEV is synonymous with the terms *total invested capital* and *market value of invested capital.*

Buy–Sell Agreement – A contract that sets forth the conditions under which a shareholder must first offer his or her shares for sale to the other shareholders before being allowed to sell to entities outside the company.

Capital Expenditures – Expenditures that result in other assets that benefit several future periods. They reduce cash flows but do not impact the income statement. Also referred to as *CapEx.*

Capital Structure – The composition of the invested capital of a business enterprise; the mix of debt and equity financing.

Capitalization – A conversion of a single-period stream of benefits into value.

Capitalization Rate – Any divisor (usually expressed as a percentage) used to convert anticipated benefits into value. This rate is often calculated as the discount rate less a long-term sustainable rate of growth.

Capitalization Table – A table showing the owners of a company's shares and their ownership percentages. It also lists the forms of ownership, such as common stock, preferred stock, warrants, and options.

Carried Interest – A share in the profits of a private equity fund. Typically, a fund must return the capital given to it by limited partners before the general partner can share in the profits of the fund. The general partner will then receive a 20% carried interest, although some firms may receive up to 25 or 30%. Also known as a *carry* or a *promote.*

Cash Flow – Cash that is generated over a period of time by an asset, group of assets, or business enterprise. It may be used in a general sense to encompass various levels of specifically defined cash flows. When the term is used, it should be supplemented by a qualifier (for example, discretionary or operating) and a definition of exactly what it means in the given valuation context.

Closing – The conclusion of a transaction whereby all necessary legal documents are signed.

Common Size Statements – Financial statements in which each line is expressed as a percentage of the total. On the balance sheet, each line item is shown as a percentage of total assets, and on the income statement, each item is expressed as a percentage of sales.

Control – The power to direct the management and policies of a business enterprise.

Control Premium – An amount (expressed in either dollar or percentage form) by which the pro rata value of a controlling interest exceeds the pro rata value of a noncontrolling interest in a business enterprise, that reflects the power of control.

Cost of Capital – The expected rate of return (discount rate) that the market requires in order to attract funds to a particular investment.

Cost of Equity Capital – The rate of return that an equity investor in a company would require to compensate for the risks of investing in that company.

Data Room – A central electronic storage location for due diligence materials provided by a company to all potential purchasers or investors in connection with an acquisition or investment.

Deal Flow – A measure of the number of potential investments or transactions that a fund, lender, advisor, or buyer reviews in any given period.

Debt – Interest-bearing obligations of a company, including bank loans, notes, and capital leases; but not including working capital liabilities such as payables and accrued expenses.

Definitive Agreement – The final, fully negotiated agreement between parties, containing all material terms, conditions, and agreements relating to the subject matter of the transaction in question.

Discount – A reduction in value or the act of reducing value.

Discount for Lack of Control (DLOC) – An amount or percentage deducted from the pro rata share of value of 100% of an equity interest in a business to reflect the absence of some or all of the powers of control. This term is synonymous with a *minority discount*.

Discount for Lack of Marketability (DLOM) – An amount or percentage deducted from the value of an ownership interest to reflect the relative absence of marketability. This term is synonymous with an *illiquidity discount*.

Discount Rate – A rate of return (cost of capital) used to convert a monetary sum, payable or receivable in the future, into present value. It can be synonymous with either the cost of equity capital or the weighted average cost of capital, depending on the level of cash flows to which it is being applied.

Discounted Cash Flow (DCF) Method – A method within the income approach whereby the present value of the future expected net cash flows is calculated using a discount rate.

Due Diligence – The investigatory process performed when considering a transaction with a third party to evaluate the business and finances of a company. In M&A, traditional or technical due diligence focuses on financial information, taxes, legal and regulatory compliance, environmental compliance, human resources, contracts, information technology, and so on. Strategic due diligence explores whether the potential of the deal is realistic by testing the rationale.

EBIT – Earnings before interest and taxes. A measurement of the operating profit of a company. One possible valuation method is based on a comparison of private and public companies' value as a multiple of EBIT.

EBITDA – Earnings before interest, taxes, depreciation, and amortization. A measurement of the cash flow of a company. One possible valuation method is based on a comparison of private and public companies' value as a multiple of EBITDA less funded debt.

Economic Depreciation – The reduction in value resulting from reductions in economic life. This is commonly different than accounting depreciation, which is the recovery of an item's original cost, through periodic depreciation charges against the item and the earnings of the business enterprise. The pace at which the cost is so recovered is generally dictated by the Internal Revenue Service's regulations regarding depreciation that are subject to change from time to time, without being motivated by any change in the economic life of the item.

Economic Income – For a given period, the amount of funds that may be withdrawn from a firm without changing its future ability to generate income.

Economic Life – The period over which property may generate economic benefits.

Equity – The owner's interest in property after deduction of all liabilities.

Equity Risk Premium – A rate of return in addition to a risk-free rate to compensate for investing in equity instruments because they have a higher degree of probable risk than risk-free instruments (a component of the cost of equity capital or equity discount rate).

ESOP – Employee stock ownership plan. An equity plan established by a company that permits the grant of options on stock of the company for long-term incentive compensation for employees.

Excess Earnings – That amount of anticipated benefits that exceeds a fair rate of return on the value of a selected asset base (often net tangible assets) used to generate those anticipated benefits.

Exit Planning – The process of determining how a business owner will successfully retire from the business and generate enough liquidity from that exit to provide the financial security to fund the owner's retirement goals.

Exit Strategy – The plan for generating profits for owners and investors of a company. Typically, exit strategies include mergers and acquisitions, recapitalizations, ESOPs, and initial public offerings (IPOs).

Fair Market Value – The price, expressed in terms of cash equivalents, at which property would change hands between a hypothetical willing and able buyer and a hypothetical willing and able seller, acting at arm's-length in an open and unrestricted market, when neither is under compulsion to buy or sell and when both have reasonable knowledge of the relevant facts. It is the most commonly used standard of value in the appraisal of closely held businesses, and is the standard of value being used in this appraisal report.

Fairness Opinion – An opinion as to whether the consideration in a transaction is fair from a financial point of view.

Financial Engineering – Refers to the financial structuring of a company or particular transaction.

Financial Intermediaries – Institutions that provide the market function of matching borrowers and lenders or traders.

Financial Investor – An investor interested solely in achieving a financial return from an investment, rather than a return coupled with a strategic benefit associated with the investment.

Free Cash Flow – The amount of cash a company has after expenses, debt service, capital expenditures, and dividends. Free cash flow measures the financial comfort level of the company as a going concern.

Going Concern – An ongoing operating business enterprise, as opposed to a collection of assets and liabilities.

Going Concern Value – The value of a business enterprise that is expected to continue to operate into the future. The intangible elements of Going Concern Value result from factors such as having a trained workforce, an operational plant, and the necessary licenses, systems, and procedures in place.

Goodwill – That intangible asset arising as a result of name, reputation, customer loyalty, location, products, and similar factors not separately identified.

Guideline Public Company Method – A method within the market approach whereby market multiples are derived from market prices of stocks of companies that are engaged in the same or similar lines of business, and that are actively traded on a free and open market.

Horizontal Integration – The merger of companies at the same stage of production in the same or different industries.

Human Capital – People. The background, knowledge, creativity, skills, influence, experience, education, training, communication, and other attributes that people bring to a business.

Income Approach – A general way of determining a value indication of a business, business ownership interest, security, or intangible asset using one or more methods that convert anticipated benefits into a present single amount. Two of the most common methods used in the income approach are the discounted cash flow (DCF) method and the capitalization of cash flow method.

Intangible Assets – Nonphysical assets (such as franchises, trademarks, patents, copyrights, goodwill, equities, mineral rights, securities and contracts as distinguished from physical assets) that grant rights, privileges, and have economic benefits for the owner.

Intermediary – A firm or person (such as a broker or investment banker) who acts as a mediator between parties in a business transaction.

Internal Rate of Return (IRR) – A discount rate at which the present value of the future cash flows of the investment equals the cost of the investment.

Intrinsic Value – The value that an investor considers, on the basis of an evaluation or available facts, to be the true or real value that will become the market value when other investors reach the same conclusion. When the term applies to options, it is the difference between the exercise price or strike price of an option and the market value of the underlying security.

Invested Capital – The sum of equity and debt in a business enterprise. (Technically, this means debt and equity on a long-term basis; however, realizing the manner in which many closely held businesses use short-term borrowing, this term, unless stated otherwise, will be used to represent equity plus all debt.)

Investment – Money or other assets committed to a business to generate future income. If the company is incurring losses or generating inadequate profits, it is measured by the current value of the tangible assets used in operations. If the company's operations generate intangible value, it is measured by the present value of the company's future returns.

Investment Banker – A financial intermediary who performs a variety of services, including aiding in the sale of securities, facilitating mergers and other corporate reorganizations, acting as a broker to both individual and institutional clients, and trading for their own accounts.

Investment Value – Also known as *strategic value* or *synergistic value*. The value to a particular buyer based on individual investment requirements and expectations. This is in contrast to the population of hypothetical willing buyers, as is the case in fair market value.

Lack of Control – The inability to control some aspect of either operational matters or matters outside the ordinary course of business due to contractual restrictions, statutory limitations, or concerns related to a possible reaction by other shareholders. (While this term can be used to encompass a minority interest discount, it can also reflect limitations in majority interests.)

Leveraged Buyout (LBO) – The purchase of a company or a business unit of a company by an outside investor using mostly borrowed capital.

Levered Basis – Use of cash flows that are available only to equity shareholders of the company. In the income approach, the applicable discount rate is the cost of equity capital. In the market approach, the numerator in the multiples is stock's value (prices) times common shares outstanding and the denominator is typically some level of earnings available to equity shareholders such as net income or net cash flow. The resulting value is one of the equity.

Liquidity – The ability to quickly convert property to cash or pay a liability.

Liquidation Value – The net amount that can be realized if the business is terminated and the assets are sold piecemeal. Liquidation can be either orderly or forced.

M&A – Acronym for mergers and acquisitions. Used in the middle market to mean the buying and selling of companies.

Management Buyout (MBO) – A leveraged buyout controlled by the members of the management team of a company or a division.

Market Approach – A general way of determining a value indication of a business, business ownership interest, security, or intangible asset by using one or more methods that compare the subject to similar (guideline) businesses, business ownership interests, securities, or intangible assets that have been sold. Two of the most common methods used in the market approach are the guideline public company method and the transaction multiple method.

Mezzanine – A layer of financing that has intermediate priority (seniority) in the capital structure of a company. For example, mezzanine debt has lower priority than senior debt, but higher priority than equity. Mezzanine debt usually has a higher interest rate than senior debt and often includes warrants. In venture capital, a mezzanine round is generally the round of financing that is designed to fund the operations of a company to a liquidity event such as an IPO.

Mid-Year Discounting/Convention – A convention used in the discounted cash flow method that reflects economic benefits being generated at mid-year, approximating the effect of economic benefits being generated evenly throughout the year.

Middle Market – The term generally refers to companies with revenues ranging from $5 million to $1 billion. For purposes of this book, we define the middle market as companies with a total enterprise value of

$250 million to $1 billion, lower middle market at $10 million to $250 million, lower-lower middle market at $3 million to $10 million, and small-cap or micro companies under $3 million.

Net Assets – Total assets less total liabilities.

Net Present Value (NPV) – The sum of the discounted present values of the expected cash flows of the investment.

Net Tangible Assets – Total assets less intangible assets and total liabilities.

Noncontrolling Interest – An ownership interest less than 50% of the voting interest in a business enterprise. Also referred to as a *minority interest.*

Nonmarketable – An interest in a business enterprise for which a freely and actively traded market does not exist. Synonymous with *illiquid.*

Nonoperating Assets – Assets not necessary to ongoing operations of the business enterprise.

Normalized – Booked amounts, adjusted to remove elements which are nonrecurring, nonoperating, or different than amounts estimated to represent the values which would be put upon them in the marketplace, or otherwise different than amounts estimated for the future.

Normalized EBITDA – EBITDA adjusted with add-backs and other adjustments so that the operating EBITDA of the business fairly represents the financial performance of the business independent of the specific costs related to the owners (in a privately held company). A mental framework from which to view this concept is to consider what costs the business would incur as a stand-alone entity of a larger company. For example: What is market rate compensation for the individual(s) that will replace the current owners? What perquisites (cars, planes, country club, excess insurance premiums, compensation for other family members, etc.) are beyond market expectations that would go away when the current owner no longer works there?

Normalized Financial Statements – Financial statements adjusted for nonoperating assets and liabilities and/or for nonrecurring, noneconomic, or other unusual items to eliminate anomalies and/or facilitate comparisons.

Opportunity Cost – The cost assigned to a project resource that is already owned by the firm. It is based on the next best alternative use.

Present Value – The value, as of a specified date, of future economic benefits and/or proceeds from sale, calculated using an appropriate discount rate.

Private Placement Memorandum (PPM) – A document explaining the details of an investment to potential investors. Also known as an *offering memorandum.*

Pro Rata – Shared or divided according to a ratio or in proportion to participation.

Rate of Return – An amount of income (loss) and/or change in value realized or anticipated on an investment, expressed as a percentage of that investment.

Recapitalization – The reorganization of a company's capital structure.

Representations and Warranties – Representations are statements of fact by the seller regarding the condition of its business, covering virtually all aspects of the company. Warranties are the seller's assurances to the buyer that the representations are true, and that if they are not, the buyer will be entitled to seek legal remedies.[2]

Return – The spendable cash that a company generates after allowing for payment of all expenses, taxes, and reinvestment requirements for working capital and capital expenditures.

Risk-Free Rate – The rate of return available in the market on an investment free of default risk.

Risk Premium – A rate of return in addition to a risk-free rate to compensate the investor for accepting risk.

Rule of Thumb – A mathematical formula developed from the relationship between price and certain variables based on experience, observation, hearsay, or a combination of these, usually applicable to a specific industry.

Standard of Value – The identification of the type of value being utilized in a specific engagement (i.e. fair market value, fair value, investment value).

Stock Option – A right to purchase or sell a share of stock at a specific price within a specific period of time. Stock purchase options are commonly used as long-term incentive compensation for employees and management of fast-growth companies.

Succession Planning – The process of determining how a business owner can be removed from the day-to-day operations of the business and who will take over running the business when the current owner is no longer in charge.

SWOT – Strengths, weaknesses, opportunities, and threats. The examination of a company's internal strengths and weaknesses in conjunction with its external opportunities and threats to qualitatively assess its position and set a strategy.

Synergy – The additional value created by bringing together two entities and pooling their strengths. In the context of a merger, synergy is the difference between the values of the merged firm and the sum of the values of the firms operating independently.

Term Sheet – A document confirming the intent of an investor to participate in a round of financing or for one party to purchase or sell a company to the other party. More broadly, a term sheet refers to a summary of the most important terms and conditions that the parties are agreeing to for a transaction. By signing this document, the subject company agrees to begin the legal and due diligence process prior to the closing of the transaction. Very similar to a letter of intent.

---

[2] Shareholder Representative Services LLC, *2010 SRS M&A Deal Terms Study.*

Terminal Value – The prospective value as of the end of the discrete projection period in a discounted benefit streams model. Sometimes referred to as *residual value*.

Total Invested Capital (TIC) – The value of the entire business enterprise (i.e. the total interest-bearing debt and equity capital of a business enterprise). It could be stated on a number of premises, including: (1) closely held; (2) as is freely traded, such as shares in a publicly traded company on an exchange; (3) as a controlling interest; or (4) as a minority interest, or some combination thereof. TIC is synonymous with the terms *business enterprise value* and *market value of invested capital*.

Transaction Multiple Method – A method within the market approach whereby pricing multiples are derived from transactions of significant interests in companies engaged in the same or similar lines of business.

Unlevered Basis – Use of predebt cash flows that are available to both holders of debt and equity shareholders of the company. In the income approach, the applicable discount rate is the weighted average cost of capital. In the market approach, the numerator in the multiples is total invested capital and the denominator is typically predebt levels of earnings such as EBIT and EBITDA. The resulting value is one of the entire business enterprise. As such, the level of debt on the valuation date must be subtracted to obtain the value of the equity.

Warrant – A security that gives the holder the right to purchase shares in a company at a predetermined price. A warrant is a long-term option, usually valid for several years. Typically, warrants are issued concurrently with debt instruments in order to increase the appeal of the debt instrument to potential investors.

Valuation Approach – A general way of determining a value indication of a business, business ownership interest, security, or intangible asset using one or more valuation methods.

Valuation Method – Within approaches, a specific way to determine value.

Vertical Integration – The merger of companies in the same industry but at different stages of production and/or distribution.

Weighted Average Cost of Capital (WACC) – The cost of capital (discount rate) determined by the weighted average, at market value, of the cost of all financing sources in the business enterprise's capital structure. It considers the cost of both debt and equity used by the firm, and it is a weighted average because it reflects the proportions of both debt and equity that are used.

Working Capital – The amount by which current assets exceed current liabilities.

Yield – The percentage return paid on a stock in the form of dividends, or the effective rate of interest paid on a bond or note.

Index

Printed and bound by CPI Group (UK) Ltd, Croydon, CR0 4YY

23/04/2025

14661000-0005